The Foundations
Science and

CC Card.
  634-6671 @Penrose

Jas. 505-758-2790

GLENN

IB

The Foundations of Dialogue in Science and Religion

Alister E. McGrath

Wycliffe Hall, Oxford University

BLACKWELL
Publishers

First published 1998

Reprinted 1999 (twice)

Blackwell Publishers Inc
350 Main Street
Malden, Massachusetts 02148, USA

Blackwell Publishers Ltd
108 Cowley Road
Oxford OX4 1JF, UK

Library of Congress Cataloging in Publication Data
McGrath, Alister E., 1953–
The foundations of dialogue in science and religion /Alister E. McGrath
p. cm.
Includes bibliographical references and index.
ISBN 0–631–20853–4 (alk. paper) — ISBN 0–631–20854–2 (pbk: alk. paper)
1. Religion and science. 2. Theology—Methodology. 3. Science—
Methodology. I. Title.
BL240.2.M4 1998
261.5'5—DC21   98–9207
                                                                CIP

British Library Cataloguing in Publication Data
A CIP catalogue record for this book is available from the British Library

Typeset in 10 on 12 pt Ehrhardt
by Ace Filmsetting Ltd., Frome, Somerset
Printed and bound in Great Britain
by MPG Books Ltd, Bodmin, Cornwall

This book is printed on acid-free paper

Contents

Acknowledgments

It is with great pleasure that I acknowledge the kindness of many individuals who have contributed to the writing of this book. My interest in the natural sciences was reinforced and sustained during my time at Oxford by Professors Jeremy R. Knowles, George K. Radda, and R. J. P. Williams. I am deeply grateful to Professor R. J. Berry, Professor John Polkinghorne, Professor Keith Ward, and Rt. Revd Rowan Williams for reading the first draft of this work, and offering corrections. I also gladly acknowledge the invaluable financial support made possible by the John Templeton Foundation, and the tireless labors of Dr Sebastian Rehnman, who tracked down and copied material in even the most obscure scientific journals. Any errors of judgment and fact are entirely my responsibility.

1

Starting All Over Again

This book is the first of what is envisaged as a series of works which aim to explore the relationship of the natural sciences and religions from a variety of standpoints – historical, philosophical, scientific, and theological. In view of the extensive scope of this project, the present chapter will aim to introduce it and explain the particular role played by the first volume in the series.

Science and Religion: The Challenge and Opportunity

The relation of religion and the natural sciences is one of the most complex, fascinating, controversial and potentially enriching subjects it is possible to study. It is true that some writers have defined "natural science" in strongly anti-religious terms, and then proceeded to demonstrate that the natural sciences are opposed to religion. This has not been a unduly taxing intellectual feat. Nevertheless, it must be pointed out that to define the sciences in such a manner in the first instance prejudges the issue, and in the second goes far beyond any existing consensus on what constitutes a "science" or a "scientific" method or outlook.

One might reasonably define a "science" as "any systematic field of study or body of knowledge that aims, through experiment, observation and deduction, to produce reliable explanation of phenomena with reference to the material or physical world" (Lafferty and Rowe 1993) or "the systematic observation of natural events and conditions in order to discover facts about them and to formulate laws and principles based on these facts" (Morris 1992). In general terms, the natural sciences are neutral towards religion, requiring neither a prior or consequent acceptance or rejection of any religious beliefs.[1] Most natural scientists will assume that considerations of divine influence upon or involvement within the natural order are largely irrelevant to the specific task of searching for a natural explanation of the patterns which are to be discerned therein. This is best regarded as a working assumption concerning the proper sphere of the natural sciences, rather than any deeply held convictions concerning the nature and activity of God.

There is no doubt that the interaction of religion and the natural sciences has become one of the most significant areas of intellectual research in the last decade. A surge of scholarly activity in the social and intellectual history of the Middle Ages and Renaissance, a new interest in the history and philosophy of the natural sciences, and a growing awareness of the shortcomings of the traditional stereotypes of the "science and religion" debates have eroded what once seemed secure boundaries between the disciplines, and opened up new possibilities of dialogue. It is no accident that a small torrent of works has been published in the last decade exploring the contours of dialogues, both actual and potential, between the two disciplines (see, for example, O'Hear 1984; Schoen 1985a; Clayton 1989; Huyssteen 1989; Banner 1990; Murphy 1990; Richardson and Wildman 1996), often focusing on individual scientists or theologians of especial importance to the dialogue (see for example, Avis 1990; Polkinghorne 1996; Worthing 1996).

A further development of major importance is the general abandonment of what might be called "Whiggish" or "presentist" modes of historiography. Such approaches aim to trace the emergence of present understandings of issues (which are assumed to be correct) in the past. The past is thus interpreted – and judged – from the standpoint of the present, in effect praising those who had the foresight to get things right, and writing off those who developed hypotheses or lines of inquiry which proved to be incorrect. It is now widely accepted that the task of the historian of science is to attempt to understand what scientists were thinking and doing within their own historical context (Kragh 1987). It often requires an act of considerable historical empathy to understand what was plausible in the past, especially when viewed against the present-day understanding of the matter. Nevertheless, such an understanding is essential, not least because it offers insights into the way in which the plausibility of scientific approaches – whether in the past or in the present – is significantly affected by prevailing social, religious, and economic assumptions.[2]

A realization of this point has contributed in no small manner to the rehabilitation of religious beliefs as a factor of significance in relation to the historical and contemporary development of the natural sciences. It is a simple matter of fact that religious beliefs have influenced and continue to influence scientific thinking, irrespective of whether this is considered to be a proper or improper influence. An understanding of the types of role which religious beliefs have exercised and now exercise in relation to the natural sciences (for example, in affecting or determining plausibility structures) is therefore of considerable interest and importance.

No apology is therefore needed for adding to the growing body of literature concerning science and religion. The importance of further exploration of the interface between science and religion is not merely intellectually stimulating; it is of considerable importance to the future of human civilization. The past history of that relationship has been marred through the dominant use of militaristic and imperialist metaphors (most notably that of "warfare") in its description, along with a general mutual lack of knowledge and respect. The 1960s fostered the belief, largely engendered and sustained by certain influential schools of sociology, that religion was in permanent decline, with a secularized world lying only a short distance in the future (Bruce 1992).

That belief seemed entirely credible at the time. For a few weeks in 1965, theology hit the national headlines in the United States, when *Time* magazine ran a front cover story declaring that God was dead. Slogans such as "God is dead" and "the death of God" became of national interest. In its issue of February 16, 1966, the journal *Christian Century* provided a satirical application form for its readers to join the "God-Is-Dead-Club." New words began to appear in the learned journals: "theothanasia," "theothanatology," and "theothanatopsis" became buzz words, before happily lapsing into obscurity.

A further indicator of the likely futility of any serious dialogue between science and religion was the widely held belief that, as the beliefs and practices of the "scientific" worldview became increasingly accepted within western culture, the number of practising scientists with any form of religious beliefs would dwindle to the point of insignificance. This assumption can be discerned as lying behind a survey of the religious views of scientists, undertaken in 1916, which showed that about 40 percent of scientists had some form of personal religious beliefs (Leuba 1916). At the time, this was regarded as demonstrating that natural scientists represented a shocking confirmation of the tendency towards disbelief within a highly significant section of the population of a country noted for its religious commitments.[3] The survey was repeated in 1996, and showed no significant reduction in the proportion of scientists holding such beliefs (Larson and Witham 1997), seriously challenging the popular notion of the relentless erosion of religious faith within the profession. If some 40 percent of those actively working in the natural sciences have serious religious beliefs, the issue of the relationship of the natural sciences and religion clearly remains significant.

In the light of such the confident expectations of the imminent demise of religion in western culture which were typical of earlier this century, there seemed to be little to be gained through such a dialogue. What was the point in exploring a frontier which would soon disappear? Yet the revival of religion worldwide since then has made the need for such a dialogue imperative. For example, Christianity, Islam, and Judaism have all undergone surges of renewal, often in quite militant forms (Kepel 1991). The perpetuation of the simplistic "warfare of science and religion" metaphor is now not merely historically and intellectually questionable (see the substantial body of materials collected by Lindberg and Numbers 1984; Numbers 1985); it could also be argued to lend indirect encouragement to the extension of such "warfare" from the realm of pure ideas to that of flesh and blood. In this new cultural situation, it is of the utmost importance that the dialogue between science and religion proceeds on the basis of mutual respect, shot through with a large dose of humility on all sides. The past decade has witnessed a subtle yet unmistakable change in mood along such lines, evident in important works by leading natural scientists such as David Bohm's *On Dialogue* (Bohm 1996), which this book aims to encourage and address.

Yet before setting out the distinctive approach of this book, it is appropriate to explain how it came to be written.

The Genesis of a Project

The project of which the present work is the first section began to take shape nearly twenty years ago. As the background against which it has emerged has gone some way to shaping its approach and structure, it seemed appropriate to begin by explaining how it came to be written. I have always been fascinated by the natural world. When I was about ten years old, I built a small telescope so that I could begin to explore the heavens. An old microscope, originally belonging to a great-uncle who was a pathologist at the Royal Victoria Hospital, Belfast, allowed me to begin the serious study of biology around the same time.

At the age of thirteen, the earliest stage possible within the British educational system, I chose to specialize in mathematics and the natural sciences. By the age of fifteen, I limited my interests still further, focusing on mathematics, chemistry and physics. In 1970, aged seventeen, I won a major scholarship to Oxford University to study chemistry. I had no interest in religion at this time, tending to regard Christianity and the natural sciences as mutually incompatible on the basis of the incorrigible certainties about life widely entertained by teenagers.

My attitude towards Christianity altered decisively during my first term at Oxford, late in 1971, as I began to realize that it possessed a far greater attraction and intellectual integrity and resilience than I had appreciated. The relationship between Christian theology and the natural sciences thus became of particular concern to me, and I devoted much of my spare time to dabbling in Christian theology, while getting on with my scientific studies. At this stage, the Oxford University Final Honour School in Natural Philosophy (Chemistry) was taken over a four-year period, of which the final year was dedicated to a research project. The first three years focused on the three major disciplines of organic, inorganic and physical chemistry, and permitted a degree of specialization through the study of "special subjects." I chose to specialize in the field of quantum theory during this first part of the course, and then moved into the field of biochemistry and biophysics for my final year research project.

After graduating with First Class Honours in 1975, I went on to undertake doctoral research in the Department of Biochemistry at Oxford, focusing on aspects of molecular biophysics, with a particular interest in the biophysical properties of biological membranes and their models. A major concern was the manner in which artificial models of complex biological membranes could be designed, validated and deployed. I was awarded an E. P. A. Cephalosporin Research Studentship to allow me to undertake this work, on the basis of a research paper prepared during my final year as an undergraduate. Although my work largely took the form of practical empirical research, I also found time to work systematically on aspects of the history and philosophy of the natural sciences. On the basis of this work, I was awarded a Fellowship by the European Molecular Biology Organization to work for several months at the University of Utrecht in the Netherlands, and a Senior Scholarship at Merton College, Oxford.

The time spent at Utrecht was formative. While working on aspects of phosphatidylcholine transport in biological membranes and their models, I had time to reflect on the more philosophical and theological issues which were raised by molecular biophysics in general. I returned to England at the end of the summer of 1976 convinced that I would need to study theology in some depth if I was going to wrestle with the issues with any degree of depth or integrity. But how? And who would teach me? As it happened, the answer lay to hand, in the small print of the terms of reference of the Senior Scholarship at Merton College, which I took up on September 1, 1976.

The scholarship in question was unusual, in that it allowed its holder either to undertake advanced research, or to study for a second undergraduate degree. Having dabbled in theology in a very amateurish manner for five years or so, I decided that the time had come to treat the subject with the seriousness it deserved. I therefore asked permission to continue my research in molecular biology, while at the same time beginning the formal study of theology at Oxford. The request caused a degree of consternation and bewilderment among the fellows of the college; nevertheless, they gave me the permission I needed. And so, from October 1976, I spent part of the day working in the Oxford University Department of Biochemistry, and the remainder of my time trying to master the basics of Christian theology. I benefitted considerably here from Oxford's commitment to the tutorial system, in that I was able to study the subject at the feet of some of the finest scholars in the field.

The Oxford theology syllabus at that time permitted specialization in the area of the relationship between theology and the natural sciences, which allowed me to explore at least some of the questions which interested me in further detail. Aware of the importance of the late medieval period to the development of the natural sciences, I also chose to specialize in scholastic theology, with particular reference to Duns Scotus and William of Ockham. It was probably the most intellectually exhilarating and challenging period of my life.

In December 1977, I was awarded my doctorate in molecular biology, having published three papers in my field, including what was believed to be the first use of anti-matter to investigate the physical aspects of biological systems (McGrath, Morgan and Radda 1976; de Kreef et al. 1977). In June 1978, I faced my examiners in theology, and was awarded First Class honours, as well as the Denyer and Johnson Prize for the best examination performance that year. As a result, I was invited to lunch by an editor at Oxford University Press, who asked me to consider writing a book on the theme of Christianity and the natural sciences, responding to a book which had recently been published by the Press, written by a rising young Oxford zoologist – Richard Dawkin's *Selfish Gene*. I declined, feeling that I still lacked the theological competence required; the idea, however, remained with me, and can ultimately be seen as lying behind the present project.

On the basis of my work at Oxford, I was awarded the Naden Studentship in Divinity at St John's College, Cambridge. This studentship, established in the eighteenth century, was intended to support original theological research. My initial intention had been to plunge immediately into the detailed investigation of the relation between the natural sciences and Christian theology, focusing particularly on the debates of the sixteenth century. However, I was advised to develop a thorough familiarity with every aspect of historical and systematic theology before doing so. It would be a mammoth task, taking years, and I recall to this day the disappointment with which I received this advice and the reluctance with which I subsequently accepted it. It was unquestionably correct. I would have to be taken seriously as a theologian before I could make a significant contribution to this immensely complex field.

My initial intention had been to begin work at Cambridge in September 1978 on the Copernican debate of the sixteenth century. Professor E. Gordon Rupp, recently retired as Dixie Professor of Ecclesiastical History at Cambridge University, had agreed to supervise the project. Rupp, however, was England's leading expert at the time on the thought of the major German reformer and theologian Martin Luther (1483–1546). It was perhaps inevitable that I would find myself diverted from Copernicus to Luther. One of Luther's particular concerns was the doctrine of justification, and I soon found myself immersed in the intricacies of the subtle shifts in Luther's thinking on this issue over the period 1509–19 (McGrath 1985). This subsequently developed into a major investigation of the history of this specific doctrine throughout the entire period of Christian history (McGrath 1986a), and a particular interest in the intellectual history of the Middle Ages and Renaissance.

After a period (1980–3) spent working in a parish in the East Midlands city of Nottingham, I returned to take up a teaching position at Wycliffe Hall, Oxford. This allowed me time to begin to engage with detailed issues of historical and systematic theology, including further engagement with the intellectual history of the sixteenth century (McGrath 1987), and the development of aspects of German-language theology since the Enlightenment (McGrath 1986b). The invitation to give the Bampton Lectures at Oxford University in 1990 allowed me to begin to explore the origins and functions of Christian doctrine (McGrath 1990). In addition to a series of articles dealing with aspects of Christian theology in relation to modern thought forms, I published several major introductions to Christian theology which are currently used widely in seminaries, colleges and universities (McGrath 1993a; McGrath 1995a; McGrath 1996).

Throughout this period of twenty years, I continued to work at the general theme of "science and religion," attempting to clarify in my own mind the nature of the central themes and issues. By the middle of 1996, I finally felt that I was in a position to return to the writing project which I had reluctantly postponed twenty years earlier. An invitation to deliver a lecture at the University of Utrecht in January 1997 on "The Relation of the Natural Sciences and Christian Theology" provided the stimulus to begin assembling the ideas and resources which now appear in this book.

Starting all over again

In part, the present project has been undertaken because of my growing conviction of the need to start things all over again. What once seemed as if it might be a wonderfully creative and interesting discussion appears to have degenerated into little more than a slanging match between a group of natural scientists bent on eliminating religion from cultural and academic life, and a group of religious people who seem to know (and care) nothing for the natural sciences. What the Renaissance envisaged as a dialogue has degenerated into what is depressingly often a mutual display of ignorance, hostility and spite. The debate has aimed to score points, not to advance understanding. There is little point in getting involved in such debates, in which the conclusions seem to be predetermined by personal agendas, rather than by a love of learning, a deep sense of humility and personal limitation, and above all a concern to foster understanding and mutual enrichment. This work is written in such a spirit, which may seem hopelessly out of place in the polarized climate which some have succeeded in creating. Nevertheless, I believe passionately that the dialogue which this book seeks to advance is of such importance that I am perfectly happy to be thought foolish or naïve in writing it.

There is a sense in which the dialogue between religion and science is dominated by the lengthening shadows of a complex and ambivalent past. Even to mention the phrase "science and religion" evokes charged memories and polarized images which predispose attitudes even before discussion has begun. As modern scholarship has made clear, it is perhaps perceptions of the past, rather than the past itself, which cast such a powerful spell on the present. It is inevitable that certain stereotypes of the past are perpetuated through the simplifications of individuals and schools of thought with quite definite agendas; perhaps one of the most pressing tasks for those committed to dialogue in this critically important field is the exorcism of the past, in which the vested interests of certain groups can be purged in order that real progress can be made. Many works dealing with this field can be shown to perpetuate yesterday's mistakes, judgments and agendas through a lack of willingness to engage with primary sources and come to terms with the complexity of the past.

Yet the need for a fresh start rests on more than the growing realization of the extent to which perceptions have been shaped by vested interests. There have been remarkable advances made in our understanding of the intellectual background against which the interaction of religion and the natural sciences developed, particularly during the Middle Ages and Renaissance. The development of the field of the sociology of knowledge has posed some significant challenges to the received views, most notably in demonstrating the ethnocentricity and culturally-conditioned nature of what had once been assumed to be the universal rationality of the Enlightenment (Manicas and Rosenberg 1985). Furthermore, unchallenged (often implicit) assumptions about the nature of "religion," often resting on rationalist or Marxist preconceptions of what religion *ought* to be, have seriously prejudiced the dialogue between science and religion by laying down in advance what religion can and cannot do and say, rather than being prepared to engage with religion as it actually exists in the real world of social and individual experience and life.

In what follows, we shall explore some reasons for suggesting that a major revision of the state of the relationship between the religions and natural science is required. In every case, the precipitating cause for revision is a growing realization of the insecurity of the inherited assumptions on which prevailing understandings rest. In some cases, this rests on the revision of presuppositions resulting from more accurate historical scholarship than that available to earlier generations; in others, on significant cultural and intellectual shifts which undermine the plausibility of hitherto widely accepted assumptions.

The four considerations to be noted in this section are the following. It must be stressed that others could easily be added to this list (which is illustrative, rather than exhaustive).

1 The rise of "postmodernism" has had important implications for both the natural sciences and religion. Although its implications for the latter have been thoroughly explored, they are poorly understood in the case of the natural sciences – and hence in relation to the dialogue between the two disciplines.
2 In recent years, there has been growing dissatisfaction expressed with the philosophical foundationalism upon which much thinking of the relation between the sciences and religion has been based. The implications of this shift for the dialogue are potentially highly significant, and require illustration.
3 Previous discussions of the relationship of religion and science have, as we noted earlier, been disproportionately influenced in a negative direction by the dominance of "conflict" models and imagery, resting on the agendas of an earlier period in western culture.
4 The existing literature shows an alarming tendency to perpetuate outdated and misleading stereotypes, in that it is often dependent upon what are often incorrect assumptions, findings, and assertions in earlier works. In consequence, misunderstandings and simple errors are often repeated, to the general detriment of the dialogue which is so urgently needed.

In what follows, we shall explore these points briefly, to indicate some of the cumulative pressures for a fresh approach to this theme. Others could easily be added to this list, further demonstrating the need for reappraisal and fresh approaches to such an important theme.

It must be stressed that it will not be possible to address each of these concerns in the present work. Some – for example the growing reaction against foundationalism – will be dealt with in later volumes in this series. It is, however, important to gain an appreciation of the nature of the factors which point to the need for revision and re-examination, even if some issues cannot be dealt with in the earlier stages of the project.

A Cultural Shift: The Inexorable Rise of Postmodernism

It is impossible to explore any aspect of modern western culture without coming to terms with what has often been termed "the postmodern shift'. Although the origins of this trend can be traced back at least to the early 1970s, its full impact would not be felt until the late 1980s. Postmodernism is generally taken to be something of a cultural sensibility without absolutes,

fixed certainties or foundations, which takes delight in pluralism and divergence, and which aims to think through the radical "situatedness" of all human thought. In each of these matters, it may be regarded as a conscious and
deliberate reaction against the totalization of the Enlightenment. To give a full
definition of postmodernism is virtually impossible (although useful surveys
and critiques abound: see, for example, Hassan 1982; Harvey 1989; Bauman
1993; Norris 1993; Fairlamb 1994; O'Neill 1994; Thiselton 1995; Eagleton
1996). Perhaps the most important distinguishing characteristic of the movement is its contention that claims to truth often represent disguised attempts
to justify the power, status or vested interests of the claimants. Nevertheless,
there remains a genuine question as to whether "postmodernism" can indeed
be seen as a coherent or distinctive movement (Hoesterey 1991).

This being the case, the relevance of this "postmodern shift" for the philosophy of science (and the ensuing dialogue with religion) remains unclear,
although at least some scholars believe that it has the potential to promise
much (see, for example, Toulmin 1982; Griffin 1989; Sassower 1993; Sassower
1995). If the natural sciences can be demarcated from all other forms of intellectual discourse and investigation (on account of their subject matter or modes
of investigation), then the "postmodern shift" will have little impact upon
them. However, there are reasons for thinking that such a total conceptual
hermetic isolation is not possible, leading to the suggestion that the rise of
postmodernism must raise questions for both science and religion, and especially their mutual relationship, even if there are excellent reasons for suggesting that a "postmodern philosophy of science" is impossible (Parusnikova
1992).

Yet many discussions of the relationship between science and religion remain firmly grounded in a set of presuppositions which can only be described
as "modern" (as opposed to "postmodern": see Levenson 1984; Calinescu
1987). Without in any way wishing to imply that this somehow invalidates
their conclusions, it must be pointed out that it certainly requires their re-
examination in the light of the sometimes subtle and always complex shifts in
patterns of thought and inherited assumptions which has accompanied (or
perhaps shaped?) the rise of postmodernism.

Yet the "postmodern" discussion to date of the methods and epistemic
achievements of the natural sciences (especially the physical sciences) has seemed
to some to be somewhat hasty and superficial in its analysis. An excellent
example is provided by Lyotard's significant essay *The Postmodern Condition*
(originally published in French in 1979), which argues that one immediate
result of the inherent diversity of the postmodern world must be the abandonment of any notion of a moral or intellectual "consensus" (Lyotard 1992, 66).
Lyotard himself seems reluctant to press this notion to its limits, for example
by drawing the conclusion that "justice" ceases to be a universal notion. Nev-

ertheless, he seems to have little hesitation in applying this approach to the natural sciences. For Lyotard, the natural sciences depend upon "paralogy" – that is, faulty or even contradictory reasoning, which abandons any claim to be in possession of or governed by centralizing narratives (Lyotard 1992, 60):

> Postmodern science – by concerning itself with such things as undecidables, the limits of precise control, conflicts characterized by incomplete information, "*fracta*", catastrophes and pragmatic paradoxes – is theorizing its own evolution as discontinuous, catastrophic, non-rectifiable, and paradoxical. It is changing the meaning of the word *knowledge*, while expressing how such a change can take place. It is producing not the known, but the unknown.

This account of the methods, goals and achievements of the natural sciences is simply not taken seriously within the scientific community, nor by many others outside it. The suggestion that any analysis – whether sociological or philosophical – which denies to the natural sciences any capacity to make true statements concerning the nature of the world inevitably calls into question the credibility of that same analysis to make true statements concerning the nature of science. The reflexive vitiation of such critiques of science remains a serious point of difficulty for the kind of postmodern relativization of the natural sciences favored by Lyotard.

In any case, Lyotard creates the impression of being somewhat muddled concerning the goals and scope of the natural sciences. As Steven Connor points out, there is a clearly a serious disjunction between Lyotard's approach and the realities of the empirical sciences (Connor 1989, 35).

> Lyotard paints a picture of the dissolution of the sciences into a frenzy of relativism in which the only aim is to bound gleefully out of the confinement of musty old paradigms and to trample operational procedures underfoot in the quest for exotic forms of illogic. But this is simply not the case. If some forms of the pure sciences, mathematics and theoretical physics again being the obvious examples, are concerned with the exploration of different structures of thought for understanding reality, then this still remains bound, by and large, to models of rationality, consensus and correspondence to demonstrable truths.

This work aims to at least begin to explore some of these issues, in the belief that they are genuinely important and illuminating.

A Philosophical Shift: The Lingering Death of Foundationalism

One of the most significant developments in recent philosophical discussions (especially in the field of the philosophy of religion) is the growing critique of what is generally known as "foundationalism" (see, for example, Williams

1977; Frankenberry 1987; Crook 1991; Uebel 1996). The background to this development is complex; in general terms it can be conceived of the sustained critique of the entire Enlightenment worldview, founded on a belief in the existence of certain foundational universal rational beliefs, which could be ascertained by due intellectual process, and thence function as the basis of human knowledge. Foundationalism can be thought of as the pervasive western philosophical doctrine that every non-basic belief must ultimately be accepted on the basis of universally compelling beliefs or realities, which are themselves in need of no support, and which transcend the particularlities of culture, chronology, and geography. The Enlightenment generally regarded such beliefs as being limited to those which were self-evidently true, or which related directly to one's own sense-experience, or which were evident to the senses. Foundational beliefs thus function as the necessary substructure on which the edifice of philosophy may be erected.

The origins of foundationalism are usually traced back to Descartes' concern to establish a basis of knowledge which did not rest upon the authority of the church or state, and was valid for all people in all places at all times (Sosa 1980). As Stephen Toulmin has shown, the history of philosophy at this stage was deeply affected by an interest in mathematics, with the certainties of this discipline being seen as pointing to potential comparable successes in such fields as philosophy and theology. All the fundamental truths of science and theology could therefore be established in a quasi-geometrical manner (Toulmin 1990, 1–87). The geometrical axioms of Euclid could find their counterparts in philosophical and ethical axioms, most notably those set out by Spinoza.

The appeal to geometry is of particular importance. It is known that the development of non-Euclidian geometry during the nineteenth century was of particular importance in eroding confidence in Kant's notion of synthetic *a priori* intuitions (which can be regarded as significant in relation to the general foundationalist programme), in that Kant had treated Euclidian geometrical axioms as non-empirical notions which therefore had the status of universal and necessary truths. The five axioms of Euclidian geometry were held to give rise to a set of necessarily true beliefs, which were not subject to the contingency of statements derived from experience. However, by about 1865 it was clear that the situation was far from as simple as Kant had imagined. Euclid's axioms applied in the special case of zero curvature, whereas those of Bolya and Lobachevksy applied in the case of negative curvature, and those of Riemann where the curvature was positive. By 1915 the situation became even more complex, through Einstein's postulation in his general theory of relativity that the true geometry of space was Riemannian, not Euclidian, and of variable curvature.

In recent years, the notion of a necessarily-true (yet non-trivial) belief has come under sustained attack on several grounds. Although the idea remains influential in some quarters, it is being treated with increased suspicion and wariness in others. What is "obviously true" seems to many to depend on the inherited assumptions concerning evidence and warranty on the part of the thinker, including (as Sigmund Freud stressed) a cluster of beliefs which may not be consciously articulated. As the anthropologist Clifford Geertz pointed out, the idea of "common sense" is actually a cultural concept, reflecting the beliefs, norms and values of a societal group (Geertz 1983). It is a form of "local knowledge", which cannot be extrapolated into some universal globally-valid truth.

As writers such as Alasdair MacIntyre have stressed, the Enlightenment appeal to "reason" or "rationality" gave rise to a set of expectations concerning the competence and scope of reason which has not, in fact, been matched by its results. Both the thinkers of the Enlightenment and their successors proved unable to agree as to precisely what those principles were which would be found undeniable by all rational persons, so that the legacy of the Enlightenment has actually been the affirmation of an theoretical ideal of rational justification which it has proved quite impossible to attain in practice (MacIntyre 1988). It must be stressed that there remain writers of importance who are committed to foundationalism in some form, most notably William P. Alston (Alston 1989; Czapkay Sudduth 1995a); nevertheless, one gains the distinct impression that there is a major re-orientation taking place, involving a shift in at least a non-foundationalist, and possibily an anti-foundationalist, approach. The implications of such a shift are of major importance to our theme, and therefore require careful study.[4]

The specific form of foundationalism associated with the Enlightenment has had a deep impact on modern Christian theology, and it is entirely possible that we are only beginning to appreciate the extent to which many of the set habits and modes of thought of recent Christian theology has been predetermined by such presuppositions (Thiemann 1985, 9–46; Thiel 1994, 38–78). The habits of thought and discourse typical of much Christian writing during the present century have been shaped by paradigms of rationality which owe their existence and form to the presuppositions of the Enlightenment. One of the distinguishing features of the complex and somewhat fragmented movement often referred to as "postmodernity" is its rejection of Enlightenment paradigms of knowledge, and especially its appeal to "universal and necessary" truths as oppressive or illusory (see Connor 1989; Griffin 1989; Jameson 1992; Norris 1993; Fairlamb 1994; Lyon 1994).

A number of works which deal with the general theme of "the rationality of science" (see, for example, Newton-Smith 1981; Trigg 1993) in fact address the more specific issue of "entitlement" or "justification," in that "rationality" is being held to be synonymous with (or at least broadly equivalent to) the related (but not identical) idea of "being entitled to hold some belief". Given the growing criticism of the uncritical use of the word-group which includes "rational" and "rationality," I propose to avoid using them in this work, and instead deploy more meaningful and appropriate terms such as "justification," "warrant," and "entitlement" (Gilbert and Mulkay 1982; Alston 1989; Huyssteen 1989; Plantinga 1993a).

It is fair to suggest that the implications of this turn away from foundationalism have yet to be explored in relation to the philosophy of science (but see Murphy 1987; Murphy 1988; Clayton 1989, 150–3), even though it has had considerable impact on recent discussions in the philosophy of religion (especially in the field of Reformed epistemology: see Philips 1988; Alston 1991; Hoitenga 1991; Czapkay Sudduth 1995a; Grube 1995) and systematic theology (especially in relation to the "Yale School": see Lindbeck 1984; Thiemann 1985; McGrath 1996b). Yet there is already clearly a widespread perception that a non-foundationalist epistemology requires a non-realist metaphysics, just as there is a clear association between epistemological foundationalism and metaphysical realism (Searle 1993; Alston 1996, 65–84). This perception is, in fact, quite unwarranted. One of the major issues which would therefore need to be addressed in the project is the question of precisely what the implications might be for theology and for the natural sciences of this retreat from foundationalism.

The Perpetuation of Outdated Stereotypes

The past continues to influence the present in ways additional to those noted above, of which the most disturbing is the uncritical repetition of material of questionable authenticity from older sources, without troubling to ascertain whether the material in question is reliable. The inevitable result is the perpetuation of certain traditions, often resting on serious factual errors. An assertion is repeated by successive authors, often in variant forms, without the application of the critical norms which are normally held essential for good scholarship. The popular perception of the relation of science and religion thus rests, at least in part, on what are little more than urban myths, tales which are told and told again, and gain their plausibility through frequency of repetition rather than any foundation in fact.

This is a matter of especial importance in relation to the relation of the natural sciences and religion. Many works in this field are written by scientists with little knowledge of religion; they often prove extraordinarily dependent upon secondary sources and textbooks for their religious information. Similarly, most religious writers lack sufficient competence in the natural sciences, and thus show an excessive dependence on secondary sources for their material. Serious errors of fact and judgment are thus perpetuated or generated through a lack of competence and confidence on the part of a scholar familiar with the complexities of one field, but not those of another.

Examples of serious errors in supposedly reliable scientific textbooks are legion. For example, consider a series of experiments carried out by Walter Kaufmann (1871–1947) on electrons. In his textbook *Einstein's Theory of Relativity* (1965), the outstanding physicist Max Born made the following assertion (Born 1965, 278):

> Experiments by Kaufman (1901) and others who have deflected cathode rays by electric and magnetic fields have shown very accurately that the mass of electrons grows with velocity according to Lorentz's formula.

This is factually incorrect; the achievement of Kaufman and others was to show that Lorentz's formula *was wrong*. Yet Max Born was one of the most distinguished figures in the field, who was of major importance in the development of the Copenhagen school of quantum theory. On the basis of his authority, this totally erroneous account of the significance of the Kaufmann experiment became standard fare in physics textbooks until it was eventually corrected (Cushing 1981). If this serious misreading of the historical material passed unnoticed by physicists for fifteen years, what hope do those who specialize in religious studies have of noticing and rectifying them? It is little cause for surprise that many serious errors of judgment concerning scientific matters are either perpetrated and perpetuated by well-meaning theologians.

This particular difficulty is, of course, two-sided. The complexities of both theology and religious history are perhaps too much to expect them hard-pressed natural scientists to deal with. Inevitably, one finds the same pattern of perpetuation of outdated textbook studies and judgments, with no real awareness of the progress of scholarship in recent years. A particularly interesting example concerns the legendary encounter between Bishop Samuel Wilberforce and T. H. Huxley during the meeting of the British Association at Oxford on June 30, 1860. Popular versions of this encounter (excellently illustrated by Irvine 1956, 6) depict Wilberforce as an ignorant cleric trying to score cheap points off Huxley, before being famously silenced by the latter. In fact, Wilberforce had written an extended review of Darwin's *Origin of Species* five weeks prior to this encounter, which he summarized in his speech. Darwin himself regarded the review as "uncommonly clever," identifying "with skill all the most conjectural parts," and identifying some serious weaknesses which needed to be addressed. Darwin's 1868 tract *The Variation of Animals and Plants under Domestication* can be seen as a response to the criticisms made by Wilberforce (Lucas 1979).

Contemporary accounts of that meeting of the British Association make no recognizable reference to such an encounter (Livingstone 1987, 33–5). It was during the 1890s that one particular version of the event was published which appears to have acquired canonical status, significantly, at a time at which Wilberforce was particularly unpopular. As J. R. Lucas remarks of the legend of the Wilberforce–Huxley encounter, having surveyed the credibility of the primary sources upon which it was grounded: "About what actually happened in Oxford on 30 June 1860 it tells us very little; but about currents of thought in the latter part of the century, it tells us a lot" (Lucas 1979, 330).

It could, of course, be argued that the urban myth of this encounter is merely iconic, and has no intellectual significance. The situation, however, is often rather more serious than this, involving significant misrepresentation of the intellectual positions of individuals or schools of thought of direct relevance to the relation of science and religion. An example will illustrate the nature and the extent of the problem. In the final edition (1961) of his *History of Western Philosophy*, the British philosopher Bertrand Russell provides a highly influential popularized account of the complex evolution of modern western philosophy, and the various obstacles which it faced as it developed. One such major obstacle, in Russell's view, was Christian theology. Russell illustrated the "bigoted" nature of Christian theology with a racy account of the early fortunes of the Copernican theory of the solar system, and singled out Calvin's critique of the theory for special criticism (Russell 1961, 515):

> Calvin, similarly, demolished Copernicus with the text: "The world also is stablished, that it cannot be moved" (Psa. xciii.I), and exclaimed: "Who will venture to place the authority of Copernicus above that of the Holy Spirit?"

The influence of Russell's book (which was widely used as an introduction to this important subject) was such that this account of Calvin's simplistic dismissal of scientific advances received wide dissemination.

The quotation which Russell attributes to Calvin is not, however, sourced. This need not appear to be a matter of major importance, in that Russell did not trouble his readers with any form of critical apparatus, presumably wishing to enhance the readability of the work. Nevertheless, the question must be asked: did Calvin ever write the words which Russell attributed to him? And if not, what is Russell's source for the alleged attribution? A routine search of Russell's writings reveals that the same attribution is to be found in his 1935 study *Religion and Science* (Russell 1935, 23):

> Melanchthon was equally emphatic; so was Calvin, who, after quoting the text: "The world also is stablished, that it cannot be moved" (Ps. 93:1), triumphantly concluded: "Who will venture to place the authority of Copernicus above that of the Holy Spirit?"

Once more, the source is not cited. The intellecual authority of Russell was such that few bothered to check him out.

Perhaps this was unwise. This particular urban myth was not challenged until Thomas S. Kuhn attempted to track it down as part of his exploration of the background to the Copernican Revolution. Kuhn did not find the quotation in Calvin, but in Andrew Dickson White's *History of the Warfare of Science with Theology in Christendom* (1896), noted above. It seems that Russell derived his information at second hand from the following passage in White's work (White 1896, vol. 1, 127):

> Calvin took the lead, in his *Commentary on Genesis*, by condemning all who asserted that the earth is not at the centre of the universe. He clinched the matter by the usual reference to the first verse of the ninety-third Psalm, and asked, "Who will venture to place the authority of Copernicus above that of the Holy Spirit?"

White, it will be noted, does not provide a source for his citation, other than an allusion to Calvin's comments on Psalm 93: 1. It might therefore reasonably be asked where within the extensive body of Calvin's writings did White himself encounter the quotation in question. The answer to this question is depressing. In a remarkable piece of literary detective work, Edward Rosen showed that the quotation could be traced back, not to the works of Calvin, but to a work published in 1886 by F. W. Farrer. Once more, no source was provided for the citation. For Rosen, the trail ended there. Farrer was a cleric at Westminster Abbey in London, who perhaps lacked the will and resources to check his facts. The remark attributed to Calvin thus had to be dismissed as pure invention (Rosen 1960). While Rosen's study is of considerable interest, I have to confess that I am unpersuaded that White drew his citation directly from Farrer's work. Rosen's research suggests to me that both Farrer and White are more likely to have drawn on a third source, common to both, yet at present unknown to us.

The attribution of this opinion to Calvin is therefore intensely problematical. Not only is the citation unknown within Calvin's works, and has its origins in an unreliable secondary source; it is inconsistent with Calvin's known approach to such matters. As Hooykaas pointed out in 1956, the alleged opinion is quite incompatible with Calvin's exegetical principles (Hooykaas 1956). Further intense study has shown that Calvin makes no such specific comment on Copernicus at that juncture or at any point in his writings. This does not mean that Calvin was ignorant of Copernicus; he simply appears to have felt that it was inappropriate for him to comment on it, even at points in his discussion of the book of Genesis, where it might have seemed in place (Stauffer 1971, 31).[5]

We are therefore confronted with the unsettling fact that a significant quotation which has been widely attributed to Calvin cannot be found in his writings, and seems to rest on scholarly laziness. A remark attributed to Calvin, on the basis of which he and religion in general have been judged, is in reality spurious. How many more urban myths such as this litter works on this theme? And how many more underlie the popular perception of the relation of science and religion? It is no easy matter to quantify the damage done to the possibilities of dialogue in this field on account of the urban myths of the amateur historians of the last century. The surge in professional scholarship in this field in recent years will unquestionably purge many of these myths from the literature, and lead to a more informed and balanced treatment of the subject.

At this point it is perhaps important to achieve at least a degree of clarity between two quite distinct (although clearly related) matters: the general body of beliefs and behavior which could reasonably be designated "Christianity"; and the institutions which are generally referred to as "the Christian church." If the emphasis in the former case falls on the idea of a set of ideas, in the latter case that emphasis falls upon an organization which cannot avoid becoming involved in social, political, financial, and even military matters. While fully conceding that it is impossible to achieve an absolute separation of these matters (in that Christianity is not simply a set of ideas, but a way of life: McGrath 1996c), it is nevertheless important to at least discern the danger in arguing that a criticism of the specific historical action of the Christian church can be directly transposed into a fundamental challenge to the core ideas of Christianity. At times in its history, the institution of the church proved to have lost sight of distinctively Christian ideas, and needed to be recalled to them through criticism.

The European Reformation of the sixteenth century will serve as an excellent illustration of this point. The Reformation represented a sustained critique of the medieval church on a number of issues, including its structures, ethics and at least some of its beliefs (McGrath 1987; Cameron 1991, 9–93). The beliefs in question tended to be medieval accruals, which were rejected in favor of what were regarded as more authentic versions of Christian belief and practice. The underlying assumption was that a distinction could be drawn between the fundamental ideas of Christianity, especially as they were found in the Bible and the thinking of the early church, and the later developments of those ideas and their institutional embodiments in the institution of the church. It was therefore possible to mount a critique of the late medieval church and its ideas on the assumption that the church had somehow departed from its foundational ideas and vision, and required to be corrected. Many late medieval theologians were actively critical of the teachings of the church of the time, and campaigned for review of some of its official doctrines.

It is clear that several of the major "science and religion" controversies of the past rest on the *church as an institution* feeling threatened by developments which called its position and authority into question. The Copernican debate illustrates this point particularly well, as we shall explore presently. A further point here is that the policies of institutions in certain specialist areas are often determined by small groups of people, or occasionally even individuals. The manner in which the medieval church was organized often meant that decisions on certain matters would be heavily influenced by key advisors. In the case of the Copernican controversy, there are grounds for thinking that major changes within the papal household in the 1530s and 1540s may have played a significant role in shifting official church thinking against Copernicus. It is known that Johann Albrecht Widmanstetter, who served as secretary to Pope Clement VII, explained Copernicus' theory to the pope in the gardens of the Vatican in 1533, apparently eliciting a positive and interested response (Striedl 1953). Yet within ten years, the atmosphere within the papal household had changed significantly.

In July 1542, a new Master of the Sacred Palace took up his position. Bartolomeo Spina appears to have been instrumental in bringing about a negative shift of opinion towards the Copernican theory on the eve of its publication in 1543 (Kempfi 1980–1). Perhaps more significantly, a new pope was in place. Paul III (1534–49) was well aware of the threat posed to the church through the rise of the Reformation, and was concerned to take steps to secure the situation in the face of the threat which loomed from northern Europe. The Roman Inquisition was re-established in 1542 to enforce doctrinal orthodoxy in Italy; the Council of Trent met in 1545 to begin to plan a sustained response to the challenge of the Reformation. Paul III felt himself to be under threat, and was not in any mood to deal sympathetically with Copernicus.

Yet this cannot be regarded as *prima facie* evidence of a fundamental conflict between the Copernican system and Christianity. Other Christian writers of the period (including Tiedemann Giese, the strongly anti-Lutheran bishop of Chelmno) regarded Copernicus' theory as consonant with Christianity, and argued so in a now-lost treatise. Indeed, it is highly likely that Giese advised Copernicus on how best to achieve acceptance for his theory with the papacy, based on his knowledge of procedures within papal circles (Westman 1990, 189–92). It is fascinating to consider what would have happened if Copernicus has made his suggestion at a time when the Roman Catholic church did not feel itself under such a threat from Lutheranism. With the benefit of hindsight, it must be asked whether it was entirely wise to allow the prominent Lutheran writer Andreas Osiander to write a prefatory letter to *De Revolutionibus*, at a time when the papacy was so concerned at the threat posed by Lutheran ideas.

The point at issue is the way in which the conflict between church authorities and new ideas (whether those ideas emanated from the religious writers of the Reformation or the writers of the "scientific revolution') is interpreted. Senior figures within the Roman Catholic church accused Luther of being "non-biblical" in his teaching, meaning that he placed unacceptable interpretations on biblical passages (Bagchi 1991); precisely the same criticism was directed by church authorities against Copernicus and subsequently Galileo (Blackwell 1991), even if attention focused on different passages of Scripture in each case. Indeed, there are remarkable parallels between the modes of response on the part of the church to the Lutheran and Copernican revolutions, in each case reflecting a perception of a threat to the privileged position of the church. Both were generally dismissed by those in authority as non-Christian innovations, despite the wiser counsels of senior figures within the church who regarded them as *bona fide* corrections to the then dominant (mis)readings of Scripture at certain points.

One of the most scandalous and distressing perpetuations of outdated stereotypes in the field of science and religion relates to the stale repetition of the myth that science and religion are locked in mortal combat. It is thus appropriate at this point to note the continuing impact of generally negative models of the interaction of the natural sciences and religion. These "conflict" or "warfare" models, which are grounded in and shaped by social forces which were particularly significant in the nineteenth century, remain influential in popular presentations of the relation of science and religion. It is therefore important to explore the origins of such models, in order to move beyond the conflict which they presuppose and reinforce towards a more positive mode of interaction.

The Continuing Dominance of "Conflict" Models in Science and Religion

There is no doubt that one of the most significant barriers to dialogue in science and religion has been the baleful presence of a "warfare" school of interpretation. Although widely regarded as fatally wounded, both historically and intellectually, through a sustained assault mounted by historians and others during the last thirty years, the image continues to exercise a lingering shadow over the field, seriously prejudicing the possibilities of progress within it. If the relationship of science and religion is perceived (or, better, prejudged) to be one of "conflict," there is a corresponding predisposition to discount in advance the potential of "dialogue." The popular understanding of the relationship continues to be deeply shaped by images of tension, conflict, and warfare. Despite the fact that roughly 40 percent of active natural scientists profess religious beliefs of some form or another (Larson and Witham 1997), the predominant perception is that the natural sciences are opposed to religious beliefs. The threat which this imagery poses to contemporary dialogue between the sciences and religion will be clear. It is therefore important to understand how this imagery came to develop.

It is clear that there remain some within the natural sciences – perhaps most notably the Oxford molecular biologist Richard Dawkins – who remain firmly and loudly committed to a warfare model (see Dawkins 1986; Dawkins 1989; Poole 1994; Dawkins 1997). Yet it must be appreciated that the perpetuation of the imagery is not due simply to anti-religious scientists; it also reflects deeply-held anti-scientific views on the part of a group within North American fundamentalism, a form of Christianity which is characterized by its aggressive rejection of science as anti-Christian (Numbers 1982; Gatewood 1984; Numbers 1992; Davis 1995). In what follows, we shall explore both aspects of this complex issue. We may begin by considering the way in which some natural scientists began to perceive religion as an enemy to their progress.

Religion as the Enemy of Science

As Freeman Dyson points out in his superb recent essay "The Scientist as Rebel" (Dyson 1995), a common element of most visions of science is that of "rebellion against the restrictions imposed by the local prevailing culture." Science is thus a subversive activity, almost by definition – a point famously stated in a lecture delivered to the "Society of Heretics" at Cambridge by the biologist J. B. S. Haldane in February 1923. For the Arab mathematician and astronomer Omar Khayyam, science was a rebellion against the intellectual constraints of Islam; for nineteenth century Japanese scientists, science was a rebellion against the lingering feudalism of their culture; for the great Indian physicists of the twentieth century, their discipline was a powerful intellectual force directed against the fatalistic ethic of Hinduism (not to mention British imperialism, which was then dominant in the region). And in western Europe, scientific advance inevitably involved confrontation with the culture of the day – including its political, social, and religious elements. In that the West has been dominated by Christianity, it is thus unsurprising that the tension between science and western culture has often been viewed as a confrontation between science and Christianity.

In part, this antagonism can be seen in sociological terms as reflecting a struggle between two elites in early nineteenth century English society (Turner 1974; Turner 1978; Welch 1996). From a sociological perspective, scientific knowledge can be seen as a cultural resource which was constructed and deployed by particular social groups towards the achievement of their own specific goals and interests (Rudwick 1981). This approach casts much light on the growing competition between two specific groups within English society in the nineteenth century: the clergy and the scientific professionals. The clergy were widely regarded as an elite at the beginning of the century, with the "scientific parson" a well-established social stereotype (Cannon 1978, 2).

With the appearance of the "professional scientist," however, a struggle for supremacy began, to determine who would gain the cultural ascendancy in the second half of the century. The "conflict" model can be understood in terms of the specific conditions of the Victorian era, in which an emerging professional intellectual group sought to displace a group which had hitherto occupied the place of honour (Heyck 1982, 87–8). The rise of Darwinian theory appeared to give added scientific justification to this model: it was a struggle for the survival of the intellectually most able. In the early nineteenth century, the British Association had many members who were clergy; indeed, the "naturalist-parson" was an accepted social category of the time. By the end of the century, the clergy tended to be portrayed as the enemies of science – and hence of social and intellectual progress.[6]

The general tone of the encounter between religion (especially Christianity) and the natural sciences can be argued to have been set by two works published in the final section of the nineteenth century – John William Draper's *History of the Conflict between Religion and Science* (1874) and Andrew Dickson White's *History of the Warfare of Science with Theology in Christendom* (1896). Both works reflect a strongly positivist and "Whiggish" view of history, and a determination to settle old scores with organized religion (Russell 1989), which contrasts sharply with the much more settled and symbiotic relationship between the two typical of both North America and Great Britain up to around 1830 (Lindberg and Numbers 1984). These images of "conflict" and "warfare" have become embedded in the popular consciousness, and have been reinforced by some recent writers wishing to perpetuate the stereotype, despite the emergence of a vast body of literature urging a more nuanced and informed reading of the situation.[7] To understand how this symbolism arose, we need to explore the ideology of the Enlightenment in a little more detail.

The eighteenth-century Enlightenment is without question one of the most significant intellectual movements to have affected western culture (see, for example, Cassirer 1951; Chitnis 1976; May 1976; Sher 1985; Gascoigne 1989). At its heart, the movement can be seen as a quest for liberation from the political, religious, social and intellectual *ancien régime*. The ideas of "authority" and "tradition" were seen as tantamount to the fettering of the present by a dead past. As Jeffrey Stout points out, "modern thought was born in a crisis of authority, took shape in flight from authority, and aspired from the start to autonomy from all traditional influence whatsoever" (Stout 1981, 2–3). This was a substantial agenda, requiring engagement with just about every aspect of traditional thought. As Thomas Reid, one of the leading figures of the Scottish Enlightenment commented: "To throw off the prejudices of education, and to create a system of nature, totally different from that which had subdued the understanding of mankind, and kept it in subjection for so many centuries, required an uncommon force of mind" (Reid 1969, 138–9).

For writers sympathetic to the Enlightenment, the past was something profoundly oppressive, wedded to ideas and values which merely perpetuated the interests of those in power. There was a need to break free from the authority of traditional ideas and institutions, and usher in a period of liberation and revolution. The apparent rapture with which news of the French Revolution was received in England and Germany clearly demonstrates the importance of the theme of "liberation" for many young people at the time. When the news of the French Revolution reached the universities of Germany, a sense of standing on the threshold of a new era appears to have dawned. Europe had come of age. The ideas of the Enlightenment seemed about to be transformed into social and political action. A collective historical transformation seemed possible. The war between France and the German princes of 1792 seemed poised to effect this transition for once and for all. No longer were children obliged to resign themselves to the authority structures and outlooks of their parents' generation.

The Christian churches were regarded as the bastions of conservative thinking, and the most significant obstacles to the process of liberation and liberalization which many wished to unleash in western Europe and elsewhere. It was therefore seen as a matter of some importance to undermine the authority of the church. The most effective means of achieving this goal was by the erosion of its intellectual credentials – with the natural sciences being seen as a potential weapon of assault in this task. The process of gradual intellectual and institutional distancing of science from religion can be discerned to be clearly under way by the end of the eighteenth century (Gieryn 1988). At this stage, there is no sign of the emergence of a "warfare" metaphor; it can be argued that this owed more to the social, economic, and political situation which emerged during the early nineteenth century, and which the Darwinian debate served to crystallize further.

Many of the attacks mounted on traditional Christian theology in Germany during the 1830s – an especially significant period in this respect – can be seen to represent a desire to destabilize the existing social and political order, thereby facilitating the transition to more liberal and equitable social structures. The close links between Christianity and the political and social establishment in western Europe during the late eighteenth and early nineteenth century resulted in Christianity being subjected to particular attack and criticism by those with progressive agendas. It is against this background that the emergence of the "warfare" metaphor is to be seen; the growing influence of the natural sciences led to their being seized upon by those with vested interests in the discrediting of the establishment through an indirect assault on the churches (see Massey 1979).

The centrality of the theme of liberation – whether political, social or religious – can be seen in the images in which the ideology of the Enlightenment was expressed. The dawn of the Enlightenment witnessed the rise of a number of significant images of liberation, of which perhaps the most significant for our discussion is that of Prometheus (Trousson 1976; Lewis 1992; Pisi 1994). In Greek mythology, Prometheus was the hero who stole fire from the gods (according to one tradition, from the forge of Hephaestus), thus making this technological advance available to mere mortals who were thus able to safeguard their autonomy. Ludwig van Beethoven composed an overture by this name. In his significantly-titled *Prometheus Unbound*, the English poet Percy Bysshe Shelley defined human nature as "free, uncircumscribed, equal, unclassed, tribeless and nationless." It was freed from all oppression and bondage imposed by traditional practices and beliefs.

It will be clear that this appeal to Prometheus as an icon of liberation had a natural affinity with the notion of a freedom gained through scientific advance. Might not the natural sciences make available the fire necessary to liberate humanity from bondage to the superstitions and irrational traditions of the past? And was not the Christian church the chief institutional embodiment of traditional values and beliefs in western culture? Although "the simplistic idea that science marches undeviatingly down an ever-broadening highway can scarcely be sustained by the historian of ideas" (Eiseley 1985, 5), it was a profoundly attractive idea to many in the nineteenth century. For part of that "undeviating advance" was a relentless erosion of the intellectual credibility and social influence of religion.

The first icon we may note is John William Draper's *History of the Conflict between Religion and Science*, which was published in 1874. For Draper, the natural sciences were Promethean liberators of humanity from the oppression of traditional religious thought and structures, particularly Roman Catholicism. "The history of science is not a mere record of isolated discoveries; it is a narrative of the conflict of two contending powers, the expansive force of the human intellect on one side, and the compression arising from traditionary faith and human interests on the other" (Draper 1874, vi). Draper was particularly offended by developments within the Roman Catholic church, which he regarded as pretentious, oppressive, and tyrannical. The rise of science (and especially Darwinian theory) was, for Draper, the most significant means of "endangering her position," and was thus to be encouraged by all means available (Draper 1874, 332). Like many polemical works, the work is notable more for the stridency of its assertions rather than the substance of its arguments; nevertheless, the general tone of its approach would help create a mindset.

The origins of Andrew Dickson White's *History of the Warfare of Science with Theology in Christendom* (1896) lie in the circumstances surrounding the foundation of Cornell University. Many denominational schools felt threatened by the establishment of the new university, and encouraged attacks on the fledgling school and White, its first president, accusing both of atheism. Angered by this unfair treatment, White decided to launch an offensive against his critics in a lecture delivered in New York on December 18, 1869, entitled "The Battle-Fields of Science." Once more, science was portrayed as a liberator in the quest for academic freedom. The lecture was gradually expanded until it was published in 1876 as *The Warfare of Science*. The material gathered in this book was supplemented by a further series of "New Chapters in the Warfare of Science," published as articles in the *Popular Science Monthly* over the period 1885–92. The two-volumed book of 1896 basically consists of the material found in the 1876 book, to which this additional material was appended.

White himself declared that the "most mistaken of mistaken ideas" was that "religion and science are enemies." Nevertheless, this was precisely the impression created by his work, whether he himself intended it or not. The crystallization of the "warfare" metaphor in the popular mind was unquestionably catalyzed by White's vigorously polemical writing, and the popular reaction to it. The popular late nineteenth-century interpretation of the Darwinian theory in terms of "the survival of the fittest" also lent weight to the imagery of conflict; was this not how nature itself determined matters? Was not nature itself a spectacular battlefield, on which the war of biological survival was fought? Was it not therefore to be expected that the same battle for survival might take place between religious and scientific worldviews, with the victor sweeping the vanquished from existence, the latter never to appear again in the relentless evolutionary development of human thought and knowledge?

Yet the image of "conflict" must be challenged. We are no longer under any obligation to respect the dominant images of the late Victorian period, which were shaped by cultural, economic and social factors as much as they were by any of a more explicitly scientific or religious nature.[8] The dominance of "conflict" imagery is, quite simply, socially conditioned (Russell 1989), and need not be perpetuated by those living in more enlightened times. While Richard Dawkins asserts ("argues" is hardly an appropriate word) that faith is "one of the world's great evils, comparable to the smallpox virus but harder to eradicate" (Dawkins 1997, 26), this is not a view that commands much support within the scientific community, not least because the language of "eradication" has uncomfortable associations with the rhetoric of the Nazi Holocaust, to date the most systematic attempt to eradicate a religious community from the face of the earth.[9]

Yet the perpetuation of the myth of perennial conflict between science and religion is not sustained purely by scientists who dislike religion. There are some on the religious side of the debate who have their own reasons for wanting to keep the conflict alive, as we shall see in the following section.

Science as the Enemy of Religion

It is often suggested, especially by those of a religious way of thinking, that the continuing popularity of "warfare" imagery is due to the propagandist methods of certain natural scientists. It is therefore important to note that certain types of religious belief are implacably opposed to the natural sciences, and actively promote the concept of conflict. Consider, for example, a work recently published by Henry Morris, President of the Institute for Creation Research (for details, see Numbers 1982, 541–4), with the title *The Long War against God* (Morris 1989), which represents a sustained critique of modern evolutionary theory. In an appreciative foreword to the book, a conservative Baptist pastor declares that "modern evolutionism is simply the continuation of Satan's long war against God" (Morris 1989, 10). This proves to be a fair summary of the general thrust of the work, which seems to assume that Darwinian evolution brings together the occult, magic and every conceivable human depravity. In a remarkably speculative and exegetically dubious analysis, Morris invites us to imagine Satan imagining the idea of evolution as a means of dethroning God (Morris 1989, 258–9). It will be clear that it is thus quite improper to suggest that the persistence of "warfare" imagery is solely due to a group of anti-religious scientists. A significant minority of religious activists insist that science has declared war on religion, and that a vigorous counterattack is the most appropriate form of defense.

The plausibility of warfare imagery is especially linked with a style of North American Protestant Christianity which is generally known as "fundamentalism." In view of the importance of this movement, it is important to understand its origins and development. "Fundamentalism" arose as a religious reaction within American Protestant culture during the 1920s to the rise of a secular culture in society at large (Marsden 1970; Marsden 1980; Marsden 1987; Rawlyk 1990; Marty 1992). It derived its name from a series of twelve books entitled *The Fundamentals*, which set out a conservative Protestant perspective on cultural and theological developments at this time.[10] Despite the wide use of the term to refer to religious movements within Islam and Judaism, the term originally and properly designates a movement within Protestant Christianity in the United States, especially during the period 1920–40, noted for its determination to confront secular culture wherever possible. This inbuilt propensity towards confrontation inevitably led to the reinforcement of a "warfare" model of the relation of religion and society – with the natural sciences (and supremely the theory of biological evolution) being seen as the advance guard of the secularizing trend within society as a whole.

The incident which has since become an icon of this confrontationalism was the infamous Scopes Trial of 1925. Thus caused the "warfare" image to gain further credibility, not least on account of the tactics used inside and outside the courtroom by anti-evolutionists. In May 1925, John T. Scopes, a young high-school science teacher, fell foul of a recently adopted statute which prohibited the teaching of evolution in Tennessee's public schools. The American Civil Liberties Union moved in to support Scopes, while William Jennings Bryan served as prosecution counsel. It proved to be the biggest public relations disaster of all time for fundamentalism. Bryan, who had billed the trial as a "duel to the death" (note again the explicit use of conflict imagery) between Christianity and atheism, was totally wrongfooted by the celebrated agnostic attorney Clarence Darrow. The legal move was as simple as it was brilliant: Bryan was called to the stand as a witness for the defence, and interrogated concerning his views on evolution. Bryan was forced to admit that he had no knowledge of geology, comparative religions or ancient civilizations, and showed himself to have hopelessly naïve religious views. In the end, Bryan succeeded in winning the trial in the courtroom; Scopes was fined $100.

But a much greater trial was taking place in the nation's newspapers, in which Bryan was declared to be unthinking, uneducated, and reactionary. Fundamentalism might make sense in a rural Tennessee backwater, but had no place in sophisticated urban America. In particular, the journalist and literary critic H. L. Mencken (to whom Sinclair Lewis later dedicated his anti-fundamentalist satire *Elmer Gantry*) successfully portrayed fundamentalists as intolerant, backward, and ignorant dolts who stood outside the mainstream of American culture. From that moment onward, fundamentalism became as much a cultural stereotype as a religious movement. It could not hope to win support among the educated and cultural elites within mainline Protestantism.

During the 1980s, North American conservative Protestant writers found themselves enmeshed in what some of their number styled the "Battle for the Bible" (again, note the explicit use of conflict imagery) – including a somewhat curt and simplistic dismissal of evolutionary theories in favor of "creationism" (Kitcher 1982; Morris 1985; Dolby 1987). Nevertheless, it must be recalled that many leading conservative evangelical writers, including Benjamin B. Warfield and others influenced by him, adopted positive or conciliatory attitudes towards Darwinism (Livingstone 1992; Livingstone 1987). The current attempt within conservative Protestantism to make sense of the biblical creation accounts in the light of evolutionary theories continues (Pinnock 1989; Santmire 1991), despite the polarizion of the debate through the deployment of "warfare" imagery.

Towards Conflict Resolution?

As has often been pointed out, recent scholarship has seriously eroded the credibility of the "warfare" metaphor as a framework for the understanding of the interaction of science and religion, even in the nineteenth century, whether in England or Germany (Moore 1979; Barbour 1990, 3–30; Gregory 1992). It also fails to distinguish between different views (agnostic, theistic, and atheistic) held within the scientific community itself; the crude portrayal of "science versus religion" overlooks important and serious debates between natural scientists over the religious implications of their work. Yet this tired old stereotype continues to linger on, often linked to – and putatively reinforced by – what Mary Midgley has styled the "modern myth" of science as the saviour of humanity (Midgley 1992), generally present as a subliminal perception rather than a consciously articulated belief.

This uncritical perpetuation of "warfare" imagery leads to a further inference, which is as unwelcome as it is unwarranted. It implies that those who are able to appreciate the outlooks and methods of both science and religion are somehow, like the unfortunate wounded of the First World War, stranded in an untenable "no man's land" between two deeply entrenched and well defended positions. Whether intentionally or not, the symbolism which has been inherited from an earlier generation erodes the intellectual credibility of those who genuinely believe that the natural sciences and religion have much to learn from each other, and can even learn to appreciate themselves and their perspectives more thoroughly through an intellectually honest and humble dialogue with each other.

The imagery of "dialogue" is thus vastly to be preferred to the unhelpful (and frankly rather outdated) image of "warfare." The history of the interaction of the natural sciences and religion in the last century suggests that a decision to wage war was generally taken in advance of any attempt to understand the other perspective. It is entirely possible that a major contributing factor to this situation is that there are relatively few who are sufficiently well qualified to understand and appreciate the perspectives of both the natural sciences and religion. But if western academia has fostered a climate of opinion which dismisses such dialogue in advance, is it entirely surprising that there are so few who are willing to undertake the very substantial intellectual and scholarly investment required to be able to contribute? The precondition for further advance in understanding and mutual appreciation is the creation of a climate, both in the academy and in the wider culture, which believes that such a dialogue is proper and profitable.

It will be clear then, that this book has set itself a broad agenda. In beginning to deal with the general theme of "science and religion," appeal has already been made to the related disciplines of history and philosophy. Perhaps it is now appropriate to set out in more detail the general approach to be adopted in this work.

The Approach to be Adopted

The present work is long and complex, and it will be helpful to its readers to clarify its approach in advance. The present work aims to establish the foundations for dialogue in science and religion by exploring the critically important area of methodology. Much work in the field of "science and religion" has focused on single issues, perhaps most importantly the issue of compatibility. For example, is the Christian understanding of human nature compatible with the neo-Darwinian theory of evolution? Or can the Christian doctrine of creation be related to the new developments in cosmology, especially in relation to the origins of the universe? More generally, attention has increasingly focused on ethical matters, including such questions as whether recent scientific developments (such as genetic engineering) raise fundamental religious and moral issues.

These are, of course, important and intrinsically fascinating questions, which merit (and, it must be said, are receiving) attention (see, for example, Nelson 1978; Drees 1990; Craig 1991; Smith 1991; Soontiëns 1992; Inwagen 1993; Quinn 1993; Brun 1994; Craig 1994; Dennett 1995; Berry 1996). At least some of these questions will be addressed at a later stage in the project, as it is currently envisaged. Yet the level at which most work requires to be done seems to me to be much more fundamental. Systematic engagement with the issues just noted rests upon a prior substantial engagement with questions of *method* – including such issues as the way in which knowledge is gained and confirmed, the manner in which evidence is accumulated and assimilated, and particularly the manner in which the world is represented.

It is this specific agenda which I propose to address in the present volume. In many ways, the present study can be regarded as a clearing of the ground, both in terms of attempting to eliminate the numerous misunderstandings which have crept into the literature dealing with "science and religion," and of engaging with some of the foundational issues relating to this theme. Some of the issues identified as needing attention (most notably, the impact of the growing criticism of foundationalism) will have to be addressed more fully in a later volume; nevertheless, it seemed right to note this theme at this preliminary stage, even it if cannot be properly addressed until later.

Addressing the theme of "science and religion" immediately raises the question of how religion is to be defined. This question is made substantially more problematical on account of the fact that no universally-accepted definition has emerged. A number of significantly different understandings of the nature of

religion, each claiming to be "scientific" or "objective," has emerged during the
last century (Preus 1987; Harrison 1990; Masuzawa 1993; Pals 1996). Certain of
these attempts (most notably those of Karl Marx, Sigmund Freud, and Emile
Durkheim) have been strongly reductionist, generally reflecting the personal or
institutional agendas of those who developed them. These reductive approaches
have been subjected to severe criticism by writers such as Mircea Eliade
(Wachtmann 1996) on account of their obvious inadequacies. Robert Towler
has observed that Thomas Luckmann's *The Invisible Religion* (1967) was the
last major contribution to the sociology of religion to use the word religion in a
Durkheimian manner to denote "beliefs with no super-empirical or supernatural reference"; the term "religion" has now generally been accepted to refer to
"beliefs and practices with a supernatural referent" (Towler 1984, 3–5).

It must be stressed that definitions of religion are rarely neutral, but are
often generated to favor beliefs and institutions with which one is in sympathy
and penalize those to which one is hostile (Devine 1986, 271). As Clarke and
Byrne point out, definitions of religions "depend on the particular purposes
and prejudices of individual scholars" (Clarke and Byrne 1993, 3–27). Thus a
writer who has a particular concern to show that all religions give access to the
same divine reality will develop a definition of religion which embodies this
belief (for example, F. Max Mueller's famous definition of religion as "a dispo-
sition which enables men to apprehend the Infinite under different names and
disguises"). A similar agenda underlies more recent writings which are committed to the view that all religions are simply local culturally-conditioned
responses to the same basic transcendent ultimate reality (see, for example,
Hick 1973; Knitter 1985). Such attempts often rest on what might be considered an excessive reliance upon a Kantian distinction between "phenomena"
and "noumena," with the various religions corresponding to the former and
"ultimate reality" to the latter. This distinction has been challenged by the rise
of the type of holistic linguistic interpretative approach found in the writings
of Donald Davidson and others (Godlove 1989), raising serious doubts concerning the coherence of the Kantian viewpoint when applied to the case of
religions.

Writers specializing in fieldwork anthropology (such as E. E. Evans-Pritchard
and Clifford E. Geertz) have offered more complex and reflective models of
religion (Evans-Pritchard 1965; Sharpe 1975). A major debate within contemporary anthropology and sociology of religion concerns whether religion is to
be defined "functionally" (religion has to do with certain social or personal
functions of ideas and rituals) or "substantially" (religion has to do with certain beliefs concerning divine or spiritual beings). Despite widespread differences in terminology (many writers disagreeing over the propriety of key terms
such as "supernatural," "spiritual," and "mystical"), there appears to be at
least some measure of genuine agreement that religion, however conceived, in

some way involves belief and behavior linked with a supernatural realm of divine or spiritual beings (Peterson 1991, 4–5).[11]

The generality of this definition clearly raises some difficulties for the present study, however, in that it threatens to make investigation of the theme "science and religion" intensely confusing. From the preceding discussion, it will be clear that I see no reason to share in the simplistic affirmation that "all religions are saying the same thing, really." My perception is that, as a matter of observation, they are not, and that a proper appreciation of the differences among the religions is essential to understand the historical development of the sciences in different regions of the world, including their relation to the religions. It is also a matter of considerable importance to respect the distinct identities of the different religions, rather than crudely attempting to force them all into the same mould.

Greek mythology tells of one Procrustes, who had the disagreeable habit of sawing off the feet of dinner guests who were too big to fit in the bed which he provided. Procrustes was disposed of by the hero Theseus; nevertheless, distinctly Procrustean habits of thought persist in the study of religions, with several prominent writers in this field being prepared to eliminate aspects (including key beliefs) of religions which are not easily accommodated to their reductionist approaches to the subject (Bernhardt 1989; Tanner 1993). It can be argued that a failure or lack of willingness to respect the distinct identities and integrities of the different religions of the world as a consequence of the pressure to harmonize their teachings through precommitment to one specific model of "religion" is one of the most serious impediments to positive advances in this critical field of "science and religion."

The approach adopted through this project, including the present volume, reflects such considerations, and supremely the necessity of respecting religious integrity as a precondition for a meaningful discussion of the complex dynamics of the science-religion interaction. It aims to focus initially on one specific religion – Christianity, especially in its western forms. The reasons for this will be obvious. In the first place, Christianity has had the greatest impact on those regions of the world most deeply affected by the rise of the natural sciences. In the second, Christianity is at present the only religion upon which I feel competent to comment; like any scholar, I am under an obligation to acknowledge my own limitations, while nevertheless still trying to remedy them. In the third place, focusing on a single major religion allows for a more manageable research project. It is firmly intended to extend this in later phases of the project to include other religious traditions, including Hinduism, Buddhism and Islam; for the moment, however, the analysis is firmly anchored in the Christian tradition, fully recognizing and acknowledging any limitations which may result from this specific approach.

The decision to focus primarily on Christianity has one significant terminological consequence, which needs to be noted at this early stage – the extensive use of the word "theology" and its cognates. The term "theology" has become widely accepted within the Christian community to refer to intellectual reflection on the content of the Christian faith (McGrath 1996a, 143–51).

It may therefore be helpful to think of the present work as a "single case study," which it is hoped to extent in due course to other religions. In exploring the contribution of Christianity to this dialogue, I shall appeal to what is generally known as the "grand tradition" in Christian theology, which can be thought of as the great tradition of theological reflection which is rooted in the Christian Bible, and can be traced through (while not being limited to) leading thinkers such as Augustine of Hippo (354–430), Anselm of Canterbury (c.1033–1109), Thomas Aquinas (c.1225–74), John Calvin (1509–64), Karl Barth (1886–1968) and Karl Rahner (1904–84). In recent years, the most distinguished explorations of issues relating to this work is generally agreed to have been undertaken by philosophers of religion, especially William P. Alston, Alvin Plantinga, Richard Swinburne and Nicholas Wolterstorff, and this is reflected in the approach adopted at a number of significant junctures.

The scientific counterpart to the question "which religion?" cannot be overlooked. Which science is to be examined, if we are to come to a properly informed understanding of the theme "science and religion"? It can easily be argued that physics and cosmology stands in a very different relation to religious thought than biology or psychology (Watts 1997, 127–9). The historical development of certain scientific disciplines has proceeded in such a manner as to reinforce a number of historically contingent matters (such as terminology) within the community dedicated to that discipline, resulting in the emergence of a series of scientific sub-cultures with significantly different approaches and understandings to related material. The outcome of any study of the interaction of "science and religion" could therefore be argued to be dependent to a significant degree upon both the science and the religion selected for study.

It is also important to appreciate that there is considerable debate, even within a single field of scientific inquiry, concerning the metaphysical (and especially the ontological) presuppositions and implications of the discipline. As Roger Jones has pointed out, "the diversity of ontological commitment in contemporary physics – diversity both in the nature of the things physicists claim to be committed to and in the nature of their commitments – makes any global characterization of science's activities dubious, whether it be of general criteria for observability or of overall aims and goals" (Jones 1991, 198–9). While the present work focuses on the interaction of one religious tradition with the natural sciences, it attempts to engage with a broad spectrum of the natural sciences. Inevitably, this runs the risk of the resulting interaction being inadequate at points; nevertheless, the risk seemed worth taking.

While the present book is written in the belief that dialogue between science and the religions is a good thing, it nevertheless adopts a studied indifference to the question of what precise model is appropriate to understanding the relation of the religions and the natural sciences. I fully concede that a number of approaches can be identified and evaluated (including those noted by Barbour 1990, 3–30; Peterson 1991, 198–207 Reich 1996; Fantino 1997; Peters 1997); nevertheless, I do not feel the need to commit myself to any of them for the specific and limited purposes of this exploration. The minimalist affirmation that dialogue is an inherently excellent and potentially illuminating process does not involve a precommitment to any one way of conceptualizing the grounds of this dialogue.[12]

An important consideration here is that precommitment to any such model generally ends up leading to the raw data of history being prioritized or interpreted in such a way that they are accommodated to fit the requirements of the model (Brooke 1991a, 16–51). Those committed to demonstrating the fundamental harmony of science and religion tend to end up emphasizing the religious faith of those at the forefront of scientific advance; those preferring to see the two disciplines as being permanently opposed to each other tend to dwell more on the conflicts and tensions of the past and present. Both faith and conflict are unquestionably present in the history of this interaction; the model adopted by the historian, however, leads to a certain accentuation of parts of the story, so that the full story is not told.

I have no doubt that the quest for a model to allow at least a degree of insight into the enormously complex interaction of science and religion is profoundly worthwhile; nevertheless, its pursuit lies beyond the limited scope of this book. My intention is to explore the areas in which science and religion can be seen to converge, and those in which they diverge, believing that this illuminates the distinctive characteristics of each, without in any way compromising their integrities.[13] The present study aims to set out the possibilities for dialogue – and at least some potential results of that dialogue – between the natural sciences and religion, using philosophy and history as catalysts to and participants in that dialogue. It respects the integrity of all participants to the dialogue, and does not seek to minimize the complexity of the issues to be discussed in the interests of some preconceived agenda or interest.

In working on this material over the last twenty years, I have gradually come to the following conclusions. (I hope I may be forgiven for stressing that they are indeed conclusions, reached in the light of research, rather than presuppositions which have been reinforced by selective appeal to evidence.) They can be set out very briefly as follows.

1   The natural sciences and the religions are quite distinct in terms of their methodologies and subject matters. It is quite improper to attempt to limit them, for example by suggesting that the sciences have to do with the physical world and the religions with a distinct spiritual world. The distinction between "science" and "religion" concerns more than subject-matter.

2   At points, despite their clear differences, those working in the fields of science and religion find themselves facing similar issues, especially in relation to issues of representation and conceptualization. At point after point, those interested in science and religion find themselves facing very similar questions, and even adopting similar approaches in the answers which they offer.

3   At points of major importance, the methods and theories of the natural sciences are genuinely illuminating to those concerned with religious matters. Equally, there are points where religious beliefs and approaches cast considerable light on issues of scientific method. The investigation of these convergences is mutually enlightening and significant.[14]

Perhaps these three conclusions may seem minimalist, stating some very obvious points. Nevertheless, I am convinced that the closer investigation of these issues is of major interest and importance.[15]

In many ways, this work develops the agenda set out by the leading British theologian Thomas F. Torrance in his 1969 work *Theological Science*, based on his 1959 Hewett Lectures on the general theme of "The Nature of Theology and Scientific Method." In this important study, Torrance argued that "theological and natural sciences share the same basic problem: how to refer our thoughts and statements genuinely beyond ourselves, how to reach knowledge of reality in which we do not intrude ourselves distortingly into the picture, and yet how to retain the full and integral place of the human subject in it all" (Torrance 1969, xiii).

Like Torrance, I have come to the conclusion that there is a remaining need to explore the fundamental relationship between Christian theology and natural sciences at the level of method – that is to say, the way in which reality (if I may be forgiven for using such a tendentious word at this stage; it will be explored further in due course) is apprehended, investigated, and represented. The agenda set by Torrance thus remains significant. The three major points of the investigation undertaken in the present work are the following (which are clearly related to Torrance's agenda, even if they do not correspond to it precisely):

1   The explicability of the world – that is to say, the simple fact that there is, or appears to be, some form of ordering to the world, and that human

beings are capable of uncovering such an order.

2   The way in which our reflection on the nature of things is controlled or modulated by the way things are. In other words, there are external factors which limit and guide our thinking. Here I am addressing the fundamental question of experimentation – that is, the empirical investigation of the world in order to ascertain what may be known of it, in the knowledge that such experiments may destroy existing ideas, or force them to be radically modified – and the complex issue of revelation. There is an extra-systemic reality which modulates responsible discourse, and which is treated by the sciences, and many within religious traditions, as possessing ontological finality.

3   The way in which the external world is represented. Both the natural sciences and Christian theology are obliged to deal with the way in which human words can in some way point to or represent something which goes far beyond those words.

With this substantial agenda in mind, I turn immediately to consider the enormously complex and intellectually fascinating question of the intelligibility of the world, and supremely the search for order amidst that complexity.

2

The Quest for Order

"The God of the physicists is cosmic order" (Pagels 1984, 83). It could be argued that the natural sciences are founded on the *perception of explicable regularity to the world, which is capable of being represented mathematically*. In other words, there is something about the world – and the nature of the human mind – which allows us to discern patterns within nature, for which explanations may be advanced and evaluated. One of the most significant parallels between the natural sciences and religion is this fundamental conviction that the world is characterized by regularity and intelligibility (Peacocke 1981, xii; Rolston 1987, 22; Johnson 1955). This perception of ordering and intelligibility is of immense significance, both at the scientific and religious levels. As Paul Davies points out, "in Renaissance Europe, the justification for what we today call the scientific approach to inquiry was the belief in a rational God whose created order could be discerned from a careful study of nature" (Davies 1992, 77).

This insight is directly derived from the Christian doctrine of creation, and reflects the deeply religious worldview of the medieval and Renaissance periods, which ensured that even the most "secular" of activities – whether economic, political or scientific – were saturated with the themes of Christian theology (McGrath 1987, 32–68). This foundational assumption of the natural sciences – that God has created an ordered world, whose ordering could be discerned by humanity, which had in turn been created "in the image and likeness of God" – permeates the writings of the period, whether it is implicitly assumed or explicitly stated. The secularization of western thought has meant that the controlling influence of such leading ideas has been removed from the public realm, and effectively relegated to the world of the private views of individuals (Pratt 1970; Chadwick 1975; Pickering 1993).

Yet this modern shift in the social function or corporate plausibility of foundational religious beliefs cannot be equated with a demonstration of their falsity or their marginalization within the reflection of individual natural scientists. A Christian doctrine of creation (in various forms, and to various extents) can be shown to remain a significant element in the thinking of many natural scientists. It is an intellectual consideration and influence which is by no means restricted to past epochs in cultural or intellectual history, such as the Renaissance. It is our concern in this chapter to explore the complex nature of this interaction, and indicate its importance for our theme.

Richard Swinburne sets out what may be regarded as a consensual approach to this matter, seen from a Christian perspective. For Swinburne, it is manifestly clear that there is a high degree of ordering within the natural world :

> Regularities of succession are all-pervasive. For simple laws govern almost all succession of events. In books of physics, chemistry and biology we can learn how almost everything in the world behaves. The laws of their behaviour can be set out be relatively simple formulae which men can understand and by means of which they can successfully predict the future. The orderliness of nature to which I drew attention here is its conformity to formula, to simple, formulable, scientific laws. The orderliness of the universe in this respect is a very striking fact about it. The universe might so naturally have been chaotic, but it is not – it is very orderly.

Perhaps some of these statements will seem slightly tendentious, and may require modification or more extensive justification. Nevertheless, they express one of the most striking features of the scientific observation of the world – its regularity.

It could, of course, be argued that this perception of "orderliness" reflects a propensity to discern patterns and impose coherence within the human mind, rather than any intrinsic structuring of the natural world itself. Regularity is thus an imposition of the human observer, rather than a feature of the world which is being observed. For Immanuel Kant, "ordering" was not to be seen as something which exists in the world independently of human minds. Rather, Kant argues that things in the world owe their fundamental structure or ordering to the noetic activity of the human mind. In other words, the existence and fundamental structure of natural entities are not intrinsic to them, but have been conferred upon them by the conceptual activity of human agents. The phenomenal world receives its fundamental "structure" from the constitutive activity of the human mind. Thus Kant regards the category of "quantity" as a human category which is imposed upon the world (Wolff 1963; Bennett 1974, 9–65). In this, Kant clearly builds on foundations erected by David Hume (Gaskin 1976; Doore 1980; Urbach 1988; Carroll 1990).

Kant's use of the "imposition" model is complex, and occasionally difficult to interpret (in part, due to Kant's evolving views on the matter: de Vleeschauwer 1962). The fundamental distinction which Kant wishes to draw is between a "thing in itself (*Ding an sich*)" and things "as they appear." For Kant, the appearance is what may be known (or, better, experienced) on account of the organizing, imprinting and shaping activity of the human mind. The mental interpretation of sense-data as representing something such as "order" involves the imposition of something which is not itself given empirically in the sense-data.

It must, of course, be conceded that the human mind is perfectly capable of discerning order or imposing patterns which are entirely of its own making. The popular image of the "man in the moon" rests on the perception that the features of the lunar surface, viewed around the time of a full moon, resemble a human face. Ancient astronomers saw patterns in the heavens, and created the constellations, which they believed to resemble the physical appearances of mythological heroes. The nineteenth-century Italian astronomer Schiaparelli saw "canals" on the surface of the planet Mars, and created a new genre of science fiction focusing on the mysterious beings who had created them; subsequent close-range exploration of the planet revealed that these were simply patterns created by an order-imposing human mind on unconnected surface features of the planet.

It could therefore be argued that, since it belongs to human nature to impose patterns upon our experience, "order" would be identified even if the universe were disordered. The perception of order is therefore not to be explained in terms of the way the world is, but in terms of the way in which the human mind works. While it must be conceded immediately that the human mind does indeed demonstrate a propensity to identify patterns and impose structure, this cannot be taken to mean that no such patterns or structures exist within nature. The explanatory and predictive successes of the natural sciences pose a serious difficulty to this position, in that they posit the existence of a publicly observable and replicable regularity to the world. This ordering would then be held to be true even if there were no human mind to discern it; on the basis of contemporary cosmological theories, it can reasonably be argued that the laws of physics operated long before human minds evolved in order to notice them. As Heinz Pagels has pointed out, the hidden order of the world has only proved amenable to interpretation in the last three centuries; this cannot by any stretch of the imagination be taken to mean that they were not present before then (Pagels 1984, 156):

> Although the idea that the universe has an order that is governed by natural laws that are not immediately apparent to the senses is very ancient, it is only in the last three hundred years that we have discovered a method for uncovering the hidden order – the scientific-experimental method. So powerful is this method that virtually everything scientists know about the natural world comes form it. What they find is that the architecture of the universe is indeed built according to invisible universal rules, what I call the cosmic code.

Pagel's language of the "architecture of the universe . . . built according to invisible universal rules" immediately established a connection between order and fabrication, and naturally leads us into a discussion of the vitally important theme of "creation."

The Doctrine of Creation

There is no doubt that interest in the doctrine of creation has been stimulated by the emergence of the "big bang" theory of the origin of the universe. The question of the origin of the universe is without doubt one of the most fascinating areas of modern scientific analysis and debate. That there are religious dimensions to this debate will be self-evident (Wilkinson 1990). Bernard Lovell, the distinguished British pioneer of radio astronomy, is one of many to note that discussion of the origins of the universe inevitably raises fundamentally religious questions (Lovell 1961, 125). More recently, Paul Davies, professor of physics at the University of Adelaide, has drawn attention to the implications of the "new physics" for thinking about God (Davies 1984; Davies 1992). In the present section, we will explore one aspect of this important debate, focusing on the question: did the universe happen – or was it created? Despite a number of significant objections against a theistic interpretation of a "big bang" cosmology (see, for example, Grünbaum 1989; Smith 1991), there is a wide body of opinion which holds that this theory naturally lends itself to such an interpretation (most ably represented by William Lane Craig: see, for example, Craig 1991; Craig 1992; Craig 1993).

The origins of the "big bang" theory may be argued to lie in the general theory of relativity proposed by Albert Einstein. Einstein's theory was proposed at a time when the scientific consensus favored the notion of a static universe. The equations which Einstein derived to describe the effects of relativity were interpreted by him in terms of a gravitional and levitational equilibrium. However, the Russian metereologist Alexander Friedman noticed that the solutions to the equations which he himself derived pointed to a rather different model. If the universe was perfectly homogenous and expanding, then the universe must have expanded from a singular initial state at some point in the past characterized by zero radius, and infinite density, temperature, and curvature (Friedman 1922). Other solutions to the equations suggested a cycle of expansion and contraction. The analysis was disregarded, probably because it did not conform to the consensus viewpoint within the scientific community. All that began to change with the astronomical observations of Edwin Hubble (1889–1953), which led him to interpret the red shifts of galactic spectra in terms of an expanding universe.

A further major development took place in 1964. Arno Penzias and Robert

Wilson were working on an experimental microwave antenna at the Bell Laboratories in New Jersey. They were experiencing some difficulties: irrespective of the direction in which they pointed the antenna, they found that they picked up a background hissing noise which could not be eliminated. Their initial explanation of this phenomenon was that the pigeons roosting on the antenna were interfering with it. Yet even after the enforced removal of the offending birds, the hiss remained (Bernstein 1984). It was only a matter of time before the full significance of this irritating background hiss was appreciated. It could be understood as the "afterglow" of a primal explosion – a "big bang" – which had been proposed in 1948 by George Gamow, Ralph Alpher, and Robert Herman. This thermal radiation corresponded to photons moving about randomly in space, without discernible source, at a temperature of 2.7 K. Taken alongside other pieces of evidence, this background radiation served as significant evidence that the universe had a beginning (and caused severe difficulties for the rival "steady state" theory advocated by Thomas Gold and Hermann Bondi, with theoretical support from Fred Hoyle).

It is now widely agreed that the observable universe had a beginning. Yet that brief statement may well be judged to raise far more questions than it answers. While it is not my intention to enter into a detailed analysis of the evidence for any one cosmological model, it is of considerable importance to note the deeply religious questions which are raised by modern cosmology, even if that same discipline is seen to experience difficulty in answering them (see, for example, Trefil 1983; Drees 1990; Craig 1991; Smith 1991; Q. Smith 1992; Grünbaum 1993; Quinn 1993; Craig 1994). We may explore these points by considering Stephen Hawking's *Brief History of Time*, which is alert to the philosophical and theological issues raised by modern cosmology.[1] The general perception of Hawking's own views has been somewhat skewed by an introduction by Carl Sagan, which suggests that Hawking's work leaves no place for a God. In view of the fact that many readers of the work appear to have penetrated no further than this preface, it is important to note its tone (Hawking 1988, x):

> This is also a book about God . . . or perhaps about the absence of God. The word God fills these pages. Hawking embarks on a quest to answer Einstein's famous question about whether God had any choice in creating the universe. Hawking is attempting, as he explicitly states, to understand the mind of God. And this makes all the more unexpected the conclusion of the effort, at least so far: a universe with no edge in space, no beginning or end in time, and nothing for a Creator to do.

It is fair to argue that this is not an accurate summary of Hawking's conclusions, nor of the general tone of the work (Craig 1990).[2] When a reader of an early draft of *Brief History* suggested that it left no place for God, Hawking replied that he "had left the question of the existence of a Supreme Being completely open" (Hawking 1985, 12).

So what is to be understood by the idea of "creation"? Although the idea of "creation" can be found in classic secular philosophy – for example, in the writings of Aristotle (Ehrhardt 1968, 107–40) – it is generally regarded as a distinctly religious notion. The idea that the world was created is one of the most foundational of religious ideas (Hamilton 1988; Sproul 1991; Leeming 1995; Ward 1996b). The notion finds different expressions in the various religions of the world. Religions of the Ancient Near East often take the form of a conflict between a creator deity and the forces of chaos (Dalley 1989; Müller 1989). Variants on this theme are associated with specific geographical regions, such as Africa (Beier 1966), the Indian subcontinent (O'Flaherty 1975, 25–55), North America (Erdoes and Ortiz 1984; Zolbrod 1984) and Australasia (Berndt 1940). The dominant form of the doctrine of creation is that associated with Judaism, Christianity, and Islam. In what follows, I shall set out the basic features of this doctrine from a specifically Christian perspective, and explore its implications for the natural sciences.

The theme of "God as creator" is of major importance within the Old Testament (Herrman 1961; Napier 1962; Fishbane 1971; Thompson 1971; Anderson 1977; Steck 1978; Bazer 1980; Bird 1981; Brooke 1987; Santmire 1991; Deroche 1992). Attention has often focussed on the creation narratives found in the first two chapters of the book of Genesis, with which the Old Testament canon opens. However, it must be appreciated that the theme is deeply embedded in the wisdom and prophetic literature.[3] Job 38: 1 – 42: 6 sets out what is unquestionably the most comprehensive understanding of God as creator to be found in the Old Testament, stressing the role of God as creator and sustainer of the world. It is possible to discern two distinct, though related, contexts in which the notion of "God as creator" is encountered: first, in contexts which reflect the praise of God within Israel's worship, both individual and corporate; and secondly, in contexts which stress that the God who created the world is also the God who liberated Israel from bondage, and continues to sustain her in the present (Lohfink 1994).

Of particular interest for our purposes is the Old Testament theme of "creation as ordering," and the manner in which the critically important theme of "order" is established on and justified with reference to cosmological foundations (Knight 1985; Millar 1987). It has often been pointed out how the Old Testament portrays creation in terms of an engagement with and victory over forces of chaos (Day 1985; Niditch 1985; Anderson 1987; Deroche 1992). It has been shown that this establishment of order is generally depicted in two different ways (Levenson 1994):

1   Creation is an imposition of order on a formless chaos. This model is espe-
    cially associated with the image of a potter working clay into a recognizably
    ordered structure (e.g., Genesis 2: 7; Isaiah 29: 16; 44: 8; Jeremiah 18: 1–6).
2   Creation concerns conflict with a series of chaotic forces, often depicted as
    a dragon or another monster (variously named "Behemoth," "Leviathan,"
    "Nahar," "Rahab," "Tannim," or "Yam") who must be subdued (Job 3: 8;
    7: 12; 9: 13; 40: 15–32; Psalm 74: 13–15; 139: 10–11; Isaiah 27: 1; 41: 9–10;
    Zechariah 10: 11).[4]

It is clear that there are parallels between the Old Testament account of God
engaging with the forces of chaos and Ugaritic and Canaanite mythology (Clifford
1984; Day 1985). Nevertheless, there are significant differences at points of
importance, not least in the Old Testament's insistence that the forces of chaos
are not to be seen as divine. Creation is not be to understood in terms of
different gods warring against each other for mastery of a (future) universe,
but in terms of God's mastery of chaos and ordering of the world.[5]

The concept of "world-order" is closely linked with two concepts which play a
major role in the Old Testament, and in the thought of the Ancient Near East in
general – "righteousness" and "truth" (Kaiser 1965; Schmid 1968; Hommel 1969;
Schmid 1973). While generalizations are dangerous, it seems that "righteousness"
can be thought of as ethical conformity to the world-ordering established by God,
while "truth" can be considered to be its metaphysical counterpart. The theme of
"conforming to the order of the world" can be seen as underlying both.

This theme is developed subsequently within the tradition of theological
reflection on the Old Testament, and is perhaps seen at its clearest in the
writings of the eleventh-century theologian Anselm of Canterbury (Söhngen
1970; Chiste 1985; McGrath 1986a, vol. 1, 55–7). For Anselm, the concept of
"rectitude" corresponds to the fundamental ordering of the world, as intended
by God. "Truth" may then be considered to be metaphysical, and righteousness to be moral, rectitude. The theme of "natural order" is also particularly
significant in the writings of the leading Reformed theologian John Calvin
(Schreiner 1991), and is widely thought to have been of importance in stimulating Calvin's positive attitude towards the close study of nature as a means of
learning more about God.

Having briefly introduced some aspects of the concept of creation, particularly within a Jewish or Christian context, we may now pass on to consider
some of its aspects in a more theological manner.

Creation: A Brief Theological Analysis

As we have seen, the doctrine of God as creator has its foundations firmly laid
in the Old Testament (e.g., Genesis 1, 2). In the history of theology, the

doctrine of God the creator has often been linked with the authority of the Old Testament. The continuing importance of the Old Testament for Christianity is often held to be grounded in the fact that the god of which it speaks is the same god to be revealed in the New Testament. The creator and redeemer god are one and the same. In the case of Gnosticism, which became especially influential during the second century, a vigorous attack was mounted on both the authority of the Old Testament, and the idea that God was creator of the world (Logan 1996). We shall explore the importance of this in what follows.

The Challenge of Gnosticism

For Gnosticism, in most of its significant forms, a sharp distinction was to be drawn between the God who redeemed humanity from the world, and a somewhat inferior deity (often termed "the demiurge") who created that world in the first place. The Old Testament was regarded by the Gnostics as dealing with this lesser deity, whereas the New Testament was concerned with the redeemer God. As such, belief in God as creator and in the authority of the Old Testament came to be interlinked at an early stage. Of the early writers to deal with this theme, Irenaeus of Lyons is of particular importance (Fautino 1994).

A distinct debate centered on the question of whether creation was to be regarded as *ex nihilo* – that is to say, out of nothing (May 1995). In one of his dialogues (*Timaeus*), Plato developed the idea that the world was made out of pre-existent matter, which was fashioned into the present form of the world. This idea was taken up by most Gnostic writers, who were here followed by individual Christian theologians such as Theophilus of Antioch and Justin Martyr, professed a belief in preexistent matter, which was shaped into the world in the act of creation. In other words, creation was not *ex nihilo*; rather, it was to be seen as an act of construction, on the basis of material which was already to hand, as one might construct an igloo out of snow, or a house from stone. The existence of evil in the world was thus to be explained on the basis of the intractability of this preexistent matter. God's options in creating the world were limited by the poor quality of the material available. The presence of evil or defects within the world are thus not to be ascribed to God, but to deficiencies in the material from which the world was constructed.

However, the conflict with Gnosticism forced reconsideration of this issue. In part, the idea of creation from pre-existent matter was discredited by its Gnostic associations; in part, it was called into question by an increasingly sophisticated reading of the Old Testament creation narratives. Writers such as Theophilus of Antioch insisted upon the doctrine of creation *ex nihilo*, which may be regarded as gaining the ascendency from the end of the second century onwards. From that point onwards, it became the received doctrine within the church (van Bavel 1990).

The importance of the decisive rejection of Gnosticism by the early church for the development of the natural sciences has been explored by Thomas F. Torrance, who points out that the affirmation of the fundamental goodness of creation "established the reality of the empirical, contingent world, and thus destroyed the age-old Hellenistic and Oriental assumption that the real is reached only by transcending the contingent" (Torrance 1985, 6). Against any idea that the natural order was chaotic, irrational or inherently evil (three concepts which were often regarded as interlocking), the early Christian tradition affirmed that the natural order possessed a goodness, rationality and orderedness which derived directly from its creation by God.

A radical dualism between God and creation was thus eliminated, in favor of the view that the truth, goodness, and beauty of God (to use the Platonic triad which so influenced many writers of the period) could be discerned within the natural order, in consequence of that order having been established by God. For example, Origen argued that it was God's creation of the world which structured the natural order in such a manner that it could be comprehended by the human mind, by conferring upon that order an intrinsic rationality and order which derived from and reflected the divine nature itself.

Three Models of Creation

Three main ways of conceiving the creative action of God became widely established within Christian circles by the end of the fifth century. We shall note them briefly, and identify their relevance to our theme.

1 *Emanation.* This term was widely used by early Christian writers to clarify the relation between God and the world on the one hand, and the divine Logos on the other (Sorabji 1983). Although the term is not used by either Plato or Plotinus (Dörrie 1965), many patristic writers sympathetic to the various forms of Platonism saw it as a convenient and appropriate way of articulating Platonic insights. The image that dominates this approach is that of light or heat radiating from the sun, or a human source such as a fire. This image of creation (hinted at in the Nicene Creed's phrase "light from light') suggests that the creation of the world can be regarded as an overflowing of the creative energy of God. Just as light derives from the sun and reflects its nature, so the created order derives from God, and expresses the divine nature. There is, on the basis of this model, a *natural* or *organic* connection between God and the creation.

However, the model has weaknesses, of which two may be noted. First, the image of a sun radiating light, or a fire radiating heat, implies an involuntary emanation, rather than a conscious decision to create. The Christian tradition has consistently emphasized that the act of creation rests upon a prior decision on the part of God to create, which this model cannot adequately express. This naturally leads on to the second weakness, which relates to the impersonal nature of the model in question. The idea of a personal God, expressing a personality both in the very act of creation and the subsequent creation itself, is difficult to convey by this image. Nevertheless, the model clearly articulates a close connection between creator and creation, leading us to expect that something of the identity and nature of the creator is to be found in the creation. Thus the beauty of God – a theme which was of particular importance in early medieval theology, and has emerged as significant again in the later writings of Hans Urs von Balthasar – would be expected to be reflected in the nature of the creation (Sherry 1992; Barrett 1996).

2   *Construction.* Many biblical passages portray God as a master builder, deliberately constructing the world (for example, Psalm 127: 1). The imagery is powerful, conveying the ideas of purpose, planning, and a deliberate intention to create. The image is important, in that it draws attention to both the creator and the creation. In addition to bringing out the skill of the creator, it also allows the beauty and ordering of the resulting creation to be appreciated, both for what it is in itself, and for its testimony to the creativity and care of its creator.

However, the image has a deficiency, which relates to a point made earlier concerning Plato's dialogue *Timaeus*. This portrays creation as involving preexistent matter. Here, creation is understood as giving shape and form to something which is already there – an idea which, we have seen, causes at least a degree of tension with the doctrine of creation *ex nihilo*. The image of God as a builder would seem to imply the assembly of the world from material which is already to hand, which is clearly deficient. Nevertheless, despite this slight difficulty, it can be seen that the model expresses the insight that the character of the creator is, in some manner, expressed in the natural world, just as that of an artist is communicated or embodied in her work. In particular, the notion of "ordering" – that is, the imparting or imposing of a coherence or structure to the material in question – is clearly affirmed by this model. Whatever else the complex notion of "creation" may mean within a Christian context, it certainly includes the fundamental theme of ordering – a notion which is especially significant in the creation narratives of the Old Testament.

3   *Artistic expression.* Many Christian writers, from various periods in the history of the church, speak of creation as the "handiwork of God," comparing it to a work of art which is both beautiful in itself, as well as expressing the personality of its creator. This model of creation as the "artistic expression" of

God as creator is particularly well expressed in the writings of the eighteenth-century North American theologian Jonathan Edwards, as we shall see presently.

The image is profoundly helpful, in that it supplements a deficiency of both the two models noted above – namely, their impersonal character. The image of God as artist conveys the idea of personal expression in the creation of something beautiful. Once more, the potential weaknesses need to be noted: for example, the model could easily lead to the idea of creation from pre-existent matter, as in the case of a sculptor with a statue carved from an already existing block of stone. However, the model offers us at least the possibility of thinking about creation from nothing, as with the author who writes a novel, or the composer who creates a melody and harmony. It also encourages us to seek for the self-expression of God in the creation, and gives added theological credibility to a natural theology (see pp. 98–118). There is also a natural link between the concept of creation as "artistic expression" and the highly significant concept of "beauty" (Sherry 1992; Barrett 1996), which will feature prominently in our discussion in this chapter.

The doctrine of creation has been further developed in subsequent theological reflection within the Christian tradition (Gilkey 1959; Peacocke 1979; Heyd 1982; Baur 1986; Pannenberg 1988; van Bavel 1990; Gehrke 1993; Webster 1993; Brun 1994; Mutschler 1995; van Till 1996). It must, however, be stressed that the twentieth century has witnessed a considerable degree of theological speculation which often seems to have little direct linkage or connection with the Christian tradition. For example, the rise of the movement known as "process theology" seems to have little place for the idea of "God as creator" or the notion of creation *ex nihilo* (Ford 1981; Ford 1991).[6] Indeed, it seems clear that the theologically most significant analyses of the notion of "creation" since the Second World War are due to Christian philosophers of religion. In what follows, we shall focus on the "grand tradition" approach to the notion of creation, and avoid engaging with some of the more speculative (and, if the truth is to be told, ephemeral) recent accounts of the doctrine offered by theologians.

Creation and Time

One of the most significant debates within Christian theology for the purposes of our discussion focusses on the complex issue of the relation of creation and time (Pike 1970; O'Donnell 1983; Leftow 1991; Craig 1996). We have already noted the use of the image of "emanation" in early Christian thinking on the nature of creation, and its background in Platonic thought. One of the most significant critics of this view was Augustine of Hippo, who held that the view presupposed or implied a change in the divine substance itself. In order to uphold what he believed to be integral to the doctrine of creation, Augustine argued that God could not be considered to have brought the creation into being at a certain definite moment in time, as if "time" itself existed prior to creation. For Augustine, "time" itself must be seen as an aspect of the created order, to be contrasted with the "timelessness" which he held to be the essential feature of "eternity." This has important implications for his understanding of the nature of history, and especially his interest in the idea of "memory" (Pelikan 1986).

This notion of "time as created" can probably be seen at its most clearest in Augustine's musings in the *Confessions*, an extended soliloquy which takes the form of a prayer to God (Augustine 1991, 229–30):

> You have made time itself. Time could not elapse before you made time. But if time did not exist before heaven and earth, why do people ask what you were then doing? There was no "then" when there was no time. . . . It is not in time that you precede times. Otherwise you would not precede all times. In the sublimity of an eternity which is always in the present, you are before all things past and transcend all things future, because they are still to come, and then they have come they are past . . . You created all times and you exist before all times. Nor was there any time when time did not exist. There was therefore no time when you had not made something, because you made time itself.

Augustine thus speaks of the creation of time (or "creation with time"), rather than creation in time. There is no concept of a period intervening before creation, nor an infinitely extended period which corresponds to "eternity." Eternity is timelessness. Time is an aspect of the created order. To speak of $t = 0$ is to speak of the origin, not merely of the creation, but of time as well.

Augustine's ideas have enjoyed a new surge of popularity and plausibility in the light of the new insights offered by modern cosmology. For example, consider the comments of Paul Davies on this point (Davies 1992, 50):

> People often ask: When did the big bang occur? The bang did not occur at a point in space at all. Space itself came into existence with the big bang. There is a similar difficulty over the question: What happened before the big bang? The answer is, there was no "before." Time itself began at the big bang. As we have seen, Saint Augustine long ago proclaimed that the world was made with time and not in time, and that is precisely the modern scientific position.

My concern here is not to enter into the specifics of this cosmological debate. Rather, it is to note that the new directions in cosmological thinking can prompt a positive and critical re-reading of the Christian, leading to the discovery that it already possesses resources which are relevant and appropriate to the new scientific debates which are taking place.

Creation and Ecology

At this point, we may pause to consider an issue of some importance: the question of the relationship of the doctrine of creation to the exploitation of nature. In 1967, Lynn White published an influential article in which he asserted that Christianity was to blame for the emerging ecological crisis on account of its using the concept of the "image of God', found in the Genesis creation account (Genesis 1: 26–7), as a pretext for justifying human exploitation of the world's resources (White 1967). Genesis, he argued, legitimated the notion of human domination over the creation, hence leading to its exploitation. Despite (or perhaps on account of?) its historical and theological superficiality, the paper had a profound impact on the shaping of popular scientific attitudes towards Christianity in particular, and religion in general.

With the passage of time, a more sanguine estimation of White's argument has gained the ascendancy (summarized in Whitney 1993). The argument is now recognized to be seriously flawed.[7] A closer reading of the Genesis text indicated that such themes as "humanity as the steward of creation" and "humanity as the partner of God" are indicated by the text, rather than that of "humanity as the lord of creation" (Barr 1968; Preuss 1995, vol. 2, 114–17). Far from being the enemy of ecology, the doctrine of creation affirms the importance of human responsibility towards the environment. In a widely-read study, the noted Canadian writer Douglas John Hall stressed that the biblical concept of "domination" was to be understood specifically in terms of "stewardship" (Hall 1986). To put it simply: creation is not the possession of humanity; it is something which is to be seen as entrusted to humanity, who are responsible for its safekeeping and tending (Nash 1991; Cobb 1992). Similar lines of thought can be found in other religions, with discernible differences of emphasis and grounding; the Assisi Declaration (1986) may be noted as a case in point (Rinpoche et al. 1986).

Although the pursuit of this point lies beyond the scope of this study, it is important to notice how the creation narratives can function as the basis of a rigorously-grounded approach to ecology (see, for example, Oeschlaeger 1994). In an important recent study, Calvin B. DeWitt has argued that four fundamental ecological principles can readily be discerned within the biblical narratives (DeWitt 1995).

1   The "earthkeeping principle": just as the creator keeps and sustains humanity, so humanity must keep and sustain the creator's creation;
2   The "sabbath principle": the creation must be allowed to recover from human use of its resources;

3 The "fruitfulness principle": the fecundity of the creation is to be enjoyed, not destroyed;
4 The "fulfilment and limits principle": there are limits set to humanity's role within creation, with boundaries set in place which must be respected.[8]

A further contribution has been made by the noted German theologian Jürgen Moltmann (born 1926), noted for his concern to ensure the theologically rigorous application of Christian theology to social, political, and environmental issues (Bauckham 1993; Bouma-Prediger 1997). For example. In his 1985 work *God in Creation*, Moltmann argues that the exploitation of the world reflects the rise of technology, and seems to have little to do with specifically Christian teachings. Furthermore, he stresses the manner in which God can be said to indwell the creation through the Holy Spirit, so that the pillage of creation becomes an assault on God. On the basis of this analysis, Moltmann is able to offer a rigorously Trinitarian defense of a distinctively Christian ecological ethic. Such is the importance of this point that it merits further discussion.

A fundamental theme of modernism – a term which is usually taken to refer to the cultural mood which began to emerge towards the opening of the twentieth century – is its desire to control, perhaps seen at its clearest in the Nietzschean theme of "will-to-power". Humanity needs only the will to achieve autonomous self-definition; it need not accept what has been given to it, whether in nature or tradition. In principle, all can be mastered and controlled. As we noted earlier (see pp. 23–4), this desire for liberation was often linked with the mythical figure of Prometheus, who came to be seen as a symbol of liberation in European literature. Prometheus was now unbound, and humanity poised to enter a new era of autonomy and progress. The rise of technology was seen as a tool to allow humanity to control its environment, without the need to respect natural limitations.

This desire to master led to a reaction against traditional religious belief, which often stressed the need to respect the "givenness" of the created order. A major theme of direct relevance to this point can be seen emerging in the writings of Ludiwg Feuerbach and Karl Marx during the 1830s and 1840s: the deification of humanity. For Feuerbach, the notion of "God" arises through an error in the human analysis of experience, whereby experience of oneself is misinterpreted as experience of God (Feuerbach 1973, vol. 5, 46–7):

Religion is the *earliest* and *truly indirect* form of human *self-consciousness*. For this reason, religion precedes philosophy in the history of humanity in general, as well as in the history of individual human beings. Initially, people mistakenly locate their essential nature as if it were *outside* of themselves, before finally realizing that it is actually within them ... The historical progress of religion consists therefore in this: that what an earlier religion took to be objective, is later recognized to be subjective; what formerly was taken to be God, and worshipped as such, is not recognized to be something human. What was earlier religion is later taken to be idolatry: humans are seen to have adored their own nature. Humans objectified themselves but failed to recognize themselves as this object.

In the end, therefore, it is humanity itself which is "God," not some objective external reality (Bradley 1980; Wartofsky 1982). In the Marxian development of Feuerbach's theme, the origins of the religious experience which is interpreted as "God" lie in socioeconomic alienation. Marx comments thus on the Feuerbachian approach to alienation (Marx 1932, vol. 1, 553–5):

Feuerbach sets out from the fact of religious self-alienation, the replication of the world in religious and secular forms. His achievement has therefore consisted in resolving the religious world into its secular foundation . . . Feuerbach therefore fails to see that "religious feeling" is itself a social product, and that the abstract individual who he is analysing belongs to a particular form of society . . . The philosophers have only *interpreted* the world in different ways; the point is to change it.

By changing the world, the human experience which is conceptualized as "God" will be removed. Socioeconomic transformation therefore allows the mastery of religion, which will be eliminated along with its causes. The mastery of religion therefore lies within the grasp of humanity, allowing the Promethean dream to be realized by revolutionary activity.

This vital theme of "the human right to mastery" is intimately connected with the rise of technology in the modern period (Cooper 1991; Ferre 1993; Postman 1993). In a remarkably astute analysis of the social role of technology, written in 1923, the Roman Catholic theologian and philosopher Romano Guardini (1885–1968) argues that the fundamental link between nature and culture has been severed as a result of the rise of the "machine." Humanity was once prepared to regard nature as the expression of a will, intelligence and design that are "not of our own making." Yet the rise of technology has opened up the possibility of *changing* nature, of making it become something which it was not intended to be. Technology offers humanity the ability to impose its own authority upon nature, redirecting it for its own ends. Where once humanity was prepared to contemplate nature, its desire now "is to achieve power so as to bring force to bear on things, a law that can be formulated rationally. Here we have the basis and character of its dominion: arbitrary compulsion devoid of all respect." No longer does humanity have to respect nature; it can dominate and direct it through the rise of technology (Guardini 1994, 46).

Materials and forces are harnessed, unleashed, burst open, altered, and directed at will. There is no feeling for what is organically possible or tolerable in any living sense. No sense of natural proportions determines the approach. A rationally constructed and arbitrarily fixed goal reigns supreme. On the basis of a known formula, materials and forces are put into the required condition: machines. Machines are an iron formula that directs the material to the desired end.

This ability to dominate and control nature will inevitably, according to at least some cultural analysts, lead to the deification of technology, resulting in a culture which "seeks its authorization in technology, finds its satisfaction in technology, and takes its orders from technology" (Postman 1993, 71). As Moltmann correctly observes, blame for this development can hardly be laid at the door of Christianity, or any other religion.

The ecological debate is one clear example of a modern discussion in which science and religion interact. The debate demands a thorough and clear understanding of the history of religious traditions and their implications. Lynn White's article has probably had an influence which is inversely proportional to its accuracy and reliability; there is a clear need for an informed contribution to this debate which avoids the rhetoric, inaccuracy, and simplistic assertions of the past.

Having explored some classical models of creation within the Christian tradition, we may now turn to considering their potential relevance to the theme of religion and science. We shall do so under the aegis of two general themes – creation and order, and creation and beauty.

Aspects of Creation: Order

We have already noted (pp. 41–2) how the theme of "order" is of major importance within the Old Testament, and noted briefly how it was incorporated into subsequent theological reflection. In view of its importance to our theme, we shall consider it in more detail. One of the most sophisticated explorations of the centrality of the concept of ordering for Christian theology and moral reasoning is to be found in Oliver O'Donovan's *Resurrection and Moral Order* (1986), now firmly established as a classic work in the field. In this work, O'Donovan – Regius Professor of Moral and Pastoral Theology at Oxford University – establishes the close connection between the theological notions of "creation" and "order" (O'Donovan 1986, 31–2):

We must understand "creation" not merely as the raw material out of which the world as we know it is composed, but as the order and coherence *in* which it is composed. . . . To speak of this world as "created" is already to speak of an order. In the first words of the creed, before we have tried to sketch an outline of created order with the phrase "heaven and earth," simply as we say "I believe in God the Creator," we are stating that the world is an ordered totality. By virtue of the fact that there is a Creator, there is also a creation that is ordered to its Creator, a world which exists as his creation and in no other way, so that by its existence it points to God.

Three highly significant themes of major relevance to our theme can be discerned as emerging from O'Donovan's analysis (O'Donovan 1986, 31–52).

1 The concept of creation is understood to be focused on the establishment of ordering and coherence within the world.
2 The ordering or coherence within the world can be regarded as expressing or reflecting the nature of God himself.
3 The creation can thus be seen as pointing to God, in that the exploration of its ordering or coherence leads to an understanding of the one who ordered it in this manner.

O'Donovan explicitly engages with the Humean suggestion that such "ordering" as can be discerned is, in fact, a creation of the human mind, rather than an objective reality in itself. While we are free to ignore this ordering, both intellectually and morally, its existence is not thereby called into question (O'Donovan 1986, 36–7).

> In speaking of the order which God the Creator and Redeemer has established in the universe, we are not speaking merely of our own capacities to impose order upon what we see there. Of course, we can and do impose order on what we see, for we are free agents and capable of creative interpretation of the world we confront. But our ordering depends upon God's to provide the condition for its freedom. It is free because it has a given order to respond to in attention or disregard, in conformity or disconformity, with obedience or rebellion.

It will be clear that O'Donovan therefore places considerable weight upon the dual notions of the *discernment* and *interpretation* of the ordering of the world. The observation of "forms of order," "relations of order," or "apparent objectivity of order" (O'Donovan 1986, 35) may be interpreted simply as the imposition of such order upon raw experience by "the will-to-order of the observing mind." Or they can be seen as of considerable import for the natural sciences, religion, and morality.

The present work endorses the widely-held view that the perception of such order cannot be explained simply by an appeal to an order-loving mind, but is a publicly observable matter, open to empirical analysis by the scientific community. Regularity exists within nature, prior to our observation of its patterns. The particular issue concerns the significance of this order. In what follows, we shall begin our exploration of the significance of this understanding of an "ordered" creation for the relation of religion and the sciences.

Created Order and the Uniformity of Nature

The philosophical relevance of the doctrine of creation to the natural sciences was explored in a classic yet neglected article published in 1934, entitled "The Christian doctrine of Creation and the Rise of Modern Science" (Foster 1934). In this paper, Foster set out the way in which a belief that the natural order was created had major consequences for scientific inquiry. While Foster focused his attention particularly on the developments of the seventeenth and eighteenth centuries, it will be clear that his analysis continues to have relevance for subsequent developments. Foster's argument identifies weaknesses in both the rationalism and empiricism of the period, which prevented either from drawing certain conclusions that seemed desirable. "The work of criticism very speedily showed that neither the Rationalist nor the Empiricist philosophy was really based upon the evidence upon which it pretended to rely. No experience, to take one example, could serve as evidence to Locke of the existence of material substances, nor any reasoning demonstrate to Descartes the existence of a material world."

Foster's argument is based on his observation that the "metaphysical implications of Christian dogma," especially in relation to the notion of creation, provided an intellectual foundation for their analysis which went beyond what their own systems or approaches could not supply. In effect, the methods of the natural sciences rest upon or reflect a series of assumptions about nature which rested on Christian beliefs concerning God and creation. As part of his analysis, Foster offers the observation that the displacement of pagan ideas of creation (especially those resting on the idea of a "demiurge") by Christian ideas was an essential historical precondition for the emergence of the natural sciences. Other writers have, of course, argued along similar lines (Hooykaas 1956).

Despite its importance, Foster's argument is a little abstract and theoretical at points, and is not adequately illustrated with historical examples. It may therefore prove helpful to explore the point in more detail, and attempt to give greater substance to what is potentially a somewhat elusive issue. To do this, we may turn to the writings of Bertrand Russell dating from the second decade of the twentieth century, which focus on the issue of induction in relation to the theme of "the uniformity of nature." Russell's analysis, set out in his 1912 work *The Problems of Philosophy*, indicates the way in which apparently unjustifiable assumptions prove essential to the scientific enterprise.

The essential difficulty noted by Russell is that the scientific method is obliged to assume the uniformity of nature in order to proceed, yet cannot itself substantiate this implicit assumption. Russell's particular formlation of this principle takes the following form: "The belief in the uniformity of nature is the belief that everything that has happened or will happen is an instance of some general law to which there are *no* exceptions" (Russell 1912, 99). But what are the grounds of this belief? Science may uncover regularities and uniformities; nevertheless, past patterns of regularity cannot be regarded as leading to any degree of certainty. "The man who has fed the chicken every day throughout its life wrings its neck instead, showing that more refined views as to the uniformity of nature would have been useful to the chicken" (Russell 1912, 98). The fundamental problem is that much scientific analysis is predicated on an assumption of uniformity which cannot itself be demonstrated:

> Our inductive principle is at any rate not capable of being disproved by an appeal to experience. The inductive principle, however, is equally incapable of being *proved* by an appeal experience. . . . Thus all knowledge which, on a basis of experience, tells us something about what is not experienced, is based upon a belief which experience can neither confirm nor confute, yet which, at least in its more concrete applications, appears to be as firmly rooted in us as many of the facts of experience.

Russell thus argues that empirical investigation cannot provide a justification of induction (or associated concepts such as the uniformity of nature) in that any such inductive or empirical justification of induction would simply beg the question. As Russell would put the point in a later work, "the principle itself cannot, without circularity, be inferred from observed uniformities, since it is required to justify any such inference."

The question of whether an appeal to induction is, in fact, circular has been debated ever since Russell's classic statement of his anxieties over the issue. Paul Edwards and Max Black argued that the difficulties could be evaded (Edwards 1949; Black 1958); Peter Achinstein among others has restated and developed Russell's misgivings concerning the legitimacy of the procedure (Achinstein 1962); Karl Popper expressed grave doubts about the validity of inductive logic in the first place, arguing that its difficulties were nothing less than "insurmountable" (Popper 1961, 29).[9]

An especially significant contribution has been made by the Oxford philosopher J. R. Lucas, who stresses that many of the difficulties associated with the notion of induction rest on the egocentricity of the observer, and a failure to "decentre." Lucas notes the parallels between many contempory anxieties concerning induction and the classic problems of solipsism (Lucas 1984, 22–3):

> The guiding principle [of the argument set forth] is non-egocentricity. The distinction between the future and the past, being a projection of one's own temporal position, is irrelevant. The particular instances I happen to know of are not thereby distinguished from those I happen not to know of. My particular observations are

typical of the general run, because the fact of my observing them is completely unimportant, and therefore, the ones I happen to observe are bound to be a random sample. The problem of induction, it is suggested, is like other problems raised by sceptics, not a real problem at all, but only the symptom of the philosopher's neurotic obsession with his own self. The sceptic about induction keeps on asking "How can I know about what I have not myself observed?" just as the phenomenologist and solipsist do. To such a question no answer is necessary for the man who does not regard himself as absolutely a special case, and no answer is possible for the man who does. Scepticism is thus seen as sort of pride, the epistemological form of original sin . . . Rationality is opposed to egocentricity, and to the extent a man is being rational, he must come out of himself.

Our concern here, however, is not to consider this continuing debate about induction (Hacking 1975; Levi 1980; Millar 1980; Holland et al. 1986; Howson 1991), but rather to note the contribution that a doctrine of creation can make to the issue at stake, especially in relation to the connection between induction and the concept of "laws of nature." This can be seen more clearly by considering the question of inductive scepticism – that is, the problem of how to proceed from the observation that "all Xs have been Ys" to the conclusion that "the next X will be a Y." We have already noted that Lucas's plea for "decentering" observation offers a helpful response to this point; we shall now consider the approach adopted by John Stuart Mill, especially in his 1843 classic *A System of Logic, Ratiocinative and Inductive* (Gower 1997, 109–29). Mill argued that "every well-grounded inductive generalization is either a law of nature, or a result of laws of nature, capable, if these laws are known, of being predicted from them" (Mill 1974, vol. 7, 318). In other words, a one-step inferential sequence of the following form (Armstrong 1983, 56):

observed situations $\Rightarrow$ non-observed situations

can be replaced by a two-set inferential sequence of the following nature:

observed situations $\Rightarrow$ laws of nature $\Rightarrow$ non-observed situations.

This procedure draws attention to the importance of "laws of nature" in relation to induction. In a sense, the very idea of a "law of nature" may be regarded as an affirmation of "uniformity through ordering." This naturally leads us to consider the idea of a "law of nature" in more detail.

Ordering and the Laws of Nature

A Christian understanding of the concept of creation is, as we have seen, closely linked with the concept of ordering. We have already drawn attention to the notion of the explicable regularity of the world, and linked this with the concept of "creation as ordering" (pp. 41–2). As Stephen Hawking, among many others, has pointed out, the existence of God is easily and naturally correlated with the regularity and ordering of the world. "It would be completely consistent with all we know to say that there was a Being who is responsible for the laws of physics" (Hawking 1985, 12). The noted theoretical physicist Charles A. Coulson pointed out the importance of "religious conviction" in explaining the "unprovable assumption that there is an order and constancy in Nature" (Coulson 1955, 57). In what follows, we shall explore the idea of the "laws of nature," a highly significant way of depicting (and interpreting) the order found within the world. We may begin, however, by noting the significance of the theories of chaos which have emerged since about 1960, which are clearly of significance in this matter.

Order and Chaos

The theme of cosmic order is of major importance within the writings of Isaac Newton, who argued that the regularity and predictability of the world were a direct consequence of its created origins. Pope's celebrated epitaph for Newton captures aspects of this point well (Pope 1963, 808):

> Nature and Nature's Law lay hid in Night
> God said, let Newton be, and all was Light.

The universe is not "random," but behaves in a regular manner which is capable of observation and explanation. This led to the widespread belief that systems which satisfied Newton's laws of motion behaved in ways which were predetermined, and which could therefore be predicted with considerable accuracy – a view which is often represented at a popular level in terms of the image of a "clockwork universe." As recent studies of Newton's natural philosophy have stressed (McGuire 1968; Heimann 1973), Newton and his followers found it appropriate to portray the laws of nature as dependent upon the continual exercise of God's will. This "voluntarist" approach to the laws of nature may have been intended to stress God's providence, rather than the regularity of nature; within a generation, however, God came to be seen simply as a creator or mechanic.

One of the most fascinating paradoxes of the religious thought of the eighteenth century is the manner in which Newton's mechanical conception of the universe was initially interpreted as supportive of the Christian understanding of God, yet within a generation was seen as rendering such a concept unnecessary. The uncovering of the regularity and rationality (in the sense of an ordering which the human mind could discern and appreciate) of the world, as expressed in Newton's laws of planetary motion, were widely interpreted as a powerful confirmation of the Christian doctrine of creation. This can be seen, for example, by considering the way in which Newtonian ideas were handled in the writings of Richard Bentley, especially the published version of the Boyle Lectures of 1692 (Gascoigne 1988; Hall 1996, 246–8). This should not be regarded as a distortion of Newton's ideas, in that Newton himself was inclined to take such a position (Schöpf 1991). The writings of William Paley may be seen as a popular exposition of the theological implications of an ordered Newtonian universe (Gillespie 1990).

Nevertheless, Newton's work could also be interpreted in another manner. The essential point concerns the existence of what appeared to be self-sustaining principles within the world. Traditional Christian conceptions of divine providence postulated the need for the sustaining and regulating hand of God to be present and active throughout the entire existence of the world. The Newtonian worldview thus encouraged the view that, although God may well have created the world, there was no further need for divine involvement. The discovery of the laws of conservation (for example, the laws of conservation of momentum) seemed to imply either that God had endowed the creation with all the mechanisms which it required in order to continue.[10] Related ideas would later be developed in biological sciences . While the concept of God was held to be significant in relation to the creation of the world, it seemed to have no necessary place in its conservation. It is this point which is encapsulated in Laplace's famous comment, made in relation to the idea of God as a sustainer of planetary motion: *nous n'avons pas besoin de cette hypothèse-là* (Hahn 1981). Although Newtonian natural theology continued to enjoy considerable popularity in England until the early Victorian period, it is clear that it had been considerably undermined from within (Gascoigne 1988). A further difficulty lay in the emergence of a critique of the notion of teleology within nature on account of its anthropomorphic associations. Writers as diverse as William of Ockham, Galileo Galilei, and Francis Bacon argued that the assumed link between intentionality and teleology was vulnerable, and could not be maintained (Soontiëns 1992, 396–7).

In terms of the development of Christian theology, it is widely agreed that the triumph of the Newtonian mechanistic worldview led to the rise of the movement generally known as "Deism" (Gay 1968; O'Higgins 1971; Sullivan 1982; Byrne 1989). Although "Deism" is perhaps less theologically coherent than has been assumed, it is known to have defended the idea that God created the world, and endowed it with the ability to develop and function without the need for his continuing presence or interference. This viewpoint, which became especially influential in the eighteenth century, regarded the world as a watch, and God as the watchmaker. God endowed the world with a certain self-sustaining design, such that it could subsequently function without the need for continual intervention. The undermining of the predictability of the

Newtonian mechanical system, evident in the rise of "chaos theory" in the present century, represents a major challenge to deism; this could not have been foreseen at the time.

The origin of chaos theory remains controverted. Writers such as Ilya Prigogine have argued that the emergence of chaos theory marks a remarkable and irreversible break with the "closed universe" or deterministic modes of thought which have characterized the classical origins of modern science (Prigogine 1997). Nevertheless, other writers have suggested that the *origins* of the discipline are thoroughly classical, in that they can be seen to emerge from attempts to understand the long-term stability of the solar system on the basis of an essentially Newtonian model. Thus Diacu and Holmes argue that the critically important notion of non-linear dynamics had its origins within a traditional classical model of the solar system (Diacu and Holmes 1997).

On the basis of this second approach, the origins of modern "chaos theory" can be traced back to 1892. One of the most important early studies of the relation between non-linearity and sensitive dependence on initial conditions was due to the French mathematician Henri Poincaré. Poincaré was especially concerned with what is known as the "Kepler problem" – that is, the problem of orbital motion which centers on three bodies interacting by the force of Newtonian gravity (Poincaré 1892). Poincaré's analysis of the problem suggested that, under certain conditions, this "classic" system could develop a potentially explosive instability. A further major development took place in 1961. Edward Lorenz, then a meteorologist at the Massachusetts Institute of Technology, noted that the use of mathematical modeling and computer prediction in the specific field of weather forecasting was subject to severe limitations (Lorenz 1963).

It was soon realized that this was not a matter which could be confined to the somewhat limited field of meteorology (Gleick 1987); the general principles could easily be applied to all systems governed by Newtonian dynamics, yielding the alarming result that they do not necessarily exhibit the "predictability" which would once have been regarded as an integral aspect of their behavior (Lighthill 1986). Even the simple instance of the oscillation of a pendulum can be shown to be prone to unpredictability under certain conditions (Crutchfield et al. 1986, 38). More complex systems – such as the growth of animal populations and non-equilibrium thermodynamics – showed the same propensity to unpredictability due to a critical dependence on the precise initial conditions of the system (May 1976; Prigogine and Stengers 1984; Stewart 1989; Ruelle 1993).

This does not mean that the world is chaotic in the sense of "inexplicable". At a mathematical level, the origins of "chaos" may be argued to lie in the complexity of the solutions to non-linear equations. Whereas linear equations offer exact solutions, their non-linear counterparts often defy precise solution.

It must be stressed that the difficulty is intrinsic to the mathematics, and does not result from a lack of precision concerning the parameters of the equations in question. The origin of the unpredictability does not lie in the "disorder" of the world, but in the intrinsic difficulty of predicting behavior in complex systems on account of acute sensitivity to their initial conditions. This view is especially associated with the Brussels School, led by the Nobel Prize winning physicist Ilya Prigogine, noted for his work on non-equilibrium thermodynamics. As Prigogine argues forcefully, non-equilibrium is "the source of order" (Prigogine and Stengers 1984, 287), so that one may speak of the spontaneous generation of order "on the edge of chaos."

The religious implications of chaos theory have only begin to be explored, and it is likely that further investigation of this area will be highly fruitful. An early contribution from Thomas F. Torrance (Torrance 1979) was followed by more detailed exploration (Ward 1990, 74–133; Russell, Murphy, and Peacocke 1995), especially in relation to the area of divine providence (Bartholomew 1984). Arthur Peacocke has offered an especially promising analysis of the creative interaction of chance and law to yield "an ordered universe capable of developing within itself new modes of existence" (Peacocke 1993, 65). The interaction and interrelation of "law" and "chaos" is pregnant with theological significance, and is clearly going to be of major importance in the future. Always keenly aware of the broader implications of his theories, Prigogine himself spoke of the "re-enchantment of nature" (Prigogine and Stengers 1984); perhaps the time has come to develop such insights to lead to a new awareness of the profound religious dimensions of the natural order.

The Laws of Nature: The Theoretical Foundations
The phrase "law of nature" appears to have begun to be used systematically during the early eighteenth century. It is generally agreed that the phrase reflects the widely-held notion, prevalent within both orthodox Christianity and Deism, that the world was ordered by a divine law-giver, who laid down the manner in which the creation should behave. A "law of nature" was thus held to be more than a description or summary of observable features of the world; it reflected a divine decision that the world was intended to behave in this manner (Ayer 1956, 211; Fraassen 1989, 1–14). With the widespread secularization of western culture, this general belief has been eroded, both inside and outside the scientific community. The phrase "laws of nature" remained, nevertheless, although it has acquired something of the status of a dead metaphor. It remains, however, a concept with profound theological implications.[11]

We may begin by attempting to clarify what a "law of nature" might be. The term is used widely, and consequently with a degree of imprecision, not least on account of the variety of nuanced meanings associated with the word

"law" (Achinstein 1971, 2). It can be used to refer to universally true statements of non-limited scope that embody only qualitative predicates (Hemel
and Oppenheim 1970). Examples of this might include "all metals conduct
electricity" or "at constant pressure any gas expands with increasing temperature." This approach to a definition excludes what might be termed "accidental laws," such as "all the animals in my garden this afternoon are cats," or
"vacuously true generalizations," such as "all solid gold spheres are less than
ten meters in diameter," or "all unicorns weigh five kilograms" (Ayers 1956;
Carroll 1990, 191–2).

The general consensus on the nature and scope of the "laws of nature"
within the scientific community has been set out by Davies (Davies 1992, 72–
92). In general terms, the "laws of nature" can be considered to have the
following features.

1   They are *universal*. The laws of physics are assumed to be valid at every
    place and every time. They are held "to apply unfailingly everywhere in
    the universe and at all epochs of cosmic history" (Davies 1992, 82). There
    is an interesting parallel here with the criterion introduced in the fifth
    century by Vincent of Lérins for Christian doctrines, which were required
    to be things which were believed "everywhere, always and by all (*quod
    ubique, quod semper, quod ab omnibus creditum est*)."

2   They are *absolute* – that is to say, that they do not depend on the nature of
    the observer (for example, his or her social status, gender, or sexual orien-
    tation). The state of a system may change over time, and be related to a
    series of contingent and circumstantial considerations; the laws, which
    provide correlation between those states at various moments, do not change
    with time. This aspect of the laws of nature causes serious difficulties for a
    postmodern worldview, which we shall examine in a later section of this
    project.

3   They are *eternal*, in that they are held to be grounded in the mathematical
    structures which are used to represent the physical world. The remarkable
    correlation between what we shall loosely term "mathematical reality" and
    the observed physical world is of considerable significance, and we shall
    return to this matter later. It is of considerable importance in this context
    to note that all known fundamental laws are mathematical in form.

4   They are *omnipotent*, in that nothing can be held to be outside their scope.

It will not have escaped the reader's notice that these attributes which are, by
common agreement and convention, applied to the "laws of nature," show remarkable affinities with those which are traditionally applied to God in theistic
religious systems, such as Christianity. Davies' analysis thus raises the question
of the relation between God and the "laws of nature," to which we now turn.

God and the Laws of Nature

We may take as our starting point a statement of Davies, who argues that God cannot "be omnipotent, for he could not act outside the laws of nature" (Davies 1984, 209). This, however, fails to take account of a fundamental debate within both Christian theology and the philosophy of religion, focussing on the question of the power of God (Oakley 1984; van den Brink 1993; Moonan 1994). In what follows, we shall explore this major discussion, and indicate its relevance to the relation of God and the laws of nature.

How can God act absolutely reliably, without being subject to some external agency which compels God to act in this way? This question was debated with some heat at Paris in the thirteenth century, in response to a form of determism linked with the writer Averroes. For Averroes, the reliability of God ultimately rested upon external pressures. God was compelled to act in certain ways – and thus acted reliably. This approach was, however, regarded with intense suspicion by most theologians, who saw it as a crude denial of the freedom of God. But how could God be said to act reliably, unless it was through external compulsion?

In what follows, we shall consider the answer given during the thirteenth and fourteenth centuries by writers such as Duns Scotus and William of Ockham. The fundamental principle which is stated by these writers is that the reliability of God is ultimately grounded in the divine nature itself. God does not act reliably because someone or something makes God act in this way, but because of a deliberate and free divine decision to act like this. This decision was not a result of coercion or external constraint, but a free decision reflecting the nature of God himself.

In his discussion of the opening line of the Apostle's Creed – "I believe in God the Father almighty" – Ockham asks precisely what is meant by the word "almighty (*omnipotens*)." It cannot, he argues, mean that God is presently able to do anything and everything; rather, it means that God was once free to act in this way. God has now established an order of things which reflects a loving and righteous divine will – and that order, once established, will remain until the end of time.

Ockham uses two terms to refer to these different options. The "absolute power of God (*potentia Dei absoluta*)" refers to the theoretical possibilities prior to commitment to any course of action or world ordering. The "ordained power of God (*potentia Dei ordinata*)" refers to the way things now are, which reflects the order established by God their creator. These do not represent two different sets of options now open to God. They represent two different moments in the great history of salvation. And our concern is with the ordained power of God, the way in which God orders the creation at present.

The distinction is important, yet difficult. In view of this, we shall explore it in a little more detail. Ockham is inviting us to consider two very different situations in which we might speak of the "omnipotence of God." The first is this: God is confronted with a whole array of possibilities – such as creating the world, or not creating the world. God can choose to actualize any of these possibilities. This is the absolute power of God, which refers to a situation in which God has not yet acted. (It should be noted that, for the sake of clarity of explanation of this specific issue, we have disregarded the question of whether God be said to "create time" or "create *within* time." This is an immensely important debate, which cannot be considered fully at this point).

We now move away from this scenario, in which we were invited to consider a range of possibilities which God had the potential to enact. We now consider the scenario in which God acts – for example, by ordering the universe. God has chosen some options, and brought them into being, with the result that certain potentialities are now actualities. We are now in the realm of the ordained power of God – a realm in which God's power is restricted, by virtue of God's own decision. Ockham's point is that by choosing to actualize some potentialities, God has implicitly chosen not to actualize others. Choosing to do something means choosing not to do something else. Once God has chosen to create the world, the option of not creating the world is set to one side. This means that there are certain things which God could do once that can no longer be done. Although God could have decided not to create the world, God has now deliberately rejected that possibility. And that rejection means that this possibility is no longer open.

This leads to what seems, at first sight, to be a paradoxical situation. On account of the divine omnipotence, God is not now able to do everything. By exercising the divine power, God has limited options. For Ockham, God cannot now do everything. God has deliberately limited the possibilities. God chose to limit the options which are now open. Is that a contradiction? No. If God is really capable of doing anything, then God must be able to become committed to a course of action – and stay committed to it. God can thus be said to act according to established laws – but these are not laws which somehow have their origination outside God, or which can be thought of as contrary to the nature of God. They themselves are the creation of God, and reflect the nature and character. In acting according to established laws, God is remaining faithful to an expression of his own nature, brought about by his own free decision. Ockham expresses this as follows (Ockham 1966, vol. 9, 585–6):

> God is able to do some things by his ordained power (*de potentia ordinata*) and others by his absolute power (*de potentia absoluta*). This distinction should not be understood to mean that there are actually in God two powers, one of which is "ordained" and the other of which is "absolute," because there is only one power of God directed towards the external world, the exercise of which is in all respects God himself. Nor should this be understood to mean that God can do

some things by his ordained power, and others by his absolute, not his ordained, power, in that God does nothing without having first ordained it. But it should be understood in this way: God can do something in a manner which is established by laws which were ordained and established by God. In this respect, God acts according to his ordained power.

The relevance of this analysis to Davies' statement will be clear. Within a theistic perspective, such as that offered by Christianity, it is quite misleading to posit a tension between God and the laws of nature, as if the latter were somehow independent of the former, or in some way contradicted each other. We could thus say that the absolute power of God refers to $t = 0$, whereas the ordained power of God refers to $t > 0$. The Christian will hold that God's nature is somehow *expressed and embodied in the ordering of the world*, which underlies the laws of nature. That God "obeys" such laws cannot conceivably be taken to mean that God is subservient to another being, or is obligated or otherwise constrained to work within an alien framework which is not of his own making. There is a fundamental line of continuity between the creator, the regularity of the creation, and the human perception and expression of this regularity in the form of "laws of nature."

Philosophical Approaches to the Laws of Nature
Three somewhat different approaches to the "laws of nature" have been set out in recent studies exploring the more philosophical aspects of the matter. In the first place, there is continued support for the Humean approach, which discerns regularity in the ordering process of the human mind, rather than any independently-existing natural ordering (Urbach 1988). For such writers, "laws of nature" merely record actual or *de facto* regularities. Since there is no necessity in nature, the "laws" in question can only describe what is observed, and nothing more. Observation may thus be regarded as a process which aims to impose order on the extra-mental world. This kind of approach can be found in the writings of Ernst Mach (Mach 1898):

> The communication of scientific knowledge always involves description, that is, a mimetic reproduction of facts in thought, the object of which is to replace and save the trouble of new experience. Again, to save the labour of instruction and acquisition, concise abridged description is sought. This is really all that natural laws are.

For Mach, the "laws of nature" are thus nothing more than "concise abridged descriptions" of reality, a convenient and helpful manner of depicting reality which has no ontological significance. They are purely heuristic in character, and cannot be held to correspond to anything that exists independent of the mind of the observer.

Other writers adopt a viewpoint which is more sympathetic to a realist interpretation. David Lewis may be regarded as developing some insights of John Stuart Mill, who argued that the question about "laws of nature" may be reduced to the simpler question: "What are the fewest and simplest assumptions, which being granted, the whole existing order of nature would result?" (Mill 1974, vol. 7, 317). Lewis suggests that "a contingent generalization is a *law of nature* if and only if it appears as a theorem or (axiom) in each of the true deductive systems that achieves a best combination of simplicity and strength" (Lewis 1973, 73). A "law of nature" is thus understood to be a contingent generalization which possesses an appropriate balance of "simplicity" and "strength', which can be formulated in a propositional manner allowing it to function within a deductive system. As Lewis himself later acknowledged, this seems to introduce a significant degree of subjectivity into the definition of such a law, in that the "best combination of simplicity and strength" is left to the judgment of the observer. The distinction between what is a genuine law of nature and what is simply an accidental regularity thus remains unclear.

A third approach argues that the laws of nature are to be thought of as relations between universals (Dretske 1977; Tooley 1977; Armstrong 1983). These laws of nature are assumed to exist independently of the human minds which attempt to discern them. Armstrong draws a fundamental distinction between "laws of nature" and "law-statements" (Armstrong 1983, 8). A law of nature is thus a feature of the real world; a law-statement is a human creation which attempts to express these features. Regularities reflect the way in which certain universals stand in a relation of "nomic necessitation" (Lange 1992, 154–5). For Armstrong, a statement p (a "law-statement") affirms a cosmic uniformity ("a law of nature") if (i) p is universally quantified; (ii) p is true; (iii) p is contingent; and (iv) p contains only non-local empirical predicates (apart from logical connectives and quantifiers) (Armstrong 1983, 12). This allows Armstrong to affirm fundamental ordering in nature, while maintaining the provisionality of human attempts to express and articulate such regularities.

It is beyond the scope of this work to enter into this debate, although we shall be considering the merits of a realist approach in due course. The Humean suggestion that "laws of nature" are imposed on nature is widely regarded as implausible within the scientific community. Regularity, according to this viewpoint, is not to be seen as a feature of the "real world," but as a construct of an order-imposing human mind. It is widely-held within the scientific community that regularity (including statistical regularity) is an intrinsic feature of the world, uncovered (not imposed) by human investigation. For example, consider the comments of Paul Davies, which would be widely endorsed by natural scientists (Davies 1992, 82–3):

It is important to understand that the regularities of nature are real . . . I believe any suggestion that the laws of nature are similar projections of the human mind is absurd. The existence of regularities in nature is an objective mathematical fact. On the other hand, the statements called laws that are found in textbooks clearly *are* human inventions, but inventions designed to reflect, albeit imperfectly, actually existing properties of nature. Without this assumption that regularities are real, science is reduced to an absurdity. Another reason why I don't think the laws of nature are simply made up by us is that they help us to uncover new things about the world, sometimes things we never suspected. The mark of a powerful law is that it goes beyond a faithful description of the original phenomenon it was invoked to explain, and links up with other phenomena too . . . The history of science shows that, once a new law is accepted, its consequences are rapidly worked out, and the law is tested in many novel contexts, often leading to the discovery of new, unexpected and important phenomena. This leads me to believe that in conducting science we are uncovering real regularities and linkages out of nature, not writing them into nature.

It will be clear that a religious (and especially a Christian) approach to the debate will focus on the idea of the ordering of the world as something which exists in that world, independent of whether the human mind recognizes it or not, and that this ordering can be understood to be related to the doctrine of creation. While many natural scientists have discarded the original theological framework which led their predecessors of the seventeenth and eighteenth centuries to speak of "laws of nature," there is no reason why such an insight should not be reappropriated by those natural scientists sensitive to the religious aspects of their work.

Recent studies of the "laws of nature" have stressed their role in reflecting and conceptualizing order (Harré 1993; Carroll 1994). This "ordering" can be discerned at several levels, including the general principles which appear to govern the universe and the classification systems or "taxonomies" which play such an important role in laying the foundations for the exploration of the laws of nature (Harré 1993, 10–11). In view of the importance of such taxonomies, we shall explore their role in the thought of a leading botanist, noting especially the theological aspects of the matter.

The Analysis of Order: The Case of Linnaeus
One of the most significant interpretations of the observation of ordering within the natural world is due to the eighteenth-century Swedish naturalist Carl von Linné (1707–78), more generally known by the Latinised form of his name, "Carolus Linnaeus" (Anderson 1997). Despite the muddled account of his significance offered by some English theologians (most notably, that found in Raven 1953, vol. 1, 152–8), it is clear that Linnaeus is an important witness to a potentially creative and illuminating mode of interaction between theo-

logical beliefs and empirical analysis. It is widely agreed that Linnaeus' starting point is his perception of some form of ordering within the natural world.
Linnaeus was not really an "experimentalist', as that term is now understood;
for him, an "experiment" referred primarily to the observation or experience
of the natural world (Broberg 1975, 38). Linnaeus brought to his taxonomical
task an acute ability for accurate observation and logical analysis, allowing him
to categorize and classify what might otherwise not be recognized as possessing
any form of regularity.

So how is this ordering to be explained? Although Linnaeus was somewhat
unorthodox by the norms of contemporary Swedish Lutheranism (Frängsmyr
1969, 216–17; Broberg 1975, 141–9), there is no doubt that a strongly religious
belief system, particularly in relation to a doctrine of creation, informs his
analysis of nature. Indeed, it is significant to observe the form of argumentation deployed in the 1743 essay "Oratio de telluris habitabilis incremento."
Linnaeus does not make an appeal to the Christian doctrine of creation in
establishing his argument; rather, he considers that doctrine to be confirmed
and strengthened by his arguments concerning the relation of plants and animals (von Hoftsen 1938, 35). Linnaeus regards the world as being much older
than a purely literal reading of the Genesis creation account would suggest
(Frängsmyr 1969, 223–5); his concern, however, does not focus on issues of
chronology, but rather the perception of ordering within nature, which Linnaeus
believes to rest upon, or somehow reflect, the divine creation of the world.
Indeed, it has been persuasively argued that the perception and explanation of
order within nature is the most single important question to be addressed by
Linnaeus (Larson 1971).

Linnaeus' taxonomic system is grounded in the assumption that creation is
fixed and rational. As it happened, the first of these assumptions would be
challenged in the subsequent generation, with the rise of evolutionary thinking
(Larson 1994). Nevertheless, the time-scale envisaged for the evolutionary
process was so enormous that a mere human life-span was insignificant in
comparison. In effect, Linnaeus' assumption of fixity proved to be adequate
for his specific purposes. It may be noted that this assumption of an orderly
world, capable of rational investigation through acute observation and logical
categorization, resonates with both the Christian doctrine of creation and the
Enlightenment belief in the harmony and rationality of the world.

Linnaeus' views on the origins of the order he perceived were soon subjected to criticism, most notably by George-Louis Leclerc, Comte de Buffon
(Sloan 1976). Our particular interest, however, concerns the importance of the
observations of regularity within nature, and the perceived consistency of such
ordering with a Christian doctrine of creation. At some times in history, the
religious significance of this regularity might be construed in a highly pragmatic manner, as with Gregory of Tours in the seventh century, who noted the

value of astronomy in determining the correct times for monastic prayers (McCluskey 1990); at others, this regularity was interpreted in more theological terms, as the divine imposition of order on the world. Many other such examples could be given, in which the perception of ordering and regularity is of foundational importance to scientific advance. Nevertheless, it must be appreciated that the perception of ordering can also lead to difficulties for a religious perspective, as will become clear in what follows.

Ordering and Mechanism: From Newton to Paley
It is a simple matter of historical fact that the relationship between "natural theology" and the "natural sciences" has been remarkably ambivalent in terms of its intentions and outcomes. One the one hand, a strategy originally devised by religious writers to heighten the awareness of a religious dimension to nature ended up offering new opportunities for a purely secular interpretation of the world; on the other, one intended to accentuate a purely naturalistic interpretation of the world has proved remarkably amenable to a religious position (Brooke 1989). Nevertheless, it can be shown without difficulty that one of the most distinctive features of British intellectual life from the late seventeenth to the late nineteenth centuries was a pervasive belief that science was allied to the cause of religion.

The origins of this trend are generally agreed to lie particularly with the use made of Newton's *Principia* by the Anglican apologists of the late seventeenth and early eighteenth centuries (Metzger 1938; Jacob 1976; Jacob and Jacob 1980). The factors which led to this development are not fully understood, although there is agreement that they probably include the following (Gascoigne 1988, 222–4):

1   A focus on natural theology led to public interest in the interpretation of the natural world, rather than the more controversial matter of the interpretation of the Bible (see further below) or matters of doctrinal disagreement between various church groupings or theological schools.
2   The nature of ecclesiastic politics in England following the post-1688 constitution favoured that section of the Church of England which placed an emphasis on the role of reason, rather than those which stressed the transcendental character of divine revelation (Jacob 1976).
3   The Newtonian concept of gravity, interpreted within a theological framework which stressed the operation of divine providence, seemed to offer a means by which divine involvement in the world could be maintained without lapsing into monism or dualism.

Yet it was not long before what had seemed to be a promising alliance between science and religion led to a growing and potentially irreversible estrangement

(Odom 1966). The Newtonian system seemed to many to suggest that the world was a self-sustaining mechanism which had no need for divine governance or sustenance for its day-to-day operation. By the end of the eighteenth century, it seemed to many that Newton's system actually led to atheism or agnosticism, rather than to faith. This can be seen reflected both in Laplace's *Treatise of Celestial Mechanics*, which effectively eliminated the need for God (either as explanatory hypothesis or as active sustainer) in cosmology (Odom 1966; Hahn 1981), and in the writings of the poet William Blake, in which the Newtonian worldview is occasionally equated with Satan (Ault 1974). Percy Bysshe Shelley famously remarked that "the consistent Newtonian is necessarily an atheist," while Samuel Taylor Coleridge conceded that Newton's general approach obviated the need for God (Force 1985, 155; Gascoigne 1988, 234).

Yet the rise of a mechanistic view of the world offered another approach to natural theology, which was seized upon by some of the leading apologists of the late eighteenth and early nineteenth century (Bennett 1986). The metaphor of the universe as clockwork had already been deployed before the advent of its most famous exponent (Mayr 1986); nevertheless, it was in the writings of William Paley that it found its most celebrated presentation (Clarke 1974; LeMahieu 1976; Gillespie 1990). For Paley, the Newtonian image of the world as a mechanism immediately suggested the metaphor of a clock or watch, raising the question of who constructed the intricate mechanism which was so evidently displayed in the functioning of the world. Although it is currently fashionable to deride Paley's natural theology, this generally rests on a failure to recognize how he managed to transform the "clockwork" metaphor from an icon of scepticism and atheism to an apologetic affirmation of the existence of God. As Mayr has demonstrated, the English tradition of natural theology had, up to this point, shied away from an appeal to mechanism, apparently for fear of its philosophical implications (Mayr 1986, 90–101). Paley saw an apologetic opening, and seized it.

One of Paley's most significant arguments is that mechanism implies contrivance. Writing against the backdrop of the emerging Industrial Revolution, Paley sought to exploit the apologetic potential of the growing interest in machinery – such as "watches, telescopes, stocking-mills, and steam engines" – within England's literate classes (Gillespie 1990, 216–17). For some, the mechanistic model of the universe implied a lifeless deity (famously derided by Blake as "Nonbodaddy"). For Paley, the model offered a new defense of the existence of God.

The general thrust of this defense is well known. Noting the proliferation of machinery in the England of his time, Paley argues that only someone who is mad would suggest that such complex mechanical technology came into being by purposeless chance. Mechanism presupposes contrivance – that is to say, a sense of purpose and an ability to design and fabricate. Both the human body in particular, and the world in general, could be seen as mechanisms which had been designed and constructed in such a manner as to achieve harmony of both means and ends. It must be stressed that Paley is not suggesting that there exists an analogy between human mechanical devices and nature. The force of his argument rests on an identity: nature *is* a mechanism, and hence was possessed of an intelligent design (Gillespie 1990, 222–7).

In the end, Paley's defence of divine design may be judged to have failed, partly on account of the rise of Darwinism in the second part of the nineteenth century. It is, nevertheless, an interesting episode in natural theology, which cannot be seen simply as part of the traditional cosmological argument (which antedated the mechanical revolution) nor traditional natural theology (which focused on natural history, following a pattern established by John Ray in his classic *Wisdom of God Manifested in the Works of Creation* (1691)). It also illustrates the manner in which "order" and "mechanism" were seen as closely related, for theological reasons.

It is interesting to note how similar issues arise in relation to the issue of symmetry in modern physics, to which we now turn.

On Symmetry in Physics and Mathematics
The importance of symmetry in physics has been the subject of considerable interest in the past (for example, see Lee 1971; Brereton 1974). Symmetry can be discerned even in situations in which change is taking place; as has often been pointed out, the laws which appear to govern such changes can be represented as invariances of the natural order in relation to all possible changes that respect a particular intrinsic pattern (Barrow 1991, 20–1). This interest in symmetry has been given new impetus through the emergence of theories of "supersymmetry" in the early 1970s, initially through the work of Pierre Raymond, and subsequently through that of Julius Wess and Bruno Zumino (Wess and Bagger 1992; Witten 1997). The subsequent extension of the approach in the late 1970s to include gravity ("supergravity") further deepened this interest in symmetry (Gates et al. 1983), which became especially marked during the period 1984–5 through the emergence of the "superstring revolution." More recently still (roughly over the period 1994–5) what might be called the "second superstring revolution" has taken place (Witten 1997), offering new perspectives on the quest for superunification, from which it is believed that a unified description of natural law may emerge. What were previously regarded as separate or weakly-coupled theories can now be seen as possible low-energy manifestations of one underlying theory.

Two quite distinct (yet ultimately complementary) understandings of the role of symmetry can be discerned within modern physics, as follows:

1 An *a priori* approach, which aims to derives laws or basic principles of nature from some foundational symmetry principles which are prior to (or

in some sense underlie) the phenomena to be explained. Leibniz' Principle of Sufficient Reason could be argued to fall into this category, in that there is an implicit assumption that nature itself is symmetrical, leading to the expectation that our knowledge of nature should exhibit a corresponding symmetry.

2 An *a posteriori* approach, which derives symmetry principles from the observation of phenomena, especially as these are expressed in laws of nature. This empirical approach is perhaps the more widely encountered in the modern period, and can be found instanced in the writings of Galileo.

From the standpoint of the history of the natural sciences, the complex nature of the interaction of these two approaches is perhaps best seen from the early development of the special theory of relativity – specifically, the significance of Lorentz transformations. Were these transformations simply an expression of the mathematical properties of Maxwell's equations? This was the view of Lorentz and Poincaré (Lorentz 1904; Poincaré 1906); if correct, it followed that symmetry resulted from the laws of nature. On the other hand, Einstein argued that the transformation reflected the derivation of new laws from an observed symmetry (Einstein 1905). More recently, the development of "supersymmetry" (a conjectured quantum mechanical symmetry between fermions and bosons) offers an explanation for the existence of fermions.[12] To put it very crudely: supersymmetry demands their existence.

It is possible to argue that observed symmetries can be categorized in a number of ways. On the one hand, there are symmetries which appear to be essentially accidental, in that they do not seem to correspond to something fundamental which acts, for example, as a constraint on general theory construction. Examples of such symmetries would include the SU(3) symmetry of a three-dimensional harmonic oscillator (Jauch and Hill 1940); the conformal invariance of Maxwell's equations in free space, first noted by Bateman and Cunningham (Cunningham 1909; Bateman 1910); and the Fock symmetry for the motion of an election in a Coulomb potential, which underlies the degeneracy of the hydrogen spectrum with respect to angular momentum (Fock 1935). Nevertheless, caution must be exercised here, in that what might initially appear to be an accidental symmetry may subsequently prove to reflect something more fundamental.[13]

The significance of such symmetries has been the subject of considerable discussion within physics for some time. In a famous paper dating from 1894, Pierre Curie argued that effects cannot be more symmetric than their causes (Curie 1894; Chalmers 1970). Curie's argument involves the assertion that symmetry is transmitted from a cause to its effect. For Curie, an effect could not possess a greater degree of symmetry than its cause. This should not be taken as an assertion that symmetry is *always* transmitted in this manner: the important phenomenon of "spontaneous symmetry breaking" in condensed matter phsyics should be noted here (Weinberg 1993, 152–67). Curie's principle has been used with some success in various fields of theoretical science, perhaps most notably the question of inter-theory relations (Post 1971; Redhead 1975). Yet it is also of considerable interest from a religious perspective, as will become clear. In what follows, I shall consider the following question: what are the implications for theism if Curie is right?

The Religious Significance of Natural Order
As we have seen, there has been considerable interest in the existence and significance of symmetry within the natural order in recent years (Curie 1894; Chalmers 1970; Post 1971; Redhead 1975; Wess and Bager 1992; Witten 1997). It will be clear that there is an immediate affinity between the notions of "symmetry" and "order." The symmetries of objects can be defined mathematically in terms of group theory – a highly significant aspect of mathematics which proves to be of major relevance to many aspects of both classical physics and quantum mechanics (Cotton 1990; Inui, Tanabe, and Onodera 1990; Altmann 1992; Atkins and Friedman 1997, 122–63). What is the religious significance of this analysis?

My particular interest here is to explore the metaphysical and theological dimensions of "Curie's Principle" (see p. 70), which can be stated in the form that symmetries are transmitted from a cause to its effect. This general principle can easily be understood within the context of the kind of theological framework set out by Thomas Aquinas, especially in his *Summa contra Gentiles*, written during the period 1259–61, initially at Paris and subsequently at Naples. This work is generally regarded as representing a classic statement of the general themes of natural theology (Kretzmann 1997, 23–53). One of its most significant discussions concerns the manner in which God may be understood to be related to the creation – a relationship which Aquinas analyses in terms of causality. Similar arguments are set out in the more comprehensive *Summa Theologiae* (Davies 1992; Elders 1997).

For Aquinas, there exists a fundamental "likeness (*similitudo*) to God" within the created order as a consequence of God being the cause, in some sense of the word, of all created things. In that no created thing can be said to come into existence spontaneously, the existence of all things can be considered to be a consequence of a relationship of causal dependence between the creation and its creator. Using what are essentially Aristotelian categories of causality, Aquinas sets out a position which we may summarize as follows:

1   Suppose that A causes B;
2   Suppose also that A possesses a quality Q;
3   Then B will also possess that quality Q as a result of its being caused by A.

The full argument set out by Aquinas is complex, and not without its difficulties (Kretzmann 1997, 139–60); nevertheless, its conclusion is clear. As Kretzmann puts it, there is a "presence in the effect of characteristics that could serve to identify, or at least to type, the agent – physical or metaphysical fingerprints providing the basis for an inductive argument to the agent's existence and some aspects of its nature" (Kretzmann 1997, 146). This does not mean that there is a similarity between all causes and effects; Aquinas notes that what he terms "accidental effects" may arise, in which no such similarity exists. It is clear, however, that Aquinas regards creation as perhaps the clearest example of a purposeful causation, in which qualities of the agent are to be found in the generated outcome.

For Aquinas, one of the most fundamental qualities which is to be attributed to God is that of "perfection." Although this concept can clearly be understood in moral terms, Aquinas uses it to characterize the distinctiveness of God in respect to the created order. "Perfection" is a quality which is possessed by God, and is possessed by that which God has created:

(a) to a lesser extent than it is possessed by God, and;
(b) as a result of its having been created by God.

In this sense, "perfection" may be thought of as an attribute which is characteristic of God, but is reflected in the created order on account of the metaphysically primary relationship of God to all other things.[14] Yet it is clear that the concept of "perfection" carries with it both moral and aesthetic connotations, which requires further investigation (Swinburne 1977, 179–209).

There has been a long association between "perfection" and "symmetry" in Christian thought. Origen (c.185–c.254) argued that the resurrection body should be spherical, on the grounds of the following (somewhat tendentious) argument:

1   The resurrection body will be perfect;
2   Perfection implies a certain shape;
3   The most perfect shape is a sphere, which is perfectly symmetrical;
4   Therefore the resurrection body will be spherical.

It is clear that point (3) reflects the influence of Platonism. It is well known that the development of Christian thought during the patristic period (usually taken to refer to the period AD c.100–451) was significantly (and sometimes unconsciously) influenced by secular Greek philosophical ideas, and this particular example may be taken as an illustration of this trend (documentation needed here).

The essential point to be made here concerns the connection between symmetry, order, and God. The Curie Principle affirms that effects cannot be more symmetric than their causes; symmetries are transmitted from a cause to its effect. The fundamental Christian conception of God as the creator and giver of order resonates with this kind of thinking about symmetry. It could be re-expressed in terms of one of the "Five Ways," in which Thomas Aquinas set out the reasons for supposing that there was indeed a God. (I have avoided using the term "argument" as it is clearly inappropriate; Aquinas believed in God long before he developed any "arguments" in support of that belief.)

Aquinas sets out "Five Ways" of arguing that the Christian understanding of God is coherent and credible (Rowe 1975; Swinburne 1979; Craig 1980; MacDonald 1991; Kretzmann 1997, 60–4). Each of these arguments is *a posteriori*, in that it is based on some aspect of a sense-perceptible reality. The fifth argument – which is based on the perception of purpose, ordering, or directedness in the world – is of particular interest, and has probably been the most influential, particularly in relation to the religious implications of the natural sciences.

Our interest here lies with the observation of ordering (or, more specifically, symmetry) within the world – not simply at the level of the structure of the world, but at the level of theories themselves. Specifically, we are interested in the suggestion that symmetry is always transmitted from cause to effect. The general approach adopted by Aquinas in his "fifth way" is to argue that this observed symmetry owes its origins to the perfection of God. If the general pattern is that a cause exhibits greater perfection than its effect, Aquinas' general line of argument would lead to the conclusion that there must exist a perfect original cause, from which all effects derive their perfection. It must be stressed that Aquinas' argument is vulnerable in terms of some of its assumptions. For example, the argument does not necessarily lead to the conclusion that there is only one God. Nevertheless, the new interest in symmetry offers a new lease of life – not to mention an important new perspective – on this longstanding philosophical approach to the question of God's existence and nature.

Symmetry can be seen as an aspect of the ordering of the world; it can also be seen as an aspect of its beauty. The symmetry of crystals – whether in the form of a snowflake or a gemstone – has long been seen as a matter of aesthetic appreciation. In what follows, we shall explore this second aspect of the concept of creation.

Aspects of Creation: Beauty

The theoretical chemist Charles A. Coulson, bringing together his scientific and theological concerns, once commented that observations of the world "set us going on a strange voyage where imagination, beauty and pattern are our signposts" (Coulson 1960, 11). The very idea of "beauty" is remarkably complex (Stolnitz 1961; Carritt 1962). Indeed, for some writers, the concept has become so difficult to define that it has ceased to be meaningful. Especially in the twentieth century, recognition of the importance of such issues as cultural conditioning and growing suspicion of the power of those cultural elites who determine taste have combined to bring about something of "a crisis not merely in the theory of beauty but in the very concept itself" (Tatarkiewicz 1972, 169). In addition, the Humean critique of the objectivity of beauty has continued to have a significant influence on contemporary reflection. For Hume, "beauty is no quality in things themselves; it exists merely in the mind which contemplates them" (Kerr 1993). Just as Hume argued that the perception of "order" within nature was the imposition of the human mind, so "beauty" was to be seen as a concept imposed upon, rather than discerned within, the natural world.

It might therefore seem a little unwise to invest any effort in exploring such a controverted and nuanced concept in this work. However, despite the difficulties attending the notion, it seems essential to include reflection on its relevance to our theme. There has been a growing interest within the learned literature in the linkage between theology and aesthetics – for example, in the way in which Victorian aesthetics were shaped by religious beliefs (Fraser 1986). The Humean critique of beauty as an intrinsic property of things has itself been subjected to criticism – from within both a Thomist and the Anglo-American analytical tradition – and the idea of beauty as an intrinsic property of things vigorously defended (Sircello 1975; Maurer 1983; Mothersill 1984). More importantly for our purposes, the notion of beauty has come to play a significant role within the philosophy of science itself (Zee 1986; McAllister 1989). In what follows, we shall explore this fascinating aspect of the relationship between religion and the sciences. We may therefore begin by considering the religious aspects of the matter.

The Religious Aspects of Beauty

The theme of "the beauty of God" has figured prominently in Christian thinking (Sherry 1992; Kerr 1993). The Old Testament frequently dwells upon the "beauty of the Lord", particularly in the Psalter (Reines 1975; von Rad 1975, vol. 1, 364–8). Augustine of Hippo argued that there was a natural progression from an admiration of the beautiful things of the world to the worship of the one who had created these things, and whose beauty was reflected in them (von Balthasar 1982–, vol. 2, 123–9). The great medieval theologian Thomas Aquinas set out "Five Ways" of inferring from the orderliness of the world to the reality of God; the fourth of those ways is based upon the observation of the existence of perfection in the world. Although Aquinas does not specifically identity "beauty" as one of these perfections at this point, it is clear that this identification can be made without difficulty, and is made elsewhere in Aquinas' works. This general line of argument was developed in the early twentieth century by the noted philosophical theologian F. R. Tennant, who argued that part of the cumulative case for the existence of God was the observation of beauty within the world (Tennant 1930, vol. 2, 89–93).

Within the Reformed tradition, a recognition of the importance of "beauty" as a theological theme can be discerned in the writings of Calvin (Wencelius 1979). However, its most powerful exposition within this tradition is generally agreed to be found in the writings of the leading eighteenth-century American theologian Jonathan Edwards (Delattre 1968). Edwards argues that the beauty of God is to be expected – and duly found – in the derived beauty of the created order (Edwards 1948, 61–9).

> It is very fit and becoming of God who is infinitely wise, so to order things that there should be a voice of His in His works, instructing those that behold him and painting forth and shewing divine mysteries and things more immediately appertaining to Himself and His spiritual kingdom. The works of God are but a kind of voice or language of God to instruct intelligent beings in things pertaining to Himself. And why should we not think that he would teach and instruct by His works in this way as well as in others, viz., by representing divine things by His works and so painting them forth, especially since we know that God hath so much delighted in this way of instruction. . . . If we look on these shadows of divine things as the voice of God purposely by them teaching us these and those spiritual and divine things, to show of what excellent advantage it will be, how agreeably and clearly it will tend to convey instruction to our minds, and to impress things on the mind and to affect the mind, by that we may, as it were, have God speaking to us. Wherever we are, and whatever we are about, we may see divine things excellently represented and held forth.

The most theologically sustained and sophisticated exploration of the significance of "beauty" of the present century can be found in the writings of the Swiss Roman Catholic theologian Hans Urs von Balthasar (1905–88). The theme of "beauty" dominates his *magnum opus* (von Balthasar 1982– ; O'Donaghue 1986; O'Donnell 1992, 18–34). "The fundamental principle of a theological aesthetics . . . is the fact that, just as this Christian revelation is absolute truth and goodness, so also it is absolute beauty" (von Balthasar 1982– , vol. 1, 607). Von Balthasar thus describes his own work as "an attempt to develop a Christian theology in the light of the third transcendental, that is to say: to complement the vision of the true and the good with that of the beautiful" (von Balthasar 1982–, vol. 1, 9). There are obvious parallels here with the Platonic triad of truth, goodness and beauty, which has led some critics to suggest that von Balthasar has himself adopted a form of Platonism, similar to that which is so striking a feature of the writings of pseudo-Dionysius.

Beauty in the Natural Sciences

It will therefore be clear that the concept of beauty is of major importance to a religious understanding of the nature of the world. Its importance has long been appreciated in pure mathematics (Penrose 1974), although the new interest in fractals has opened up the issue in a new and highly exciting manner (Penrose 1990, 98–128; Moon 1992; Peitgen, Jürgens, and Saupe 1992). In the present century, that interest in beauty has also become significant for the natural sciences. While "beauty" can be understood to refer to the natural world itself, it is generally understood to refer to the manner in which that world is to be interpreted, especially at the theoretical level (Zee 1986; McAllister 1989; Barrett 1996). The beauty of theories is often associated with their symmetry, as we noted when dealing with the elegance of Maxwell's equations (Penrose 1974, 270–1). Steven Weinberg, who received the 1979 Nobel Prize for physics, comments as follows on the beauty of scientific theories (Weinberg 1993, 119):

> The kind of beauty that we find in physical theories is of a very limited sort. It is, as far as I have been able to capture it in words, the beauty of simplicity and inevitability – the beauty of perfect structure, the beauty of everything fitting together, of nothing being changeable, of logical rigidity. It is a beauty that is spare and classic, the sort we find in the Greek tragedies.

This point is especially clear from the writings of Paul Dirac, who managed to establish a connection between quantum theory and general relativity at a time when everyone else had failed to do so. Dirac's approach appears to have been based on the concept of "beauty," in that an explicitly aesthetic criterion is laid down as one (not the only) means of evaluating scientific theories (Dirac 1963, 47):

> It is more important to have beauty in one's equations than to have them fit experiment . . . It seems that it one is working from the point of view of getting beauty in one's equations, and if one has a really good insight, one is on a sure line of progress.

At first, this might seem an outrageous suggestion. Surely it is the degree of empirical fit which determines the adequacy of a theory, rather than its intrinsic beauty? However, the situation is not quite as simple, as a cursory survey of the history of science will make clear. We shall consider two aspects of early twentieth-century physics, each of which is rightly regarded as being of foundational importance.

Our first example is *Einstein's theory of general relativity*. This theory allowed three correlations with empirical data: a retrodiction (i.e., accounting for something which was already known) of the anomalous precession of the planet Mercury (which had been known, but now accounted for, since about 1865); the prediction of the deflection of a beam of light on account of the gravitational mass of the sun; and the prediction of a solar gravitational redshift of light. The theory also possessed considerable conceptual elegance and simplicity. The noted physicist H. A. Lorentz commented that it "has the very highest degree of aesthetic merit: every lover of the beautiful must wish it to be true" (Lorentz 1920, 23).

Perhaps they did; but the experimental evidence did not support it. Popular accounts of the acceptance of general relativity from about 1920 tend to focus on the retrodiction of the anomalous motion of Mercury and the prediction of the deflection of light rays (apparently confirmed by observations of a solar eclipse in 1919). Yet the third predicted effect could not be detected. In the case of light emitted from the sun, general relativity predicted that there should be a gravitational redshift due to the reduction of the velocity of light by 2.12 parts in a million. No such redshift was observed (a fact which weighed heavily in the deliberations of the Nobel Prize committees in 1917 and 1919). This seemed to be a classic instance of T. H. Huxley's famous aphorism concerning "the great tragedy of science – the slaying of a beautiful hypothesis by an ugly fact" (Huxley 1894, 244). But this was not, in fact, the case. It is now known that the techniques available in the 1920s simply were not good enough to allow the predicted effect to be observed; it was not until the 1960s that final confirmation was forthcoming. The intrinsic beauty of the theory could at last be seen to be correlated with its truth.

Our second example is provided by the early history of quantum theory, focusing particularly on the *interpretation of atomic spectra*, especially that of atomic hydrogen. The remarkable advances made in spectroscopy during the nineteenth century allowed the spectrum of the sun to be examined for the first time, with results which proved to be of foundational importance. The presence of a hitherto unknown yellow line in that spectrum, without any known terrestial parallel, led to the discovery of helium. Over the period 1859–60, the frequencies of a series of four lines observed in the solar spectrum were measured with what, for those days, was amazing accuracy – roughly one part in ten thousand (Ångström 1868). The precision of these measurements of the visible line spectrum of atomic hydrogen led to the development of a new science: "spectral numerology" (Pais 1991, 142). This was an attempt to account for the relationship of the observed spectral lines with some fundamental mathematical equation.

The breakthrough, when it came, was simple and elegant. Working only on the basis of the four frequencies reported by Ångström, J. J. Balmer found that he could exactly reproduce the frequencies by means of the following formula:

$$v = R \left(\frac{1}{b^2} - \frac{1}{a^2} \right)$$

where R is a constant now known as the "Rydberg constant" (3.29163×10^{15}), b = 2, and a = 3, 4, 5 and 6 respectively. It must be stressed that this was an *exact* fit, not an approximation! Balmer (who was then a teacher in a Basle high school) mentioned his observations to the professor of physics at the University of Basle. By this time (1885), 12 more frequencies had been established, although this was unknown to Balmer. On learning of them from his colleague, Balmer found that they could all be fitted into his equation – again, *exactly* – without any difficulty, by setting a = 2 and b = 5, 6, . . . 15, and 16. In fact, Balmer's formula allows an entire series of spectral lines to be predicted (one of which is now known by his name), as follows:

b = 1, a = 2, 3 . . .   Lyman series (ultraviolet)
b = 2, a = 3, 4 . . .   Balmer series (visible)
b = 3, a = 4, 5 . . .   Paschen series (infrared)
b = 4, a = 5, 6 . . .   Brackett series (far infrared)
b = 5, a = 6, 7 . . .   Pfund series (far infrared)
b = 6, a = 7, 8 . . .   Humphreys series (far infrared)

The sheer beauty of the equation – matched, it has to be said, by experimental evidence, both retrodictive and predictive – will be clear. An elegant formula proved capable of representing something fundamental, which subsequently proved to be of major importance in uncovering the principles of atomic structure (Condon and Shortley 1964; Cowan 1981; Atkins and Friedman 1997, 202–39).

Our interest now focuses on the interpretation of such spectra. Such was the interest in Balmer's analysis that his results were published in the 1912 edition of the *Encyclopaedia Britannica*. It was clear that the elegance of the mathematical formula was such that it was saying something very important about something very fundamental. *But what?* By March 6, 1913, the Danish physicist Niels Bohr realized the significance of what Balmer had uncovered (Pais 1991, 143–55). On the basis of a quantum mechanical interpretation of the hydrogen atom, Bohr was able to derive Balmer's formula in two manners. For the first time, it became clear that Balmer's formula corresponded to aspects of the fundamental structure of the hydrogen atom.

The discovery opened the way to rapid development. Once more, the concept of "beauty" played an important part. During the period 1925–6, Werner

Heisenberg and Erwin Schrödinger were both working on ways of describing atomic events (Pais 1991, 267–89), especially in the light of the work of Louis de Broglie. Their younger colleague Paul Dirac describes their different approaches as follows (Dirac 1963, 46–7):

> Heisenberg worked keeping close to the experimental evidence about spectra . . . Schrödinger worked from a more mathematical point of view, trying to find a beautiful theory for describing atomic events . . . He was able to extend de Broglie's ideas and to get a very beautiful equation, known as Schrödinger's wave equation, for describing atomic processes. Schrödinger got this equation by pure thought, looking for some beautiful generalization of de Broglie's ideas, and not by keeping close to the experimental development of the subject in the way Heisenberg did.

The differences in approach are highly significant. Heisenberg worked outwards from the experimental evidence; Schrödinger sought an elegant theory which would then account for that evidence. The two, as it proved, converged. The quest for beauty and the quest for truth met at a common point. This point is clearly hinted at in Heisenberg's reflections on his work (Heisenberg 1971, 59, 68):

> I had the feeling that, through the surface of atomic phenomena, I was looking at a strangely beautiful interior, and felt almost giddy at the thought that I now had to probe this wealth of mathematical structures nature had so generously spread out before me . . . If nature leads to mathematical forms of great simplicity and beauty – coherent systems of hypotheses, axioms, etc. – . . . we cannot help thinking that they are "true," that they reveal genuine features of beauty.

The general drift of this analysis will be clear. A strong doctrine of creation (such as that associated with Christianity) leads to the expectation of a fundamental convergence of truth and beauty in the investigation and explanation of the world, precisely on account of the grounding of that world in the nature of God. The correlation in question is not arbitrary or accidental, but corresponds to the reflection of the nature of the creator in the ordering and regularity of creation. It is a simple, yet important, indication of an area in which there is clearly convergence between the sciences and a religious worldview.

Conclusion

The present chapter has explored the critically important theme of the regularity of the world, disclosed by the experimental-scientific method, and anticipated and given a rigorous foundation by a Christian doctrine of creation. It would be foolish to draw the hasty conclusion that this correlation constitutes some kind of proof of the existence of God, although this conclusion can clearly be given some form of warrant on the basis of the kind of considerations set out in this chapter. My intention is not, in fact, to draw such a conclusion, but rather to stress the convergence or complementarity of scientific and religious viewpoints at this point. As a matter of historical fact, the assumption of some such complementarity was commonplace in an earlier period of western culture. While the continuing secularization of western culture has meant that such beliefs have been largely eliminated from public discourse (see the classic study of Neuhaus 1986), including that of the academy, it is clear that they remain significant and illuminating for many. Perhaps there is a case to be made for the reappropriation of the ethos of an earlier age, which saw knowledge of God and an understanding of the world as natural partners.

Our attention now turns to exploring the manner in which the natural sciences and theology suppose that such a knowledge and understanding of reality are gained.

3

The Investigation of the World

In the previous chapter, we noted a high degree of convergence between the natural sciences and religion in relation to the critically important area of the ordering of the world, and its amenability to investigation and explanation. We now move on to consider an area in which there is clearly divergence between the disciplines – the question of how information about the world is obtained and its reliability assessed. I see no pressing reason for underplaying the divergence which is evident at this point; part of the purpose of the present study has been to identify areas of divergence, as well as convergence. Nevertheless, there is perhaps more convergence than might at first appear to be the case.

Experimentation and Revelation: A Fundamental Divergence?

We begin our analysis by considering the tension between the notions of "experimentation" and "revelation," often regarded as the distinguishing features of the natural sciences and religions respectively. It must be made clear from the outset that this is a simplistic judgment: for example, the mere observation of nature is often held to be integral to at least some of the natural sciences, while some religions understand "revelation" simply as the teachings of their founders, without any necessary transcendent dimension. Nevertheless, for the purposes of our analysis, we shall take these notions to be significant elements of the natural sciences and religions, and attempt to explore their significance.

The Natural Sciences: Experimentation

"Experiments are the only means of knowledge at our disposal. The rest is poetry, imagination" (Max Planck). Even those who are supportive of a "strong program" in the sociology of knowledge have drawn attention to the serious danger which it brings in its wake – the devaluation of an engagement with nature as a means of advancing scientific knowledge (Rudwick 1985, 450–6). One of the serious weaknesses in the programme advanced by Thomas Kuhn (which has had considerable impact on the thinking of many interested in the science-religion interaction) is his failure to show how critically important experimentation was to the emergence of new ways of thinking. For example, Kuhn's book-length study of the black-body radiation problem in relation to the development of quantum theory (Kuhn 1978) makes hardly any mention of the critical experiments which showed that there was a serious discrepancy between theoretical predictions on the basis of a classical model, and the actual outcome of experimental observation, which led Planck to formulate the quantization of energy; even the most elementary introduction to the develop-ment of quantum theory would treat these experimental observations as of critical importance (see the discussion in Atkins and Friedman 1997, 1–2).

Although the close link between scientific advance and experimentation is widely assumed, it is widely agreed that insufficient attention has been paid to the epistemological and sociological aspects of the question. Why do we be-lieve that experiments "work"? At first sight, this question might seem easy to ask; on closer examination, however, it is found to be exceptionally complex, with the history of the advance of scientific theory through experimentation offering no simple patterns (see the studies of Zahar 1978; Hacking 1983; Franklin 1986; Hon 1987; Ackermann 1988; Ackermann 1989; Goloding, Pinch and Schaffer 1989; Hon 1989; Worrall 1989a; Hones 1990; Franklin 1993; McAllister 1996).

The popular view of the matter is that theory proposes; experiment deter-mines. There is no doubt that the history of science provides a very large number of examples of precisely this pattern: the Compton effect provided important confirmation of the "photon" theory of light, and resulted from an experiment designed to confirm or refute this theory. Yet other patterns can easily be discerned. For example, the advance of the perihelion of Mercury was known as a phenomenon before it was explained by Einstein's theory of relativity. Experiments can be in error, due to flaws in their design or instru-mentation (Zahar 1978; Hon 1989; Hon 1995). Occasionally – especially in popular accounts – actual events are made to conform to the pattern demanded by a "theory then experiment" model. For example, the discovery of the 2.9 K background radiation by Arno Penzias and Robert Wilson in 1964 took place by accident, while they were working on an experimental microwave antenna at the Bell Laboratories in New Jersey. At least one account of that observation interprets this as a deliberate attempt to confirm a theory: "Radioastronomers believed that if they could aim a very sensitive receiver at a blank part of the sky that appeared to be empty, it might be possible to determine whether or

not the theorists were correct" (Branley 1979, 100). The importance of serendipity in experimental advance cannot be overlooked (Kantorovitch and Ne'eman
1989)!

Despite the enormous complexity of the relation between experiment and
theory, it needs to be said that there is a widespread consensus that theory
must be grounded in or consistent with experimental observations. In this
sense, Planck is correct. At least in principle, theories either account for what
is already known through experimentation or observation, or predict hitherto
unknown results (Worrall 1989a), which may be confirmed or refuted by experiments. Nevertheless, even this modest correlation of theory and experimentation runs the risk of gross simplification.

For example, it is not true that all experiments are unequivocal in their
results or their interpretation. "A sufficiently determined critic can always find
a reason to dispute any alleged result" (MacKenzie 1989, 412). In recent years,
considerable attention has been paid to Walter Kaufman's famous experiment
of 1905, in which he attempted to distinguish between Max Abraham's classic
theory of the electron, developed in 1902 (Goldberg 1970), and the new relativistic approach of H. A. Lorenz and Albert Einstein (Kaufmann 1906;
Zahar 1978; Hon 1995). At the time, the result of the experiment was seen
as decisively counting against the relativistic interpretation; the status of
the experiment is now viewed in a more negative light, and is seen to reflect a
subtle combination of experimental error and unacknowledged theoretical
precommitments.

Nor does it mean that a theory can only find acceptance when it is totally
consistent with experimental observations. As we noted earlier (p. 77), Einstein's general theory of relativity allowed three correlations with empirical
data: an explanation of the anomalous precession of the planet Mercury (which
had been known, but now accounted for, since about 1865: see Zahar 1973);
the prediction of the deflection of a beam of light on account of the gravitational mass of the sun; and the prediction of a solar gravitational redshift of
light. This third predicted effect – a gravitational redshift due to the reduction
of the velocity of light by 2.12 parts in a million – could not be detected. It is
now known that the techniques available in the 1920s simply were not good
enough to allow the predicted effect to be observed; it was not until the 1960s
that final confirmation was forthcoming using the then newly discovered
Mössbauer effect (Glymour 1980b, 98–99). Yet Einstein's theory was widely
accepted by 1920, more than forty years before one of its predictions could be
confirmed.

Recent studies, drawing on the insights of the social sciences, have also
brought out the manner in which the design and interpretation of experiments
are significantly affected by social and cultural factors Collins 1985; Golinski
1990; Pickering 1990). One such factor which is of particular importance is

group loyalty. "Scientific communities tend to reject data that conflict with group commitments and, obversely, to adjust their experimental techniques to tune in on phenomena consistent with those commitments" (Pickering 1981a, 236). Such studies do not in any way point to an "irrational" view of science, but indicate that the idea that "experimentation" constitutes an unproblematic link between theory and the realities of the natural world may require revision (for example, see Lenoir 1988).

We shall have cause to return to the exploration of some of these themes in a later section, especially when we turn to deal with the analysis of experience. We may now turn to a brief discussion of the religious concept of revelation.

Religion: Revelation

Central to most of the religious traditions of the world is the notion of "revelation" (see the excellent survey provided in Ward 1994). Although there are significant variations from one religious tradition to another, it is clear that a fundamental common theme is that of the impartation of information concerning the nature of the world, and especially in relation to God or the spiritual dimension of things, which would otherwise be inaccessible or hopelessly obscure. As had been made clear, the present study will work within a specifically Christian framework; it will entail dealing with Christian understandings of the notion of "revelation." This will include certain themes that are generally agreed to be distinctively Christian (such as the emphasis on the person of Jesus Christ as the self-disclosure of God), as well as others that can be argued to be present, at least to some extent, in other religious traditions (such as the belief, shared with Judaism, that the will of God was made known through the prophets of Israel).

The Christian concept of "revelation" is complex and highly nuanced (Niebuhr 1960; Dulles 1983; Trembath 1991; Swinburne 1992; Gunton 1995; Torrance 1996b). To understand its significance for our discussion, we shall focus on one of the many themes in a consensual classic Christian understanding of the nature of revelation: the critical idea that in, some manner, the nature of God is disclosed in the person and the work of Jesus Christ.

A study of the development of Christian thought indicates that one of the most significant precipitating factors for the emergence of the central doctrines of Christianity was the death and resurrection of Jesus Christ (McGrath 1990, 1–7). Something happened which required interpretation and explanation, and was found to be impossible to accommodate within the existing conceptual structures of the day. In our earlier analysis of the relation of "experimentation and revelation," we noted the manner in which a radical revision of existing patterns of thought can be precipitated by an observation which calls those patterns into question. There is no doubt that the particularities and distinctives of Jesus of Nazareth (especially his resurrection) posed a formidable challenge to the received understanding of the nature of God, and forced a revision of ideas.

The nature of that debate focused particularly on the concepts of "divinity" and "humanity," both of which were "classical" notions, firmly grounded in the philosophical matrix of the Greek-speaking world of the eastern Mediterranean. The extent to which classic Greek philosophical concepts (especially the concept of divinity) influenced the development of Christian theology during the patristic era is relatively well understood see, for example, Chadwick 1966; Pannenberg 1971), and can be illustrated in a number of ways. Perhaps the clearest example of the influence of a "classic" concept of God, largely determined by the modes of thought and philosophical conventions of secular Greek philosophy, relates to the question of whether God may be said to suffer (on which see McWilliams 1985; Creel 1986; Fiddes 1988).

The patristic discussion of this question is deeply influenced by the idea that God is perfect. So how is "perfection" to be defined? Greek patristic writers felt that contemporary classical philosophy offered a reliable answer: to be perfect is to be unchanging and self-sufficient. It is therefore impossible for a perfect being to be affected or changed by anything outside itself. Furthermore, perfection was understood in very static terms within classical philosophy. If God is perfect, change in any direction is an impossibility. If God changes, it is either a move *away from* perfection (in which case God is no longer perfect), or *towards* perfection (in which case, God was not perfect in the past). Aristotle, echoing such ideas, declared that "change would be change for the worse," and thus excluded his divine being from change and suffering.

This understanding passed into Christian theology at an early stage. Philo, a Hellenistic Jew whose writings were much admired by early Christian writers, wrote a treatise entitled *Quod Deus immutabilis sit*, "That God is unchangeable," which vigorously defended the impassibility of God. Biblical passages which seemed to speak of God suffering were, he argued, to be treated as metaphors, and not to be allowed their full literal weight. To allow that God changes was to deny the divine perfection. "What greater impiety could there be than to suppose that the Unchangeable changes?', asked Philo. It seemed to be an unanswerable question. For Philo, God could not be allowed to suffer, or undergo anything which could be spoken of as "passion."

This "classic" idea of God thus precludes the notion of the suffering of God, in much the same way as the particle model of an electron precluded it from demonstrating diffraction patterns. This prohibition of divine suffering is perhaps most clearly seen in the writings of Benedict Spinoza, which strongly reflect the "classic" view of God (Spinoza, vol. 2, 526–8):

> Proposition: God is without passions, nor is he affected with any experience of joy or sadness.

Demonstration: All ideas, in so far as they have reference to God, are true, that
is, they are adequate: and therefore God is without passions. Again, God cannot
pass to a higher or lower perfection: and therefore he is affected with no emotion
of joy or sadness. Q.E.D.
Corollary: God, strictly speaking, loves no one nor hates any one. For God is
affected with no emotion of joy or sadness, and consequently loves no one nor
hates anyone.

The classic model of God possessed logical rigor and philosophical consistency, and was capable of expressing at least some of the insights concerning
God which derived from divine revelation. But not all. Some were inconsistent. The process of criticizing the shortcomings of the "classic" concept of
God can be explored from the writings of Martin Luther, who mounted a
sustained critique of the Aristotelian model of God (McGrath 1985, 136–41),
and in the writings of such twentieth-century theologians as Eberhard Jüngel
and Jürgen Moltmann, both of whom were criticical of the Cartesian concept
of God, which can be seen to be anticipated in Spinoza (Moltmann 1974;
Jüngel 1983; Bauckham 1987). It is of no small significance that the precipitating cause of this criticism of "classic" model was, in every case, reflection on
the identity and significance of Jesus Christ. Revelation in Christ is thus the
precipitant of a process of criticism and engagement with the received view of
God, with a view to retaining that word, while determining the limitations
which are to be placed upon its use within the Christian tradition.

It is of considerable importance to observe that while the Old Testament
uses the term "god" to refer to its deity, its most characteristic way of referring
to that god is in terms of the name YHWH – usually translated as "the Lord
God" – which is a proper name, referring *only* to the covenant God of Israel.
The redefinition of the "classic" concept of God within the Christian tradition
can be argued to lead to the formulation of the doctrine of the Trinity, which
identifies the distinctive and distinguishing characteristics of the Christian god
(Jenson 1982; Thompson 1994; Weinandy 1995; McGrath 1996, 292–318;
Torrance 1996a, 1–111). In Thomas Aquinas' celebrated *Summa Theologiae*, an
exposition of "the one god" (*de deo uno*, fundamentally an exploration of a
classic model of God) is followed by a discussion of "the triune god" (*de deo
triuno*, in which the distinctively Christian understanding of the godhead is
explored). We can see here the modulation of a classic concept in the light of
perceived inadequacies and limitations. Once more, it is widely agreed that the
development of the doctrine of the Trinity is a response to sustained reflection
on the identity and significance of Jesus Christ.

We have thus seen how the figure of Jesus acts as a precipitant and stimu-
lant to modification of the classic concept of God, especially in the areas of the
suffering of God and the doctrine of the Trinity. This may be regarded as

illustrative of the concept of revelation in general, which serves both as the foundation and criterion of distinctively Christian understandings of God, human nature, and so forth. This brief illustrative account of the role of revelation (which must be supplemented with reference to the more substantial accounts noted above) allows us to begin to mount a systematic comparison of the roles of experimentation and revelation.

This very brief account of the roles of experimentation and revelation suggests certain fundamental divergences between the natural sciences and religion. The most fundamental of these may be stated as follows: experimentation and revelation appear to offer radically divergent approaches to the acquisition and verification of knowledge. Yet it must be pointed out that divergent approaches to the acquisition of information does not necessarily imply a contradiction in the information which is thereby acquired. In what follows, we shall explore the ways in which the natural sciences interpret and address the question of "experience."

The Interpretation of Experience

It will be clear that the natural sciences are correctly described as "empirical – that is, as resting on an analysis of experience, gained through observation.[1] It will be clear that there is a danger of simplification here, in that experimental data do not necessarily wear their meanings on their sleeves, so that a complex interaction between "experiment" and "interpretation" is an inevitable aspect of the experimental method. This is often expressed in terms of the "theory-laden nature of observation" (Hanson 1961; Shapere 1982; Fodor 1984; Pinch 1985; Kosso).

The importance of "religious experience" for theology will also be clear (Huyssteen 1988; Alston 1991; McGrath 1993c; Grube 1995). There is a close semantic connection between "experimentation" and "experience." When the eighteenth-century writer John Wesley spoke of "experimental religion," he intended us to understand a form of the Christian faith which had a strongly experiential element. The term "empirical theology" is sometimes used to designate a specific approach to theology associated with the University of Chicago Divinity School (Meland 1969), but can in principle be applied to any theology which takes its starting point in human experience (Ammermann 1997).

Both the scientific and religious communities can be thought of as attempting to wrestle with the ambiguities of experience, and offering what are accepted as the "best possible explanations" for what is observed. The point that we particularly wish to make at this early point is that the analysis of experience can lead to the generation of conceptualities which are often very complex, and occasionally quite counter-intuitive. Many natural scientists hostile to religion deride the complexity of its conceptualities. As we have seen, two such areas of doctrine originating from within the Christian tradition can be singled out as being of particular complexity: the doctrine of the Trinity, which can be regarded as an attempt to articulate the richness and mystery of the Christian understanding of God, and the doctrine of the "two natures" of Jesus Christ. Each of these is unquestionably counter-intuitive. Science, some argue, deals with simple ideas, and avoids such extravagant ventures into such realms. Others, however, are not so sure. Bas van Fraassen is intensely skeptical of those who suggest that science is justifiably simple whereas religion is unjustifiably complex (Fraassen 1985, 258):

> Do the concepts of the Trinity, the soul, hæcceity, universals, prime matter, and potentiality baffle you? They pale beside the unimaginable otherness of closed space-times, event-horizons, EPR correlations and bootstrap models.

Fraassen clearly considers that the conceptual and imaginative demands of some areas of modern physics exceed those traditionally associated with even the most labyrinthine theological and philosophical systems of the Middle Ages. The point which emerges from his comments is that the engagement with the world of experience and phenomena throws up concepts and ideas which are far from simple, yet which appear to be inevitable if the phenomena are to be preserved. For an orthodox Christian theologian, the doctrine of the Trinity is the inevitable outcome of intellectual engagement with the Christian experience of God; for the physicist, equally abstract and bewildering concepts emerge from wrestling with the world of quantum phenomena. But both are committed to sustained intellectual engagement with those phenomena, in order to derive and develop theories or doctrines which can be said to do justice to them, preserving rather than reducing them.

Both the sciences and religion may therefore be described as offering interpretations of experience. This is not to say that both or either may be reduced to such interpretations, but simply to note that both possess explanatory elements. This being the case, a comparison of the way in which the two disciplines deal with the complexities of experience is of considerable interest to our study. We may begin by considering the contribution of the French philosopher of science Pierre Duhem (1861–1916) to the interaction of theory and experience.

Pierre Duhem on Theory and Experience

The name of Duhem has been invoked frequently in Anglo-American discussions of empiricism since about 1955, apparently largely due to the influence of Willard Van Orman Quine's seminal essay "Two Dogmas of Empiricism." The doctrine traditionally, yet misleadingly, known as the "Duhem–Quine thesis" asserts that, if incompatible data and theory are seen to be in conflict, one cannot draw the conclusion that any particular theoretical statement is responsible for this tension, and must therefore be rejected. The root of the problem may lie in an auxilliary assumption used in the theoretical analysis, or the manner of observation which leads to the suggestion that such a conflict does in fact exist. The Duhem–Quine thesis is of fundamental importance to any attempt to correlate theory and experience, whether in science or religion. It also indicates a significant degree of convergence in relation to the problems which both the natural sciences and religions are forced to engage with.

Quine has provided us with what is undoubtedly one of the finest accounts of the way belief systems or worldviews relate to experience (Quine 1953, 42–3):

> The totality of our so-called knowledge or beliefs, from the most casual matters of geography and history to the profoundest laws of atomic physics . . . is a man-made fabric which impinges on experience only along the edges . . . A conflict with experience at the periphery occasions adjustments in the interior of the field . . . But the total field is so underdetermined by its boundary conditions, experience, that there is much latitude of choice as to what statements to reevaluate in the light of any single contrary experience.

In other words, experience often has relatively little impact upon worldviews. (Imre Lakatos made a related point in connection with his discussion of the "protective belt" of auxiliary hypotheses in scientific reasoning.) Where experience seems to contradict a worldview or system of beliefs, the most likely outcome is an internal readjustment of the system, rather than its rejection. Quine thus points to some of the difficulties in refuting a theory on the basis of experience, which must be addressed by any empirical approach.

Quine's analysis has given rise to what is often referred to as the "underdetermination thesis" – the view, especially associated with sociological approaches to the natural sciences, which holds that there are, in principle, an indefinite number of theories that are capable of fitting observed facts more or less adequately (see, for example, Boyd 1973; Newton-Smith and Lukes 1978; Pickering 1981b; Laudan and Leplin 1991). The choice of theory can thus be explained on the basis of sociological factors, such as interests. According to this view, experimental evidence plays a considerably smaller role in theory generation and confirmation than might be thought. As Mary Hesse has pointed out, some form of relativism is the inescapable consequence of the thesis of the underdetermination of theory by evidence (Hesse 1989, xiv) – a conclusion which has admirably suited certain sociological interpretations of the natural sciences. The strongest form of this approach ("maximal underdetermination") would take the following form (C. Wright 1993, 287):

> For any theoretical statement S and acceptable theory T essentially containing S, there is an acceptable theory T¢ with the same testable consequences but which contains, essentially, the negation of S.

Many writers have, of course, been strongly sceptical of this approach (see Grünbaum 1960; Glymour 1989b; Fraassen 1983; Greenwood 1990). Nevertheless, it continues to be highly influential, and therefore merits critical examination. In what follows, we shall explore the views of Duhem and Quine, and establish their relevance to the interaction between the natural sciences and religion.

It is of critical importance to appreciate that it is highly improper to attribute the "underdetermination thesis" in any of its developed forms to Pierre Duhem. Its philosophical origins lie with Quine; its sociological applications with relativists such as David Bloor and Harry Collins. As a number of careful studies have indicated, neither Duhem and Quine can legitimately be cited as advocates of the view that a hypothesis can be made irrefutable by experimental evidence, or that any theory can be maintained in the face of any evidence (see especially Laudan 1965; Ariew 1984; Needham 1996). There is no doubt that such an intellectual pedigree has been asserted by relativists; nevertheless, both Duhem and Quine are quite clear that, in practice, the natural sciences are not reduced to such relativistic meanderings, but have established quite definite procedures for coping with the issues involved (Balashov 1994).

It is clear that Quine based his understanding of Duhem on secondary English language sources, in particular some references to Duhem in Philip Frank's *Modern Philosophy and Its Science* (1940) and Arnold Lowinger's more substantial 1940 study of the methodology of Duhem (Lowinger 1940; Frank 1941). Quine's most succinct summary of Duhem's position can be found in his "Two Dogmas of Empiricism." One of Quine's objectives in this seminal essay is to demonstrate the weakness of the "empiricist dogma" that each theoretical statement, considered in isolation, can be confirmed or falsified. Quine asserts that this view has been effectively countered by Duhem, who demonstrated that "our statements about the external world face the tribunal of sense experience not individually, but only as a corporate body" (Quine 1953, 41). Adolph Grünbaum mounted a powerful challenge to what he termed "Duhem's thesis," demonstrating that it is either empirically false or trivially true. Yet this is actually a criticism of Quine's presentation of the thesis, which introduces ideas which cannot be attributed to Duhem himself (Grünbaum 1960).[2]

Since then, there has been a growing awareness of the divergence between

Quine and Duhem at a number of critical junctures (see most notably Tuana 1978; Vuillemin 1979). In general terms, Quine's interpretation of Duhem is much stronger than Duhem himself would allow. For example, Duhem explicitly distinguishes a number of different sciences, arguing that his thesis has greater applicability, for example, in physics than in physiology (Duhem 1954, 180). In making this distinction, it is clear that Duhem was responding to a series of crucial experiments by Claude Bernard. Quine, however, appears to extend Duhem's thesis to embrace "the whole body of our knowledge" (Vuillemin 1979). Rather than attempt to disentangle the complex question of the extent to which Quine misunderstood Duhem, and subsequently diverged from this misinterpretation, I propose to engage directly with Duhem, with a view to clarifying his relevance to our themes.

Duhem's most fundamental assertion could be stated in terms of "the thesis of inseparability." According to Duhem, the physicist simply is not in a position to submit an isolated hypothesis to experimental test. "An experiment in physics can never condemn an isolated hypothesis but only a whole theoretical group" (Duhem 1954, 183). The physicist – and we note at this point that Duhem deliberately chose to restrict his analysis to this discipline, and declined to extend it to physiology or certain branches of chemistry – cannot subject an individual hypothesis to an experimental test, in that the experiment can only indicate that one hypothesis within a larger group of hypotheses requires revision. The experiment does not itself indicate which of the hypotheses requires modification (Duhem 1954, 187). Even when a strict deductive consequence of a theory is shown to be false (assuming, of course, that a "crucial experiment" can be devised which allows such an unequivocal conclusion to be drawn), that falsity cannot be atttributed (for example, by *modus tollens*) to any specific site in the theory itself or its ancilliary assumptions.

Yet can such a "crucial experiment" be devised? Duhem's argument needs closer examination at this point. In the section of his *Aim and Structure of Physical Theory* entitled "A 'Crucial Experiment' is Impossible in Physics," Duhem argues that we do not have access to the full list of hypotheses which underlie our thinking. It might at first seem that we could enumerate all the hypotheses than can be made to account for a phenomenon, and then eliminate all of these hypotheses except one by experimental contradiction (Duhem 1954, 188). However, the physicist is never in a position to be sure that all the hypotheses have been identified and checked (Duhem 1954, 190). More significantly, Duhem insists that no theoretical hypothesis, considered in isolation, has observational consequences. An experiment is not simply about the observation of phenomena; it is about their interpretation. There is no direct logical bridge between concepts and experience.

An excellent illustration of the manner in which Duhem's theory applies to an allegedly "crucial" experiment can be seen in the case of the Michelson–

Morley experiment of 1887 (Hirosige 1968; Hirosige 1976). The essential issue concerned the nature of the "luminiferous ether" – that is, the medium through which light travelled. As a result of their experiment, Michelson and Morley concluded that "the ether is at rest with regard to the earth's surface" (Michelson and Morley 1887). This experiment was designed to test some of the ideas set out in a paper published in the previous year by H. A. Lorentz, with the title "On the Influence of the Motion of the Earth on Luminiferous Ether." This paper set out a theory of the ether which rested on a series of hypotheses: for example, that the ether surrounding the earth is in motion; that the ether possesses a velocity potential; that the relative motions of the earth and ether can differ close to the earth's surface; and that when the ether moves through a transparent body, the light waves are affected by the resulting change in relative motion. Underlying these explicitly stated hypotheses were a number of unstated and auxiliary hypotheses, such as (it turned out) the critically important assumption that light required a medium for its transmission.

The Michelson–Morley experiment called this cluster of hypotheses into question. But which one was wrong? Lorenz dealt with the experimental result by introducing the hypothesis of the contraction of moving bodies, leading Henri Poincaré to comment that Lorentz's theory seemed to acquire new hypotheses in the light of each experimental result (Hirosige 1976, 41). George FitzGerald argued along similar lines in 1889, arguing that the extent of such a contraction was precisely equal to the expected ether displacment, so that the two effects cancelled each other out (Hunt 1988). Although this idea did not receive much support (Warwick 1991, 43–5), it was nevertheless developed still further by Joseph Larmor in his widely-read book *Aether and Matter*, in which he also argued that the null-result obtained by Michelson and Morley was the result of matter contracting when it moved through the ether (Larmor 1900, 64; Warwick 1991).

With the benefit of hindsight, it is possible to argue that the Michelson–Morley experiment disproved the existence of the ether. But was not the way things were seen at the time. It was, quite simply, too radical a conclusion. The interpretation of the observation statement resulting from the experiment clearly indicated the need for the modification of either hypotheses or the theory itself. But which one? For example, Lorenz's contraction hypothesis was investigated in 1904 by D. B. Brace, who failed to observe the predicted effects, and concluded that the contraction hypothesis could not be sustained. This conclusion was immediately challenged by Larmor, who argued that the experimental observation could be accounted for by the theory of corresponding states. The theoretical site of the difficulty raised by the experiment thus could not be easily identified.

We may summarize Duhem's thesis as follows. Let us define a theory, T, which consists of a group of hypotheses, H_1, H_2, H_3 . . . H_n. An example of such a theory might be Newton's theory of optics, or the rival theory proposed by Huygens. Each theory consists of such a group of explicitly stated interrelated hypotheses. It also consists of a number of auxiliary hypotheses, which are sometimes not formulated explicitly. We might refer to these as A_1, A_2, A_3 ... A_n. Now consider an observation statement O. What is the impact of this statement on the group of hypotheses? Is it the theory which requires modification? Or merely one of its hypotheses? And if so, which one?

To give a specific historical example: let us consider Newton's theory of planetary motion, which can be thought of as a composition of his three laws of motion and the gravitational principle. An observation is now made which seems inconsistent with this theory (Hanson 1971, 31):

O = the observed orbit of the planet Uranus is not consistent with its predicted theoretical values

This therefore calls into question the group of hypotheses consisting of both the explicit hypotheses of the Newtonian theory , H_1, H_2, H_3 ... H_n and the auxiliary hypotheses as A_1, A_2, A_3 ... A_n.

But which of these hypotheses were wrong? Is it the entire theory which requires to be abandoned, or is a modification required to only one hypothesis, which allows the theory as a whole to be saved? In this specific case, it was an auxiliary assumption which proved to be incorrect – namely, the assumption that there was no planet beyond Uranus. When a trans-Uranic planet was postulated, the anomalous orbital parameters of Uranus could be explained by the existence of this planet, which exercised a gravitational pull on Uranus. The planet in question (now named "Neptune") was duly discovered in 1846 by German astronomers on the basis of more sophisticated calculations by Adams and Leverrier.

Duhem's thesis is also of considerable importance to Karl Popper's theory of falsifiability (Swinburne 1964; Grünbaum 1976). In his 1983 work *Realism and the Aim of Science*, Popper noted that Duhem's work made it impossible to falsify individual hypotheses within a group (Popper 1983, 187):

> [I here note a serious] objection closely connected with the problem of *context*, and the fact that my criterion of demarcation applies to *systems of theories* rather than to statements out of context. This objection may be put as follows. No single hypothesis, it may be said, is falsifiable, because every refutation of a conclusion may hit any single premise of the set of all premises used in deriving the refuted conclusion. The attribution to the falsity to some particular hypothesis that belongs to this set of premises is therefore risky, especially if we consider the great number of assumptions which enter into every experiment ... The answer is that we can indeed falsify only *systems of theories* and that attribution of falsity to any particular statement within such a system is always highly uncertain.

Duhem was quite clear that his thesis did not apply to all sciences, but only to those that "require an interpretative chunk of theory in order for their theoretical hypotheses to confront observation" (Ariew 1984, 323). Yet it will be clear that Duhem's thesis can also be applied to other disciplines which seek to approach experience by means of a complex raft of theoretical assumptions – such as Christian theology. We shall therefore turn to explore the potential of Duhem's approach for theology.

Can Experience Falsify Doctrine? A Case Study

It may initially seem quite inappropriate to use Duhem's ideas in a religious context. After all, Duhem was a physicist, and did not concern himself with matters of theology. However, this is not strictly correct. In 1905 Duhem wrote a short work entitled "The Physics of a Believer," in which he sought to clarify the manner in which science and religion interacted (Gillies 1993, 201–4). In this essay, Duhem argued for the separation of science and religion, in effect anticipating the approach later advocated by Ludwig Wittgenstein. This was regarded with distaste by the Catholic Church, which saw this attempt to separate science and theology as damaging the cause of natural theology. Nevertheless, Duhem was not entirely consistent in this matter, and elsewhere in the same essay argued that the teachings of general thermodynamics and Aristotelian scholasticism could be seen as "two pictures of the same ontological order, distinct because they are each taken from a different point of view, but in no way discordant."

In what follows, we propose to explore the manner in which Duhem's thesis can be used to address the enormously complex matter of the relationship between Christian doctrine and religious experience. This must be seen as an extension of Duhem's approach, in that Duhem did not himself apply his thesis to religion. It may be useful to reiterate that we shall be using Duhem's thesis in the form in which he himself developed and limited it, rather than the more expansive and ambitious version set out by of Willard Van Orman Quine in his seminal essay "Two Dogmas of Empiricism." Our attention will focus on a question which has been much debated in the recent scholarly literature (Plantinga 1979; Fitzpatrick 1981; Martin 1984; Rowe 1986; Draper 1989; O'Connor 1990; Alston 1991b; Nelson 1991): does the existence of evil constitute empirical evidence against the existence of God?

In a major recent study, William P. Alston points out how two quite distinct approaches to the problem of evil have been adopted in the present century (Alston 1991, 29):

1   A *logical* argument, which attempts to show that evil is logically incompatible with the existence of God. Alston reports that it "is now acknowledged

on (almost) all sides" that this argument is bankrupt.

2   An *empirical* argument which asserts that the empirical evidence of evil is incompatible with the existence of God.

Stephen J. Wykstra has suggested that these two approaches might be designated as "logical" and "evidential" (Wykstra 1984). It is this second "empirical" or "evidential" approach which will concern us especially in this section.

It may, however, be helpful to explore the distinction between these two types of argument before proceeding further. First, let us state the logical aspects of the problem of evil, as it is traditionally formulated. Consider the following three hypotheses:

H_1 God is omnipotent and omniscient;
H_2 God is completely good;
H_3 The world contains instances of suffering and evil.

The traditional logical formulation of the problem of suffering is that the third of these propositions is held to be inconsistent with the first two by critics of theism.

In fact, this is a relatively unsatisfactory statement of the problem of suffering, as has often been pointed out (see Sutherland 1984, 22). At least one further hypothesis needs to be added before the possibility of evil can be regarded as constituting a potential logical difficulty for the theory, such as:

H_4 A good omnipotent God would eliminate suffering and evil.

This would clearly raise the question of whether this supplementary hypothesis is correct (the "greater good" argument would certainly suggest that it is not), and how it can be known in the first place with the necessary degree of certainty to cause any difficulties for theism.

However, closer examination reveals that the four propositions just noted are different in their nature. Three (H_1, H_2, and H_4) could be defined as "ideas" or "propositions." The fourth (H_3) is actually an observation statement, making an empirical rather than theoretical affirmation. The three propositions H_1, H_2, and H_4 all make affirmations concerning the attributes of a (putative and hypothetical) god. The remaining statement H_3 takes the form of a report, based on experience and observation, of the way things are.

It will be clear that the fundamental question being addressed is the relation between a theory and observation. The issue is not to be confused with a logical riddle, stated or conceived in terms of propositions, in which the manner in which those propositions are related is seen to give rise to an inconsistency (as, for example, in the statement "I propose to draw a three-sided square" or "Everything stated in this sentence is false"). The issue is more complex than this, and involves the attempted correlation between the world of ideas and empirical observations concerning the external world. As Thomas F. Torrance has argued in the course of a careful comparison of the methods of theology and the natural sciences, "there is not and cannot be any logical bridge between ideas and existence" (Torrance 1985, 76). This is not to deny any correlation between concepts and experience, either in theology or the sciences, but to note a serious difficulty concerning the direct linking of logic and observation.

It is therefore appropriate to reformulate the problem in a more empirical manner, as follows. Consider the following hypotheses, which we shall group together:

H_1 God is omnipotent and omniscient;
H_2 God is completely good.

Now add the following observation statement:

O = the world contains instances of suffering and evil

The fundamental question which must be addressed in the problem of evil can be formulated, in a Duhemian manner, as follows. Does the observation statement O require that the group of hypotheses (H_1 and H_2) be abandoned? Or that just one of them should be revised? And if so, which one? Or is there a problem with an auxilliary hypothesis, which needs to be considered?

An example will make this difficult point clearer. Duhem's approach to the relationship of theory and experience allows us to suggest that there is indeed a problem somewhere along the line in relation to the experienced presence of evil in the world and the existence of an omniscient and omnipotent God. But it does not identify the specific point at which those difficulties are encountered. In the case of Christianity, even the simple term "God" is associated with a complex matrix of interconnected notions which cannot be clinically isolated from each other and subjected to empirical testing. Critics of a theistic position tend to allow it to be understood that the perceived existence of suffering seriously erodes the plausibility of the God-theory; Duhem reminds us that this conclusion simply cannot be drawn in this manner or on the basis of such considerations. We must have access to all the hypotheses to handle the question. Yet, as Duhem pointed out in the case of physics, it is impossible to enumerate such hypotheses exhaustively. Limitations on our part seriously prejudice our ability to interpret the significance of empirical observations. Even if all are agreed on the following observation statement:

O = there exists evil and suffering in the world

it is far from clear as to how this is to be interpreted.

One of the most careful statements of an empirical approach to the problem of evil can be found in the writings of William Rowe (see, for example, Rowe 1979; Rowe 1984; Rowe 1986). In what follows, we shall set out his formulation of the problem as it is found in his 1979 essay "The Problem of Evil and Some Varieties of Atheism" (Rowe 1979). In this essay, Rowe sets out his argument as follows (Rowe 1979, 336):

1   There exist instances of intense suffering which an omnipotent, omniscient being could have prevented without thereby losing some greater good or permitting some evil which is equally bad, if not worse.
2   An omniscient, wholly good being would prevent the occurrence of any intense suffering it could, unless it could not do so without thereby losing some greater good or permitting some evil which is equally bad or worse.
3   There does not exist an omnipotent, omniscient, wholly good being.

The argument is, of course, vulnerable. Objections can easily be raised against each of Rowe's assertions. For example, note how his first assertion combines an observation statement with a hypothesis. We can disentangle them by suggesting that the first statement could more properly be expressed as an empirical observation statement O and a hypothesis H:

O = There exist instances of intense suffering;
H = An omnipotent, omniscient being could have prevented instances of intense suffering without thereby losing some greater good or permitting some evil which is equally bad, if not worse.

How, we might reasonably ask, can Rowe know H? A number of writers have pointed out that the force of Rowe's objection would seem to be vitiated by an unwarranted confidence in a human ability to determine that God has (or could have) no good reason to allow some of the suffering we experience in the world (Wykstra 1984).

As Alston points out (Alston 1991b), one of Rowe's difficulties is that he is obliged to rely on inference in establishing his case against God. Arguments from experience must be accompanied by an acceptance of the cognitive limits which are imposed upon us. Alston notes three areas of limitation: a lack of data (such as the nature of the universe, the reasons behind divine behavior, and the nature of the afterlife); complexity beyond human capacity (in that the factors involved are too complex and nuanced to permit easy analysis); and difficulty in determining what is metaphysically possible or necessary (in that we are in no position to determine what can and cannot be the case). Alston (1991, 61) concludes that:

> we are simply not in a position to justifiably assert, with respect to . . . suffering that God, if he exists, would have no sufficient reason for permitting it. And if that is right, the inductive argument from evil is in no better shape than its late lamented deductive cousin.

This brief discussion of the role of experience in science and religion also invites the question of whether there may be any middle ground on which the somewhat different approaches of the natural sciences and religion might meet. One obvious possibility calls out for examination – natural theology.

A Middle Way? Natural Order and Natural Theology

In previous sections, we have noted the manner in which the concepts of "revelation" and "experimentation" operate as sources of knowledge within the religions and natural sciences. It will be clear from that analysis that there is a considerable degree of divergence between these approaches. This does not, however, mean that the two disciplines are to be seen as lacking common ground. In this present section, we propose to explore the idea of a natural theology as a mediating principle between science and religion, offering a theoretical justification of this approach, and dealing with some criticisms which might be offered against it. Once more, we shall offer a specifically Christian approach, while noting that similar insights could be offered from other religious traditions.

We have already stressed the importance of the doctrine of creation as a theological foundation for the natural sciences (see pp. 39–79). The observation of ordering and beauty of the world naturally raises a significant theological question. What can be known of the creator from the creation? In other words, in what ways can the God who created this world, and whose nature is in some manner reflected in its structures, be known from that world? The doctrine of creation is generally regarded as providing a rigorous theological foundation to the notion of a natural knowledge of God (Robinson 1972; Corr 1973; Blaisdell 1982; Clarke 1983; Long 1992; J. E. Smith 1992; Barr 1993; Gingerich 1994). As the leading Anglican writer F. J. A. Hort argued in his 1871 Hulsean Lectures, "it is not too much to say that the Gospel itself can never be fully known till nature as well as man is fully known; and that the manifestation of nature as well as man in Christ is part of his manifestation of God" (Hort 1893, 83). If God created the world, it is to be expected that this creation should bear the mark of God's handiwork. Just as an artist's distinctive style might be evident in her sculpturing, or a painter might sign his name on his work, so the presence of God, it is argued, can be discerned within his creation. But what part of creation?

Three Approaches to Natural Theology

Three answers may be picked out from the considerable variety offered by Christian theology down the centuries. It will be clear that the second two such answers are of especial importance, given our analysis of the implications of the doctrine of creation in an earlier section of this chapter.

In the first place, we may note an appeal to *human reason*. Augustine of Hippo addresses this question at some length in his major work *De Trinitate*. The general line of argument developed by Augustine can be summed up as follows. If God is indeed to be discerned within his creation, we ought to expect to find him at the height of that creation. Now the height of God's creation, Augustine argues (basing himself on Genesis 1 and 2), is human nature. And, on the basis of the neo-Platonic presuppositions which he inherited from his cultural milieu, Augustine further argued that the height of human nature is the human capacity to reason. Therefore, he concluded, one should expect to find traces of God (or, more accurately, "vestiges of the Trinity") in human processes of reasoning. On the basis of this belief, Augustine develops what have come to be known as "psychological analogies of the Trinity" (Zekiean 1981).

In the second place, we may consider the *ordering of the world*. This is one of the most significant themes for our study, in the light of its close connection with the findings of the natural sciences. We have already seen how Thomas Aquinas' arguments for the existence of God base themselves on the perception that there is an ordering within nature, which requires to be explained (Kretzmann 1997). Equally, the fact that the human mind can discern and investigate this ordering of nature is of considerable significance. There seems to be something about human nature which prompts it to ask questions about the world, just as there seems to be something about the world which allows answers to those questions to be given. The noted theoretical physicist and Christian apologist John Polkinghorne comments on this point as follows, in his *Science and Creation* (Polkinghorne 1988, 20):

> We are so familiar with the fact that we can understand the world that most of the time we take it for granted. It is what makes science possible. Yet it could have been otherwise. The universe might have been a disorderly choas rather than an orderly cosmos. Or it might have had a rationality which was inaccessible to us. . . . There is a congruence between our minds and the universe, between the rationality experienced within and the rationality observed without.

There is a deep-seated congruence between the rationality present in our minds, and the *orderedness* which we observe as present in the world. One of the most remarkable aspects of this ordering concerns the abstract structures of pure mathematics – a free creation of the human mind – which, as Polkinghorne stresses, nevertheless provide important clues to understanding the world. One thinks, for example, of Paul Dirac's 1931 explanation of a puzzling aspect of an equation he had derived to explain the behavior of an electron. It had *two* types of solution, one with positive energy and the other with negative energy. The latter class could be interpreted as implying the existence of a particle which was identical to an electron in every respect, save that it was positively charged. This point was brought out clearly by Hermann Weyl's demonstration that such "negative energy solutions" had electron mass. In 1932, Carl Anderson observed real-life effects which led him to postulate the existence of the positive electron, corresponding to Dirac's postulated particle. The new particle was observed only in cloud chamber experiments; this was accounted for by Blackett's observation that Dirac's theory indicated that the particle would soon annihilate itself on collision with a negatively-charged electron, and was therefore not (as some had thought) a constituent element of stable matter. In a sense, the positron can thus be said to have been known to the mathematicians before the physicists discovered it (Hanson 1963).

In the third place, natural theology has appealed to *the beauty of the world*. A number of theologians have developed natural theologies, based on the sense of beauty which arises from contemplating the world. As we noted in an earlier section (pp. 75–6), Hans Urs von Balthasar and Jonathan Edwards offered such an approach in the twentieth and eighteenth centuries respectively, the former from a Roman Catholic and the latter from a Reformed perspective (Butler 1990).[3]

These, then, are merely some of the ways in which Christian theologians have attempted to describe the manner in which God can be known, however fleetingly, through nature. Within a specifically Christian perspective, these insights (which may be obtained into the existence and nature of God) are to be seen as pointers to the greater reality of God's self-revelation, rather than as complete in themselves. We shall explore this point briefly in what follows.

Natural and Revealed Theology

In the writings of both Thomas Aquinas and John Calvin, a distinction is drawn between a valid yet partial knowledge of God available through the observation of the world and a fuller knowledge of God resulting from God's decision to reveal himself. As we considered Aquinas in some detail earlier in relation to the issue of ordering, it is appropriate to illustrate the point at issue in this later section of the work from Calvin.

Calvin draws a fundamental distinction between a general "knowledge of God the creator," which can be had through reflection on the created world, and a more specifically Christian "knowledge of God the redeemer," which can only be had through the Christian revelation. Calvin argues that the latter is consistent with the former, and extends its insights (Dowey 1952; Parker 1969).

The first book of Calvin's *Institutes of the Christian Religion* (1559) opens with discussion of this fundamental problem of Christian theology: how do we know anything about God? Calvin affirms that a general knowledge of God may be discerned throughout the creation – in humanity, in the natural order, and in the historical process itself. Two main grounds of such knowledge are identified, one subjective, the other objective. The first ground is a "sense of divinity (*sensus divinitatis*)" or a "seed of religion (*semen religionis*)," implanted within every human being by God. God has thus endowed human beings with some inbuilt sense or presentiment of the divine existence. It is as if something about God has been engraved in the hearts of every human being. The second ground lies in experience of and reflection upon the ordering of the world. The fact that God is creator, together with an appreciation of the divine wisdom and justice, may be gained from an inspection of the created order, culminating in humanity itself.

It is important to stress that Calvin makes no suggestion whatsoever that this knowledge of God from the created order is peculiar to, or restricted to, Christian believers. Calvin is arguing that anyone, by intelligent and rational reflection upon the created order, should be able to arrive at the idea of God. The created order is a "theatre" or a "mirror" for the displaying of the divine presence, nature and attributes (Schreiner 1991). Although God is invisible and incomprehensible, God wills to be known under the form of created and visible things, by donning the garment of creation. It is of the utmost significance to observe that Calvin therefore commends the natural sciences (such as astronomy), on account of their ability to illustrate further the wonderful ordering of creation, and the divine wisdom which this indicates (see pp. 51–72). Significantly, however, Calvin makes no appeal to specifically Christian sources of revelation at this stage in his argument. His argument up to this point is based upon empirical observation and ratiocination. If Calvin introduces scriptural quotations, it is to consolidate a general natural knowledge of God, rather than to establish that knowledge in the first place. There is, he stresses, a way of discerning God which is common to those inside and outside the Christian community.

Having thus laid the foundations for a general knowledge of God, Calvin stresses its shortcomings; his dialogue partner here is the classical Roman writer Cicero, whose *On the Nature of the Gods* is perhaps one of the most influential classical expositions of a natural knowledge of God (Grislis 1971).

Calvin argues that the epistemic distance between God and humanity, already of enormous magnitude, is increased still further on account of human sin. Our natural knowledge of God is imperfect and confused, even to the point of contradiction on occasion. A natural knowledge of God serves to deprive humanity of any excuse for ignoring the divine will; nevertheless, it is inadequate as the basis of a fully-fledged portrayal of the nature, character and purposes of God.

Having stressed this point, Calvin then introduces the notion of revelation; scripture reiterates what may be known of God through nature, while simultaneously clarifying this general revelation and enhancing it. "The knowledge of God, which is clearly shown in the ordering of the world and in all creatures, is still more clearly and familiarly explained in the Word." It is only through scripture that the believer has access to knowledge of the redeeming actions of God in history, culminating in the life, death and resurrection of Jesus Christ. For Calvin, revelation is focused upon the person of Jesus Christ; our knowledge of God is mediated through him. God may thus only be fully known through Jesus Christ, who may in turn only be known through scripture; the created order, however, provides important points of contact for and partial resonances of this revelation. The basic idea here, then, is that a knowledge of God the creator may be had both through nature and through revelation, with the latter clarifying, confirming and extending what may be known through the former. Knowledge of God the redeemer – which for Calvin is a distinctively *Christian* knowledge of God – may only be had by the Christian revelation, in Christ and through Scripture.

This general approach was developed with particular rigour within the Reformed tradition. The importance attached to the notion of natural theology in the writings of Jean-Alphonse Turrettini (1671–1737), the leading Genevan theologian of the eighteenth century illustrates this point particularly clearly (Heyd 1982; Klauber 1994). Thomas Chalmers, the leading Scottish nineteenth-century Presbyterian theologian, also adopted a strongly positive approach to the matter (Cairns 1956).

Particular attention should be paid to the "two books" tradition, which is known to have been of importance to English natural theology during the seventeenth and early eighteenth centuries. This approach can be argued to draw on Calvin's theological approach, which we have just explored above. It was also influential in Protestant circles after Calvin. For example, the "Belgic Confession" (1561), a Reformed confession of faith which had its origins in the Lowlands, spoke of nature as being "before our eyes as a most beautiful book in which all created things, both great and small, are like characters leading us to contemplate the invisible things of God" (Müller 1903, 233). This idea of the "book of nature" which complemented the "book of Scripture" rapidly gained popularity. Francis Bacon commended the study of "the book of God's word" and the "book of God's works" in his *Advancment of Learning* (1605). This latter work had considerable impact on English thinking on the relation of science and religion. Thus in his 1674 tract *The Excellency of Theology compared with Natural Theology*, Robert Boyle noted that "as the two great books, of nature and of scripture, have the same author, so the study of the latter does not at all hinder an inquisitive man's delight in the study of the former" (Boyle 1772, vol. 4, 1–66). Similar thoughts can be found expressed in Sir Thomas Browne's 1643 classic *Religio Medici* (Fisch 1953, 258):

> There are two books from whence I collect my divinity. Besides that written one of God, another of his servant, nature, that universal and publick manuscript, that lies expansed unto the eyes of all. Those that never saw him in the one have discovered him in the other.

Note especially the idea of the world as "God's epistle written to mankind" (Boyle). This metaphor of the "two books" with the one author was of considerable importance in holding together Christian theology and piety and the emerging interest and knowledge of the natural world at this time (Manuel 1974, 31; Peacocke 1979, 1–7).

Yet if this positive approach to a natural knowledge of God represents the majority report within the Christian tradition, it is important to acknowledge that there have been other views. In what follows, we shall explore three significant (although ultimately not decisive) objections to natural theology, reflecting theological and philosophical concerns respectively.

Objections to Natural Theology: Theological

Perhaps the most negative attitude to have been adopted in recent Christian theology is that of the leading Swiss Reformed theologian Karl Barth, whose controversy with Emil Brunner over this matter illustrates some of the serious concerns associated with it within the Protestant theological community. Barth's stringent and strident criticisms of natural theology can be answered effectively, and are often regarded as lying at the extreme end of the theological spectrum. Nevertheless, they merit consideration, not least on account of the fact that they have become "landmarks" in the discussion of the matter.

In 1934, the Swiss theologian Emil Brunner published a work entitled *Nature and Grace*, in which he argued that "the task of our theological generation is to find a way back to a legitimate natural theology" (Lehmann 1940). Brunner located this approach in the doctrine of creation, specifically the idea that human beings are created in the *imago Dei*, "the image of God'. Human nature is constituted in such a way that there is an analogy with the being of God. Despite the sinfulness of human nature, the ability to discern God in nature remains. Sinful human beings remain able to recognize God in nature and the events of history, and to be aware of their guilt before God. There is thus a what Brunner termed "a point of contact (*Anknüpfungspunkt*)" for divine revelation within human nature.

In effect, Brunner was arguing that human nature is constituted in such a way that there is a ready-made point of contact for divine revelation. Revelation addresses a human nature which already has some idea of what that revelation is about. For example, take the gospel demand to "repent of sin." Brunner argues that this makes little sense, unless human beings already have some idea of what "sin" is. The gospel demand to repent is thus addressed to an audience which already has at least something of an idea of what "sin" and "repentance" might mean. Revelation brings with it a fuller understanding of what sin means – but in doing so, it builds upon an existing human awareness of sin.

Barth reacted with anger to this suggestion (Barth and Brunner 1947). His published reply to Brunner brought their long-standing friendship to an abrupt end. Barth was determined to say "no!" to Brunner's positive evaluation of natural theology. It seemed to imply that God needed help to become known, or that human beings somehow cooperated with God in the act of revelation. "The Holy Spirit . . . needs no point of contact other than that which that same Spirit establishes," was his angry retort. For Barth, there was no "point of contact" inherent within human nature. Any such "point of contact" was itself the result of divine revelation. It is something that is evoked by the Word of God, rather than something which is a permanent feature of human nature (Torrance 1970).

Underlying this debate is another matter, which is too easily overlooked (O'Donovan 1986). The Barth–Brunner debate took place in 1934, the year in which Hitler gained power in Germany. Underlying Brunner's appeal to nature is an idea, which can be traced back to Luther, known as "the orders of creation." According to Luther, God providentially established certain "orders" within creation, in order to prevent it collapsing into chaos. Those orders included the family, the church, and the state. (The close alliance between church and state in German Lutheran thought reflects this idea.) Nineteenth-century German Liberal Protestantism had absorbed this idea, and developed a theology which allowed German culture, including a positive assessment of the state, to become of major importance theologically. The "orders of creation" seemed to be interpreted in such a manner as to justify a racial ideology. A further aspect of Barth's concern at this point is that Brunner, perhaps unwittingly, may have laid a theological foundation for allowing the state to become a model for God. And who wanted to model God on Adolf Hitler?

An equally critical approach to natural theology has been developed on

other grounds by the noted Scottish theologian Thomas F. Torrance. There
are clear parallels between Torrance and Barth. Thus Torrance sets out what
he understands to be Barth's fundamental objection to natural theology – the
radical separation which some writers assert between "revealed theology"
and a totally autonomous and unconnected "natural theology" (Torrance 1980,
90–1):

> Epistemologically, then, what Barth objects to in traditional natural theology is
> not any invalidity in its argumentation, nor even its rational structure, as such,
> but its *independent* character – i.e., the autonomous rational structure that
> natural theology develops on the ground of "nature alone," in abstraction from
> the active self-disclosure of the living and Triune God – for that can only split
> the knowledge of God into two parts, natural knowledge of the One God and
> revealed knowledge of the triune God, which is scientifically as well as theo-
> logically intolerable. This is not to reject the place of a proper rational struc-
> ture in knowledge of God, such as natural theology strives for, but to insist
> that unless that rational structure is intrinsically bound up with the actual
> content of knowledge of God, it is a distorting abstraction. That is why Barth
> claims that, properly understood, natural theology is included within revealed
> theology.

Torrance also stresses that Barth's criticism of natural theology does not rest
on any form of dualism – for example, some kind of deistic dualism between
God and the world which implies that there is no active relation between
God and the world, or with some form of Marcionite dualism between redemption and creation implying a depreciation of the creature (Torrance
1980, 87). It is clear that Torrance himself sympathizes with Barth at these
points.

Torrance also notes a fundamental philosophical difficulty which seems to
him to lie behind the forms of natural theology rejected by Barth. This kind of
autonomous natural theology is, he argues, a "desperate attempt to find a
logical bridge between concepts and experience in order to cross the fatal separation between God and the world which it had posited in its initial assumptions, but it had to collapse along with the notion that science proceeds by way
of abstraction from observational data" (Torrance 1985, 38). It attempted, by
means of establishing a logical bridge between ideas and being, to reach out
inferentially towards God, and thus to produce a logical formalization of empirical and theoretical components of the knowledge of God. For Torrance,
this development was assisted considerably by the medieval assumption that
"to think scientifically was to think *more geometrico*, that is, on the model of
Euclidean geometry, and it was reinforced in later thought as it allowed itself
to be restricted within the logico-causal connections of a mechanistic universe"
(Torrance 1985, 41–2).[4] It will thus be clear that Torrance sees the "traditional

abstractive form" of natural theology as resting on a "deistic disjunction between God and the world" (Torrance 1985, 40) .

What is of especial interest is the manner in which Torrance identifies a parallel between the theological status and significance of natural theology and the empirical challenge to the unique status of Euclidian geometry, which was challenged through the rise of non-Euclidian geometry in the nineteenth century, and Einstein's argument for the Riemannian geometry of space–time (Torrance 1985, 41).

> If in the relation of geometry to physics, as Einstein pointed out, it was forgetfulness that the axiomatic construction of Euclidean geometry has an empirical foundation that was responsible for the fatal error that Euclidean geometry is a necessity of thought which is prior to all experience, theological science ought to be warned against the possibility of regarding natural theology in the heart of dogmatic theology as a formal system which can be shown to have validity on its own, for that would only serve to tranpose it back into an *a priori* system that was merely an empty scheme of thought.

It will be clear that Torrance accepts that a natural theology has a significant place within Christian theology, in the light of an understanding of the nature of God and the world which rests on divine revelation, and which cannot itself be ascertained by human inquiry.

Torrance can therefore be thought of as moving natural theology into the domain of systematic theology, in much the same manner as Einstein moved geometry into the formal content of physics. The proper locus for the discussion of natural theology is not debate about the possibility of a hypothetical knowledge of God, but within the context of the positive and revealed knowledge of creator God. A proper theological perspective on nature allows it to be seen in its proper light (Torrance 1985, 39):

> So it is with natural theology: brought within the embrace of positive theology and developed as a complex of rational structures arising in our actual knowledge of God it becomes "natural" in a new way, natural to its proper object, God in self-revealing interaction with us in space and time. Natural theology then constitutes the epistemological geometry, as it were, within the fabric of revealed theology.

The Barthian challenge can thus be met, in a manner which Torrance believed had Barth's support (Torrance 1976, ix–xi).

Other objections, however, have been raised against the idea of a "natural theology" from within Protestantism, particularly those found in the writings of the leading Reformed philosopher of religion Alvin Plantinga. We may turn to consider these before proceeding further.

Objections to Natural Theology: Philosophical

In recent years, philosophers of religion working within a Reformed theological perspective have risen to considerable prominence. Alvin Plantinga and Nicholas Wolterstorff are examples of writers belonging to this category of thinkers, who have made highly significant contributions to the philosophy of religion in recent decades. Plantinga understands "natural theology" to be an attempt to prove or demonstrate the existence of God, and vigorously rejects it on the basis of his belief that it depends on a fallacious understanding of the nature of religious belief (Plantinga 1983). The roots of this objection are complex, and can be summarized in terms of two foundational considerations (H. Brown 1991; Hoitenga 1991; Fales 1996; Todd 1996):

1 Natural theology supposes that belief in God must rest upon an evidential basis. Belief in God is thus not, strictly speaking, a basic belief – that is, something which is self-evident, incorrigible or evident to the senses. It is therefore a belief which requires to be itself grounded in some more basic belief. However, to ground a belief in God upon some other belief is, in effect, to depict that latter belief as endowed with a greater epistemic status than belief in God. For Plantinga, a properly Christian approach is to affirm that belief in God is itself basic, and does not require justification with reference to other beliefs.
2 Natural theology is not justified with reference to the Reformed tradition, including Calvin and his later followers.

The latter point is inaccurate historically (see our analysis above and Beversluis 1995, 193–9), and need not detain us. However, the first line of argument has met with growing interest.

Plantinga clearly regards Aquinas as the "natural theologian *par excellence*" (Plantinga 1983, 40), and directs considerable attention to his methods. For Plantinga, Aquinas is a foundationalist in matters of theology and philosophy, in that "*scientia*, properly speaking, consists in a body of propositions deduced syllogistically from self-evident first principles." The *Summa contra Gentiles* shows, according to Plantinga, that Aquinas proceeds from evidential foundations to argue for a belief in God, which clearly makes such belief dependent upon appropriate evidential foundations (H. Brown 1991). We have already noted the importance of the growing criticism of classic foundationalism in modern philosophy and theology (pp. 11–14); our concern here is to note that Plantinga's conception of natural theology involves his belief that it intends to *prove* the existence of God.

It is clearly not necessary that a natural theology should make any such assumption; indeed, there are excellent reasons for suggesting that, as a matter of historical fact, natural theology is to be understood as a demonstration, from the standpoint of faith, of the consonance between that faith and the structures of the world. In other words, natural theology is not intended to prove the existence of God, but presupposes that existence; it then asks "what should we expect the natural world to be like if it has indeed been created by such a God?" The search for order in nature is therefore not intended to demonstrate that God exists, but to reinforce the plausibility of an already existing belief. This kind of approach can be found in the writings of William P. Alston, who can be seen as sharing at least some of Plantinga's commitments to a Reformed epistemology, while tending to take a considerably more positive attitude to natural theology.

In his major study *Perceiving God*, Alston sets out what he regards as a responsible and realistic approach. Alston defines natural theology as "the enterprise of providing support for religious beliefs by starting from premises that neither are nor presuppose any religious beliefs" (Alston 1991a, 289). Conceding that it is impossible to construct a demonstrative proof of the existence of God from extra-religious premises, Alston argues that this is not, in any case, a proper approach to natural theology.

Properly speaking, natural theology begins from a starting point such as the existence of God or the ordering of the world, and shows that this starting point leads us to recognize the existence of a being which would be accepted as God. There is thus, in Alston's view, a strong degree of convergence between natural theology and traditional arguments for the existence of God, particularly those deriving from Thomas Aquinas. Yet his conception of natural theology goes beyond such narrow proofs, and encourages the engagement with other areas of human life and concern, amongst which he explicitly includes science . Natural theology thus offers "metaphysical reasons for the truth of theism as a general world-view" (Alston 1991a, 270), and allows us to build bridges to other disciplines.

Objections to Natural Theology: Historical
A third objection to natural theology, which is of particular relevance to our discussion, may also be noted. This objection rests on the emergence of "Deism" (Gay 1968; O'Higgins 1971; Sullivan 1982; Byrne 1989), a form of Christianity which placed particular emphasis on the regularity of the world, yet which was widely regarded by its critics as having reduced God to a mere clockmaker. The term "deism" (from the Latin *deus*, "god") is often used in a general sense to refer to that view of God which maintains God's creatorship, but denies a continuing divine involvement with, or special presence within, that creation. It is thus often contrasted with "theism" (from the Greek *theos*, "god"), which allows for continuing divine involvement within the world.

In its more specific sense, Deism is used to refer to the views of a group of English thinkers during the "Age of Reason", in the late seventeenth century and early eighteenth centuries. In his *Principal Deistic Writers* (1757), John Leland grouped together a number of writers – including Lord Herbert of Cherbury, Thomas Hobbes, and David Hume – under the broad term "deist." Whether these writers would have approved of this designation is questionable. Close examination of their religious views shows that they have relatively little in common, apart from a general skepticism of specifically Christian ideas. John Locke's *Essay concerning Human Understanding* (1690) developed an idea of God which became characteristic of much later Deism. Indeed, Locke's *Essay* can be said to lay much of the intellectual foundations of Deism. Locke argued that "reason leads us to the knowledge of this certain and evident truth, that there is an eternal, most powerful and most knowing Being." The attributes of this being are those which human reason recognizes as appropriate for God. Having considered which moral and rational qualities are suited to the deity, Locke argues that "we enlarge every one of these with our idea of infinity, and so, putting them together, make our complex idea of God." In other words, the idea of God is made up of human rational and moral qualities, projected to infinity.

Matthew Tindal's *Christianity as Old as Creation* (1730) argued that Christianity was nothing other than the "republication of the religion of nature." God is understood as the extension of accepted human ideas of justice, rationality, and wisdom. This universal religion is available at all times and in every place, whereas traditional Christianity rested upon the idea of a divine revelation which was not accessible to those who lived before Christ. Tindal's views were propagated before the modern discipline of the sociology of knowledge created scepticism of the idea of "universal reason," and are an excellent model of the rationalism characteristic of the movement, and which later became influential within the Enlightenment.

The ideas of English Deism percolated through to the continent of Europe through translations (especially in Germany), and through the writings of individuals familiar with and sympathetic to them, such as Voltaire's *Philosophical Letters*. Enlightenment rationalism is often considered to be the final flowering of the bud of English Deism. For our purposes, however, it is especially important to note the obvious consonance between deism and the Newtonian worldview; indeed, it is possible to argue that deism owed its growing intellectual acceptance in part to the successes of the Newtonian mechanical view of the world.

The amalgam of Newtonian natural philosophy and certain forms of Anglican theology proved popular and plausible in post-revolutionary England (see further pp. 67–8). Nevertheless, it was an unstable amalgam. As Odom has pointed out, it was not long before the "estrangement of celestial mechanics and religion" began to set in (Odom 1966). Celestial mechanics seemed to many to suggest that the world was a self-sustaining mechanism which had no need for divine governance or sustenance for its day-to-day operation. This danger had been recognized at an early stage by one of Newton's interpreters, Samuel Clark. In his correspondence with Leibniz, Clark expressed concern over the potential implications of the growing emphasis on the regularity of nature (Alexander 1956, 14):

> The notion of the world's being a great machine, going on without the interposition of God, as a clock continues to go on without the assistance of a clockmaker; is the notion of materialism and fate, and tends (under the pretence of making God a supramundane intelligence) to exclude providence, and God's government in reality of the world.

The image of God as a "clockmaker" (and the associated natural theology which appealed to the regularity of the world) was thus seen as potentially leading to a purely naturalist understanding of the universe, in which God had no continuing role to play.

An appeal to natural theology might therefore be argued, on historical grounds, to lead to a form of Christianity which seriously distorted the traditional orthodox understanding of the nature of God, and especially the criticial issue of God's continuing involvement in the world. The term "deism" now has strongly pejorative overtones to many Christian theologians. So does not an emphasis on natural theology risk the introduction of a similar distortion today? For at least some contemporary writers, there exists a significant historical precedent which suggests that an emphasis on natural theology is associated with a mechanistic worldview and a significantly reduced conception of God.

That this is a serious objection must be conceded. But it need not be a serious issue. The objection is easily resolved along the following lines. It has often been pointed out that we are more often wrong in what we deny than in what we affirm. Deism affirmed a series of significant and authentically Christian notions – for example, God as creator, and the orderedness of the world. It chose to deny (or radically marginalize) others, including the continuing involvement of God in the world, the need for redemption, and so forth. There is no compelling reason why the affirmation of the former should be understood to necessarily entail the denial of the latter. As we have seen, the exploration of the affinities between Christianity and the natural sciences leads to an emphasis being placed on the doctrine of creation; this does not mean the denial or marginalization of the doctrine of redemption. Rather, it entails recognizing that one broad area of Christian thought has particular relevance to this significant issue, resulting in a focusing on the doctrine of creation for the specific purpose of the dialogue in question.

It will be clear from the above discussion that both Plantinga and Barth have raised significant concerns about the nature and scope of natural theology.

Equally, many orthodox Christian theologians would express concern at the possible revitalization of a deist world view resulting from an emphasis on the regularity of nature. Yet these are criticisms which seem to concern potential abuses of natural theology, rather than its actual use within responsible Christian thinking, whether Protestant or Roman Catholic (Clarke 1983; Gill 1984; Long 1992; J. E. Smith 1992; Czapkay Sudduth 1995b).

In many ways, the analysis which has just been presented is something of a digression; it has, however, been necessary to attempt to clarify the status of natural theology (including noting certain objections) before making a firmer connection between natural theology and the natural sciences. In what follows, we shall attempt to indicate the importance of this point.

Natural Science and Natural Theology: The Anthropic Principle

There is no doubt that the rise of the natural sciences has been a significant stimulus to reflection within the field of natural theology (see for example, Cairns 1956; Gascoigne 1988; Brooke 1989; Wilkinson 1990). One of the most significant functions of natural theology is that it offers a point of contact between religion and science. While the concepts of "special revelation" and "experimentation" can be seen as pointing in significantly different and diverging directions, the area of natural theology can equally be seen as offering a common ground between these different disciplines with their distinctive methodologies. In effect, reflection on the natural order prompts lines of thought and inquiry which lead the two disciplines to undertake further exploration in the light of their different methodologies. The same observations of order in nature prompt one group to explore the matter further in terms of divine revelation, and another in terms of the design and implementation of experiments. Indeed, there is no fundamental reason why, for example, a natural scientist who happens to be a Christian should not see these as complementary insights.

In what follows, we shall explore one of the most interesting themes to emerge in the discussion of the interaction of the sciences and religion: the "anthropic principle." The term is used in a variety of ways by different writers, leading to occasional confusions (Gardner 1987); nevertheless, the term is generally used to refer to the remarkable degree of "fine-tuning" observed within the natural order. We have already noted the considerable emphasis on regularity within nature to be found in the writings of the physicist and philosopher Paul Davies, and the significance which he attaches to the "laws of nature" (see pp. 60, 64–5). Davies argues that the remarkable convergence of certain fundamental constants is laden with religious significance. "The seemingly miraculous concurrence of numerical values that nature has assigned to her fundamental constants must remain the most compelling evidence for an element of cosmic design" (Davies 1984, 189). What Davies is describing here is the "anthropic principle," which has been the subject of considerable discussion since about 1980 (Carr and Rees 1979; Barrow and Tipler 1986; Craig 1988; Harris 1990; Smith 1994). In what follows, we shall consider this principle, and its implications for the dialogue between religion and science.

The most accessible introduction to the principle is widely agreed to be the 1986 study of John D. Barrow and Frank J. Tipler, entitled *The Anthropic Cosmological Principle*. The basic observation which underlies the principle may be stated as follows (Barrow and Tipler 1986, 5):

> One of the most important results of twentieth-century physics has been the gradual realization that there exist invariant properties of the natural world and its elementary components which render the gross size and structure of virtually all its constituents quite inevitable. The size of stars and planets, and even people, are neither random nor the result of any Darwinian selection process from a myriad of possibilities. These, and other gross features of the Universe are the consequences of necessity; they are manifestations of the possible equilibrium states between competing forces of attraction and compulsion. The intrinsic strengths of these controlling forces of Nature are determined by a mysterious collection of pure numbers that we call the *constants of Nature*.

The importance of this point can be seen from an important review article published by B. J. Carr and M. J. Rees in 1979 (Carr and Rees 1979). Carr and Rees pointed out how most natural scales – in particular, the mass and length scales – are determined by a few physical constants. They concluded that "the possibility of life as we know it evolving in the Universe depends on the values of a few physical constants – and is in some respects remarkably sensitive to their numerical values" (Carr and Rees 1979, 612). The constants which assumed a particularly significant role were the electromagnetic fine structure constant, the gravitational fine structure constant, and the electron-to-proton mass ratio.

If the situation is represented graphically by a size–mass diagram, an interesting point can be observed. It might be expected that such a diagram would show a fairly random distribution of observed points; in fact, the diagram reveals a significant degree of ordering, with some specific regions being heavily populated, and others unpopulated. The particular distribution actually observed reflects the inevitable equilibrium between competing natural forces of attraction and repulsion. The sizes of people and planets are not accidental coincidences, but rest on the inevitablities of cosmological constants. Thus the size of a planet is the geometric mean of the size of the universe and the size of an atom, whereas the mass of a human being is the geometric mean of the mass of a planet and the mass of a proton (Carr and Rees 1979, 605).

Examples of the "fine tuning" of fundamental cosmological constants include the following:

1   If the strong coupling constant was slightly smaller, hydrogen would be the only element in the universe. Since the evolution of life as we know it is fundamentally dependent on the chemical properties of carbon, that life could not have come into being without some hydrogen being converted to carbon by fusion. On the other hand, if the strong coupling constant were slightly larger (even by as much as 2 percent), the hydrogen would have been converted to helium, with the result that no long-lived stars would have been formed. In that such stars are regarded as essential to the emergence of life, such a conversion would have led to life as we know it failing to emerge.

2   If the weak fine constant was slightly smaller, no hydrogen would have formed during the early history of the universe. Consequently, no stars would have been formed. On the other hand, if it was slightly larger, supernovae would have been unable to eject the heavier elements necessary for life. In either case, life as we know it could not have emerged.

3   If the electromagmetic fine structure constant was slightly larger, the stars would not be hot enough to warm planets to a temperature sufficient to maintain life in the form in which we know it. If smaller, the stars would have burned out too quickly to allow life to evolve on these planets.

4   If the gravitational fine structure constant were slightly smaller, stars and planets would not have been able to form, on account of the gravitational constraints necessary for coalescence of their constituent material. If stronger, the stars thus formed would have burned out too quickly to allow the evolution of life (as with the electromagnetic fine structure constant).

This evidence of "fine-tuning" has been the subject of considerable discussion among scientists, philosophers, and theologians (perhaps most interestingly in Swinburne 1990). It will be clear that the considerations are actually quite anthropocentric, in that the observations derive their significance partly on account of their assumption that life is carbon-based.[5]

So what is the significance of this? There is no doubt that these coincidences are immensely interesting and thought-provoking, leading at least some natural scientists to posit a possible religious explanation for these observations. "As we look out into the Universe and identify the many accidents of physics and astronomy that have worked together to our benefit, it almost seems as it the Universe must in some sense have known that we were coming" (Freeman Dyson, cited in Barrow and Tipler 1986, 318). It must be stressed, however, that this does not command general assent within the scientific community, despite its obvious attractions to a significant subset of that community which endorses the notion of a creator God.

The anthropic principle, whether stated in a weak or strong form, is strongly consistent with a theistic perspective. A theist (for example, a Christian) with a firm commitment to a doctrine of creation will find the "fine-tuning" of the universe to be an anticipated and pleasant confirmation of his religious beliefs. This would not constitute a "proof" of the existence of God, but would be a further element in a cumulative series of considerations which is at the very least consistent with the existence of a creator God. This is the kind of argument set forth by F. R. Tennant in his important study *Philosophical Theology*, in which the term "anthropic" is thought to have been used for the first time to designate this specific type of teleological argument (Tennant 1930, vol. 2, 79):

> The forcibleness of Nature's suggestion that she is the outcome of intelligent design lies not in particular cases of adaptedness in the world, nor even in the multiplicity of them . . . [but] consists rather in the conspiration of innumerable causes to produce, either by united and reciprocal action, and to maintain, a general order of Nature. Narrower kinds of teleological arguments, based on surveys of restricted spheres of fact, are much more precarious than that for which the name of "the wider teleology" may be appropriated in that the comprehensive design-argument is the outcome of synopsis or conspection of the knowable world.

This does not mean that the factors noted above constitute irrefutable evidence for the existence or character of a creator God; few religious thinkers would suggest that this is the case. What would be affirmed, however, is that they are consistent with a theistic worldview; that they can be accommodated with the greatest of ease within such a worldview; that they reinforce the plausibility of such a worldview for those who are already committed to them; and that they offer apologetic possibilities for those who do not yet hold a theistic position.

But what of those who do not hold a religious viewpoint? What status might the "anthropic principle" have in relation to the longstanding debate about the existence and nature of God, or the divine design of the universe? Peter Atkins, a physical chemist with stridently anti-religious views, notes that the "fine-tuning" of the world may appear to be miraculous; however, he argues that, on closer inspection, a purely naturalist explanation may be offered (Atkins 1994, 153). Perhaps the most significant discussion of this point may be found in the major work by Barrow and Tipler on this theme, which we shall explore in what follows. The basis argument deployed by Barrow and Tipler is that there is no need to seek any further explanation of the existence of the universe as it presently exists, in that if it was not as it presently is, we would not be able to observe it (Barrow and Tipler 1986, 566):

The enormous improbability of the evolution of intelligent life in general and *Homo sapiens* in particular at any randomly chosen point in space–time does *not* mean we should be amazed we in particular exist here. This would make as much sense as Elizabeth II being amazed she is Queen of England. Even though the possibility of a given Briton being monarch is about 10^{-8}, *someone* must be. Only for the person who is monarch is it possible is it possible to ask, "how improbable is it that I should be monarch?" Similarly, only if an intelligent species of a particular kind does evolve in a given space–time location is it possible for its members to ask how probable it was for intelligent life of some form to evolve there.

Barrow and Tipler here make the foundational assumption (which they do not seem to explicitly justify) that our existence as human observers is itself an adequate basis for explaining the fundamental features of the universe (a point stressed by Craig 1988). The argument set out above seems to take the following form:

1   There are roughly 10^8 people in England.
2   One of these people is the monarch.
3   There is therefore a 10^{-8} probability of any one of these people being the monarch.
4   Therefore it should not be a cause for surprise to that one person to find that they are the monarch. Someone has to be.

The argument is not especially persuasive, in that it rests upon the conceded plausibility of an existing situation to render plausible a much more complex and contested situation. In effect, the argument presupposes an analogy between one person in Great Britain having to be the monarch, given the current constitutional situation of that country (a matter of contingency, not necessity) and the emergence of humanity in the universe. The analogy is vulnerable at critical points. To explore this matter in more detail, let us consider a central feature of the argument: the role of the observer.

In opening their extensive presentation of the anthropic principle, Barrow and Tipler stress the importance of the observer in the analysis of the universe (Barrow and Tipler 1986, 1–2, emphasis in original):

The basic features of the Universe, including such properties as its shape, size, age and laws of change, must be *observed* to be of a type that allows the evolution of observers, for if intelligent life did not evolve in an otherwise possible universe, it is obvious that no one would be asking the question for the observed shape, size, age and so forth of the Universe. At first sight such an observation might appear true but trivial. However, it has far-reaching implications for physics. It is a restatement of the fact that any observed properties of the Universe that may initially appear astonishingly improbable, can only be seen in their true perspective after we have accounted for the fact that certain properties of the Universe are necessary prerequisites for the evolution and existence of any observers at all.

It will be clear that the basic line of argument here is that the fact that anyone is doing any observing at all reflects the fact that the universe possesses certain features which permits the evolution of life forms capable of observing at least some of those features.

William Lane Craig has offered a response to this position which merits consideration (Craig 1988). Let us concede, he argues, the following:

(1) We should not be surprised that we do not observe features of the universe that are incompatible with our own existence.

If such features existed and were incompatible with our existence, it is unlikely that we would be here to observe them. In effect, this is the central line of argument offered by Barrow and Tipler, although there are numerous digressions and sub-arguments en route. Craig points out that (2) does *not* in any way follow from (1):

(2) We should not be surprised that we do observe features of the universe which are compatible with our existence.

As a simple matter of fact, (2) is *not* a contrapositive of (1); whereas the assumption that it *is* underlies the approach of Barrow and Tipler.

As this is not a particularly easy point to appreciate, it will be helpful to consider some illustrations which bring out the point at issue. Craig himself offers the following. Suppose that you are dragged in front of a firing squad, consisting of 100 trained marksmen, all of whom are in possession of fully loaded and functioning rifles, which they duly aim at your heart. You hear the command to fire. There is a deafening noise. You open your eyes, and to your amazement, discover that you are still alive. All 100 marksmen missed their target. Improbable though that may seem, it is what has actually happened. Now consider the following statements.

(3) You should not be surprised that you do not observe that you are dead.

And

(4) You should be surprised that you do observe that you are alive.

Both these statements are true. The element of surprise in (4) rests on the highly improbable event of 100 trained marksmen missing an easy target; the lack of this element of surprise in (3) rests on the fact that dead people do not observe anything.

On the basis of this line of thought, Craig argues that the anthropic principle does not in any way conflict with the following statement:

(5) We should be surprised that we do observe features of the universe which are compatible with our existence.

in the light of the exceptionally high degree of improbability that such features should be present in the universe. It does not follow that our surprise at the basic features of the universe is unwarranted or inappropriate. Craig concludes by amending (5) slightly to yield (6), which clarifies the nature of the grounds of such surprise more explicitly:

(6) We should be surprised that we do observe basic features of the universe which individually or collectively are excessively improbabe and are necessary conditions of our own existence.

A related analogy is deployed by Richard Swinburne, making a similar point, although perhaps a little more clearly, especially in relation to the critical point concerning the existence of an *observer*. In view of its clarity and importance, we shall cite him directly and at length (Swinburne 1979, 138):

Suppose that a madman kidnaps a victim and shuts him in a room with a card-shuffling machine. This machine shuffles ten packs of cards simultaneously and then draws a card from each pack and exhibits simultaneously the ten cards. The kidnapper tells the victim that he will shortly set the machine to work and it will exhibit the first draw, but that unless the draw consists of an ace of hearts from each pack, the machine will simultaneously set off an explosion which will kill the victim, in consequence of which he will not see which cards the machine drew. The machine is then set to work, and to the amazement and relief of the victim the machine exhibits an ace of hearts drawn from each pack. The victim thinks that this extraordinary fact needs an explanation in terms of the machine having been rigged in some way. But the kidnapper, who now reappears, casts doubt on this suggestion. "It is hardly surprising," he says, "that the machine only draws aces of hearts. You could not possibly see anything else. For you would not be here to see anything at all, if any other card had been drawn." But of course the victim is right and the kidnapper is wrong. There is indeed something extraordinary in need of explanation in ten aces of hearts being drawn. The fact that this peculiar order is a necessary condition of the draw being perceived at all makes what is perceived no less extraordinary and in need of explanation.

Swinburne's point is that the existence of an observer has no bearing on the probability of the events being observed. If a series of highly improbable events give rise to an observer who can note this improbability, they are nonetheless improbable.

So what is the connection between the anthropic principle and natural theology? Craig argues that, once the basic philosophical fallacy is eliminated from Barrow and Tipler's work, the volume "becomes for the design argument in the twentieth century what Paley's *Natural Theology* was in the nineteenth" – that is, "a compendium of the data of contemporary science which point to a design in nature inexplicable in natural terms, and therefore pointing to the Divine Designer" (Craig 1988, 393). Perhaps there is a degree of overstatement here. For example, the evidence could conceivably be intgerpreted on the basis of a number of theories, including the idea that many different universes exist. Nevertheless, a theist would certainly feel justified in interpreting the evidence assembled in this volume as pointing to the universe having a creator. It does not prove anything, in the rigorous sense of that term. Nevertheless, it is clearly consistent with a theistic interpretation of the world (Ward 1996a, 50–60).

Our analysis up to this point has focused on the interpretation of the world of nature. This, however, is only one of the areas which requires to be interpreted from a religious perspective. One of the most significant aspects of the "science and religion" debate, seen from a specifically religious perspective, concerns the manner in which the Bible is interpreted. In view of the importance of this issue to the history and contemporary exploration of the relationship between science and religion, we may now turn to deal with it in some depth.

Creation and Biblical Interpretation

Throughout its long history, Christian theology has seen the interpretation of biblical texts as being of central importance. The subject of biblical interpretation became of major importance during the Middle Ages and the sixteenth century, both of which witnessed a significant growth of interest in the relation of Christianity and the emerging sciences of nature (Evans 1984; McGrath 1987, 152–74). The earliest period of sustained theological reflection within the Christian church is generally referred to as "the patristic period," and can be thought of as extending from roughly AD 100 to 451. This period of Christian history is widely regarded as being of constitutive importance by Roman Catholic, Protestant, and Orthodox Christian writers (McGrath 1996a, 5–25).

Augustine on Biblical Interpretation and the Sciences

It is clear that a creative interaction between biblical exposition and a contemporary scientific understanding of the world can be discerned during the patristic period – as, for example, in two significant anthropological treatises of the fourth century, Gregory of Nyssa's *de opifico hominis* and Nemesius of Emesa's *de natura hominis* (Young 1983). However, it is widely agreed that Augustine of Hippo (354–430) is of especial importance in relation to the exploration of the relationship between biblical interpretation and the sciences. Augustine stressed the importance of respecting the conclusions of the sciences in relation to biblical exegesis. As Augustine himself stressed in his commentary on Genesis, certain passages were genuinely open to diverse interpretations; it was therefore important to allow further scientific research to assist in the determination of which was the most appropriate mode of interpretation for a given passage (van Bavel 1990, 1–2):

> In matters that are so obscure and far beyond our vision, we find in Holy Scripture passages which can be interpreted in very different ways without prejudice to the faith we have received. In such cases, we should not rush in headlong and so firmly take our stand on one side that, if further progress in the search for truth justly undermines our position, we too fall with it. We should not battle for our own interpretation but for the teaching of the Holy Scripture. We should not wish to conform the meaning of Holy Scripture to our interpretation, but our interpretation to the meaning of Holy Scripture.

Augustine therefore urged that biblical interpretation should take due account of what could reasonably be regarded as established facts.

In some ways, this approach to biblical interpretation may be seen as ensuring that Christian theology never became trapped in a pre-scientific worldview. Edward Grant has shown the importance of this point in relation to the development of medieval cosmology over the period 1200–1687, noting especially the manner in which Augustine's approach was endorsed and developed by Thomas Aquinas (Grant 1996, 90–1). The general approach set out by Augustine was adopted by several influential Roman Catholic theologians of the sixteenth century, including a highly significant commentary on Genesis (Valentini 1591–5) which is known to have influenced Galileo's developing views on biblical interpretation (Blackwell 1991, 20–2). Nevertheless, it was an approach which had its difficulties, not least of which was the question of whether an allegedly "scientific" belief was a permanently valid insight into the nature of the world, or simply a culturally conditioned response to events, a traditional belief resting on the authority of an acknowledged master, or a fallacy which would be discarded by subsequent generations.

It can be shown without difficulty that all three such categories of "scientific" beliefs had a considerable influence on the Christian interpretation of the Bible, especially during the Middle Ages. The rediscovery of Aristotle seemed to make available a body of highly respectable "scientific" findings, whose validity seemed assured – a belief in which theologians were encouraged to believe by other academics of the time (Gilson 1978, 181–410). In consequence, medieval biblical exposition and systematic theology can be shown to have followed Augustine's advice in deferring to science, and thus perpetuated what can now be recognized to be the *un*scientific influence of Aristotle (Schmitt 1973; Sylla 1979; Brockliss 1981; McGrath 1984; Carroll 1994).

Augustine himself used contemporary psychological ideas in the course of his reflections on the doctrine of the Trinity in the early fifth century (Zekiean 1981); although Augustine clearly believed himself to be thoroughly up to date in his analysis, this is now regarded by some as one of the more unsatisfactory aspects of his theology. Nevertheless, it may be noted that Augustine appears to have developed these analogies largely on his own, the contrast with, for example, the "triad" proposed by Marius Victorinus being particularly important at this juncture (Ziegenaus 1972). If this is so, it is clear that there are difficulties with the argument that Augustine adopted and incorporated contemporary scientific beliefs into his theology.

It is sometimes argued that the controversy over the view of Copernicus and Galileo arose partly because biblical exposition took no account of the natural sciences. A more plausible reading of the historical data is that the controversy arose precisely because too much weight was given to what early generations of theologians and philosophers had been led to understand were the established certainties of the sciences. When those "scientific" foundations were challenged, biblical interpretation became intensely difficult at points. How could Augustine's maxim be adopted, when there was controversy over what the sciences were saying? Christian biblical exposition had allowed itself to assume that the sciences had established certain matters as fact, which could then be used as the basis of the interpretation of related biblical passages. Augustine's legacy to biblical interpretation proved to be ambivalent: designed to ensure that biblical interpretation was alert to what the sciences had established, it proved capable of enslaving Christian theology to what previous generations of scientists had believed.

The situation became more complex in the aftermath of the Council of Trent (1545–63). Responding to the challenges posed by the rise of Protestantism in the first half of the sixteenth century, the Roman Catholic church stressed the importance of maintaining continuity with the medieval church. Intending to undermine the credibility of Protestant interpretations of certain critical biblical passages (such as those relating to the disputed doctrine of justification by faith), the Council insisted that the consensus of previous generations of theologians should remain normative (Blackwell 1991, 5–22). The weapon was intended to discredit Protestant teachings, which were in effect treated as innovations – a matter to which we shall return presently. However, there was an unintended side-effect. Augustine's maxim – designed to maintain openness to the sciences – trapped theologians in the world of medieval science. If, for example, the consensus of theologians had been that the sun rotated around the earth, Trent's stipulations could only mean that that consensus must be maintained. An indirect and unintended casualty of Trent's polemic against Protestantism was thus the responsivity of theology to *new* developments in the sciences. The results were as tragic as they were unintended.

Types of Biblical Interpretation

During the patristic period, three broad methods of biblical interpretation emerged, which would be developed and refined in the centuries which followed. In what follows, we shall note their general characteristics, and indicate their relevance to our theme, focusing especially on G. J. Rheticus's *Treatise on Holy Scripture and the Motion of the Earth*, which is widely regarded as the earliest known work to deal explicitly with the relation of the Bible and the Copernican theory (Westman 1975; Wilson 1975; Hooykaas 1984, 28–35). The three approaches are:

1   A *literal* approach, which argues that the passage in question is to be taken at its face value. For example, a literal interpretation of the first chapter Genesis would argue that creation took place in six periods of twenty-four hours. This view can be found in the writings of some Christian theologians of the patristic period (Swift 1981); it remains influential today, especially within North American fundamentalism (see p. 27). It has, however, been something of a minority view, in that most Christian writers have tended to argue that biblical passages dealing with cosmological issues are generally poetic or metaphorical in nature.

2   An *allegorical* approach, which stresses that certain sections of the Bible are written in a style which it is not appropriate to take absolutely literally. During the Middle Ages, three non-literal senses of Scripture were recognized; this was regarded by many sixteenth-century writers as somewhat elaborate. This view regards the opening chapters of Genesis as poetic or allegorical accounts, from which theological and ethical principles can be derived; it does *not* treat them as literal historical accounts of the origins of the earth.

3   An approach based on the idea of *accommodation*. This has been by far the most important approach in relation to the interaction of biblical interpretation and the natural sciences. The approach argues that revelation takes place in culturally and anthropologically conditioned manners and forms, with the result that it needs to be appropriately interpreted. This approach has a long tradition of use within Judaism and subsequently within Christian theology

(Benin 1993), and can easily be shown to have been influential within the patristic period. Nevertheless, it mature development can be found within the sixteenth century. This approach argues that the opening chapters of Genesis use language and imagery appropriate to the cultural conditions of its original audience; it is not to be taken "literally," but is to be interpreted to a contemporary readership by extracting the key ideas which have been expressed in forms and terms which are specifically adapted or "accommodated" to the original audience.

In view of the importance of this third approach, we shall consider its application at a period of critical importance for our study – the Copernican and Galileian debates of the sixteenth and early seventeenth centuries.[6]

Accommodation and the Copernican Debates

How, it has often been asked, can an absolutely transcendent God be revealed to finite human beings? The idea of divine "condescension" or "accommodation" has a distinguished history of use within both Jewish and Christian philosophy. Accommodation may be defined as the controlling belief that "divine revelation is adjusted to the disparate intellectual and spiritual level of humanity at different times in history" (Benin 1993, xiv). The idea can be found within the philosophically-inclined forms of Judaism found in the city of Alexandria in the second century, but receives its most sophisticated development within the Christian tradition, including major scholastic writers, such as William of Auvergne and Thomas Aquinas. The concept was also explored thoroughly by certain medieval Jewish philosophers, most notably Maimomides.

The most significant theological exploration of the theme of accommodation around the time of the Copernican debate was due to John Calvin (1509–64), who may be regarded as developing a longstanding Christian approach to the issues involved. In revelation, Calvin argues, God adjusts himself to the capacities of the human mind and heart. God paints a portrait of himself which we are capable of understanding. The analogy which lies behind Calvin's thinking at this point is that of a human orator. A good speaker knows the limitations of his audience, and adjusts the way she speaks accordingly. The gulf between the speaker and the hearer must be bridged if communication is to take place (Battles 1977; Benin 1993, 187–95).

In the classical period orators were highly educated and verbally skilled, whereas their audiences were generally unlearned and lacked any real ability to handle words skillfully. As a result, the orator had to come down to their level if he was to communicate with them. He had to bridge the gap between himself and his audience by understanding their difficulties in comprehending his language, imagery and ideas. Similarly, Calvin argues, God has to come down to our level if he is to reveal himself to us. God scales himself down to meet our abilities. Just as a human mother or nurse stoops down to reach her child, by using a different way of speaking than that appropriate for an adult, so God stoops down to come to our level. Revelation is an act of divine condescension, by which God bridges the gulf between himself and his capacities, and sinful humanity and its much weaker abilities. Like any good speaker, God knows his audience – and adjusts his language accordingly.

An example of this accommodation is provided by the scriptural portraits of God. God is often, Calvin points out, represented as if he has a mouth, eyes, hands and feet. That would seem to suggest that God is a human being. It might seem to imply that somehow the eternal and spiritual God has been reduced to a physical human being. (The question at issue is often referred to as "anthropomorphism" – in other words, being portrayed in human form.) Calvin argues that God is obliged to reveal himself in this pictorial manner on account of our weak intellects. God has to adjust the way in which he speaks of himself to take into account our strictly limited ability to comprehend him. Images of God which represent him as having a mouth or hands are divine "baby-talk (*balbutire*)," a way in which God comes down to our level and uses images which we can handle. More sophisticated ways of speaking about God are certainly proper – but we might not be able to understand them. Thus Calvin points out that many aspects of the story of the creation and fall (Genesis 1–3) (such as the notion of the "six days" of creation, or the "waters above the earth") are accommodated to the mentality and received opinions of a relatively simple people. To those who object that this is unsophisticated, Calvin responds that it is God's way of ensuring that no intellectual barriers are erected against the gospel; all – even the simple and uneducated – can learn of, and come to faith in, God.

Calvin uses two models of God to develop this idea of divine accommodation to human capacities in revelation. God is our father, who is prepared to use the language of children in order to communicate with us. He adapts himself to the weakness and inexperience of childhood. He is our teacher, who is aware of the need to come down to our level if he is to educate us concerning him. He adapts himself to our ignorance, in order to teach us. The doctrine of the incarnation speaks of God coming down to our level to meet us. He comes among us as one of us. Calvin extends this principle to the language and images of revelation: God reveals himself in words and pictures we can cope with. God is prepared to stoop down, as a mother stoops down to meet her child, and use language which we can understand. God's concern and purpose is to communicate, to bridge the great yawning gulf between himself as creator and humanity as his creation. For Calvin, God's willingness and ability to condescend, to scale himself down, to adapt himself to our abilities, is a mark of God's tender mercy towards us and care for us.

Calvin may be regarded as making two major contributions to the Copernican debate. At one level, he positively encouraged the scientific study of nature; at the other, he removed a major obstacle to the development of that study. His first contribution is specifically linked with his stress upon the orderliness of creation; both the physical world and the human body testify to the wisdom and character of God. Calvin thus commends both astronomy and medicine – indeed, he even confesses to being slightly jealous of them – in that they are able to probe more deeply into the natural world, and thus uncover further evidence of the orderliness of the creation and the wisdom of its creator. It may thus be argued that Calvin gave a fundamental religious impulse and legitimation to the scientific investigation of nature, in that it was seen as a means of discerning the wise hand of God in creation, and thus enhancing both belief in his existence and the respect in which he has held.

An ethos which clearly reflects similar views was pervasive within the Royal Society in the seventeenth century. Thus Richard Bentley (1662–1742) delivered a series of lectures in 1692, based on Newton's *Principia Mathematica* (1687), in which the regularity of the universe, as established by Newton, is interpreted as evidence of design. In a letter written to Bentley as he was preparing his lectures, Newton declared that "when I wrote my treatise about our system, I had an eye on such principles as might work with considering men for the belief of a Deity; and nothing can rejoice me more than to find it useful for that purpose." There are unambiguous hints here of Calvin's concept of the universe as a "theatre of the glory of God."

In the second place, Calvin may also be regarded as eliminating a major obstacle to the development of the natural sciences – a simplistic form of biblical literalism, corresponding to the consistent application of a literal approach to the interpration of the Bible to the creation narratives. This emancipation of scientific observation and theory from crudely literalist interpretations of scripture took place at two distinct levels: first, by declaring that the natural subject-matter of scripture is not the structure of the world, but God's self-revelation and redemption, as concentrated in Jesus Christ; second, by insisting upon the accommodated character of biblical language. We shall consider both these points individually.

Calvin indicates (although it should be noted that he is not totally consistent in this respect) that the Bible is to be regarded as primarily concerned with the knowledge of Jesus Christ. It is not to be treated as an astronomical, geographical, or biological textbook. Perhaps the clearest statement of this principle is to be found in a paragraph added in 1543 to Calvin's preface to Olivetan's translation of the New Testament (1534): the whole point of scripture is to bring us to a knowledge of Jesus Christ – and having come to know him (and all that this implies), we should come to a halt, and not expect to learn more. Scripture provides us with spectacles through which we may view the world as God's creation and self-expression; it does not, and was never intended, to provide us with an infallible repository of astronomical and medical information. The natural sciences are thus effectively emancipated from theological restrictions.

Note also how Calvin is clearly working with the idea of "creation" as a (to use modern terminology) *theory-laden* reading or observation of nature. Calvin argues that Christian doctrine provides us with spectacles through which we may view and interpret the natural world as God's creation, in much the same way as N. R. Hanson regards scientific theories as spectacles through which the process of observation takes place (Hanson 1961; Shapere 1982).

The importance of Calvin's use of "accommodation" at this point is highly significant, and is best appreciated by comparing him with the German reformer Martin Luther (1483–1546). The latter was noted for his emphasis on the literal meaning of the Bible, which caused alarm to other theologians within the emerging Protestant movement. For example, in his controversy during the 1520s with the Swiss reformer Huldrych Zwingli over the meaning of the famous words spoken by Jesus over the bread at the last supper – "this is my body" (Matthew 26: 26) – Luther insisted that the word "is" could only be interpreted as "is literally identical with." This struck Zwingli as a religious and linguistic absurdity, totally insensitive to the various levels at which language and imagery operated. In this case, Zwingli argued that the word "is" meant "signifies" (Stephens 1986, 218–50; McGrath 1993b, 165–81). For Zwingli, the Bible was a complex document, in which the literal sense was not always the natural sense (Stephens 1986, 73–7).

Luther, however, had no time for such subtleties, and often gave the impression that the Bible had to be read literally, if its clarity and authority were to be upheld. He applied this somewhat wooden and unperceptive approach to those sections of the Bible which appeared to be of importance to astronomical matters, with results which were as historically unfortunate as they were theologically unjustified. On June 4, 1539, Luther commented caustically upon Copernicus' theory – to be published in 1543 – that the earth revolved around the sun: did not scripture insist that the contrary was the case? And so the heliocentric theory of the solar system received a somewhat curt dismissal.

This contrasts sharply with Calvin, who, as we have seen, argues that God, in revealing himself to us, has accommodated himself to our levels of understanding and our innate preference for pictorial means of conceiving him. God reveals himself, not as he is in himself, but in forms adapted to our human capacity. Thus scripture speaks of God having arms, a mouth, and so on – but these are just vivid and memorable metaphors, ideally suited to our intellectual abilities. God reveals himself in ways suitable to the abilities and situations of those to whom the revelation was originally given. Thus the biblical stories of the creation (Genesis 1–2) are accommodated to the abilities and horizons of a relatively simple and unsophisticated people; they are not intended to be taken as literal representations of reality.

The impact of these ideas upon English scientific theorizing, especially during the seventeenth century, was considerable. For example, Edward Wright defended Copernicus" heliocentric theory of the solar system against biblical literalists by arguing, in the first place, that scripture was not concerned with physics, and in the second, that its manner of speaking was "accommodated to the understanding and way of speech of the common people, like nurses to little children." Both these arguments derive directly from Calvin.

Similar arguments can be found used during the controversy over the heliocentric model of the solar system in the early seventeenth century, which led to the Roman Catholic church condemning Galileo, in what is widely regarded as a clear error of judgment on the part of some ecclesiastical bureaucrats. Although the controversy centering on Galileo is often portrayed as science versus religion, or libertarianism versus authoritarianism (Langford 1989), the real issue concerned the correct interpretation of the Bible (Blackwell 1991, 53–134). Appreciation of this point is thought to have been hindered in the past on account of the failure of historians to engage with the theological (and, more precisely, the hermeneutical) issues attending the debate (Pedersen 1983, 1–2). In part, this can be seen as reflecting the fact that many of the scholars interested in this particular controversy were scientists or historians of science, who were not familiar with the intricacies of the debates on biblical interpretation of this remarkably complex period. Nevertheless, it is clear that the issue which dominated the discussion between Galileo and his critics was that of how to interpret certain biblical passages. The issue of accommodation was of major important to that debate, as we shall see.

To explore this point, we may turn to a significant work published in January 1615. In his *Lettera sopra l'opinione de' Pittagorici e del Copernico*, the Carmelite friar Paolo Antonio Foscarini argued that the heliocentric model of the solar system was not incompatible with the Bible (Basile 1983; Caroti 1987; Blackwell 1991, 87–110). Foscarini did not introduce any new principles of biblical interpretation in his analysis; rather, he sets out and applies traditional rules of interpretation (Blackwell 1991, 94–5):

> When Holy Scripture attributes something to God or to any other creature which would otherwise be improper and incommensurate, then it should be interpreted and explained in one or more of the following ways. First, it is said to pertain metaphorically and proportionally, or by similitude. Second, it is said . . . according to our mode of consideration, apprehension, understanding, knowing, etc. Thirdly, it is said according to the vulgar opinion and the common way of speaking.

The second and third ways which Foscarini identifies are generally regarded as types of "accommodation." As we noted above, this approach to biblical interpretation can be traced back to the first Christian centuries, and was not controversial.

Foscarini's innovation lay not in the interpretative method he adopted, but in the biblical passages to which he applied it. In other words, Foscarini suggested that certain passages, which some had interpreted literally, were to be interpreted in an accommodated manner. The passages to which he applied this approach were those which seemed to suggest that the earth remained stationary, and the sun moved. Foscarini argued as follows:

> Scripture speaks according to our mode of understanding, and according to appearances, and in respect to us. For thus it is that these bodies appear to be related to us and are described by the common and vulgar mode of human thinking, namely, the earth seems to stand still and to be immobile, and the sun seems to rotate around it. And hence Scripture serves us by speaking in the vulgar and common manner; for from our point of view it does seem that the earth stands firmly in the center and that the sun revolves around it, rather than the contrary.

Galileo's growing commitment to the Copernican position (reinforced by his reflections on the phases of Venus) led him to adopt an approach to biblical interpretation similar to Foscarini's.

The official condemnation of this viewpoint was based on two considerations (Pagano 1984, 99–100):

1　Scripture is to be interpreted according "to the proper meaning of the words." The accommodated approach adopted by Foscarini is thus rejected in favor of a more literal approach. As we have stressed, both methods of interpretation were accepted as legitimate, and had a long history of use within Christian theology. The debate centered on the question of which was appropriate to the passages in question.
2　The Bible is to be interpreted "according to the common interpretation and understanding of the Holy Fathers and of learned theologians." In other words, it was being argued that nobody of any significance had adopted Foscarini's interpretation in the past; it was therefore to be dismissed as an innovation.

This second point is of major importance, and needs to be examined more carefully, in that it is to be set against the longstanding and bitter debate, fuelled during the seventeenth century by the Thirty Years War (1618–48), between Protestantism and Roman Catholicism over whether the former was an innovation or a recovery of authentic Christianity. The idea of the unchangeability of the catholic tradition became an integral element of Roman Catholic polemic against Protestantism (Chadwick 1957, 1–20). As Jacques-

Bénigne Bossuet (1627–1704), one of the most formidable apologists for Roman Catholicism, put this point in 1688:

> The teaching of the church is always the same. . . The gospel is never different from what it was before. Hence, if at any time someone says that the faith includes something which yesterday was not said to be of the faith, it is always heterodoxy, which is any doctrine different from orthodoxy. There is no difficulty about recognizing false doctrine; there is no argument about it. It is recognized at once, whenever it appears, simply because it is new.

These same arguments were widely used at the opening of the century, and are clearly reflected and embodied in the official critique of Foscarini. The interpretation which he offered had never been offered before – and it was, for that reason alone, wrong.

It will therefore be clear that this critical debate over the interpretation of the Bible must be set against a complex background. The highly charged and politicized atmosphere at the time seriously prejudiced theological debate, for fear that the concession of any new approach might be seen as an indirect concession of the Protestant claim to legitimacy. To allow that Roman Catholic teaching on any matter of significance had "changed" was potentially to open the floodgates which would inevitably lead to demands for recognition of the orthodoxy of central Protestant teachings – teachings that the Roman Catholic church had been able to reject as "innovations" up to this point.

It is a sad fact of life than many debates of intrinsic intellectual significance take place against a complex backdrop of vested interests. As a result, the outcome of the debates in question often depend on certain entrenched positions, including issues of personal allegiance and status, which have relatively little to do with the intellectual debate itself. In the case of the Galilean debate, for example, the strictly scientific aspects of the matter were overshadowed by complex issues of power and patronage, both secular and ecclesiastical (Biagioli 1993, 103–209). The "honor of patrons" was a major concern for Galileo, and can be shown to have influenced both the questions which he chose to address, and the means by which he addressed them. As Biagioli argues in the conclusion to his masterly study of the importance of patronage as a factor in early modern scientific progress, the rise of experimentation was not simply a matter of an increased interest in empirical analysis: it offered a vitally important way out of "the deadlock of noncommittal arbitration typical of patronage" (Biagioli 1993, 357).

In a society in which "truth" was often determined by the power of patronage and the rapidly changing instabilities of court politics, it is only to be expected that serious miscarriages of intellectual justice will occur. It is generally agreed that Galileo's positive reputation in ecclesiastical circles until a surprisingly late date was linked to his close relationship with the papal favorite, Giovanni Ciampoli. When Ciampoli fell from grace in the spring of 1632, Galileo found his position seriously weakened, perhaps to the point of being fatally compromised (Biagioli 1993, 329–340). Without the protection of Ciampoli, Galileo was vulnerable to the charges of "heresy through innovation" which were levelled against him by his critics.

Evangelicalism and the Natural Sciences

It is widely agreed that evangelicalism is one of the most significant forms of Christianity in the modern world, having particular influence in North America (Marsden 1980; Marsden 1987; Bebbington 1989; Stackhouse 1993; McGrath 1995b). Evangelicalism is noted for its particularly strong emphasis on the importance of the Bible in matters of belief and personal conduct, making its attitude towards the interpretation of biblical passages relating to cosmology and biology of especial interest to our study. It is therefore of considerable interest to explore the response of evangelicals to the issue of creation, and particularly the way in which the "creation texts" of the book of Genesis are handled .

Some North American evangelicals – such as those generally described as "creationists" – are adamant that all forms of the theory of biological evolution were contrary to the teaching of the Bible, and therefore are explicitly off-limits to evangelicals (Kitcher 1982; Numbers 1982; Morris 1985; Dolby 1987; Numbers 1992). This was certainly the view taken by the highly influential conservative Protestant writer Charles Hodge (1797–1878). For the later Hodge, Darwinism was simply a form of atheism (Hodge 1874, 173–7). It must, however, be pointed out that Hodge drew a distinction between "Darwinism" and "evolution," and regarded the Darwinian viewpoint as unacceptable on account of its apparent rejection of the notion of divine design (Livingstone 1987, 100–5).

Nevertheless, this was not the only view within evangelicalism on this matter, as can be seen from the writings of Benjamin B. Warfield and James I. Packer, widely regarded as the most significant evangelical writers of the nineteenth and twentieth centuries respectively. In an 1888 essay on Darwin, Warfield set out his view that the Darwinian doctrine of natural selection could easily be accommodated by evangelicals as a natural law operating under the aegis of the general providence of God (Livingstone 1986). Packer followed Warfield at this point (Packer 1978, 5):

> I believe in the inerrancy of Scripture, and maintain it in print, but exegetically
> I cannot see that anything Scripture says, in the first chapters of Genesis or

elsewhere, bears on the biological theory of evolution one way or the other. On that theory itself, as a non-scientist, watching from a distance the disputes of the experts, I suspend judgment, but I recall that B. B. Warfield was a theistic evolutionist. If on this count I am not an evangelical, then neither was he.

More generally, Packer can be seen as developing Calvin's accommodationist understanding of the way in which biblical interpretation and scientific analysis may interact. This is especially clear in a highly significant discussion of the proper approach to biblical passages regarded as crucial to the issue of biological evolution (Packer 1988, 170–1).

> It should be remembered, however, that Scripture was given to reveal God, not to address scientific issues in scientific terms, and that, as it does not use the language of modern science, so it does not require scientific knowledge about the internal processes of God's creation for the understanding of its essential message about God and ourselves. Scripture interprets scientific knowledge by relating it to the revealed purpose and work of God, thus establishing an ultimate context for the study and reform of scientific ideas. It is not for scientific theories to dictate what Scripture may and may not say, although extra-biblical information will sometimes helpfully expose a misinterpretation of Scripture.

Packer thus argues that interrogating biblical statements concerning nature in the light of scientific knowledge about their subject matter may help towards attaining a more precise exegesis of them. For though exegesis must be controlled by the text itself, not shaped by extraneous considerations, the exegetical process is constantly stimulated by questioning the text.

The views of Packer and Warfield have not met with universal assent. "Creationists" such as Henry Morris have somewhat hastily dismissed the approach adopted by Warfield as a clear case of "pervasive theological apostasy" (Morris 1984, 39). However, they are illustrative of a major trend within historical evangelicalism, which has sought to reconcile the biblical creation accounts with the insights of the natural sciences (Moore 1979; Moore 1985; Livingstone 1987). "Creationist" writers have attempted to suppress or dismiss this prominent section of the evangelical movement, often insisting that an openly anti-evolutionary stance is an essential element of evangelical identity. It is to be hoped that a more sensitive and informed reading of evangelical history will allow and encourage a more positive engagement with such issues. There are role models already available (for example, Berry 1996) ; the future could well see some important developments in this area.

Inference to the Best Explanation

In a classic study, Gilbert Harman argued that inductive inference could be described as "inference to the best explanation" (Harman 1965). This process could be described as "accepting a hypothesis on the grounds that it provides a better explanation of the evidence than is provided by alternative hypotheses" (Thagard 1976, 77). Perhaps the best-known scientific work to make extensive use of inference to the best explanation is Charles Darwin's *Origin of Species*, which sets out a substantial array of observational data which can be explained on the basis of natural selection, but which caused some difficulties for the then-prevailing theory of the special creation of individual species (Thagard 1976, 74; Banner 1990, 125–30). It may be noted at this point that William Whewell developed the notion of "consilience" as a measure of the explanatory power of explanations, and that Darwin was influenced considerably by this notion in his thinking (Ruse 1975; Yeo 1991).

Some have argued that the notion of "explanation" is not an integral aspect of religious identity. To put it crudely: religion is not primarily about explaining things. This view has been defended by a number of writers, perhaps most significantly the philosopher of religion D. Z. Phillips (Phillips 1976). The approach adopted by Phillips can also be found in the writings of Wittgenstein, especially his caustic remarks on Sir James Frazer's *Golden Bough*. This view has, however, been subjected to serious criticism in a number of recent works specifically engaging with the relationship of Christianity and the natural sciences. In his careful study *Explanation from Physics to Theology*, Philip Clayton brings out the significance of "the meaning dimension" in religion (Clayton 1989, 113–45). A number of different levels of explanation may be discerned; nevertheless, a phenomenological approach to the question definitely discloses an explanatory imperative within the religious traditions. Michael Banner offers a different approach in his *Justification of Science and the Rationality of Religious Belief*. Banner argues that the objections against explanation advanced by Phillips can be countered and refuted, both on account of internal difficulties within his approach, and the need for a more nuanced account of the nature of faith than that which he offers (Banner 1990, 67–118).

The considerations set out by Banner and Clayton are widely regarded as at least neutralizing the objections to a "religion as explanation" model. For the specific purposes of the present study, it is not my intention to argue that religion is primarily about offering explanations of the way things are. My concern is simply to note that religions offer at least some explanation of the nature of things, irrespective of the degree of comprehensiveness of that explanation or the emphasis which would be placed upon "explanation" alongside other aspects of religious existence, such as "salvation." Thus Richard

Swinburne's carefully argued defense of the existence of God makes a judicious appeal to the explanatory power of theism in relation to such matters as the existence and ordering of the universe (Swinburne 1979, 277–90). The world displays phenomena which "cry out for explanation'; part of the coherence of theism is its (alleged) ability to offer an explanation for what is observed.

So what criteria might be advanced as determining which is the "best" explanation? We have already noted the appeal to beauty which is found in the writings of some natural scientists (see p. 76). Harman himself comments that "such as judgment will be based on considerations such as which hypothesis is simpler, which is more plausible, which explains more, which is less *ad hoc*, and so forth" (Harman 1965, 89).[7] This is not especially illuminating; furthermore, as Gerd Buchdahl has pointed out, the criteria set forth here can easily conflict with one another (Buchdahl 1970). Making a theory capable of explaining more usually involves the addition of extra hypotheses – which renders the theory less simple. Further, as Nancy Cartwright has stressed, there seems to be an inverse relationship between the simplicity of a theory and its ability to represent the world (Cartwright 1983). A careful examination of the development of scientific theory makes it very difficult to generalize whether there are universally accepted critera for determining which of several explanations is "the best" ; indeed, we have already noted the tendency on the part of certain sociological schools to interpret the Duhem–Quine thesis to mean something like "all explanations are equally good, in that all are underdetermined by the evidence" (see pp. 89–91).

The simple fact of the matter seems to be that "the best explanation" is primarily a pragmatic notion (Fraassen 1977). This should not be taken to mean that the selection of the best explanation is a purely subjective matter. For example, Pierre Duhem's notion of "good sense" (*le bon sens*: see Lowinger 1940; Duhem 1954; Ariew 1984) suggests such subjectivity more by the term which he chose to apply to it, rather than the use which he chose to make of it. At the risk of appearing naïve, it is also necessary to ask whether there is, in fact, any real consensus as to what "explanation" means. Three very different approaches – which could be described as *epistemic, modal,* and *ontic* – may be discerned within the literature (Salmon 1984a). Bas C. van Fraasen, Clark Glymour, and Wesley Salmon, for example, advocate models of explanation which seem to be diametrically opposed to each other (Glymour 1980a; Fraassen 1983).

The Best Explanation: A Case Study

Given these difficulties (which are widely conceded: see Hempel and Oppenheim 1970; Friedman 1974; Mellor 1976; Railton 1978; Railton 1981; Fraassen 1983;

McMullin 1984; Salmon 1984a; Salmon 1984b; Nelson 1996; Roth 1996), there might seem to be little point in attempting some kind of comparison between explanation in religion and the natural sciences. Rather than abandoning the idea of such a comparison, however, I propose to offer an alternative – a single case study which is both historically significant and methodological illuminating.

The case study in question is Charles Darwin's appeal to the "best explanation" of a series of problems which required analysis, which led to the formulation of his theory of natural selection. For Darwin, the issues which required to be explained included the following (Kleiner 1981, 127–9):

1   The problem of explaining adaptation; that is, the manner in which organism's forms are adapted to their needs. A ready explanation of one type was available from the doctrine of special creation, which posited that the creator caused each organism's form to be related to its environmental needs.
2   The question of why some species die out. It is known that Darwin's discovery of Thomas Malthus' theories on population growth had a significant impact on his thinking on this issue (Young 1969; Kleiner 1988). It was not initially clear how the extinction of seemingly well-adapted and successful species could be explained without recourse to "catastrophe" theories.
3   The uneven geographical distribution of life forms throughout the world. Darwin's personal research trips on the *Beagle* convinced him of the importance of developing a theory which could explain the peculiarities of island populations.
4   Vestigial structures – such as the nipples of male mammals – were difficult to accommodate on the basis of the concept of special creation, in that they appeared to be redundant and serve no apparent purpose.

Darwin's task was to develop an explanation which would account for these observations more satisfactorily than the alternatives which were then available. Although the historical account of how Darwin arrived at his theory has perhaps been subject of a degree of romantic embellishment (for example, see Sulloway 1982), it is clear that the driving force behind his reflections was the belief that the morphological and geographical phenomena could be convincingly accounted for by a single theory of natural selection. Darwin himself was quite clear that his explanation of the biological evidence was not the only one which could be adduced. He did, however, believe that it possessed greater explanatory power than its rivals, such as the doctrine of special creation. "Light has been shown on several facts, which on the theory of special creation are utterly obscure" (Darwin 1968, 230).

In the end, Darwin's theory had many weaknesses and loose ends. For example, it required that speciation should take place; yet the evidence for this was conspicuously absent. Darwin himself devoted a large section of *Origin of Species* to detailing difficulties with his theory, noting in particular the "imperfection of the geological record," which gave little indication of the existence of intermediate species, and the "extreme perfection and complication" of certain individual organs, such as the eye. Nevertheless, he was convinced that these were difficulties which could be tolerated on account of the clear explanatory superiority of his approach. Yet even though Darwin did not believe that he had adequately dealt with all the problems which required resolution, he was confident that his explanation was the best available (Darwin 1968, 205):

> A crowd of difficulties will have occurred to the reader. Some of them are so grave that to this day I can never reflect on them without being staggered; but, to the best of my judgment, the greater number are only apparent, and those are are real are not, I think, fatal to my theory.

(We can, incidentally, see here a pre-Duhemian recognition of the co-existence of theory and anomalies.) At least some of the "loose ends" of his theory were tied up through the discovery of the physical basis of heredity through the cytological work of A. F. L. Weissmann in the 1880s and 1890s, and the rediscovery of Gregor Mendel's work by Carl Correns in 1900 (Wilson 1896; Correns 1900; Castle 1903; Darden 1977; Darden 1991, 49–64, 80–3).[8] Loose ends still remain; yet Darwin's "theory" is now widely regarded as a fact, capable of tolerating the remaining difficulties without necessitating an abandonment of the theory as a whole.

Yet on the basis of a naïve falsificationism, every difficulty for a theory amounts to its refutation. On the basis of his survey of the development of the natural sciences, Thomas Kuhn comments that "if any and every failure to fit were ground for theory rejection, all theories ought to be rejected at all times" (Kuhn 1970, 146). A more realistic approach, as we have seen, is to recognize that even the best explanations are attended by anomalies and difficulties. A puzzle is not necessarily counterfactual. Darwin's theory can be seen as offering a grand theory, replete with a full complement of difficulties, anomalies and puzzles. Those difficulties continue to puzzle. Nevertheless, the theory continues to be held, with the difficulties being seen as interesting puzzles which are generally expected to be resolved at some point in the future.

The nature of scientific progress is such that anomalies tend to become resolved, so that what is at present puzzling – or even could be held to call a theory into question – may well be understood tomorrow. A classic example of this trend can be seen in William Prout's famous hypothesis of 1815, according to which all elements were composed of hydrogen. On the basis of this hypothesis, it would be expected that the atomic weights of the elements would be integral multiples of that of hydrogen. The precise measurements of the Swedish chemist Jöns Berzelius called this into question, in that a number of elements clearly possessed non-integral atomic weights – such as chlorine (35.45). This was widely seen as a decisive contradiction of Prout's hypothesis. However, the discovery of isotopes in 1910 reversed this judgment. It was established that a number of elements existed with different atomic weights, while having the same atomic numbers (Pais 1991, 125–7). Each of these isotopes possessed an atomic weight which was an integral multiple of that of hydrogen. As Larry Laudan comments: "The very phenomena which had earlier constituted anomalies for Prout's hypothesis became positive instances for it" (Laudan 1977, 31).

As we have stressed, even the best explanations seem to leave a lot of loose ends lying around. Yet these loose ends – which may take the form of anomalies, inconsistencies or puzzles – need not be seen as causing undue difficulties for the theories in question. Such difficulties may be tolerated without causing the status of the theory to be called into question. It must be noted immediately, however, that what seems to be a minor inconsistency or anomaly within a theory may be precisely that, and nothing more – or it may hold the key to the unravelling of the entire theory, and open the way to its being supplanted with another. As Duhem and Quine have made clear (although in significantly different ways), the difficulty lies in knowing which is the case.

The religious implications of this discussion will be clear. Indeed, precisely the same issue arises in any religious system. The Christian understanding of the world, according to its more sympathetic exponents, offers a coherent and plausible explanation (see the classic studies of Tennant 1930; Swinburne 1977; Swinburne 1979). Yet it does not explain everything with equal plausibility – the question of suffering and evil being a luminous example of such a difficulty. So is this simply a difficulty or puzzle, which is to be tolerated as as an explanatory deficit which it is hoped will one day be resolved? Or is it to be seen as a fatal flaw, which requires the entire theory to be abandoned? We simply cannot know for certain which is the case. It is, however, important to know that precisely this same difficulty is encountered in other areas of intellectual reflection.

Explanation and Eschatology: A Theological Perspective

Yet perhaps one additional consideration may be added to our discussion, as we bring this chapter to a close. The theme of "eschatological verification', which enjoyed a degree of popularity during the period 1955–65, articulates the idea that there are many puzzles and anomalies which are noetic rather than ontic, resulting from limitations on our perception of the situation. Those puzzles or anomalies, it is argued, will be resolved at the end of time, when all is finally revealed. (The term "eschatological" derives from the Greek phrase *ta eschata*, "the last things.)" What is apparently incoherent or anomalous within a theory is held to result from the limitations imposed upon us by virtue of our finite existence; this, it is argued will be resolved after death. Such an idea can be discerned in the writings of St Paul, most notably his famous assertion that "we now see through a mirror darkly; then we shall see face to face" (1 Corinthians 13: 12). Although Paul's eschatology does not focus on the resolution of present ambiguities (see the survey in Kreitzer 1993), this aspect of eschatological thinking has been developed in recent years.

The idea can be discerned in I. M. Crombie's contribution to the debate at the Oxford University Socratic Club concerning whether the existence of God could be falsified. Commenting on the issues raised by the problem of suffering, Crombie remarked (Crombie 1955, 126):

> There is a *prima facie* incompatibility between the love of God, and pain and suffering. The Christian maintains that it is *prima facie* only; others maintain that it is not. They may argue about it, and the issue cannot be decided; but it cannot be decided, not because (as in the case of e.g. moral or mathematical judgments) the appeal to facts is *logically* the wrong way of trying to decide the issue, and shows that you have not understood the judgment; *but* because, since our experience is limited in the way it is, we cannot get into a position to decide it . . . For the Christian the operation of getting into position to decide it is called dying; and though we can all do that, we cannot return to report what we find.

This idea was developed more fully by John Hick (Hick 1957, 150–62; Hick 1964). Hick offers an analogy of two people, travelling the same road and experiencing the same difficulties and concerns. One believes that it leads to the Celestial City; the other does not (Hick 1964, 260–1).

> During the course of the journey the issue between them is not an experimental one. They do not entertain different expectations about the coming details of the road, but only about its ultimate destination. And yet when they do turn the last corner it will be apparent that one of them has been right all the time and the other wrong. Thus although the issue between them has been experimental, it has nevertheless from the start been a real issue. They have not merely felt differently about the road; for one was feeling appropriately and the other inappropriately in relation to the actual state of affairs. Their opposed interpretations of the road constituted genuinely rival assertions, though assertions whose assertion-status has the peculiar characteristic of being guaranteed retrospectively by a future crux.

It will be clear that these considerations have importance for the programe of "inference to the best explanation," in that the Christian perspective inevitably involves some kind of assertion concerning the future of creation or the ultimate goal of humanity which cannot be verified at present. Present anomalies, especially in relation to the issue of suffering, can thus be accommodated in terms of future clarification.

Curiously, a secularized version of "eschatological confirmation" is found (although in a modified form) in the natural sciences. To clarify this point, we may turn again to the famous case of the general theory of relativity (see p. 77). Einstein's theory made two predictions and one retrodiction: it retrospectively explained the (known) anomalous precession of Mercury; it predicted the gravitational bending of light; and it predicted a gravitational red-shift of light from the sun. This red-shift was not observed until the 1960s, more than 40 years after the theory received wide acceptance. Until that point, the failure to detect a predicted effect was treated as an anomaly, something which could be tolerated on account of the theory's explanatory successes elsewhere, in the general belief that, at some point in the future, clarification would be forthcoming. A present significant anomaly was tolerated, partly in the expectation of a future resolution of the anomaly, and partly on account of the present coherence of the theory.

Perhaps we might end this discussion with a thought experiment. It is the year 1930. We are considering three grand theories, each of which offers explanations of the way things are. Each has a strong degree of resonance with reality, offering a good degree of fit with experience. Yet each has difficulties which require to be accommodated.

1   The Einsteinian is passionately committed to the General Theory of Relativity, which has much to commend itself. Yet one of its core predictions has not been observed. He holds onto the theory, believing that its explanatory ability and coherence are sufficient to justify it, and that the difficulty will one day be resolved.

2   The Darwinian holds that, with some necessary modifications, the ideas set out in *Origin of Species* offer an excellent and deeply compelling account of the diversity of life forms on the earth. Yet there is a serious difficulty. The very title of the book points to an explanation of how different species come into existence. Yet speciation – the formation of a new species by the accumulation of mutations – has never been demonstrated in real life or under laboratory conditions. Yet the Darwinian holds on to the theory, believing that its explanatory ability and coherence are sufficient to justify it, and that the difficulty will one day be resolved.

3   The Christian holds that a theistic worldview, especially one which takes full account of the doctrine of the incarnation, offers a compelling and attractive understanding of things. The issue of pain and suffering in the world remains something of a puzzle, and at times troubles her considerably. Yet she holds on to her faith, believing that its explanatory ability and coherence are sufficient to justify it, and that the difficulty will one day be resolved.

In each case, there is a common structure of an explanation with anomalies, which are not regarded as endangering the theory by its proponents, but are seen as puzzles which will be resolved at a later stage. The Einsteinian was vindicated in the 1960s; yet the theory remained acceptable and attractive despite this difficulty. The Darwinian still awaits resolution of the issue of speciation; yet the theory remains potent, despite this difficulty. The Christian still awaits resolution of the difficulty posed by suffering, and is prepared to concede that it will probably never find full resolution in this life; nevertheless, she holds that the theory remains credible, despite this difficulty.

Conclusion

From this discussion, it will be clear that both the natural sciences and religions offer what they believe to be warranted, coherent and reliable explanations of the world. It is not true to state that science believes only what has been empirically proven (contra the simplistic view set out by Dawkins 1997); at points, inference is necessary, in which an hypothesis (such as a "missing link" or unobserved entity) is postulated as the "best explanation" of known facts or established observations. This is an accepted norm of scientific reasoning, and is not controversial. The same process can be seen in religious thinking: on the basis of a philosophical theism or a purely natural theology, "God" would be proposed as the best explanation of the way things are. At points, both scientific and religious theories (or "doctrines") find themselves confronted with mysteries, puzzles and anomalies, which can co-exist with theories which appear to prohibit them. These can give rise to intellectual, institutional or existential tensions. Nevertheless, it is a simple matter of fact that such anomalies exist and are tolerated on warranted grounds, whether the theorist in question is a Christian, Marxist, or Darwinian. "When science progresses, it often opens vaster mysteries to our gaze" (Eiseley 1985, 5). One does not need to be religious to appreciate the element of mystery in nature; it does, however, open some very interesting doors.

Yet it will be clear that the idea that this discussion raises the question of what such "vaster mysteries" might be. Are such entities merely intraparadigmatic constructs? Is the world to be regarded as a construct of our various discourses, conceptual schemes, and paradigms? Or is there some "ontological finality of science as we have it" (Rescher 1987, 61), which rests upon something independent of theory, to which theory is a legitimate response, and by which that theory is to be guided and judged? With such questions, we raise the complex issue of realism, which is the subject of the following chapter.

4

The Reality of the World

The remarkable explanatory and predictive successes of the natural sciences are widely held to point to the independent reality of what it describes. Aeroplanes fly, and they fly, at least in part, on account of the relation between pressure and kinetic energy first set out by Daniel Bernouilli in 1738. Television and radio work, at least partly on account of the predictions made by Maxwell's theory of electromagnetic radiation. A long list of technological developments, widely regarded as essential to modern western existence, can be argued to rest upon the ability of the natural sciences to develop theories which may initially explain the world, but subsequently allow us to transform it. And what more effective explanation may be offered for this success than the simple assertion that what scientific theories describe is really present? As John Polkinghorne comments (Polkinghorne 1986, 22):

> The naturally convincing explanation of the success of science is that it is gaining a tightening grasp of an actual reality. The true goal or scientific endeavour is understanding the structure of the physical world, an understanding which is never complete but ever capable of further improvement. The terms of that understanding are dictated by the way things are.

The simplest explanation of what makes theories work is that they relate to the way things really are. If the theoretical claims of the natural sciences were not correct, their massive empirical success would appear to be totally coincidental. "If scientific realism, and the theories it draws on, were not correct, there would be no explanation of why the observed world is as if they were correct; that fact would be brute, if not miraculous" (Devitt 1984, 108).

For reasons such as these, natural scientists tend to be realists, at least in the broad sense of that term. It seems to many that the success of the natural sciences show that they have somehow managed to uncover the way things really are, or to lock into something which is fundamental to the structure of the universe. The importance of this point is considerable, not least in that it raises the question of whether theologians wishing to argue for the independent existence of God (rather than as a construct of the human mind) may learn anything from the forms of realism associated with the natural sciences. The present chapter aims to explore this issue, beginning with an examination of the nature of realism itself.

Realism: The Affirmation of an Independent Reality

As we have seen (see p. 55), a critical question for both the natural sciences and the religions concerns the status of non-observable or theoretical entities. A strict empiricism holds that experience is our only source of knowledge concerning the world, and that such knowledge should therefore be restricted to statements directly relating to observations. The postulation of theoretical entities lying beyond or behind observations may be an interesting and possibly useful procedure, but such entities are little more than "useful fictions'. Perhaps the most celebrated statement of this position is due to Ernst Mach and we shall explore it in what follows.

For Mach, the natural sciences concern that which is immediately given by the senses. Science concerns nothing more and other than the investigation of the "dependence of phenomena on one another" (Mach 1911, 63). The world consists only of our sensations. This led Mach to take a strongly negative view of the atomic hypothesis, in which he argued that atoms were merely theoretical constructs which cannot be perceived (Hiebert 1970). To use the Kantian framework which seems to lie behind Mach's statements, he arued that it is impossible to move from the world of phenomena to the world of "things in themselves". It is not possible to move beyond the world of experience. Nevertheless, Mach allows the use of "auxiliary concepts" which serve as bridges linking one observation with another. They have no real existence, and must not be thought of as actual or existing entities. They are "products of thought" (Mach 1911, 51) which "exist only in our imagination and understanding" (Mach 1911, 50).[1]

The central distinction of importance here, as it has traditionally been stated, may be said to be between *idealism* on the one hand, and *realism* on the other. The former, while not denying that such things as physical objects exist in the world, holds that we can have knowledge of how things appear to us, or are experienced by us, but not as they are in themselves. Perhaps the most familiar version of such an approach is that espoused by Kant, who argues (although not with total consistency) that such physical things are to be considered as appearances or representations, rather than things in themselves (Bennett 1974,

52–9). The idealist will thus hold that we can have knowledge of the manner in which things appear to us, through the ordering activity of the human mind; we cannot, however, have knowledge of mind-independent realities. In developing our ideas, we are therefore building on foundations which already exist in the human mind.[2]

Realism, on the other hand, will argue to the effect that experience is knowledge of something that is independent of human minds. To use the elegant turn of phrase characteristic of older English philosophy, realism is concerned "on the one hand, to divest physical things of the colouring which they have received from the vanity or arrogance of mind; on the other, to assign them along with minds their due measure of self-existence" (Alexander 1913, 279). It is a position which often commends itself on account of its consonance with "common sense." However, it is important here to appreciate that "common sense" is a culturally-conditioned affair, rather than some globally accepted and self-evidently true scheme (Geertz 1983). Realism may have a certain intuitive plausibility, and is certainly the natural philosophy of most practising scientists (as opposed to those who "confine themselves to the study of printed scientific texts," to borrow a somewhat pointed distinction from Harré (1986, 323–4).

Nevertheless, "realism" is a term which is perhaps as easy to use as it is difficult to define. Three brief definitions could be offered of the central realist thesis, each of which will find its defenders :

1   The world is mind-independent;
2   (Only) nonmental entities exist;
3   Mental and nonmental entities exist.

Each of these statements embodies a realist thesis, although it will be clear that there is a significant difference in the level of commitment and manner of formulation which they adopt. (1) certainly gets to the heart of the matter, in that it directly counters Berkeley's denial of the real existence of unperceived things; nevertheless, it is wise to draw a distinction between "reality" and "mind-independence," which is embodied in (2) and (3).

Richard Boyd sets out the central theses of what he terms "scientific realism" as follows (Boyd 1984):

1   "Theoretical terms" (or "non-observational terms") in scientific theories are to be thought of as putatively referring expressions. Scientific theories should thus be interpreted "realistically."
2   Scientific theories, interpreted in this realistic manner, are confirmable and are in fact often confirmed as approximately true by ordinary scientific evidence interpreted in accordance with ordinary methodological norms.

3   The historical development of the mature sciences is largely a matter of successively more accurate approximations to the truth concerning both observable and unobserved phenomena. Later theories tend to build on the observational and theoretical knowledge embodied in earlier theories.
4   The reality which scientific theories describe is largely independent of thoughts or theoretical commitments.

There can be little doubt that most natural scientists espouse a range of opinions which are recognizably "realist" in their core affirmations, reflecting a common commitment to the ontological finality of the natural order (Rescher 1987). To use an example famously employed by Einstein, the moon does not exist simply because or when we look at it (Mermin 1991). Nevertheless, there is considerable variation on matters of definition within the realist camp, as we shall see. The extent of this variation is such that it once led Jarrett Leplin to comment that "scientific realism is a majority position whose advocates are so seriously divided as to appear a minority" (Leplin 1984, 1). It may therefore be helpful to begin our discussion of the general nature of realism by outlining some of the issues involved, particularly in relation to the status of theoretical entities. Perhaps one of the most helpful starting points is to be found in the writings of Michael Dummett, to which we now turn.

Michael Dummett's Critique of Realism

The debate over realism entered a new phase with Michael Dummett's famous lecture of 1959 on "Truth" (Dummett 1978, 1–24). Dummett focused the debate on the issue of certain classes of statements, such as mathematical statements or statements about the past. The question which needs to be addressed, according to Dummett, is whether statements in these classes possess an objective truth which may be held to be independent of our means of knowing it, or whether such statements cannot be true or false unless it is, in principle, possible to know whether they are so. As Dummett states this point, in concluding his lecture (Dummett 1978, 24):

> The realist holds that we give sense to those sentences of our language which are not effectively decidable by appealing tacitly to means of determining their truth-values which we do not ourselves possess, but which we can conceive of by an analogy with those which we do. The anti-realist holds that such a conception is quite spurious, an illusion of meaning, and that the only meaning we can confer on our sentences must relate to those means of determining their truth-values which we actually possess. Hence, unless we have a means which would in principle decide the truth-value of a given statement, we do not have for it a notion of truth and falsity which would entitle us to say that it must be either true or false.

That there are potentially significant theological aspects of this is made clear by Dummett's later suggestion that the truth of such a statement "involves the possibility in principle that it should be, or should have been, recognized as true by a being – not necessarily a human being – appropriately situated and with sufficient perceptual and intellectual powers" (Dummett 1978, 314). Dummett's challenge to realism is thus to explain how a statement or assertion can be capable of being true or false when the evidence which would allow such a verdict is at present unavailable.

The concepts of truth and falsity can apply only to statements which we are capable of verifying or falsifying. Consider a statement which is not accessible to such verification – for example, "there were six geese sitting on the front lawn of Buckingham Palace at 5.15 p.m. on June 18, 1865." For the realist, this statement must either be true or false, despite the unavailability of the evidence which would allow us to ascertain whether it is, as a matter of fact, true or false. Dummett himself responds to this point as follows (Dummett 1978, 364):

> Of any statement about the past, we can never rule it out that we might subsequently come upon something which justified asserting or denying it, and therefore we are not entitled to say of any specific such statement that it is neither true not false; but we are not entitled either to say in advance that is has to be either one or the other, since this would be to invoke notions of truth and falsity independent of our recognition of truth or falsity.

The truth or falsity of statements concerning the past are clearly called into question by Dummett's stringent critique, along with other statements which lack empirical assertability conditions. The difficulties which this observation raises for Dummett is considerable, and has important implications for his approach to unobservables in general. Crispin Wright argues that a series of categories of statements is rendered problematical by Dummett – including "unrestricted spatial or temporal generalizations, many subjective conditions, descriptions of the remote past, hypotheses about the mental life of others or of animals" (C. Wright 1993, 53). Certain classes of scientific statements are also vulnerable, in that they frequently offer generalizations or affirmations concerning unobservables.

Dummett's position has been criticized by a number of writers, on various grounds. William P. Alston has pointed out that Dummett's verificationist account of sentence meaning does not require the abandonment of a realist position (Alston 1996, 103–31). Anthony Appiah, focusing on Dummett's attitude to statements concerning the past, argued that the clear difficulties which Dummett experiences in this area reflects an affinity on his part with an intuitionist philosophy of mathematics, leading to the conclusion that verification – like a mathematical proof – must be an "all or nothing process" (Appiah 1986, 38–45).

It is, however, with the application of a verificationist approach to the philosophy of science that we are especially concerned in this work. We shall therefore turn to deal with the approach set out by Bas van Fraassen, especially in his celebrated *The Scientific Image* (1980).

Bas van Fraassen's Critique of Realism

Van Fraassen drew a distinction between a realist, who holds that science aims to give a literally true description of what the world is like, and a "constructive empiricist', who holds that science offers theories which are empirically adequate. For the latter, acceptance of a theory does not involve commitment to the truth of that theory, but to the belief that it adequately preserves the phenomena to which it relates. Van Fraasen thus sets out a vigorously empiricist approach to reality, in which echoes of Machean positivism can be clearly discerned (Fraassen 1980, 202–3):

> To be an empiricist is to withhold belief in anything that goes beyond the actual, observable phenomena, and to recognize no objective modality in nature. To develop an empiricist account of science is to depict it as involving a search for truth only about the empirical world, about what is actual and observable . . . it must invoke throughout a resolute rejection of the demand for an explanation of the regularities in the observable course of nature, by means of truths concerning a reality beyond what is actual and observable, as a demand which plays no role in the scientific enterprise.

To speak of "laws of nature" or theoretical entities such as electrons is to introduce an unwarranted and unnecessary metaphysical element into scientific discourse (Fraassen 1980, 204–18).

The critically important distinction concerns observation and theory. While van Fraassen concedes that observation is theory laden, he insists that only those entities which can actually be observed can have any ontological status. In common with the Vienna Circle, he stipulates that there is an epistemologically significant difference between those entities which can be observed by the human senses, and those which can not be observed in this way. His definition of the notion of "observability" (which is clearly of crucial importance here) focuses on the notion of present accessibility to the senses: "X is observable if there are circumstances which are such that, if X is present to us under those circumstances, then we observe it" (Fraassen 1980, 16). A theory can thus be said to be true if "what the theory says *about what is observable* (by us) is true." In other words, theories aim to describe the observable, and do not require the existence of any posited unobservable entities as a prior condition for their acceptance. Fraassen's ontology is summed up in his maxim: "the assertion that theory T explains fact E does not presuppose or imply that T is true" (Fraassen 1980, 100).

Clearly the issue of what is "observable" and what is not is of some importance here. Yet Fraassen seems to define observation in terms of the naked eye, unassisted by technology. This leads him to take some remarkable steps, such as his assertion that the moons of the planet Jupiter are "observable" (even though, under normal conditions, a telescope is required to see them from earth) because it would be possible to travel to that planet, and observe the moons directly from that vantage point. The role of technology in taking us there is conveniently overlooked. More remarkably, Fraassen – having allowed that we "see" through a telescope – argues that we do *not* "see" through microscopes, in that the entities which are alleged to be "observed" are not themselves visible to the naked eye. This has struck his critics as somewhat bizarre (Harré 1986, 57):

> "Observable" means "able to be observed by an unaided human being'. To argue that something unobservable may come to be observable (and so to speak have been the same thing all along) is to violate the rules of language. So the scientific ontology must be tied to current human capacities for observation. *Percipi est esse!* Van Fraassen generously allows physicists and other simpletons to think in terms of a spurious ontology, that is the realist interpretations of their theories, provided they drop it when they are called upon to say something about the furniture of the world. So the back of the moon did not exist before the Apollo fly-pasts, nor did bacteria before the invention of the microscope.

Presumably van Fraassen would not wish to defend the unsupportable idea that the far side of the moon did not exist before we were able to observe it; however, his published views certainly point in this direction. Rather than focus on this unsatisfactory aspect of his account of scientific theorizing, we shall deal with his analysis of the role of posited unobserved entities in theories.

A modest scientific realism would hold that "at least some of the theoretical terms of a theory denote real theoretical entities which are causally responsible for the observable phenomenon that prompts us to posit their existence" (Newton-Smith 1981, 46). A good example of such a "theoretical entity" or "unobservable entity" (for an account of this distinction, see Fraassen 1980, 15) is the electron. By any criterion of observability which wins van Fraassen's approval, an electron lies beyond observation. So do electrons actually exist? Michael Levin has argued that van Fraassen's approach reduces to saying that "experience is *as if* there are electrons, but that this is the strongest statement that can be made" . The electron is a posited entity with explanatory force, but no ontological status. It is not required to exist for theories which posit it to have explanatory success, or to possess empirical adequacy. This certainly sounds as if van Fraassen is suggesting that electrons have no existence outside the sphere of human mental construction (although there is no point in *The Scientific Image* at which he specifically denies the existence of electrons).[3] This certainly renders him vulnerable to the telling criticism of Nicholas Rescher, who argues that van Fraasen "tries to do for *theoretical* entities what Bertrand Russell tried to do for *fictional* entities – to reinterpret talk that is *ostensibly* about entities in terms that bear no ontological weight" (Rescher 1987, 35).

It is widely thought that one of the most effective responses to van Fraassen is an appeal to the burgeoning body of scholarship which examines the manner in which various theoretical entities were initally proposed largely as a matter of conjecture – such as electrons, neutrinos and other subatomic particles – but whose existence was subsequently confirmed through a relentless process of theoretical and empirical investigation. In his important essay on the "Epistemology of Natural Science," Wesley Salmon argues that statements concerning unobservable entities can be made without the need for a special theoretical vocabulary. He illustrates this from a variety of experimental situations, including the work of Jean Perrin on Brownian motion (Salmon 1992). Salmon noted the manner in which Perrin suspended large numbers of tiny particles of gamboge (a yellow resinous substance) in water, and observed their motion with a microscope. From their behavior, he inferred that they were being buffeted by many smaller particles. Although these particles could not be seen, their effect could be determined, allowing the value of Avagadro's number (the number of molecules in a mole of any substance) to be determined accurately across a wide range of diverse experimental situations. As Salmon notes, "the problem of the existence of entities not even indirectly observable was essentially settled for natural science as a result of the work of Perrin and others in roughly the first decade of the twentieth century" (Salmon 1992, 295).

This point is not, it must be stressed, invalidated by the agreed fact that there have been developments in what is known or thought about such entities, or that previously accepted understandings have been laid to one side in favor of others. For example, electrons were conceived in one manner by J. J. Thompson, another by Niels Bohr on the one hand, and Paul Dirac on the other, and in a radically different way by Feynman, Schwinger, and Tomonaga. Yet there is no difficulty in affirming that all were describing the same entity, yet with increasing degrees of approximation to verisimilitude as a result of an increasing accumulation of knowledge, gained through experiment and theoretical reflection. Precisely this process of refinement and elaboration points to the existence of paradigm-transcendent truths against which paradigms may be tested. There exist real-world entities independent of our theoretical constructions and mental processes, against which our ideas and theories require to be tested. For the natural sciences, "ontological finality" rests with nature itself (Rescher 1987, 61).

A Response to Dummett and van Fraassen

In response to such attacks on various forms of realism, we may begin by setting out a triadic taxonomy of scientific theories and the respective realms to which they relate, following the general lines set out by Rom Harré (Harré 1986, 70–3). This triadic approach avoids the ludicrous situation which develops when scientific realism is identified (generally by its critics, but occasionally by its less informed advocates) with one particular schema, as if such a schema constituted a universal theory of science. The unsurprising adduction of a counter-example is then held by such people to discredit the entire scientific enterprise. The suggestion that the natural sciences all, without exception, deploy the same methodology is seriously vulnerable, in that different methodologies (although sharing some common features) are regarded as appropriate to specific fields of scientific investigation. Harré's taxonomy (which he does not hold to be exhaustive) indicates the different types of theory, and the different cognitive status to be assigned to each. In what follows, we shall retain Harré's terminology.

- *Type 1 Theories*, which concern "cognitive objects with pragmatic properties." Examples would include Newton's theories of motion, which relate to the constitution, classification and prediction of observable phenomena. The referents of Type 1 Theories lie in the realm of actual and possible objects of experience to an unaided observer, such as the moon, the planet Jupiter, the human kidney, cannon balls falling from the Leaning Tower of Pisa, and the Grand Canyon.
- *Type 2 Theories*, which concern "cognitive objects with iconic properties." Theories of this type enable the representation or visualization of a certain class of entities which are themselves unobservable. The vast majority of scientific theories fall into this category. The referents of Type 2 Theories are entities which are objects of possible experience, and their confirmation as part of the real world existing independently of the observer depends on the availability of the necessary technology. Such referents would include viruses, bacteria, the moons of the planet Uranus, and X-ray stars.
- *Type 3 Theories*, which concern "cognitive objects with mathematical properties." Theories of this type enable "the representation of non-picturable systems of being and their behavior." The referents of such theories is a domain of entities which lie beyond all possible experience, such as quantum states.

The importance of Harré's analysis is that it explicitly acknowledges that the boundaries between these types of theories are historically conditioned, and will therefore vary. The moons of the planet Uranus, though real, could not be observed before the invention of the telescope; bacteria could not be observed before the invention of the microscope, nor viruses before the electron microscope, and so forth. The boundary between Type 1 and Type 2 is thus defined by technological constraints, and is thus culturally and historically conditioned. This allows us to deal with entities which could be described as "presently lying beyond experience but nevertheless anticipated to be objects of experience at some point in the future."

It will also be clear that the boundary between Type 2 and Type 3 is vulnerable to erosion through theoretical or techological advance. For example, consider the virus, which I have categorized as "Type 2." Had I been writing in 1900, I would have described it as Type 3, as theoretical physics had demonstrated that there were limits to the optical resolution of microscopes which limited the size of objects which they could discern – such as the ultra-small virus. With the unexpected discovery, of such fundamental importance to the development of quantum theory, that electrons could be diffracted, the way was opened to the visualization of a realm of optical phenomena which had hitherto been regarded , on theoretical grounds, as lying beyond such visualization. It is far from clear how many other entities, which presently might be regarded as Type 3, will eventually require recategorization.

It will therefore be clear that it is difficult to draw an explicit distinction between the realms of the "observable" and the "theoretical." Entities may begin by being regarded as explicitly "theoretical," in that they are postulated as a means of explaining certain observations, even though the entities in question themselves could not be observed. With the advance of technology, at least some of these entities have themselves become observable. The notion that there is some kind of absolute ontological distinction between the realms of the "theoretical" and the "observable" may have some appeal to logical minds, and is as a matter of fact associated with certain anti-realist philosophies which hold that a radically different epistemic status is to be ascribed to observational and theoretical assertions. Typically, the former would be held to be real and verifiable; the latter to be little more than a useful fiction which serves some purposes as a codification scheme. While this distinction may possess a certain theoretical neatness, any absolute differentiation of the concepts is difficult to maintain (see, for example, the arguments of Achinstein 1968; Hesse 1974; Churchland 1979; Newton-Smith 1981, 19–43; Newton-Smith 1988). As Newton-Smith (1981, 25) comments:

> Consider the following typical development in the history of science. At one stage genes were posited in order to explain observed phenomena. At that time

no one had in any sense observed or detected the existence of genes. However, with the development of sophisticated microscopes scientists came to describe themselves as seeing genes.

The basic issue here is that there appears to be a continuum of observability, rather than an epistemically decisive and absolute separation between "observable" and "unobservable." There is thus a spectrum of possibilities, in which the advance of technology necessarily implies that there is an irreversible trend towards the extension of the realm of the observable. As such, the distinction between "observable" and "theoretical" is not grounded on epistemic issues, but on one's historical and cultural location. It is a relative, not absolute, matter. The term "unobservable" does not mean "intrinsically lying beyond human observation" but "presently lying beyond human observation." While van Fraasen holds that it is improper to treat unobservables as putative observables, the history of the scientific project suggests that this is precisely what happens on a regular basis through technological advance. This is not to hold that all unobservables will alter their status in this manner. Yet it is not necessary to hold this in order to refute van Fraassen; it suffices to note that some have, as a matter of fact, altered in this manner, and that it is to be expected that others will in the future.

An excellent illustration of this point can be seen from the search for the "top quark," which reached its climax at the Fermi National Accelerator Laboratory in March 1995 (Liss and Tipton 1997). The existence of this particle had been inferred from the discovery in 1977 of the "bottom quark," with a mass of 4.5 GeV. Though unobservable, the quark was widely agreed to exist; it was just a matter of detecting it through the creation of appropriate experimental conditions. In the event, the mass of the missing quark was much higher than expected (175 GeV), necessitating the concentration of immense amounts of energy to cause the production of the particle from a collision. Yet the top quark has never been "seen" or "observed." What actually have been observed are a series of events, some of which are interpreted (with good reason) as the creation of a top–antitop pair, allowing the mass of the top quark to be calculated. Yet the existence of the "top quark" is widely accepted, despite lack of direct observation – and the absence of any expectation that it will ever be "seen."

It will be clear, even from the examples just noted, that the debate between realism and idealism is of considerable interest and importance to both the natural scientist and the theologian. It is also possible that their respective responses might be of interest to each other. With this point in mind, we may turn to consider the some aspects of the debate within theology over this matter.

The Realism Debate in Theology

The recognition that theological language is analogical or metaphorical in nature can be interpreted in two different manners. It be taken taken to mean that human thought and language is incapable of doing justice to the full wonder and transcendence of God – a theme to be found in the writings of theologians as diverse as Gregory of Nyssa, Thomas Aquinas, Martin Luther, John Calvin and John Henry Newman (Selby 1975, 3–11, 67–95; Louth 1981). Others would regard the metaphorical nature of theological language as an acknowledgment that the Christian language is an interesting yet outdated accumulation of images which may be useful to individuals as they think about life, but makes no reference to any world-transcending God. Each of these approaches can be discerned within two significant recent studies of the roles of metaphor in theological language (McFague 1985; Soskice 1985).

The central debate within Christian theology concerns the question of whether the language and conceptualities of Christian discourse are arbitrary constructions, reflecting the whims of historical accidents and personal preference, or whether they are in any way controlled by external, non-linguistic constraints. My concern at this juncture is not to resolve such a debate, but simply to indicate that it is taking place, paralleling a related debate in the natural sciences. In the following section, we shall explore the notion of "critical realism," with special reference to the works of Albert Einstein and Thomas F. Torrance; the present section is concerned with noting how such a debate continues to be significant in the present.

Traditional Christian theology (such as that which flourished during the High Middle Ages and the Reformation periods) regarded Christian theology as an attempt to express in the form of human words something of the ultimate reality of God. Most theologians of the medieval period understood dogma as a dynamic concept, a "perception of divine truth, tending towards this truth (*perceptio divinae veritatis tendens in ipsam*)." It is true that certain medieval writings do indeed suggest that doctrine may be treated as Euclidean theorems: Alan of Lille's *Regulae theologiae* and Nicholas of Amien's *De arte catholicae fidei* are excellent examples of this genre dating from the twelfth century, later found in such writings as Morzillus" *de naturae philosophiae* (1560) and Morinus" *Astrologia gallica* (1661). Nevertheless, a considerably more nuanced approach to the nature of theological statements is much more characteristic of the period.

Theology is here recognized to be concerned with the clarification of the manner in which affirmations about God are, in the first place, derived, and in the second place, how they relate to analogous affirmations drawn from the more familiar world of the senses. It is an attempt to achieve conceptual clarity, to avoid confusion through subjecting statements concerning God to close scrutiny. What does the word "God" stand for? How does the question, "Does God exist?," relate to the apparently analogous question, "Does Socrates exist?"? What reasons might be adduced for suggesting that "God is righteous"? And how does this statement relate to the apparently analogous statement "Socrates is righteous"? Underlying such attempts to achieve clarity of concepts and modes of discourse is the recognition that doctrinal affirmations are to be recognized as perceptions, not total descriptions, pointing beyond themselves towards the greater mystery of God himself (McGrath 1990, 15–20).

The reality of God is thus affirmed as something independent of our knowledge, existing without the need to request our permission to do so. The task of theology is to attempt to express, under the limiting conditions of human conceptualities, as much as possible of what needs to be said about God's nature and purposes. Without wishing to simplify what is a complex discussion, it can be argued that both naïve and critical forms of realism dominate the Christian tradition of theologizing until the Enlightenment. Even those Christian traditions usually characterized as "negative theology," which are strongly critical of any attempt to reduce God to human words and stress the need to preserve the mystery of the divine, operate on the assumption that there is an extra-linguistic reality, whose mystery requires to be preserved in this manner. For example, let us hear Origen on this matter (Louth 1981, 72):

> If one reflects that the richness of what there is in God to contemplate and know is incomprehensible to human nature and perhaps to all beings which are born . . . one will understand how God is enveloped in darkness, for no one can formulate any conception rich enough to do him justice. It is then in darkness that he has made his hiding place; he has made it thus because no one can know all concerning him who is infinite.

(Note that the term "incomprehensible" is to be understood as "incapable of being *grasped*" as much as "incapable of being fully understood.")

This traditional approach has been challenged by many recent writers, for a variety of reasons. Especially during the 1970s and 1980s, some religious (and anti-religious) writers argued that "God" and "religion" were human constructs, and proceeded to the conclusion that human dignity and freedom could be advanced by deconstructing both notions . Reality is something which we construct, not something to which we respond. As Don Cupitt, perhaps the most noted popular critic of religious realism, asserts: "We constructed all the world-views, we made all the theories . . . They depend on us, not we on them" (Cupitt 1985, 9). The suggestion that religious worlds are constructed (and may thus be reconstructed in manners congenial to the *Zeitgeist* or the concerns of the postmodern self) clearly has an attraction for many; nevertheless, it remains a contested issue.

A less radical approach, which is sensitive to the growing realization of the importance of communities and traditions in all areas of human reflection, is associated with Yale Divinity School, and is often referred to as "postliberalism" (Placher 1989; Hensley 1996; Wolf 1996; Kellenberg 1997). The emergence of "postliberalism" is widely regarded as one of the most important aspects of western theology since 1980. The movement had its origins in the United States, and was initially associated with Yale Divinity School, and particularly with theologians such as Hans Frei, Paul Holmer, David Kelsey, and George Lindbeck. While it is not strictly correct to speak of a "Yale school" of theology, there are nevertheless clear "family resemblances" between a number of the approaches to theology to emerge from Yale during the late 1970s and early 1980s. Since then, "postliberal" trends have become well established within North American and British academic theology.

The basic themes of "postliberalism" are generally considered to be a rejection of the totalizing projects of modernity, whether this takes the specific form of an Enlightenment-style appeal to universal reason, or a liberal appeal to "religion," "culture," or an unmediated religious experience common to all of humanity. Each of these is now recognized as a false universal, a fictitious construction of a totalizing mindset. In their place, postliberalism places religious communities and their traditions, particularly as mediated through narratives.

In his major work *The Nature of Doctrine*, Lindbeck sets out an understanding of the role of doctrine as a regulator of Christian discourse. He argues that that religions may be compared to languages, with religious doctrines functioning as grammatical rules. Religions are cultural frameworks or mediums which engender a vocabulary and precede inner experience (Lindbeck 1984, 33):

> A religion can be viewed as a kind of cultural and/or linguistic framework or medium that shapes the entirety of life and thought. . . . It is not primarily an array of beliefs about the true and the good (although it may involve these), or a symbolism expressive of basic attitudes, feelings or sentiments (though these will be generated). Rather, it is similar to an idiom that makes possible the description of realities, the formulation of beliefs, and the experiencing of inner attitudes, feelings and sentiments. Like a culture or language, it is a communal phenomenon that shapes the subjectivities of individuals rather than being primarily a manifestation of those subjectivities. It comprises a vocabulary of discursive and nondiscursive symbols together with a distinctive logic or grammar in terms of which this vocabulary can be meaningfully deployed.

Just as a language is correlated with a form of life (as Wittgenstein pointed out in relation to "language games"), so a religious tradition is correlated with the form of life it engenders, articulates, and reflects.

Lindbeck's approach has generated controversy, not least over precisely what he intends his readers to understand by some of his statements. Some (such as McGrath 1990, 14–34; Sommerville 1995; Kellenberg 1997) have interpreted him to suggest that his approach to doctrine may dispense with the question of whether the Christian idiom has any external reference. On this view, language *functions* within a cultural and linguistic world; it does not necessarily, however, *refer* to anything. Doctrine is concerned with the internal regulation of the Christian idiom, ensuring its consistency. The question of how that idiom relates to the external world is considered to be improper. Christian theology is thus talk about talk about God, not talk about God. Others (such as Hensley 1996) have argued that this represents a misreading of Lindbeck's thought, and that he is, in fact, to be interpreted as an "antifoundational thinker who is, in principle, open to metaphysical realism."

The importance of this debate is clear, in that it points to a continuing debate within Christian theology over the nature and function of theological language, and particularly its relation to any putative reality which is independent of the religious tradition with which that language is associated. This debate has a direct parallel within the scientific community. In both science and religion, a related debate is taking place. In what follows, we shall explore a possible convergence of views within at least significant sections of both communities.

Critical Realism in Science and Theology: A Convergence of Views

It will be clear from the discussion to date that it is impossible to speak of a consensus within either the natural sciences or theology concerning the issue of realism. Various forms of realism and anti-realism can be discerned within both disciplines. It is perhaps worth noting that critics of realism tend to fall within the categories of philosophers of science or historians of science, and frequently reflect concerns which have their origins outside the scientific community. Most practising natural scientists operate on the basis of some form of realism (Leplin 1984; Leplin 1986).

A similar pattern can be discerned within the Christian theological tradition. There is no consensus at present, although it is important to note the preponderance of forms of realism within the pre-Enlightenment tradition, and the growing commitment to forms of realism within both Reformed, Roman Catholic, and Orthodox circles.[4] William P. Alston's remarkable recent defense of philosophical and theological realism from within the Reformed tradition will serve as an example of the growing influence of realism in such circles, to which other examples could easily be added – such as N. T. Wright's espousal of critical realism in relation to New Testament theology (Wright 1992, 32–8), Thomas F. Torrance in relation to theology (Torrance 1985; Torrance 1988; Achtemeier 1994; Morrison 1997), John Milbank in connection with the relation of theology and social theory (Milbank 1993), and Ian Barbour and Wentzel van Huyssteen and others in their discussion of the relation of religion and science (Barbour 1974, 29–70; Huyssteen 1989, 143–97; Polkinghorne 1996, 11–25).

This does not mean that all recent Christian writers have associated themselves with such a position. For example, Nancy C. Murphy has argued against the notion of "critical realism," partly on the grounds that such an approach is characterized by modern presuppositions at a time in which there is a clear shift towards postmodern forms of reasoning (Murphy 1987; Murphy 1988). In part, Murphy's argument rests on the assumption that critical realism is grounded in a foundationalist epistemology; the growing criticism of foundationalism would therefore seem to necessitate the abandonment of critical realism.

This would seem to be a somewhat hasty conclusion. William P. Alston is one of a number of writers to uphold a commitment to a specific form of realism ("alethic realism" in Alston's case), while rejecting foundationalist assumptions (Alston 1996). Similarly, Nicholas Wolterstorff has stressed that the assumption that "anti-foundationalism in epistemology requires anti-realism in metaphysics" is unwarranted (Wolterstorff 1996b, xii). Wolterstorff further points out that anti-foundationalism is nothing new, in that it can readily be discerned within the writings of the great eighteenth-century Scottish philosopher Thomas Reid.[5]

To speak of a "prevailing consensus" on the matter of "critical realism" within Christian theology would be to exercise an unduly selective attention to the literature. Nevertheless, I propose to suggest that there is growing interest in critical realism within the field, so that an exploration of the parallels between science and religion in this respect would be of importance. Four broad categories of comparison suggest themselves, as follows.

Reality Exists Independent of Our Mental Activity

A central theme of most forms of scientific realism is that the reality which scientific theories describe is largely independent of our thoughts or theoretical commitments. Despite their clear divergences at points, both Max Planck and Albert Einstein referred to "reality," meaning a world which exists independent of human thought, and which is accessible to scientific investigation and interpretation. For Einstein, the fact that one cannot know something about an entity in no way entails the conclusion that the entity exists.[6] As John

Polkinghorne has further pointed out, difficulties in depiction cannot be taken as an indication that something does not exist (Polkinghorne 1986, 47):

> It is our ability to understand the physical world which convinces us of its reality, even when, in the elusive world of quantum theory, that reality is not picturable. This gives physics a good deal in common with theology as the latter pursues its search for an understanding of the Unpicturable.

Physics is to be understood as an attempt to grasp a reality which exists prior to and independent of the process of observation (Polikarov 1989). Nevertheless, Einstein must be understood as a critical realist, in that he insists that "reality" is not presented to us *directly*. Knowledge derives from sense-experience, from which theories may be derived. Yet the fact that our knowledge of reality takes place through our sense-experiences and reflection on them does not in any way require us to conclude that this reality does not exist independently of our minds.

A similar line of thought can be discerned within the classical theistic tradition. God is held to exist independently of our recognition of this fact. For most writers in this tradition, God cannot be known *directly*, on account of the radical ontological difference between God and humanity, or the inability of fallen or finite human nature to perceive God. The fact that knowledge of God may be analogical (Aquinas) or accommodated (Calvin) has not been understood (at least, within the classical tradition) to imply that the idea of a God who is independent of human reflection may be dispensed with. The suggestion that the notion of God is essentially a human construction is generally traced back to Ludwig Feuerbach (Bradley 1980; Wartofsky 1982; Thiselton 1995, 123–6). While certain styles of theology are vulnerable to his criticisms (particularly those which seek their starting points in subjective human experience), it must be noted that the traditional Thomist and Reformed approaches possess a certain resilience in this face of this critique (Küng 1980, 191–216).

The Intelligibility of Reality

One of the leading themes of Einstein's philosophy of science is the notion of "intelligibility (*Verständlichkeit*)" of reality. The nature of the world outside our minds is such that our minds are able to grasp at least something of its nature and ordering. There exists an objective or mind-independent domain with reference to which our theories acquire whatever truth-value is conferred upon them. Yet the attempt to understand the external world is itself governed by that world, in that we are obliged to be constrained by the way the world is, or is seen to behave, in our explanations. Explanations and analysis are not independent constructions of the human mind, but are seen to be grounded in and responsive to what can be known of reality. Einstein's understanding of the scientific method is such that (Torrance 1985, 54–5):

> we are concerned in the development of scientific theories to penetrate into the comprehensibility of reality and grasp it in its mathematical harmonies or symmetries or its invariant structures, which hold good independently of our perceiving: we apprehend the real world as it forces itself upon us through the theories it calls forth from us. Theories take shape in our minds under the pressure of the real world upon us . . . This is the inescapable "dogmatic realism" or a science pursued and elaborated under the compelling claims and constraints of reality.

A similar situation can be argued to exist within theology. On this view, theology is under an obligation to give a faithful account of the reality which requires description. Theology is held to be "responsible," in the sense that it regards itself as being accountable for its representation of the prior reality to which it is a response. This limitation placed upon theologizing runs counter to the tendency within some sections of the discipline, which follow the "postmodern turn" by stressing the importance of creativity and freedom (for some of the issues, see Wilde 1981; Hassan 1982; Bernstein 1991; Lyotard 1992; Bauman 1993; Lundin 1993). The critical realist approach in theology inevitably leads to restrictions on freedom in thinking about God on account of the obligation to remain faithful to what is, or can be, known about that God. This would be seen as repressive and restrictive by some writers. For example, when Don Cupitt asserts "the more realistic your God, the more punitive your morality" (Cupitt 1989, 168), one assumes that he is protesting against the limitations which such an understanding of God imply. Yet an entirely proper response to this objection might be that, if this is the way that God really is, then we are under an intellectual and moral obligation to tell the truth about it.

Cupitt's response, I assume, would be to deny that, as a matter of fact, this is the way things are; however, this merely invites the question of how, if this is indeed not the situation, we might go about ascertaining how things are, raising some rather uncomfortable questions for him en route. The issue of ontological finality – which is of such critical significance in relation to van Fraassen's instrumentalism – has a direct theological counterpart. At one point, Cupitt asserts that "facts" are to be thought of as "descriptive propositions whose truth is testable in ways independent of local cultural beliefs, human wishes, and so on" (Cupitt 1980, 44). However, Cupitt later seems to have come round to the view propounded by Alasdair MacIntyre, to the effect that "facts, like telescopes and wigs for gentlemen, were a seventeenth century invention" (MacIntyre 1988, 357). In his later writings, Cupitt adopts the view – associated with writers such as Foucault and Derrida – that claims about truth are really disguised claims to power. It is far from clear where this takes us in terms of attempting to investigate the world (though the omens are far from propitious: see Thiselton 1995, 104–17). Perhaps Cupitt would now stand among those "for whom phrases like 'how things stand' smack of objectivism, scientism, phallocentrism, transcendentally disinterested subjects and a number of other creepy things" (Eagleton 1996, 12).

If there is indeed a parallel between the natural sciences and religion, as I wish to suggest there is, a proper response to Cupitt's protest might take the following form. It might indeed be argued that it is repressive and uncreative to suggest that the Compton wavelength of an electron is 2.424309×10^{-12} meters, or that DNA possesses the structure of a double helix. Each of these could be argued to be intransigent, representing the interests of the western male scientific establishment, and failing to respect creativity. The intense difficulty with such objections is that experimental research, often linked with theoretical considerations, shows that this is the way they are – and further asserts that these conclusions are independent of the gender, social status, religion, and sexual orientation of the observer.

The parallel with religion is therefore not exact. The Christian doctrine of the incarnation may be taken to affirm the interaction of God with human history and culture, and thus pointing to the inevitability of the intermingling of historically and culturally conditioned elements (such as language and imagery) into the way in which God and the Christian life are conceived.[7] Nevertheless, a critically realist theology would wish to affirm that the realities which it attempts to describe and interpret are prior to such description and interpretation, and in some manner control the nature of that description and interpretation. As Torrance puts this point (Torrance 1985, 85):

> The basic convictions and fundamental ideas with which our knowledge of God is built up arise on the ground of evangelical and liturgical experience in the life of the Church, in response to the way God has actually taken in making himself known to mankind through historical dialogue with Israel and the Incarnation of his Son in Jesus Christ and continues to reveal himself to us through the Holy Scriptures. Scientific theology or theological science, strictly speaking, can never be more than a refinement and extension of the knowledge informed by those basic convictions and fundamental ideas, and it would be both empty of material content and empirically irrelevant it it were cut adrift from them.

The Relation of Theoretical and Observable Terms

Critical realism holds that "theoretical terms" (or "non-observational terms') in scientific theories are to be thought of as putatively referring expressions, so that scientific theories should thus be interpreted "realistically". We have seen how various "theoretical" entities were proposed, and subsequently observed through technological advance, whether directly or indirectly. Examples of such theoretical entities would include genes, positrons, and neutrinos. The neat distinction between "theoretical" and "observable" entities which is required or postulated by certain writers hostile to such forms of realism is difficult to sustain.

What of theology? It will be clear that theology postulates a number of entities which are unobservable – such as God himself, to give one particularly glaring example. Within the Christian tradition, God is defined not merely as being invisible as a matter of fact, but as a matter of human ability. Nevertheless, the point which we made earlier concerning the *present* unobservability of putatively observable entities becomes of particular importance at this point. Traditional Christian theology asserts that, though unobservable at present, God will not remain thus. The theme of the "beatific vision" asserts that what is currently beyond observation will finally be seen. This theme has not received much attention in modern theological discussion; nevertheless, it is of major importance to medieval Christian theology. The beatific vision is a theme of major importance in the writings of Thomas Aquinas (Hoye 1975), and figures especially prominently in the *Divine Comedy* of Dante Aligheri. Dante portrays the gradual ascent of the soul through various stages, until a final vision is obtained of "the love which moves the sun and the other stars." There has been a renewed interest in the field of eschatology in the last few decades, stimulated in no small way by the publication of Jürgen Moltmann's *Theology of Hope* (Moltmann 1967), with its distinctive emphasis on the need for eschatology to be of central importance to Christian reflection, rather than being relegated to its margins (Bauckham 1987, 3–52).

Earlier (p. 136), we noted the possible significance of the concept of "eschatological verification" in relation to the ambiguities and puzzles of human experience. The concept sets out the idea that there are many anomalies in our experience of the world which result from limitations on our perception of the situation which, it is argued, will be resolved at the end of time, when all is finally revealed. What is apparently incoherent or anomalous is argued to result from the limitations imposed by the finitude of human existence. The central error of Hume's empiricism could be said to be his demand for epistemic warrant (that is, justification in terms of presently available knowledge) for ontological claims regarding the existence of a world and its constituent features, some of which are presently unknown, and others of which may elude human understanding (Norris 1997, 211). A similar point is being made in relation to theological concepts. The key to the relation of theoretical and observable entities is thus seen to be eschatological in nature.

The Role of an Interpretative Community

In recent years, both philosophers and theologians have come to realize the importance of community and tradition in the process of interpretation and the advancement of understanding. Alasdair MacIntyre has stressed that the Enlightenment-inspired model of an isolated individual thinker, free to make intellectual judgments devoid of any explicit or implicit precommitments, is little more than a fantasy (MacIntyre 1988, 334):

> The history of attempts to construct a morality for tradition-free individuals . . . has in its outcome . . . been a history of continuously contested disputes, so that there emerges no uncontested and incontestable account of what tradition-independent morality consists in and consequently no neutral set of criteria by means of which the claims of rival and contending traditions could be adjudicated.

What is true of the quest for an indisputable morality is true also for the intellectual quest in general. The Enlightenment quest for a universal rationality, free of the limitations of culture and history, has failed (MacIntyre 1988, 6):

> Both the thinkers of the Enlightenment and their successors proved unable to agree as to precisely what those principles were which would be found undeniable by all rational persons. One kind of answer was given by the authors of the *Encyclopédie*, a second by Rousseau, a third by Bentham, a fourth by Kant, a fifth by the Scottish philosophers of common sense and their French and American disciples. Nor has subsequent history diminished the extent of such disagreement. Consequently, the legacy of the Enlightenment has been the provision of an ideal of rational justification which it has proved impossible to attain.

MacIntyre argues for the need to return to the idea of a tradition-centred rationality. There is no "view from nowhere," no rationality which is untainted by history and culture (Jones 1987). It is therefore necessary either to abandon any quest for a rationally grounded morality altogether, or to return to the approaches to rationality which were accepted before the Enlightenment insistence on the attainability of a universal rationality gained the ascendancy. For MacIntyre, this means a renewed understanding of the epistemological and moral importance of a community and of tradition.

The same themes have emerged as important within theology, particularly in the "postliberal" school. The writings of George Lindbeck and Stanley Hauerwas have stressed the importance of community and tradition for theology and ethics respectively (McGrath 1996b; Wolf 1996; Kellenberg 1997). Theological and ethical reflection are undertaken within a tradition-shaped community. A similar point is made by Thomas F. Torrance in his discussion of "the social coefficient of knowledge," where he notes the importance of a community in relation to the acquisition and interpretation of knowledge (Torrance 1985, 98–130).

At first sight, this might have no relevance to the natural sciences. Nevertheless, recent studies from the field of the sociology of knowledge have shown that the natural sciences should be recognized as community-based activities, based on shared understandings of evidence and procedures, which are adapted and developed in response to the needs of new situations. Understanding of certain conventions regarding, for example, "styles of reasoning" and "standards of demonstration" have emerged, generated and reinforced by the practice of scientific communities or teams, rather than purely theoretical considerations (Galison 1995). This is especially significant in the case of large-scale experiments (Galison 1987, 274–5):

> The history of large-scale experiments cannot be written as if the experiment issued from a single mind. We are faced with a new kind of historical phenomenon that must be accorded the multiple structures of a true and heterogeneous community.

A growing interest in the actual practice of science (rather than an abstract account of its ideas) has demonstrated the perhaps unacknowledged significance of communal norms, traditions and approaches in the scientific undertaking (Pickering 1990; Pickering 1992). Attention has been drawn to the emergence of certain definite traditions in areas such as theorizing, experimentation and the development of instrumentation (Galison 1988). Inevitably, this leads to the conclusion that such traditions are prone to a series of difficulties – such as the pursuit of community or team interests, and the protection of vested interests (see Pickering 1981). It is no accident that one can speak of "schools" of scientific interpretation – such as the Copenhagen school of quantum theory. Equally, it is clear that group loyalty among physicists at Trinity College, Dublin – including such luminaries as George FitzGerald, William Rowan Hamilton, James MacCullagh, and Frederick Trouton – played no small part in establishing the British response to the null-result of the Michelson–Morley experiment (Warwick 1995, 322–9). The recognition of the importance of interpretative communities in no way depreciates the commitment of the scientific community to the experimental method and the rigorous investigation of results. It simply reminds us that the natural sciences are like other human intellectual activities in this respect – including theology.

A related point of convergence at this point concerns the idea of "reception" – that is, the process by which an idea, perhaps originally associated with or generated by an individual or group, becomes generally accepted and adopted by a community. Within the natural sciences, it is instructive to note the way in which certain theories were initially associated with individuals or small groups, before gradually finding wider acceptance within the scientific community as a whole. This process can be seen at work in the reception of Copernican theory in the later sixteenth century (Brotóns 1995), the gradual acceptance of a wave theory of light in Britain (Cantor 1975), or the growing endorsement of Darwinian theory within popular scientific culture in the Victorian period (Ellegerd 1958).

This process of acceptance often involves considerable internal debate within the scientific community, and an accompanying shift in the paradigms which both reflect and sustain its identity and tasks. One of the achievements of Thomas S. Kuhn's *Structure of Scientific Revolutions* was to note the role of the scientific community in accepting new approaches. For example, Kuhn notes the manner in which works such as Ptolemy's *Amalgest* or Newton's *Principia* precipitated a debate within the community, eventually leading to refinements within its program (Kuhn 1962, 270):

> Their achievement was sufficiently unprecedented to attract an enduring group of adherents away from competing modes of scientific activity. Simultaneously, it was sufficiently open-ended to leave all sorts of problems for the redefined group of practicioners to resolve.

The process of reception (I use the theological term here) is often difficult and controversial, involving factors which are not necessarily "scientific" in nature – such as the vested interests of individuals and power groups (Kuhn 1962, 150–1):

> The transfer of allegiance from paradigm to paradigm is a conversion experience. Lifelong resistance, particularly from those whose productive careers have committed them to an older tradition of normal science, is not a violation of scientific standards but an index to the nature of scientific research itself.

This, it must be stressed, cannot be seen as a negation of the scientific enterprise; rather, it is a recognition of the active role of a community in the acceptance of new ways of thinking and working ("paradigms"), and the inevitable interaction of social and cultural factors in this process of evaluation and acceptance.

It is perhaps at this point that the sociology of knowledge has a genuine and significant contribution to make to our understanding of scientific development. While the assertion (typically associated with the "strong program" in the sociology of knowledge) that "scientific truth" is a purely social construct is widely rejected (Norris 1997, 218–47, 265–94), there are excellent reasons for suggesting that the plausibility of certain theories – and hence the manner and extent of their acceptance – can be accounted for, to some limited extent, by social factors.[8] Thus in their richly documented study of the controversy between Richard Boyle and Thomas Hobbes over the role of experimental evidence, Shapin and Schaffer argue that social factors helped Boyle win acceptance for his approach. In particular, Boyle's (non-scientific) argument that the experimental program was a potential guarantor of civil stability and peace is argued to have been particularly attractive to a society which had all too recent memories of a destructive civil war. Shapin and Schaffer (1985, 13) thus suggest that:

> There was nothing self-evident or inevitable about the series of historical judgements in that context which yielded a natural philosophical consensus in favour of the experimental programme. Given other circumstances bearing upon that philosophical community, Hobbes's views might well have found a different reception. They were not widely credited or believed – but they were *believeable*; they were not counted to be correct – but there was nothing inherent in them that prevented a different evaluation.

Perhaps there is a blurring here of the critical distinction between the intellectual foundations of a theory and the factors which influence its reception, so that the latter is somehow elided with the former. Yet the point made is fair: non-scientific factors affect the reception of scientific theories.

The same process (and the same determining factors) can be seen in the process of doctrinal development within Christianity, in which an interpretative and evaluative community is of critical importance. There are clear parallels between the development of doctrine and the emergence of new paradigms within the scientific community (see, for example, Knight 1994).[9] In Christian theology, an important distinction can be drawn between a "theological opinion" and a "doctrine" or "dogma" (McGrath 1990, 10–13). A theological opinion may be understood to be an idea associated with and advocated by an individual theologian or a school of opinion. It has no authority within the ecclesiastical community. Yet that community may, by an often long and complex process of "reception," come to accept that opinion as authoritative, so that a teaching originally associated with an individual or small group comes to have authority within the community (Greenacre 1988). This can be illustrated by the manner in which the early church committed itself to a "two natures" Christology; the medieval western church "received" the theological notion of transubstantiation (Plotnik 1970); Protestant churches accepted the concept of forensic justification as representing the distinctive evangelical position on this issue (McGrath 1986a, vol. 2, 20–53).

If this analysis of the significant role of interpretative communities is correct, it would indicate that future dialogue in science and religion needs to take place within a community which values and encourages such dialogue. There are severe limitations placed upon what individuals can achieve, even in dialogue. The future exploration of this critically important subject will thus depend upon the development of research programs , linked with institutions, societies, and communities. The intellectual foundations of such dialogue seem to me to be incorrigible; yet, as the complexities of the process of reception indicate, this cannot of itself be regarded as sufficient reason for it to gain widespread acceptance.

Conclusion

This chapter has noted significant parallels between the ideas and approaches of the natural sciences and one major style of theological reasoning. It is clear that the position which is generally described as "critical realism" offers considerable potential as a theoretical bridge between the two disciplines. Critical realism can be distinguished from what might loosely be called "naïve realism" by its insistence that its language, through referential, is indirect, making use of models, metaphors, and analogies. "Naïve realism," on the other hand, can be argued to rest upon the assumption that there is a direct correspondence between human mental pictures and the reality to which they refer.

It will therefore be clear that an integral aspect of critical realism, whether in the sciences or theology, concerns the use of intermediate models or analogies in the representation or depiction of reality. They are to be seen as partial, incomplete yet *necessary* ways of referring to reality (Barbour 1990, 43; Peacocke 1993, 14). In view of the importance of this matter, we shall consider the manner in which the religions and sciences represent reality in the following chapter.

5

The Representation of the World

The importance of imagery in human reflection is beyond dispute. In both science and religion, models or analogies serve as a means of visualization. Whatever other role they may play, one of their more significant functions is to offer a visual image of something which may lie beyond the natural or assisted human ability to perceive through the senses. My own research work in the design and construction of analogues of biological membranes convinced me of the need to have simplified, yet reliable, models of enormously complex systems, to allow at least some of their features to be examined and understood. But what is the status of such analogues or models? This question has been vigorously debated within the scientific community.

Ernst Mach (1838–1916) is widely regarded as one of the most robust defenders of an empirical approach to the world, arguing that our knowledge is limited to observation and sensation. A theory is thus to be understood as an economical shorthand description that could be analyzed, if necessary, in terms of an expansion of the component observation statements. Nevertheless, Mach was acutely aware of the need to *represent* the world (Mach 1906, 314–15):

> Every practical and intellectual need is satisfied the moment our thoughts have acquired the power to represent the facts of the senses completely. Such representation, consequently, is the end and aim of physics; while atoms, forces and laws are merely means of facilitating the representation.

Mach thus allowed the need for imaginative constructions – what we might now call "models" – having no actual existence, save as useful mental pictures to allow us to connect various observations.

It is therefore of considerable interest to consider the roles played by such analogies or models in the religions and sciences, and especially the critically important question of whether they are merely "imaginary constructs" or "useful

fictions" – or whether they denote something which refers, and makes ontological claims. Mach himself was fond, when debating theoretical entities (in
which category he famously and mistakenly included atoms), of asking his
colleagues the simple question: "have you seen any?" (Bernstein 1989, 60–1).
As the rise of the atomic hypothesis makes clear, the issue of visualizibility
would prove to be somewhat more complex than Mach imagined (Hiebert
1970).

A related difficulty can be seen in relation to the evaluation of the theory set
forth by Einstein, Podolsky and Rosen, which argued that the existence of
two-particle systems demonstrated either nonlocality or the theoretical incompleteness of quantum theory (Einstein, Podolsky, and Rosen 1935). The EPR
argument is complex, and is not strictly relevant to our discussion (for details
see Redhead 1987, 71–81); it is sufficient for our purposes to note that Einstein
adopted the latter interpretation, which was more congenial to his realist epistemology. Some thirty years later the Irish physicist John Bell explored the
implications of some features of two-particle systems which had experimental
consequences which could be investigated as a test for the presence of nonlocality
– the viewpoint earlier rejected by Einstein (Redhead 1987, 82–118; Laudisa
1995). These consequences have subsequently been verified experimentally.

Our concern here does not lie with the enormously complex issue of quan-
tum nonlocality and its apparent implications for the philosophy of physics.
Rather, we are concerned with the enormous difficulty in visualizing the points
at issue, for example, in Bell's theorem, or the Greenberger–Horne–Zeilinger
(GHZ) cases, which were held to lend support to Bell (Maudlin 1994, 24–8).
In response to this need, N. David Mermin devised a series of "parables" –
narratives which were designed to allow visualization of the issues involved
(Mermin 1981; Mermin 1991). The principle to appreciate here is that complex abstract ideas require visualization – not to be *correct*, but to be *grasped* by
a wider audience than those capable of thinking in highly abstract manners.
This point applies throughout the ideational spectrum, whether we are dealing
with quantum theory or ideas about God and eternal life.

It will be clear that this discussion has a profoundly religious dimension.
This can be seen immediately by considering the following statement
(Polkinghorne 1991, 20):

> We habitually speak of entities which are not directly observable. No one has
> ever seen a gene (though there are X-ray photographs which, suitably inter-
> preted, led Crick and Watson to the helical structure of DNA) or an electron
> (though there are tracks in bubble chambers which, suitably interpreted, indicate
> the existence of a particle of negative electric charge of about 4.8×10^{-10} esu and
> mass about 10^{-27} gm). No one has ever seen God (though there is the astonishing
> Christian claim that "the only Son, who is in the bosom of the Father, he has
> made him known" (John 1: 18)).

It is a matter of fact that most religions make statements which relate to a series of entities (such as "God," "forgiveness," or "eternal life") which are unobservable in themselves at present. The question of how such theoretical or unobservable entities are to be depicted, and their precise ontological status, is a matter of considerable interest and importance within both science and religion, and will occupy our attention throughout the present chapter. We may begin by considering the role played by analogies or models in science and religion.

Analogies in Science and Religion

Giovanni Vico once commented that it was a distinctive "property of the human mind, that whenever men can form no idea of distant and unknown things, they judge them by what is familiar and at hand" (Vico 1968, 60). This Vichian principle can readily be demonstrated to be of major importance in both science and religion. It is, however, important to appreciate that Vico here reflects the pervasive belief of the Italian Renaissance that the relation between symbol and original is ontologically grounded, rather than accidental. In the case of Marsilio Ficino, any resemblance between a symbol and its original rested on a neo-Platonic understanding of the relation of the world of senses and ideas (Kristeller 1943, 96–8). As E. H. Gombrich pointed out in a classic essay, the iconography of the Renaissance was ultimately grounded in the belief that there was some ontological transference between the visual image and the reality which it depicted (Gombrich 1948).

It is widely agreed that analogies play a major role in many forms of argumentation and inference, whether in philosophy, theology or the natural sciences (Lyttkens 1952; Jevons 1958, 628–43; Hempel 1965, 434–6; Pöhlmann 1965; Bunge 1967; Hesse 1967; Bunge 1973; Burrell 1973; Palmer 1973; Weitzenfield 1984; Swinburne 1992). The manner in which analogies are generated, validated, and applied provides one of the most interesting parallels between Christianity and the natural sciences, and illuminates their commonalities and divergences.

One of the central difficulties encountered in dealing with analogies is that no general theory of analogical argument is widely accepted (Shaw and Ashley 1983, 421–2). This is not to say that no such theory has been set out; the point is that none finds general acceptance today. One of the most intriguing questions is whether older justifications of argumentation by analogy can be retrieved. For example, there is a clear understanding in classical philosophy that the concept of analogy is somehow grounded in mathematical proportions, so that there is some form of proportionality between entities which are held to be analogically related (Lyttkens 1952). As we have seen, the Renaissance witnessed the growing influence of a neoPlatonic ontology, which affirmed a linkage between the icon and its original. One of the more interesting aspects of classical Christian theology concerns its grounding of the use of analogies concerning God in a series of theological beliefs, to which we shall turn presently.

The logical structure of arguments from analogy can be set out in the following manner (Shaw and Ashley 1983, 420–1):

1   Entities $E_1, E_2, E_3 \ldots E_n$ have properties $P_2, P_3, P_4 \ldots P_n$ in common.
2   Entities $E_2, E_3 \ldots E_n$ have property P_1 in common.

Therefore it is probable that

3   Entity E_1 has property P_1.

Note that the analogy is not confined to a comparison between two entities only, even though this is probably the most common type of analogy to be encountered. Indeed, the larger the number of entities between which the analogy holds, and the greater the number of respects in which the analogy may be said to hold (in other words, the greater the number of analogous properties), the stronger the analogy may be considered to be. Yet, as Shaw and others have pointed out, these considerations are essentially intuitive, and are therefore vulnerable to conflicting intuitions (Shaw and Ashley 1983, 422). It is this aspect of arguments from analogy which has led some writers to suggest that they are devoid of real significance (Beardsley 1950, 105–9). This, however, distinctly seems to be a minority view.

It is clear that the natural sciences have gone some considerable way towards establishing and regulating the use of analogies in the depiction and explanation of the world, and have led to comparisons between the ways in which analogies and models function in the sciences and religion. It is not entirely clear, however, how far these comparisons have taken us. As Janet Martin Soskice has suggested, the level of discussion on the part of theologians has tended to be little more than something along the lines of "religion need not be ashamed of its reliance on models if science proceeds in the same way" (Soskice 1987, 110). The clear (if unstated) assumption here is that the explanatory successes of the natural sciences lend credence to its use of models, and hence justify theology doing the same thing.[1]

The Use of Analogies in Science

The use of analogy in scientific thinking during the eighteenth century is a subject of major historical interest in its own right. The prevailing consensus is summarized in the standard work of reference of the period, the *Encyclopédie; ou Dictionnaire raisoné des sciences, des arts et des métiers*. This radical work of reference, edited by Denis Diderot and Jean Le Rond d'Alembert, is known to have been one of the most influential works of reference of this period, summarizing existing knowledge in many areas, and advocating future changes – often of a quite revolutionary nature – in others (Lough 1968). The article on "analogy" reflects a widely prevailing consensus of the period and that immediately preceding it, which is reflected in much of its scientific writing (de Marsais and l'Abbé Yvon 1751). Analogies illuminate things, but do not prove them; an analogy which is drawn on the basis of external appearances cannot be regarded as a foolproof demonstration of any corresponding internal similarity.[2]

Other writers of the period, however, felt able to press the implications of perceived analogies further. For example, the English astronomer John Herschel, who discovered the planet Uranus, adopted a less nuanced approach to the issue in his 1831 work *Preliminary Discourse on the Study of Natural Philosophy*. He argued that the observation of an analogy between two phenomena made it difficult to avoid the conclusion that, if the cause of one was clear, "it becomes scarcely possible to refuse to admit the action of an analogous cause in the other, though not so obvious in itself" (Herschel 1830, 142).

Such statements illustrate the general lines of the heuristic use of analogies to make sense of the natural world during the seventeenth and eighteenth centuries. Isaac Newton, an active proponent of the thesis that nature "is very conformable to herself', argued that the infinite variety of nature ultimately rested on an inner simplicity, reflected in both the mechanical and biological spheres (Guerlac 1983). Analogies drawn from the biological sphere were thus held to be appropriate in the mechanical, and vice versa. There existed a certain "analogy of nature," which was itself the consequence of the actualization in creation of certain eternal and archetypal patterns in the mind of God. This theme was developed further in George Cheyne's 1715 work entitled *The Philosophical Principles of Religion*, which asserted that the observed analogy of nature was to be accounted for theologically (McGuire 1970, 35):

This analogy of things necessarily infers the existence of the author of these things, and the wisdom of the contriver of this analogy. These things and this analogy could come from nothing else but from their original ideas and archetypal patterns in the divine mind or imagination, and their harmony and proportion can possibly arise from nothing but their being representations of his ideas.

It is important to note the explicit appeal which is made to the doctrine of creation as an intellectual foundation of both the observed regularity and intelligibility of the natural order (see p. 53).

The eighteenth-century natural historian Linnaeus used one analogy in particular (summed up in the phrase *planta est animal inversum,* "the plant is the inverse of the animal') to further his understanding of the grounds of the ordering which he observed within the natural world. This analogy can be found in his *Praeludia sponsaliorum plantarum,* one of Linnaeus" earliest writings, written when he was a mere twenty-two years of age. It has often been suggested that Linnaeus overplays his analogies, in that analogies often play the methodological role of demonstration rather than illumination (Broberg 1975, 37–8). Nevertheless, their critical role in his thinking is undisputed.

In what follows, we shall explore some aspects of the role of analogies in scientific explanation.

Analogical Thinking and Scientific Explanation
The precise role of analogies in scientific reasoning is contested. For some, reliance on analogies is inessential, and can easily be dispensed with (Hempel 1965, 439); for others, the appeal to analogies is integral to the scientific process. "Metaphoric concept formation is an essential aspect of scientific reasoning for the purpose of solving conceptual problems" (Rothbart 1984, 595). The history of science strongly suggests that analogies or models do play a significant role in scientific explanation. Millar has shown how iconic expressions have exercised a subtle yet significant influence on physical theory (Miller 1984). Often highly abstract physical concepts need to be *vizualized* if they are to be used effectively.

In what follows, we shall explore the way in which Darwin developed the notion of "natural selection" as a means of making sense of the bewildering diversity of plants and animals, both living and extinct, which had generally been a source of mystery to those who had preceded him. The analogical form of reasoning deployed by Darwin in *Origin of Species* can be set out as follows. The first chapter of the book takes the form of a substantial analysis of "variation under domestication" – that is, the way in which domestic plants and animals are bred, the manner in which variations develop in successive generations through this breeding, and how these can be exploited to bring about inherited characteristics which are regarded as being of particular value by the breeder (Darwin 1968, 71–100). The second chapter then sets out the remarkable variation and novelty which can be discerned within the natural order (Darwin 1968, 101–13), and introduces the key notions of the "struggle for existence" and "natural selection" to account for what may be observed in both the fossil records and the present biosphere (Darwin 1968, 114–72).

It is then argued that this process of "domestic selection" or "artificial selection" constitutes an analogy which can be used as a framework for understanding that a related – yet ultimately significantly different – process of selection is taking place within nature itself (Young 1971; Young 1985; Young

1993). "Variation under domestication" is presented as an analogue of "variation under nature." An unknown and unobservable process is thus posited within the natural order which is analogous to a known process, familiar to English stockbreeders and horticulturalists (Darwin 1968, 132): "As man can produce and certainly has produced a great result by his methodical and unconscious means of selection, what may not nature effect?"

A more rigorous analysis of Darwin's appeal to analogy has been presented by Rom Harré (Harré 1986, 204–7). At a basic level, the analogical argument deployed by Darwin takes the following form. The following observation statement is set out and extensively illustrated in the first chapter of the *Origins*: *Domestic variation* acted on by *domestic selection* leads *to domestic novelty*. As the second chapter unfolds, it is clear that Darwin's illustrative narrative carries the reader along with him towards the conclusion that an analogical observation statement might be applied to natural world:

Natural variation acted on by . . . *what?* . . . leads *to natural novelty*.

Two of the three elements of the analogy have been firmly set in place by the end of the second chapter, in that natural variation and natural novelty have both been established and illustrated. The question which then arises is: what is the missing middle element? What is the natural analogue of artificial or domestic selection? The fourth chapter confirms what the second suggests – that the unknown mechanism which leads to diversity within nature is "natural selection." It will be clear that the force of Darwin's argument rests on the conviction that there is a general analogy between "variation under domestication" and "variation under nature," and more specifically that there is an analogue between the specific and known productive process of artificial selection and an unknown process within nature, which Darwin terms "natural selection." (We shall explore the problems that this terminology raises presently: see pp. 172–6.)

It will be clear that this form of analogical reasoning was productive in the case of Darwin's reflections on varieties within nature. It must, however, be appreciated that the appeal to analogy in scientific reasoning has not always had positive consequences. The choice of an inappropriate analogy can lead to a series of unhelpful or misleading assumptions being generated concerning a phenomenon, hindering a proper understanding from being attained. Analogies have their limits, and can often mislead and misrepresent. In what follows, we shall use some analogies used in Darwinian and neo-Darwinian discussions to indicate the difficulties that need to be considered if analogies are to assist, rather than mislead us.

The Limits of Analogy: The Case of "Natural Selection'
As we have seen, Darwin deployed the term "natural selection" as a metaphorical or non-literal means of referring to a process which he believed to be

the most convincing means of explaining the patterns of diversity be observed within the biosphere (Young 1985). Darwin himself claimed that the concept and the term were suggested by the methods of livestock breeders and pigeon-fanciers, who used artificial selection as a means of generating and preserving desirable characteristics within the animal world. The concept of "natural selection" was thus based on the perception of an analogy between the existing and familiar notion of "artificial selection" (L. T. Evans 1984). The term first appears after Darwin's reading, in March 1840, of Youatt's standard manual of cattle management *Cattle: Their Breeds, Management and Diseases* (note the reference to him in Darwin 1968).

Darwin was quite clear that the methods of domestic animal breeders were of major importance to his thinking. "All my notions about how species changed derive from long-continued study of the works of agriculuralists and horticulturalists; and I believe I see my way pretty clearly on the means used by nature to change her species and *adapt* them to the wondrous and exquisitely beautiful contingencies to which every living being is exposed" (Darwin 1887, vol. 2, 29–30). This passage is significant, not simply on account of the parallel drawn between the familiar process of what would now be called "artificial selection" and the inferred or proposed process of *natural* selection; it also implies the notion of a conscious process of selection. Darwin, who was scrupulous in his choice of words, speaks explicitly of nature changing her species and adapting them. The analogy is apparently being allowed to imply that the active selection of the animal or plant breeder is somehow paralleled within nature itself. This is certainly suggested by his frequent references to "nature" as an agent who actively "selects" variants which she approves as good.

The analogy was regarded as seriously misleading by Alfred Russell Wallace, who was alarmed at its implication of active choice and purposefulness on the part of nature. He wrote to Darwin to express his misgivings. "I am led to conclude that the term itself, and your mode of illustrating it, however clear and beautiful to many of us, are not yet the best to impress it on the general naturalist public." For Wallace, many had been led to assume that the term "natural selection" implied an active process of selection on the part of a personified nature, which was thus conceived anthropomorphically as implying rational analysis and an intended goal. "I think this arises almost entirely from your choice of the term 'Natural Selection' and so constantly comparing it in its effects to Man's Selection, and also your so frequently personifying nature as 'selecting,' as 'preferring,' as 'seeking only the good of the species,' etc., etc. To the few, this is as clear as daylight, and beautifully suggestive, but to many it is evidently a stumbling block" (Darwin and Seward 1903, vol. 1, 267–8).

The "analogy" (L. T. Evans 1984) or "metaphor" (Young 1985) of natural selection deployed by Darwin thus carries over the notions of intention, active selection and ultimate purpose from the model (established procedures of artificial selection) to the *explicandum* (the natural order). At both the verbal and conceptual level, the anthropomorphic concept of "purpose" is retained, despite Darwin's apparent intention to eliminate this (and Wallace's more explicit views on this matter). Darwin himself realized the dangers of his somewhat anthropomorphic manner of speaking about "nature." In a preface added to the third edition of *Origin of Species* (1861), Darwin sought to correct possible misunderstandings along such lines:

> Others have objected that the term selection implies conscious choice in the animals which become modified; and it has even been urged that, as plants have no volition, natural selection is not applicable to them! In the literal sense of the word, no doubt, natural selection is a false term; but who ever objected to chemists speaking of the elective affinities of the various elements? and yet an acid cannot strictly be said to elect the base with which it in preference combines. It has been said that I speak of natural selection as an active power or Deity; but who objects to an author speaking of the attraction of gravity as ruling the movement of the planets? Everyone knows what is meant and is implied by such metaphorical expressions; and they are almost necessary for brevity. So again it is difficult to avoid personifying the word Nature; but I mean by Nature, only the aggregate action and product of many natural laws, and by laws the sequence of events as ascertained by us.

This passage is of considerable importance, on account of its explicit affirmation of the analogical or metaphorical nature of the term "natural selection." It is a "false term" – that is, a term which cannot be pressed to its literal limits of meaning. In effect, the ideas of "active choice" and any personification of the selecting agent (which might be argued to be essential to the notion of "selection") have been suppressed or eliminated from the analogy.

The concept of selection also plays a significant role in a number of flawed approaches to the use of analogy in understanding natural processes, to which we now turn.

Flawed Analogies: Neo-Darwinians and Selection
How can natural selection from simple origins lead to structures of considerable complexity, whose arrangement might lead some to suggest that they are "designed"? Richard Dawkins offers an analogy to allow insights into this process in his *Blind Watchmaker* – the "biomorph program." He asks us to imagine a computer program, in which the software has been given a few carefully chosen instructions to allow it to generate shapes. The computer operator selects those shapes which are thought to be particularly elegant, and discards the remainder. Eventually, Dawkins argues, ordered and elegant patterns will emerge.

The analogy is intended to show how beautiful or organized structures can be accounted for without invoking the contested notion of design. Indeed, the entire point of the analogy is to eliminate the idea of a "designer" or "creator" as a means of explaining apparent ordering in the world. However, it is clear that the idea of design has been suppressed only at the verbal level. The difficulty is that the analogy, while eschewing design-words, nevertheless presupposes the supervention of a computer operator who "selects" certain outcomes of the biomorph programme instructions (Ward 1996a, 124–6). Intelligence and design are thus implicitly presupposed at two points: the design of the program itself, and the intervention of the intelligent operator whose views on the merits of shapes determine the outcome of the process. "Selection" is thus "selection by someone." An unacknowledged anthropomorphism underlies the process. The idea of a "selector" or "creator" has been eliminated only at the verbal level; the analogy requires the presupposition of such an operator for it to have any plausibility.

I assume that Dawkins might wish to meet this criticism by pointing out that his analogy assumes that the "biomorphs" that are randomly varying are to be understood as *effects* (that is, as phenotypes subject to selection), so that the match which is set by the computer is analogous to the environment. Such a process can be argued to take place in selection for crypts, in that any variant which increases resemblance to the environment will be selected. (A related example would be selection for mimicry, in which case any variant which enhances resemblance to the model will increase the chances of being selected.) Nevertheless, the terms "select" and "selection" still remain laden with anthropomorphic associations.

It might, however, be argued that such a program or operator could emerge naturally in the course of time. Dawkins' approach has often been characterized as "given enough time, anything can happen." It is certainly Dawkins' view that natural selection could lead to those creatures with brains possessed of more effective algorithms having a greater propensity to survive, passing down these algorithms to their progeny and thus ensuring their survival. The process of natural selection would then favor those creatures who had developed more effective algorithms, so eventually leading to the development of the remarkably effective algorithms of the human brain. The idea may seem attractive; however, there are some serious difficulties. The most obvious analogy to such an approach to human intelligence is the "Turing Machine" (Deutsch 1985; Penrose 1990, 61–75, 534–8; Hodges 1992, 96–107). Random mutations could be argued to tend to destroy, rather than enhance, its operation. In any case, there are difficulties here in relation to the "halting problem," which we need not consider here.

The analogy offered by Dawkins thus has considerable weaknesses. It is not my intention to argue that a flawed analogy leads to a flawed argument, and hence potentially to a misguided conclusion – not least because in this particular case, the conclusion appears to have been arrived at in advance of the supporting analogy. It serves as a reminder of the need to examine the "analogies" offered by some natural scientists with the critical perspective that all analogies properly invite, if they are to serve their intended heuristic function. Dawkins' analogy gains its plausibility from the active practice of purposeful and goal-directed selection in the real world; he then asks us to abandon this specific aspect of the analogy, negating its plausibility. As one noted analytical philosopher has pointed out, just as analogies "give rise to philosophical problems, so analogies are useful in conjuring away philosophical problems" (Waismann 1965, 60). Perhaps the question here is whether a skilfully constructed and deployed analogy "conjures away" a serious issue of molecular biology, by systematically minimizing the difficulties in understanding its origins and development.

A similar difficulty can be instanced in Elliott Sober's *Philosophy of Biology*, which adopts an approach similar to Dawkins. How, he asks, can astonishingly complex biochemical systems arise? The numerical odds against it appear to be substantial. The issue to be explained, and the analogy offered to explain it, are stated by Sober as follows, drawing on the type of analogy already offered by Dawkins (Sober 1993, 37–8):

> Imagine a device that is something like a combination lock. It is composed of a series of disks placed side by side. On the edge of each disk, the twenty-six letters of the alphabet appear. The disks can be spun separately so that different sequences of letters may appear in the viewing window.

Sober then asks us to calculate the possibility of any one specific combination of letters appearing in the window – such as the 19-letter combination METHINKSITISAWEASEL (an example already used by Dawkins 1986, 47). The calculation is quite simple. As there are 26 possibilities on each disk, and 19 disks in all, it follows that there are 26^{19} different possible sequences. The probability of this one specific combination appearing is thus 26^{-19}, which is unquestionably a very small number indeed. Now Sober proposes a modification to this:

> But now imagine that a disk is frozen if it happens to put a letter in the viewing window that matches the one in the target message. The remaining disks that do not match the target then are spun at random, and the process is repeated. What is the chance now that the disks will display the message METHINKSITISAWEASEL after, say, fifty repetitions? The answer is that the message can be expected to appear after a surprisingly small number of generations of the process.

Sober clearly regards this analysis as clinching his argument that complex systems can arise much more simply than might be thought.

But the analogy is flawed. His imprecise mode of speaking of a disk being "frozen" conveniently omits reference to the means by which this selection might take place. Perhaps, somewhat like Clerk Maxwell, Sober envisages a demon watching the spinning, and influencing the outcome? Someone has to decide which disks to freeze, and the criteria determining whether it is to be frozen or not; alternatively, some directive selectional process is required, whose origins then require as much explanation as its application. "Instead of an analogy for natural selection acting on random mutation, the Dawkins–Sober scenario is actually an example of the very opposite: an intelligent agent directly the construction of an irreducibly complex system" (Shapiro 1986, 179–80; Behe 1996, 221). The notion of "selection" or "design" has merely been eliminated at the verbal level; it remains deeply embedded at the conceptual level.

Let me stress that my concern here relates to the validity of the analogy used in argumentation, not the explanation of the complexities of biological systems. The debate over how complex biochemical and biophysical systems arise is significant, and is neither assisted nor illuminated by the use of inappropriate analogies. As Mario Bunge pointed out, analogies have a marked historical propensity to mislead in the sciences (Bunge 1973, 125–6). The point is therefore to ensure that any analogies deployed or developed in this context are appropriate to the task in hand. In this case, the analogy appears to fail, if judged by this criterion, in that it implicitly presupposes precisely the agency (active selection) which it is intended to exclude.[3] All argumentation rests on the correct use of analogies, and the natural sciences are no exception. Nevertheless, the issue of "design" is so significant in contemporary debate that the careless choice (should I say "selection"?) of analogies is of critical importance.

Seeing through a Glass Darkly: The Limits of Analogies

Models and analogues possess an ability to illuminate when used rightly, and to confuse and perplex when not. The difficulty lies in knowing which is the case. In the case of the scientific community, models are *generated* with a view on the one hand to retrospectively explaining what is known about a more complex system, and on the other to predicting novel aspects of its behavior. The prediction, and subsequent verification, of such behavior is generally taken to be an important indication that a model is appropriate.

The field of theoretical physics is a particularly rich resource for those looking for examples of the positive use of analogies in scientific thinking. Indeed, in his study of elementary particles, Jeremy Bernstein comments that "it is probably no exaggeration to say that all of theoretical physics proceeds by analogy" (Bernstein 1968, vii). A good example of the positive contribution of analogical thinking can be seen in Enrico Fermi's 1933 paper, offering a model for the beta decay of radioactive nuclei (Fermi 1933). The model offered by Niels Bohr for the phenomenon involved the non-conservation of energy, and was widely regarded as unsatisfactory (Pais 1991, 369). Fermi insisted on the conservation of energy and momentum in the process of beta emission, and offered a different approach for understanding what was happening, based on an assumed analogy with a known process. Fermi's model, as he himself noted, was explicitly constructed "by way of analogy" with an aspect of electromagnetic theory.

Fermi treated the creation and annihilation of electrons in beta emission as being analogous to the creation and annihilation of photons in quantum transitions between electron orbits. The interaction of particles and fields in beta emission was assumed to be analogous to that of charged particles and fields in electromagnetic theory, with a corresponding Hamiltonian. The overall result was a model which offered a coherent account of various aspects of beta decay which had hitherto proved puzzling, and allowed further investigation of the phenomenon.

Yet analogies also possess a remarkable propensity to mislead. The choice of analogy is therefore of critical importance. The use of the word "choice" is deliberate. In part, the advance of the natural sciences has been dependent upon the selection of analogies which facilitate understanding. Yet the history of scientific understanding also indicates that analogies can cause serious difficulties for the development of scientific thought, in that the adoption of an analogy for a process may lead to the establishment of certain habits of thought which cause observers to misread. The concept of the "ether" as a medium for the propagation of electromagnetic radiation is an example of such a misleading analogy to which reference has already been made. Other examples can easily be adduced, including the now totally repudiated concepts of "phlogiston" and "caloric" (Worrall 1989b, 112).

A less often cited example is the apparent use of magnetic, mechanical, or electrical analogues during the development of genetic theory over the period 1900–26. This research eventually led to the recognition of the existence and specific function of the gene in a seminal paper published by Thomas Hunt Morgan in 1926 (Morgan 1926).[4] Yet it can be argued that this development was hindered at the time by the use of inappropriate analogies as a means of understanding the genetic mechanisms implicated. We shall explore this in a little more detail in the following paragraphs.

Following the rediscovery of the work of Gregor Mendel in 1900, considerable effort was expended in attempting to clarify the principles governing inherited characteristics or traits. By 1905, it was clear that certain traits were linked in some manner, although the pattern of coupling (later to be interpreted as "complete" and "incomplete" coupling) was far from clear (Correns 1900; Castle 1903; Bateson, Saunders and Punnett 1905). Neither the pattern nor its explanation was clear at this early stage. William Bateson, one of the more significant workers in the field, used a series of vague physical analogies – in particular, the analogies of "coupling" and "repulsion" – in an attempt to explain the puzzling observations (Coleman 1970; Darden 1977; Cock 1983). It is clear from Bateson's writings that he appears to have thought in terms of certain forces (paralleling magnetic or electrical forces) which were capable of attracting or repulsing factors of genetic significance. Although Bateson does not appear to have developed a definite hypothesis along these lines, it is clear that such analogies were of significance in shaping his thought, and (in this case) hindering him from finding a solution to the observed patterns.

At times, it is unclear whether a quality relates merely to a theory or model, or to the reality which it is intended to depict. For example, an intensely debated question within theoretical physics is whether quantum theory provides a complete theory of a fuzzy reality, or a fuzzy picture of a sharp reality. The former represents the generally dominant view, associated with Niels Bohr and the Copenhagen school, whereas the latter was the view of Einstein. The relation between "picture" and "reality" is thus of considerable significance. Does fuzziness arise from the process of depiction, or from the way things are in themselves? It is virtually impossible (to speak very loosely) to know whether fuzziness is something we impose on the world through the process of observation and depiction, or whether it is already present, prior to our observation and depiction, in reality itself.

A further serious difficulty concerns the notion of observation. Does the act of obsveration itself distort that which is thus observed, or in some way alter it? Pascual Jordan is one of a number of writers to attempt to set out the disconcerting implications of quantum theory at this point (Jammer 1974, 151):

> Observations not only disturb what has to be measured, they produce it . . . We compel [the electron] to assume a definite position . . . We ourselves produce the results of measurement.

These three terse statements set out the paradox (at least, from the standpoint of classical thinking) with which we are confronted: to measure something is to disrupt it. At the classical level, this may not be significant; at the quantum level, it cannot be ignored.

It is impossible to overlook the affinity of this point with a related concern of religious importance in the early writings of Karl Barth. In his *Romans* commentary, Barth stressed the impossibility of "pinning down" God in the act of revelation (McCormack 1995, 129–290). God's revelation impinges upon human history only as a tangent touches a circle – at a "mathematical point." God's revelation can no more be pinned down in human history than a bird in flight, concealing more than it reveals (in that it reveals the "otherness" of God in the chasm fixed between God and humanity), having no "stationary point (*Standpunkt*)." Revelation comes "perpendicularly from above (*senkrecht von oben*)." Although Barth would later move away from such radical views, they remain a fundamental stimulus to Christian theology. Can we be said to "possess" God's revelation? Is not the attempt to *depict* God in effect an unacknowledged attempt to *limit* God?

With this point, we have already begun to make the transition from science to religion. In what follows, we shall discuss the use of analogies or models in religion in a little more detail.

The Use of Analogies in Theology

A cursory example of the Bible or the Christian creeds shows up the use of what might variously be referred to as models, analogies, or metaphors. The distinction between these three terms is disputed and potentially confusing, and cannot be resolved in the present study (see the issues raised by MacCormac 1975; McFague 1983; Rothbart 1984; Soskice 1985; Vaught 1987; Hintikka and Sandu 1990; Tirrell 1991; Swinburne 1992, 39–51; Clark 1994; Fodor 1995). The Apostles' Creed, for example, opens with an affirmation of faith in "God the Father almighty," immediately suggesting that there is a similarity – the extent and nature of which remains to be determined – between "God" and a human father. The use of such metaphorical terms is, of course, by no means restricted to theology: any technical language ends up making an appeal to such ways of speaking. For example, the language of modern physics is permeated with metaphors: "In physics, we speak or a *field* of force, or of the *flow* of heat, and so on. Indeed, technical discourse cannot do without metaphorical language" (Hutten 1956, 84).[5] The use of irreducible metaphors in religious language has its direct parallels in the natural sciences (see the careful analysis in Arbib and Hesse 1986), and religions cannot be singled out for criticism in this respect (see Burgess 1972).

Janet Martin Soskice has suggested that two main types of models may be distinguished (Soskice 1985, 101–3): homeomorphic models, in which there is a clear-cut resemblance between the model and its referent – for example, a model aeroplane (which is a scaled-down version of the real thing), or perhaps a dummy used for teaching life-saving skills to students; and paramorphic models, in which "candidates for similarity" are identified – for example, in the traditional imagery used in the kinetic theory of gases, which enourages us to think of gas molecules as inelastic billiard balls. She thus argues that "an object or state of affairs is a model when it is viewed in terms of its resemblance, real or hypothetical, to some other object or state of affairs" (Soskice 1985, 101). Homeomorphic models can be understood to refer literally, and paramorphic models metaphorically, to the situation or object to be modeled.

The use of models, analogies, and metaphor in religious language is traditionally grounded in a doctrine of revelation which seeks to articulate the manner in which access to God is not to be denied to those lacking intellectual ability. The critical issue is that of "accommodation," which has already been discussed earlier (see pp. 121–9). For writers as diverse as Origen and John Calvin, God reveals himself in manners or forms which are adapted or tempered to the capacities of the human mind (Battles 1977; Benin 1993; D. F. Wright 1993). This involves the use of imagery (which is often highly anthropomorphic), which is held to be a model, analogy or metaphor for some aspect of the nature of God.

It can be shown without difficulty that the status of such imagery was often the subject of debate within the Christian tradition. For example, is the New Testament imagery relating to Jesus of Nazareth (who is referred to as "Son of God" at points) to be understood to refer literally (Jesus really is divine) or catachrestically or honorifically (Jesus is to be honoured as if he were God). This debate is an integral aspect of the Arian controversy of the fourth century, which remains a landmark in the development of the Christian theological tradition (McGrath 1996a, 332–5). As a result, Christian theology has been obliged to develop means for proceeding from imagery to theology – that is, from metaphor to thought models (Huyssteen 1989, 137–47).

One seminal question concerns the grounding of such analogies, models, or metaphors. Sallie McFague argues that "thinking metaphorically means spotting a thread of similarity between two dissimilar objects," so that "one object, event or whatever is used as a way of speaking about the other" (McFague 1983, 15). The question which arises is why one such object or activity should be privileged in this manner as a model for God, or for divine activity? The traditional answer has stressed the inextricable linkage between certain models and revelation – in other words, divine self-revelation is seen as being integrally connected with certain root metaphors. On this view, we are therefore not authorized to use metaphors for other than those which are found in the Old and New Testaments.[6]

The Christian doctrine of creation plays an integral role at this point. The idea in question is often referred to as the *analogia entis* ("analogy of being"), and is developed with particular care in the writings of Thomas Aquinas. The argument deployed by Aquinas can be summarized along the following lines. In that God created the natural order, some form of correspondence between that order and its creator is to be expected (see Mascall 1966, especially 92–121). This does not mean that God is to be considered to be identical to nature; there are areas of similarity and dissimilarity. In that the likeness between God and creatures is established by God in the act of creation, Aquinas argues that it is not proper to suggest that "God is like a creature." Rather, it is to be said that "the creature is like God," in that the act of creation established that relationship from the Godward side. Aquinas sets this out clearly in the section of his *Summa contra Gentiles* in which he deals with the issue of "the likeness of creatures to God" (Aquinas 1975, vol. 1, 138–9):

> Effects that fall short of their causes do not agree with them in name and nature. Yet some likeness must be found between them, since it belongs to the nature of action that an agent produce its like, since each thing acts according as it is in act. The form of an effect, therefore, is certainly found in some measure in a transcending cause . . . God gave all things their perfection, and thereby is both like and unlike all of them. Hence it is that Sacred Scripture recalls the likeness between God and creatures, as when it is said in Genesis 1: 26: "Let us make man to our image and likeness" . . . A creature receives from God that which makes it like him. The converse, however, does not hold. God, then, is not likened to a creature; rather, the converse is true.

For Aquinas, the use of analogies based on creatures to refer to God is thus not arbitrary, but is ultimately grounded in creation itself.

Earlier (p. 168), we noted the severe difficulty encountered in arguments from analogy – the potentially arbitrary character of the analogies employed. The assumption that "A is an analogy for B" requires justification. On what basis is the analogy posited? Is the existence of some similarity a happy coincidence? Or does it rest on something more fundamental, perhaps reflecting something deeply embedded in the structure of the universe? It is important to pause here, and note the importance of the way in which the growth of "supersymmetry" theories have posited a fundamental relationship between various aspects of modern physics. The doctrine of creation places such relationships on a secure intellectual footing, suggesting that a correlation exists within the created order prior to its being discerned through human investigation.

Analogies, models, and metaphors (and we use the three terms to refer collectively to images held to be significant in this matter) require interpretation. What aspects of the image are *intended* to be carried over? In a postmodern context, this question would be treated with suspicion. The notion of "authorial intention" is regarded as problematic (for example, in the works of Roland Barthes, and especially in Jacques Derrida's "White Mythology'); every reader is free to make of a text or image what he or she chooses (Thiselton 1992, 80–141). Without wishing to concede this point, I shall rephrase the question in a less pointed manner: what aspects of the image might be appropriately carried over, and on the basis of what criteria should this decision be made? How does one know when an analogy has been pressed too far?

The question is of some significance in theology, in that it seems that at

least some ideas which enjoyed currency in patristic theology may have involved the abuse of an analogy – the so-called "fish-hook" or "mousetrap"
theory of the atonement (Turner 1952). It must be noted that this analogy is
best seen as a highly dramatic and evocative *illustration* rather than an *explanatory model* for the meaning of the cross. Nevertheless, the reception of the
analogy suggests that, at least at the popular level, the analogy was understood
as an explanation, which would receive further development during the Middle Ages, particularly in the famous image of the "Harrowing of Hell."

The New Testament itself speaks of Jesus giving his life as a "ransom" for
sinners (Mark 10: 45; 1 Timothy 2: 6). This image of Christ's death as a
ransom came to be of central importance to Greek patristic writers, such as
Irenaeus and Origen. The word "ransom" was treated as an analogy or model
for the meaning of the death of Christ, and was taken to suggest three related
ideas.

1 Liberation. A ransom is something which achieves freedom for a person
   who is held in captivity.
2 Payment. A ransom is a sum of money which is paid in order to achieve an
   individual's liberation.
3 Someone to whom the ransom is paid. A ransom is usually paid to an
   individual's captor.

These three ideas thus seem to be implied by speaking of Jesus' death as a
"ransom" for sinners. At any rate, that was the conclusion of Origen, perhaps
the most speculative of the early patristic writers. If Christ's death was a
ransom, Origen argued, it must have been paid to someone. But who? It
could not have been paid to God, in that God was not holding sinners to
ransom. In what can only be seen as a fateful theological move, Origen
concluded that it had to be paid to the devil. Rufinus of Aquileia and Gregory
the Great developed this idea still further. The devil had acquired rights over
fallen humanity, which God was obliged to respect. The only means by
which humanity could be released from this satanic domination and oppression was through the devil exceeding the limits of his authority, and thus
being obliged to forfeit his rights. So how could this be achieved? Gregory
suggests that it could come about if a sinless person were to enter the world,
yet in the form of a normal sinful person. The devil would not notice until it
was too late: in claiming authority over this sinless person, the devil would
have overstepped the limits of his authority, and thus be obliged to abandon
his rights.

Rufinus suggests the image of a baited hook: Christ's humanity is the bait,
and his divinity the hook. The devil, like a great sea-monster, snaps at the bait
– and then discovers, too late, the hook (McGrath 1995a, 180):

[The purpose of the Incarnation] was that the divine virtue of the Son of God might be like a kind of hook hidden beneath the form of human flesh . . . to lure on the prince of this world to a contest; that the Son might offer him his human flesh as a bait and that the divinity which lay underneath might catch him and hold him fast with its hook. . . . Then, just as a fish when it seizes a baited hook not only fails to drag off the bait but is itself dragged out of the water to serve as food for others; so he that had the power of death seized the body of Jesus in death, unaware of the hook of divinity which lay hidden inside. Having swallowed it, he was immediately caught. The gates of hell were broken, and he was, as it were, drawn up from the pit, to become food for others.

The aspect of this approach to the meaning of the cross that caused the most disquiet was the apparent implication that God was guilty of deception.

It can be argued that this thoroughly unsatisfactory theory resulted from an analogy being pressed far beyond its intended limits. But how are those limits to be established in the first place? In the case of the natural sciences, an obvious answer might be: through experimentation. Sound waves were once regarded as a model for light, and it was thus argued that, just as sound requires a medium for its propagation, so must light – leading to the notion of "luminiferous ether" which was eventually discarded in the aftermath of the Michelson–Morley experiment. As we have stressed, there is no exact parallel in religious thought, which tends to focus on the theme of revelation. An answer which has found wide acceptance was proposed by Ian T. Ramsey, who pointed out that the Christian tradition was not limited to any one model of God, but was in possession of a number of such models, each of which interacted with others to build up a cumulative understanding of God. One model modified another, allowing an understanding to be gained of whether any given model was being abused or improperly interpreted (Ramsey 1957; Ramsey 1964; Gill 1976).

This observation leads us to compare the manner in which analogies and models are used in science and religion in a little more detail.

Analogies in Science and Religion: A Comparison

In his pioneering studies on the interaction of science and religion, Ian G. Barbour explored the manner in which models were used in science and religion (Barbour 1974, 29–70). On the basis of this comparison, Barbour identified three similarities and a corresponding number of differences between "religious models and theoretical models in science" (Barbour 1974, 69). In general terms, his analysis has stood the test of time remarkably well (but see the comments of Soskice 1985, 97–117), providing one is prepared to accept the implicit critical realism which underlies his analysis. Although Barbour avoids any specific commitment to a Christian perspective, the general points which he notes apply well to this specific viewpoint. The similarities which he identifies are the following.

1   In both science and religion, models are analogical in their origins, can be extended to cope with new situations, and are comprehensible as individual units.
2   Models, whether scientific or religious, are not to be taken either as literal depictions of reality, nor simply as "useful fictions." "They are symbolic representations, for particular purposes, of aspects of reality which are not directly accessible to us."
3   Models function as organizing images, allowing us to structure and interpret patterns of events in our personal lives and in the world. In the sciences, the models relate to observational data; in the religions, to the experience of individuals and communities.

Significantly, Barbour also identified three areas of difference between the use of models in scientific and religious contexts. At this point, a degree of generalization about the nature of religion may perhaps lead to some incautious conclusions, although there is no doubt that, at least in some cases, the points which Barbour makes are valid.

1   Religious models serve non-cognitive functions which have no parallel in science.
2   Religious models evoke more total personal involvement than their scientific counterparts.
3   Religious models appear to be more influential than the formal beliefs and doctrines which are derived from them, whereas scientific models are subservient to theories.

My concern, focusing on traditional Christian ways of thinking, is to draw attention to a further point of difference, which seems to me to be of considerable importance. In the sciences, analogies or models are chosen and validated partly on the basis of whether they offer a good empirical fit. These two themes – selection and validation – are of considerable importance, not least in that they highlight a significant difference between the natural sciences and religion. Analogies are generated within the scientific community; if they prove to be unsatisfactory, they are discarded, and replaced by new ones.

For example, consider the Bohr model (1913) of the hydrogen atom, which postulates that a single electron orbits a central nucleus (a feature derived from the Rutherford model of 1910), with an angular momentum which is confined to certain limited values. On the basis of this model, Bohr was able to explain the spectral formula proposed by Balmer (see p. 78), and postulate certain "quantum numbers" corresponding to the state and energy of the system (Pais 1991, 146–52; Atkins and Friedman 1997, 5). Yet the model had serious weaknesses (for example, the assumption that the electron orbited the nucleus in a circle) which had to be modified as experimental data built up.

The point here is that a model was *devised*, partly as an analogue of a simple harmonic oscillator and partly as an analogue of the solar system, which was found to have explanatory potential. Bohr's genius lay in devising the model. It was not self-evident, but rested on Bohr's belief that the application of quantum concepts to statistical mechanics by Einstein and Planck could be paralleled in the field of dynamics. Subsequent to its being formulated, the model required validation, both in terms of its ability to explain what was already known, and to predict novel phenomena.

It will also be clear that scientific models may be dispensed with when a superior model has been devised. The Rutherford model of the hydrogen atom, although regularly used at the popular level, has been discarded within professional circles on account of its obvious deficiencies. There is no commitment within the scientific community to any one model; in principle, the advancement of understanding may – but does not necessarily – lead to the discarding of earlier models.

These key themes of *formulation* and *validation* have no direct parallel in classical Christian thought. For a religion such as Christianity, it has been traditionally understood that the analogies or models in question are "given", not chosen; the two tasks which confront the theologian are those of establishing the limits of the analogy, and correlating it with other such given analogies. Let me make it clear immediately that not all theologians would support this traditional view; some would argue that we are at liberty to develop new models that avoid certain features of traditional models which are deemed to be unsatisfactory (see, for example, McFague 1985). Nevertheless, the traditional view remains influential, as can be seen from Torrance's exploration of "theological science" (Torrance 1969, 25–54).

There would be no question of abandoning a traditional Christian model of God within orthodox Christian circles – for example, the model of God as "shepherd." Such models are far too deeply embedded in the biblical material and both theological reflection and liturgical practice to be treated in this manner. They have assumed the status of "root metaphors," which are regarded as permanent and essential components of the truth of the Christian tradition. These models may prove to require reinterpretation, or the exploration of aspects which had, up to this point, been ignored – but the model itself remains fundamental for theological reflection (see, for example, Ramsey 1957; Ramsey 1964; Soskice 1985).[7]

Analogies and Visualization: Complementarity in Science and Religion

In the previous section of this chapter, we explored some aspects of the issue of visualization, and noted its importance in both scientific and religious contexts. This issue is of particular importance in relation to Niels Bohr's theory of "complementarity," suggesting that the detailed exploration of this theory might be of relevance to our study.

It is critically important to appreciate from the outset that the term "complementarity" can be used in two fundamentally different senses in discussions of science and religion. On the one hand, it can be used to refer to a model for the relationship of science and religion which stresses the positive nature of their interaction (see, for example, MacKay 1974; Reich 1990; Reich 1994; Gilbert 1995; Duce 1996; MacKinnon 1996). This approach argues that the sciences and the religions approach their subject matter in different ways, asking different questions and answering them on the basis of their distinctive methodologies – yet yielding answers which are harmonious and mutually enriching, rather than conflictual and divergent.

This approach can be found in a number of forms in contemporary writings on this theme. A modest and cautious application can be found in the writings of John Polkinghorne, who speaks of "a search for understanding which seeks to take an even-handed view of two accounts of what is going on" (Polkinghorne 1991, 27). Others have noted the importance of "complementarity reasoning" as an integral aspect of human development (Oser and Reich 1987), and argued for its application to the specific issue of the relationship of scientific theories and religious doctrines (Reich 1990; Reich 1994).

At a more theological level, Langdon Gilkey has argued for a "two-language" approach to the matter, in which both science and religion offer linguistically distinct yet complementary approaches to reality (Gilkey 1989). For Gilkey, the ideal is for someone to be bilingual, conversant with both disciplines and able to relate scientific and religious commitments without conflict. Especially at the popular level, this is often expressed in terms of "science asking *how*-questions and religion asking *why*-questions" (Gilkey 1985, 49–52, 108–13). This distinction is somewhat unhelpful, and can easily be shown to be vulnerable to erosion, especially in the light of further developments in cosmology.

A further difficulty is that the possibility of conflict seems to be ruled out in advance, at least in the stronger version of the models. This presents serious difficulties, similar to those assocuiated with the "all religions are saying the same thing" model, which rules out conflict on matters of substance or significance, occasionally in advance of having actually studied the religions in question. The approach adopted in the present work is to avoid any such assumption, and note areas of convergence and divergence without commitment to the restrictiveness of any one model for the relationship of the sciences and the religions. The general principle of the mutually enriching encounter of religion and science can be maintained without the need to adopt this specific model.

It is with the second sense of the term "complementarity" that we shall be concerned in the present section. This is found in the writings of the noted Danish physicist and philosopher, Niels Bohr (1885–1962). In view of the complexity and importance of the matter, it will be necessary to lay some foundations for our discussion of the concept.

Niels Bohr on Complementarity

The notion of "complementarity" is especially associated with the philosophical writers of Niels Bohr and the "Copenhagen School" of quantum mechanics. It must be noted, however, that there exist significant differences between Bohr and other thinkers associated with this school – such as Max Born, Paul Dirac, Werner Heisenberg, Pascual Jordan, and Eugene Paul Wigner – so that it is potentially misleading to speak of the "Copenhagen interpretation" as if this designated an unequivocally defined body of beliefs. To avoid difficulties over this point, we shall focus on the writings of the leading representative of this school, the noted Danish physicist and philosopher Niels Bohr. The development and specific nature of Bohr's philosophy of physics, and especially his notion of complementarity, has been the subject of an explosion of scholarly interest in recent years (see especially Folse 1985; Honner 1987; Krips 1987, 6–38; Murdoch 1987; Faye 1991; Pais 1991), with the result that it is now possible to establish a proper evaluation of its religious significance.

The Origins of Complementarity: Einstein to Heisenberg

It is often suggested that Bohr's theory of complementarity had its origins in Einstein's 1905 proposal that, under certain circumstances, a beam of monochromatic light of frequency v behaved as if it consists of quanta or particle-like objects, whose energy E was given by the relationship $E = hv$ where h is Planck's constant (Fölsing 1997, 134–54). It had been known for some time that electrons were emitted from metals when they were exposed to ultraviolet radiation. However, the precise patterns of emission were puzzling. The emission of electrons did not take place unless the frequency of the incident light exceeded a certain threshold value, no matter how intense the applied radiation might be. Einstein argued that the photoelectric effect could be conceived as a collision between an incoming particle-like bundle of energy and an electron close to the surface of the metal. The electron could only be ejected from the metal if the incoming particle-like bundles of energy possessed sufficient energy to eject this electon. As a result, there was a cut-off point, determined by the properties of the metal in question, known as the "work function" of the metal. (The "particle-like bundle of energy" to which we have referred was designated a "photon" by G. N. Lewis, and this term has passed into general usage. It is hoped that the anachronistic use of the term in what follows will not prove confusing.)

Einstein's theory allowed the following facts to be explained.

1 The critical factor which determines whether an electron is ejected is not the intensity of the light, but its frequency;
2 The incoming light can be treated as if it consists of particles ("photons") with a definite energy or momentum;
3 The observed features of the photoelectric effect can be accounted for by assuming that the collision between the incoming photon and the metallic electon obeys the principle of the conservation of energy, so that the kinetic energy of the emitted electon (T) can be represented as:

$$T = hv - \Phi$$

where Φ is the "work function" of the metal. If hv is less than Φ, no electrons will be emitted, no matter how intense the bombardment with photons. Above this threshold, the kinetic energy of the emitted photons can be predicted to be linearly related to the frequency of the radiation.

Einstein's brilliant theoretical account for the photoelectric effect suggested that electromagnetic radiation had to be considered as behaving as particles under certain conditions. It met with intense opposition, not least because it appeared to involve the abandonment of the prevailing classical understanding of the total exclusivity of waves and particles: something could be one, or the other – but not both. Even those who subsequently verified Einstein's analysis of the photoelectric effect were intensely suspicious of his postulation of "photons." Einstein himself was careful to refer to the light-quantum hypothesis as a "heuristic point of view" – that is, as something which was helpful as a model to understanding, but without any necessary existence on its part.

At the time (1905), Einstein's theory offered an explanation of what had been observed, and also a prediction of what had not yet been observed – the prediction that the emitted electron's energy would be governed by the relationship $T = hv - \Phi$. Yet confirmation was duly forthcoming. In 1916, R. A. Millikan confirmed its accuracy, while expressing his personal doubts about the particle-theory of light offered by Einstein. "Einstein's photoelectric equation . . . appears in every case to predict exactly the observed results . . . Yet the semicorpuscular theory by which Einstein arrived at his equation seems at present wholly untenable."

By then, however, Einstein had moved on. In an 1909 paper dealing with the energy fluctuations in a thermal cavity, he asserted that "the next phase in the development of theoretical physics will bring us a theory of light tat can be interpreted as a kind of fusion of the wave and [particle] theory." This development took place in 1925, and is to be seen as the precipitant of Niels Bohr's reflections on the concept of complementarity. It must be stressed that Bohr was strongly opposed to the notion of a "photon," holding that the observed phenomena could be explained much more convincingly by holding that energy was not necessarily conserved. His writings of the period 1920–3 show a clear hostility towards Einstein's appoach (Pais 1991, 232–9).

Major further evidence for Einstein's view came in 1923, when Arthur H. Compton extended Einstein's approach by exploring the way in which X-rays were scattered from peripheral carbon electrons in a graphite target, and showed that the pattern of scattering of the X-rays could be explained by assuming that the X-rays and electrons behaved as particles, the collision of which was subject to the principle of the conservation of energy. The results – and their interpretation – caused a sensation. Bohr, however, remained unconvinced. Together with Hendrik Kramers and John Slater, Bohr developed an account of light in atomic energy transmission which abandoned the notions of causality and the conservation of energy and momentum (Pais 1991, 235–7). In relation to the Compton scattering of X-rays, the theory required a random correlation between the production of the secondary photon and the emitted electron. It was argued that Compton's results could be interpreted if energy and momentum were conserved on average over many individual interactions, rather than conserved in each individual interaction.

Yet two experiments in the first months of 1925 showed them to be wrong. Using coincidence measurement techniques, Walther Bothe and Hans Geiger were able to confirm that a relationship of causality existed between the production of the secondary photon and electron in the Compton effect; Compton himself collaborated with Alfred Simon to demonstrate that momentum and energy were conserved in individual events. By April 1925, Bohr was clear that his explanation was inadequate. But what was the alternative? Only then did he learn of the work of a researcher in Paris, which seemed to offer, if not a solution, then at least the beginnings of one.

The origins of the developments which led Bohr to explore the notion of complementarity can be traced to two papers published by Louis de Broglie in September 1923. De Broglie had been deeply impressed by Einstein's discussion of the wave–particle duality for light. The essence of de Broglie's approach was to argue that the principle established by Einstein in 1905 was capable of generalization, and could be extended to all material particles, particularly electrons. In his first paper, published on 10 September, he suggested that it was possible to assign a "fictitious associated wave" to any moving body, whose momentum and wavelength (λ) were related as follows:

$$\lambda = h/p$$

where h is Planck's constant and p is the momentum of the moving body. What is truly radical about this proposal is that it abolishes the idea of a total distinction between particles and waves; any moving particle has an associated "de Broglie wavelength" λ. The de Broglie equation proposes a fusion of what had hitherto been considered to be opposites, in that momentum had been considered to be a property of particles, and wavelength a property of waves. De Broglie proposed a fundamental relationship between these. In his second paper, published two weeks later, de Broglie proposed a means of testing his proposed relationship. Experimental confirmation of his ideas, he wrote, could be obtained by allowing electrons to traverse an aperture whose dimensions were small in relation to the predicted de Broglie wavelength.

De Broglie's predictions were confirmed in 1925 by Clinton Joseph Davisson and Lester Halber Germer at the Bell Laboratories in New York, who observed the diffraction of electrons by atoms in a crystal of nickel. The resulting diffraction pattern was consistent with the de Broglie wavelength predicted by the equation. Further confirmation came shortly afterwards, when G. P. Thomson – son of the great physicist J. J. Thomson, who discovered the electron in 1906 (Pais 1972) – demonstrated the diffraction of electrons by thin films of celluloid and goal. (The irony of this situation has often been noted: J. J. Thompson was awarded the Nobel Prize for showing that the electron was a particle, while his son was awarded the Prize for showing that it was a wave.) In both cases, the electron velocity and its associated "de Broglie wavelength" were measured, and found to be related by the formula $\lambda = h/p$.

Matters developed further in 1926, when Werner Heisenberg and Erwin Schrödinger developed these insights into a consistent theory (independently of each other), using different (yet mathematically equivalent) formalisms . In effect, Heisenberg developed his "matrix mechanics" by beginning from the assumption that matter was particulate, whereas Schrödinger pioneered his "wave mechanics" on the assumption that matter possessed wave properties. Yet how could both be true? Was the electron a wave, or was it a particle? The two mathematical schemes proposed by Schrödinger and Heisenberg were mathematically equivalent and consistent, but seemed to begin from significantly different starting points, and reflect radically different assumptions. It seemed to Bohr that the two mathematical tools reflected different philosophical interpretations of what was happening (Pais 1991, 302–16).

Bohr's Formulation of the Complementarity Principle

Bohr and Heisenberg (who was then working in Copenhagen) argued endlessly during 1926 and the early months of 1927 over how to make sense of the experimental and mathematical materials. The central question was whether classical notions, such as "waves" and "particles," would have to be abandoned or whether they could continue to be used. Heisenberg was inclined to the view that they should be abandoned; the words simply did not make sense at the level of quantum phenomena. Bohr was quite convinced that this was not so. As he declared in a lecture given on September 16, 1927 in the Italian town of Como to mark the centenary of the death of the Italian physicist Alessandro Volta, "our interpretation of the experimental material rests essentially upon the classical concepts" – the issue concerned how these were to be related to each other in a "complementary" manner (Bohr 1972–85, vol. 6, 147):

> The very nature of the quantum theory . . . forces us to regard the space–time coordination and the claim of causality, the union of which characterizes the classical theories, as complementary but exclusive features of the description . . . complementary pictures of the phenomena . . . only together offer a natural generalization of the classical mode of description.

The decision to use the term "complementary" and related terms to refer to the way in which classical terms were to be used to describe quantum phenomena was no easy one, and caused some confusion within his audience.

As developed by Bohr in the Como lecture, the notion of "complementarity" is a means by which those conflictual aspects of quantum phenomena which cannot be accounted for within the framework of classical theories may be completely described. The term carries with it the dual associations of "the bringing together of mutually exclusive ideas" and "a completness of description," both of which can be argued to be integral to Bohr's understanding of the concept.[8] He argued that the implications of the quantum postulate were "completely foreign to the classical theories." For Bohr, "the quantum theory is characterized by the acknowledgement of a fundamental limitation in the classical physical ideas when applied to atomic phenomena." After explaining this point in more detail, Bohr argues that "the quantum postulate presents us with the task of developing a 'complementarity' theory."

The use of this term is, of course, highly significant, and it must be noted that Bohr's early attempts to set out the theory are specifically directed towards wave–particle complementarity. The two models of the nature of light can "be considered as different attempts at an interpretation of experimental evidence in which the limitation of the classical concepts is expressed in complementary ways." What was originally held to be completely separate in classical physics now appear together in "complementarity," even though, according to the classical model, they cannot be unified into a single picture (Bohr 1987, vol 2, 26). For Bohr, the "wave-picture" applies *only* when the "particle-picture" does not, and *vice versa*. The approach is complete (in that only two pictures are needed) and complementary (in that only one of these mutually exclusive pictures can apply at any one time).

This contrasts sharply with Einstein's view, for whom conceptual unity was a fundamental goal of scientific explanation. It is well known that one of the reasons why Einstein rejected Bohr's notion of complementarity was that – by stressing the need for two mutually exclusive ways of visualizing what was taking place – it rendered conceptual synthesis impossible. It may be argued that Einstein here shows a significant degree of continuity with a Hegelian idealist worldview, with its emphasis upon synthesis and continuity. As Murdoch points out in his superb study of Bohr's philosophy (Murdoch 1987, 196):

> Although Einstein was inclined to doubt whether the aim of achieving the greatest possible conceptual unity is attainable, he believed that the aim should be maintained as a regulative principle. He was greatly troubled by the lack of conceptual unity in the foundations of contemporary physics . . . The difficulty of uniting quantum theory with relativity theory was, he believed, due largely to a lack of conceptual unity: what was needed was a unified conceptual scheme subsuming the schemes of mechanics and electrodynamics and uniting the notions of electromagnetic and gravitational fields. Here Einstein differs from Bohr, for whom conceptual homogeneity *per se* was not one of the main goals of science.

In the Como lecture, Bohr moves towards a significant philosophical shift in his interpretation of quantum phenomena, in which he comes close to "instrumentalism" (Krips 1987, 22–4). Perhaps the issue at stake is not whether an electron "is" a particle or a wave, but whether – and under what conditions – it "behaves like" a wave or particle. Bohr's principle of complementarity suggests – and the contrast with Einstein will be clear – that no mathematical or conceptual model, or any properties of such models, can be regarded as having the status of physical reality. All classical concepts must be seen as idealizations. "Regarding the quantum postulate as axiomatic, Bohr believed Einstein dogmatically refused to accept its logical consequence that we must abandon the classical presupposition that the classical state of the system refers to properties possessed by an independent physical reality" (Folse 1985, 152).

Complementarity and the Indispensability of Classical Concepts

So why not simply dispense with the classical concepts? Bohr argued that they needed to be retained, while "giving them a suitable quantum-theoretical reinterpretation" (Bohr 1987, vol. 1, 8). As we have seen, Heisenberg argued for their rejection, a strategy also urged by Albert Einstein, who believed that the concepts of classical physics would have to be replaced entirely. This point has been brought out clearly in a particularly sensitive and nuanced recent study of Einstein's approach. "In the end, Einstein was more radical in his thinking than were the defenders of the orthodox view of quantum theory, for Einstein was convinced that the concepts of classical physics will have to be replaced, and not merely segregated in the manner of Bohr's complementarity" (Fine 1986, 24).[9] For Bohr, this failed to resolve the issue (Bohr 1987, vol. 1, 16):

> It would be a misconception to believe that the difficulties of the atomic theory may be evaded by eventually replacing the concepts of classical physics by new conceptual forms. Indeed . . . the recognition of the limitation of our forms of perception by no means implies that we can dispense with our customary ideas or their direct verbal expressions when reducing our sense impressions to order. No more is it likely that the fundamental concepts of the classical theories will ever become superfluous for the description of physical experience. The recognition of the indivisibility of the quantum of action, and the determination of its magnitude, not only depend on an analysis of measurements based on classical concepts, but it continues to be the application of these concepts alone that make it possible to relate the symbolism of the quantum theory to the data of experience.

It will thus be clear that one of Bohr's central concerns was how to visualize quantum phenomena. In a postcard sent to Wolfgang Pauli in the late summer of 1927, Heisenberg indicated that one of the main differences between himself and Bohr concerned the issue of how to construct "visualizable (*anschaulich*)" analogies for quantum phenomena.[10] Bohr himself had no difficulty in expressing the problem; the question was how to solve it (Bohr 1972–85, vol. 5, 311):

> [The experimental results] preclude the possibility of a simple description of the physical occurences by means of visualizable pictures . . . such pictures are of even more limited applicability than is ordinarily supposed. This is of course almost a purely negative assertion, but I feel that . . . one must have recourse to symbolic analogies to an even greater extent than hitherto.

On the basis of this analysis, it will be clear that Bohr's notion of "complementarity" is directly related to an understanding of the way in which reality is to be depicted, and the status of the depictions to what they are believed to represent. The classical models, taken individually, have their limitations; taken together, however, they offer a means of representing the behaviour observed at the quantum level. This does not mean that electrons "are" particles or that they "are" waves; it means that, whatever they ultimately are, their behavior may be described on the basis of wave or particle models, and that a complete description of that behavior rests upon the bringing together of what are, in effect, mutually exclusive ways of representing them. This is not an intellectually shallow and lazy expedient of affirming two mutually exclusive options, rather than an attempt to determine which is the superior. As has been stressed, it was, for Bohr, the inevitable outcome of a series of critical theories and experiments – most notably, those of Millikan, Compton, Davisson and Germer, and Thomson – which demonstrated the impossibility of representing the situation in any other manner.

A further issue of importance here concerns the meaning to be attached to the term "phenomenon." For Bohr, the means of observation cannot be detached from the observational result (Harré 1986, 301–6). Bohr tends to use the term "phenomenon" in the special sense of an indissoluble union of the observational apparatus, its reactions and reality itself. Bohr placed the "phenomena," in his sense of the term, at the heart of his understanding of physical science, and regarded it as the fundamental object which required description and analysis. Although this point can be discerned in Bohr's writings over the period 1925–35, it was developed more fully on the eve of the Second World War (Folse 1985). The term "phenomenon" must be used "to refer exclusively to observations obtained under specified circumstances, including an account of the whole experiment" or "the comprehension of the effects observed under given experimental conditions" (Pais 1991, 432–3). This contrasted with Einstein's insistence that one should be able to seek a deeper-lying theoretical framework which permitted phenomena to be described independently of the experimental conditions (Fine 1986a; Harré 1986, 48–50; Polikarov 1989; Laudisa 1995).

But inevitably, the question has to be asked: is Bohr right about complementarity? One difficulty which may be noted immediately concerns Bohr's understanding of concept formation. According to Bohr, we must describe quantum systems using the terms which we use for describing the classical world, in that the language we uses derives from that world and our long association with it. As Peter Gibbins explains this point, from Bohr's perspective (Gibbins 1987, 9):

> The language of classical physics is ideally suited to describing the macrophysical world, the world of medium-sized objects, in which we learn and constantly test natural language. The species has evolved classical concepts (of position, speed and so on) for so many generations that they are now an intrinsic part of our worldview. However far we travel from the world of everyday reality we are stuck with classical concepts.

For Bohr, quantum theory was able to ascertain the degree of imprecision with which classical descriptions applied to quantum systems. More seriously, even by 1934, it was clear that the "new quantum theory" derived by Born, Heisenberg, and Schrödinger could assign state vectors to quantum systems at all times. In effect, non-classical concepts were developed which were capable of fitting quantum systems precisely. Bohr's notion of "complementarity" could be retained at a secondary level, but otherwise seemed redundant. Nevertheless, it retains a degree of heuristic value, not least on account of Bohr's insistence on some form of correlation between the language and conceptualities of the macro-world of classical physics and the more mysterious world of quantum phenomena. Perhaps Bohr's lasting contribution will be seen to be his insistence that we use classical concepts (while establishing their limitations) to depict or represent the more abstract themes of quantum theory.

It is clear that this type of thinking has considerable implications for both philosophy and theology – for example, in relation to the classic "mind–body problem" (Brody and Oppenheim 1969) or the "two natures doctrine" in classical Christology (Kaiser 1976). Bohr himself never saw the need to restrict this mode of thinking to issues solely related to quantum theory, but extended it (often, it has to be said, in a rather tenuous manner) to include such areas as the problem of human consciousness, the description of living organisms, and aspects of human culture (Pais 1991, 438–47). He had occasion to develop some religious aspects of these issues in his unpublished Gifford Lectures, given at the University of Edinburgh during the period October 21–November 11, 1949.[11] The Gifford Lectures were founded in 1888 "for promoting, advancing, teaching and diffusing the study of natural theology, in the widest sense of that term." The lectures have been of considerable importance to the exploration of the relation between religion and the natural sciences (Jaki 1986); it therefore seems entirely proper to explore what the significance of Bohr's approach might be to theology. In the section that follows, we shall attempt to deal with this question.

Complementarity and Theology

It is widely agreed that the most interesting application of Bohr's principle of complementarity relates to Christology – that is, the area of Christian theology which deals with the identity of Jesus Christ, and specifically the classic Christological principle which affirms that Jesus Christ is fully divine and fully human (McGrath 1996a, 319–57). This is set out fully in the classic definition offered by the Council of Chalcedon in 451, which remains a fundamental reference point for Christian identity:

> We confess our Lord Jesus Christ to be one and the same Son, perfect in divinity and humanity, truly God and truly human, consisting of a rational soul and a body, being of one substance with the Father in relation to his divinity, and being of one substance with us in relation to his humanity, and is like us in all things apart from sin.

It will be clear immediately that this involves the bringing together of two "natures" – divinity and humanity – within a single subject, which might be thought to raise essentially the same issues as those confronted by Bohr during the late 1920s, thus raising the possibility that Bohr's approach might offer interesting or helpful insights into this important matter. The possibility has certainly been noted by theologians in the past.

Earlier Approaches to Theology and Complementarity
The potential of such an approach has been explored in two earlier studies. In 1967, W. H. Austin explored the potential of Bohr's principle of complementarity to Christology (Austin 1967). Austin's analysis was not particularly encouraging. He argued that there was no Christological equivalent to the "wave packet" which could bring two complementary (yet mutually exclusive) viewpoints together as a "compromise model" (Austin 1967, 87–92). It is not clear that Austin has understood that "wave packets" were derived by Schrödinger from linear harmonic oscillator wavefunctions. Although Austin himself offers the models of "Logos" and "Messiah" as candidates for such complementarity, his historical and theological analysis (which lacks scholarly rigor) offers little hope for encouragement. Nor is it clear that he has understood the distinctive nature of Bohr's approach, which rests on the assertion that "interpretation of the experimental material rests essentially upon the classical concepts" (Bohr 1972–85, vol. 6, 147).[12]

More promising approaches were subsequently offered by Christopher Kaiser in 1976 and Russell Stannard in 1982 (Kaiser 1976; Stannard 1982, 157–66). Nevertheless, Kaiser's approach seems to assume that Bohr understood "complementarity" in terms of some form of modalist metaphysic. "The atom is an entity in its own right, existing in the two modes of 'wave' and 'particle' " (Kaiser 1976, 38). Elsewhere, he seriously misrepresents Bohr by using a theological term ("mode of being") to describe the relation between "wave" and "particle" (Kaiser 1976, 43). This is not the interpretation which Bohr placed upon the principle of complementarity, which tends towards instrumentalism (Krips 1987, 22–4) and is often interpreted specifically as a form of non- or anti-realism (Fine 1984, 83; Fine 1986a; Fine 1986b). It is seriously confusing to introduce such modalist vocabulary in this context.

As Charles A. Coulson has pointed out, the issue must be understood to be functional and representational, not ontological: "An electron is not a particle, though it may be good enough for many purposes to treat it as if it were. An electron is not a wave, although again for certain other purposes it may be convenient to treat it as if it were" (Coulson 1955, 24). The essential point is that, despite not being able to give a precise description of what an electron is, it is possible to develop reliable models which allow its behavior to be described and predicted. It is thus not necessary to answer the question "exactly what is an electron?" to be able to describe and predict its behaviour (Coulson 1955, 71).

With the recent publication of several magisterial studies of Bohr's philosophy of physics (Folse 1985; Honner 1987; Krips 1987, 6–38; Murdoch 1987; Faye 1991; Pais 1991; Plotnitsky 1994), the strongly instrumentalist character of some aspects of Bohr's approach can be understood (especially when compared with Einstein's). Bohr can be thought of as adopting a realist approach to theoretical entities (in the sense that theoretical terms refer to something which exist independent of any theory), yet a non-realist approach to the specific models employed in their description (electrons cannot be said to "be" particles or "be" waves). The new clarity which has now been brought to understanding Bohr's anti-metaphysical understanding of complementarity allows its theological potential (and limitations) to be further appreciated. More recent studies of Bohr's relevance to religion have adopted a much more careful reading of Bohr, and allowed a more informed understanding of his approach (Loder and Neidhardt 1992; Kaiser 1996; Loder and Neidhardt 1996; MacKinnon 1996). In what follows, I shall disregard those earlier studies relating to the theme of "science and religion" on this issue which seem to misread Bohr at points of importance, rather than perpetuate the misunderstandings on which they rest.

Bohr's principle of complementarity is, as was noted earlier, concerned especially with the wave and particle models of light and matter. In order to avail ourselves of its full theological potential, it will be necessary to restate Bohr's principle in terms which extends its application beyond the specific and limited field within which it was developed. The fundamental principle is that the behavior of certain entities can be completely described by using either one of two mutually exclusive "classic" models. One aspect of its behavior may be described using model A, others with model B; yet there is no aspect of its behaviour which allows or requires *both* model A *and* model B to be true; nor are there are grounds for saying that the entity in question "is" A or "is" B or "is" A and B.

As we have stressed above, Bohr is an instrumentalist in his statements on complementarity, and was concerned with the modeling of the behavior of light and matter. Ontology could be left till later, if it was needed at all. This does *not* mean that Bohr held that electrons were constructs of the human mind. His instrumentalism relates to the specific issue of describing the behavior of electrons and other quantum phenomena. Bohr had no doubts that electrons existed; the difficulties lay in depicting or representing electrons in terms of existing conceptualities.

It is clear that Bohr was concerned to stress that the two models required to explain or depict quantum phenomena were already known and well understood. They provided a means of depicting and understanding something relatively new and unknown. Each of these models is already familiar to those attempting to understand the nature or behavior of the entity in question. Although the two models – both of which are necessary to describe the behavior of this entity – are mutually exclusive under normal circumstances, it is recognized that there are various other models or analogies which may be used to represent or depict the physical world, each with its own validity under certain circumstances and in certain manners, yet which stand in a relation of mutual exclusivity, so that if one such model or analogy may be said to apply to any situation, the other is automatically excluded.

As we have seen, it could be argued that there is no need to appeal to such "classic" models. The quantum phenomena possess an integrity of their own, and can be modeled without the need for the "principle of complementarity." In conceding this point, it is nevertheless important to note that Bohr's concern appears to have been to allow us to visualize these phenomena, using what is already known and understood as a means of understanding something novel and complex. One of Bohr's insights was that it was possible to use models which had been tried and tested in known situations to make sense of what was happening in more complex situations, providing the limits of the model were established and respected. Arthur Peacocke makes a similar point in relation to both science and theology, as follows (Peacocke 1984, 51):

> The scientific and theological enterprises share alike the tools of groping humanity – our stock of words, ideas and images that have been handed down, tools that we refashion in our own way for our own times in the light of experiment and experience to relate to the natural world and that are available, with God's guidance, to steer our own paths from birth to death.

This clearly points to at least one aspect of complementarity which has considerable theological potential, and raises the question of whether there might be others.

Bohr, Barth, and Torrance on Complementarity

Some scholars have noted a clear parallel between Bohr's "principle of complementarity" and Karl Barth's "dialectical method" (Loder and Neidhardt 1992; Loder and Neidhardt 1996) at this point. Loder and Neidhardt suggest that a number of significant points of convergence can be noted between the two writers. In the case of Bohr, the "phenomenon" to be explained is the behaviour of quantum events; for Barth, it is the relation between time and eternity on the one hand, and humanity and divinity in the person of Jesus Christ on the other (Loder and Neidhardt 1996, 282):

1 For both Bohr and Barth, classical forms of reason are pushed to their

limits to explain the phenomena in question.

2 Both writers vigorously maintain the principle that the phenomenon should be allowed to disclose how it can be known, and avoid reducing the phenomenon to known forms.

3 In both cases, the phenomenon discloses itself as an irreducible bipolar relationship which imposes itself upon the knower, and thus requires representation in terms of either the complementarity or dialectic of classical forms. The relationality between these polarities is asymmetrical.

4 Both situations require that the influence of the observer be recognized, and incorporated into what is known.

5 The observation of the phenomena requires that the knower should be able to communicate those observations in language.

There are some points which should be noted in qualifying these observations. First, both the early Barth and Bohr were receptive to the ideas of the Danish philosopher Søren Kierkegaard. It is possible that these convergences may reflect a shared affinity with the ideas of this writer, particularly his emphasis upon the "subjectivity" of truth, and its central theme of the self-involvement of the knower with the known. The early Barth (as seen in the second edition of the *Romans* commentary) can be regarded as a theological iconoclast, who was concerned to destroy theological and Christological "towers of Babel" – human constructions erected in defiance of God (Jüngel 1982). Yet Barth later appears to have realized that the decisive influence of Kierkegaard on his earlier dialectical theology may have represented the outcome of the hidden intrusion of philosophy and anthropology into theology, so that his dialectical theology, far from representing the *destruction* of anthropocentric theology, actually represented its *consolidation*. Barth may therefore be thought of as shifting the base of his theology to a *theological* rather than an *anthropological* foundation – and as identifying Jesus Christ, the Word of God, as that foundation.

This development is generally thought to have taken place in Barth's study of Anselm of Canterbury's theological method (1931), *Fides Quaerens Intellectum*. In this study, Barth argues that theology should be autonomous in relation to philosophy. At the heart of this work is the recognition of the importance of Anselm's insight that there is a "ratio peculiar to the Word of God," a "ratio of God," a "Word spoken from God" which stands over and against human concepts of "ratio" (that is, "reason"). Truth is thus the consequence of God's own action, which Barth comes to identify with the event of God's own selfrevelation in his Word in Jesus Christ (Pugh 1990).[13] This observation leads to the second point at which caution may be necessary. A critic might suggest that Loder and Neidhardt treat Barth as being a "dialectical" theologian thoughout his long and productive theological career. In fact, it is more accurate to suggest that Barth went through a "dialectical phase," which had probably ended by 1930.

These points must be understood, however, to be cautionary rather than counterfactual. There is clearly a significant degree of convergence in the methods of the two writers, despite their fundamental differences in areas of study. It clearly indicates that the "principle of complementarity" has religious utility. The question therefore arises: which area of theology is most appropriate as a "case study" of the religious application of Bohr's approach.

It is significant that the general convergences between Barth and Bohr noted above can also be discerned within the works of Thomas F. Torrance, widely respected both as an interpreter of Barth and an advocate of dialogue between theology and the natural sciences. Torrance's insistence on God's self-revelation determing our understanding shows clear parallels with the approach adopted by Barth (Torrance 1969, 26–7):

> Christian theology arises out of the actual knowledge of God given in and with concrete happenings in space and time. It is knowledge of the God who actively meets us and gives Himself to be known in Jesus Christ – in Israel, in history, on earth. It is essentially positive knowledge, with articulated content, mediated in concrete experience. It is concerned with fact, the fact of God's self-revelation; it is concerned with God Himself who just because He really is God always comes first. We do not therefore begin with ourselves or our questions, nor indeed can we choose where to begin; we can only begin with the facts prescribed for us by the actuality of the subject positively known.

Torrance thus strongly affirms the need to interpret the "phenomenon" of revelation on its own terms.

As we noted earlier (p. 195), it is widely agreed that the most obvious area of theology which is amenable to this kind of complementarist approach is Christology. Torrance illustrates this point well, in that he forges a link between the knowledge of God and Christology, which leads to an affirmation of the bipolarity of revelation.[14] As several recent studies of Torrance's doctrine of the knowledge of God have stressed (Kruger 1990; Seng 1992), the incarnation plays a central role in his understanding of how God can be known and the substance of that knowledge. It is therefore perhaps not a matter for surprise that Torrance should use this term in Christological contexts (Torrance 1969, 149): "Here we are faced with another fundamental characteristic of the truth of God as it is in Jesus: it is both divine and human. Knowledge of it is, accordingly, bipolar."

Some recent studies have confirmed the positive results which can be achieved from such an exploration (see especially Kaiser 1996; Loder and Neidhardt 1996). Christian orthodoxy has always held that Jesus Christ must be thought of as being truly divine and truly human. This simultaneous assertion of "two natures in one subject" clearly parallels Bohr's views on the complementarity of wave and particle models of light and matter.

Complementarity and the Genesis of Classical Christology
It seems to me, however, that the most promising approach to the issue of "complementarity and Christology" does not rest in an exploration of the final Christological definitions as such, but in the manner in which these emerged during the patristic period. The development of Christology during this formative period of Christian thinking is well documented and understood (see for example, Grillmeier 1975; Williams 1987; Macquarrie 1990; Marshall 1992), as is its significance for the overall development of theology. In what follows, I propose to explore the development of Christology during the patristic period, and note the manner in which Bohr-type concerns can be seen as playing a significant role in this highly significant matter. In order to allow for clarity of presentation, we shall consider two of the parallels noted by Loder and Neidhardt between Bohr and Barth, and explore the manner in which the evolution of classic Christology conforms to a similar pattern.

First, Loder and Neidhardt note that that the phenomenon to be explained should be allowed to disclose how it can be known, and avoid reducing the phenomenon to known forms. As noted earlier, Bohr's reflections on complementarity were forced upon him by the experimental evidence which accumulated during the period 1905–25. Much simpler ways of visualizing the situation could have put forward (and, as the development of quantum theory over this period indicates, were indeed adduced). Yet the simplicity of these models foundered against the experimental evidence, which ineluctably led Bohr to the conclusion that two apparently mutually exclusive ways of conceiving quantum phenomena were required.

The development of Christology during the period 100–451 shows this concern to have been of overwhelming importance. This same theme of allowing the phenomenon (if we may be allowed to use this term to refer to the complex amalgam of "historical testimony and religious experience") to dictate its own interpretation can be discerned throughout the development of patristic Christology. Simplistic reductionist modes of representing the identity and significant of Jesus of Nazareth foundered on the phenomena which they were required to represent (see for example, Wiles 1967; Marshall 1992; McGrath 1996a, 322–41). In particular, the model of Jesus of Nazareth as a purely human figure (generally held to be found in the Ebionite heresy) or as a purely divine figure (generally held to be found in the Docetic heresy) were regarded as quite inadequate. Both the representation of Jesus in the New Testament and the manner in which the Christian church incorporated Jesus into its life of prayer and worship required a more complex understanding of his identity and significance than either of these simpler models were able to offer.

The suggestion that some third model could be invoked to explain the phenomenon of Jesus of Nazareth was rejected as unsatisfactory. The debate over the teachings of Apollinarius of Laodicea (on which see Prestige 1940, 193–246) led to agreement that there was no "intermediate state," no "*tertium quid*," interposing between the two natures. The patristic period witnessed a decisive rejection of any attempt to explain Jesus in terms which involved the construction of a mediating or hybrid concept between divinity and humanity. There is a direct Christological parallel with Bohr's insistence on the completeness of the principle of complementarity. As with Bohr's complementary accounts of waves and particles, the Chalcedonian approach to Christology affirmed that the approach offered by the "two natures" doctrine was *complete* (in that only two such models or natures are needed) and *complementary* (in that only one of these mutually exclusive models or natures can apply at any one time).

Patristic writers (such as Leo I) often offered developed understandings of which aspects of the ministry of Jesus of Nazareth were to be attributed to his human, and which to his divine, nature. Such approaches were open to misunderstanding, in that they could be interpreted to mean that Jesus was divine only when acting in certain manners, and human only when acting in others. The assertion of more ontological manners of affirming both the humanity and divinity of Jesus can be understood as a means of avoiding this potentially vulnerably way of conceiving the identity of Jesus. Our point, however, concerns the development of patristic theology, not the form of its final statements.

Second, Loder and Neidhardt noted that both Bohr and Barth affirmed that the phenomenon (whether revelatory or quantum) discloses itself as an irreducible bipolar relationship which imposes itself upon the knower, and thus requires representation in terms of either the complementarity or dialectic of classical forms. The Christological issue of critical importance was that the biblical portrayal of Jesus of Nazareth at times suggested that he behaved or functioned as God, at others as human. This can be seen clearly stated in the famous letter written by Pope Leo I to Flavian, patriarch of Constantinople on June 13, 449, which is usually referred to as the "Tome of Leo." In this letter, Leo set out the prevailing Christological consensus within the Latin-speaking western church. The letter was later elevated to a position of authority by the Council of Chalcedon (451), which recognized it as a classic statement of Christological orthodoxy. The letter is primarily a critique of the views of Eutyches, especially his rejection of the true humanity of Christ. For Leo, the formula *totus in suis, totus in nostris* sums up the correct position on this matter (McGrath 1995a, 146–7):

Christ was born God of God, Almighty of Almighty, co-eternal of eternal; not later in time, not inferior in power, not different in glory, not divided in essence. The same only-begotten, eternal Son of the eternal Father was born of the Holy Spirit and the Virgin Mary. But this birth in time has taken nothing from, and added nothing to, that divine eternal nativity, but has bestowed itself wholly on the restoration of humanity . . . For we could not overcome the author of sin and death, unless he had taken our nature and made it his own, whom sin could not defile nor death retain. . . . That birth, uniquely marvellous and marvellously unique, ought not to be understood in such a way as to preclude the distinctive properties of the kind [i.e. of humanity] through the new mode of creation. . . . Thus the properties of each nature and substance were preserved in their totality, and came together to form one person. Humility was assumed by majesty, weakness by strength, mortality by eternity; and to pay the debt that we had incurred, an inviolable nature was united to a nature that can suffer. And so, to fulfil the conditions of our healing, the human being Jesus Christ, one and the same mediator between God and humanity, was able to die in respect of the one, yet unable to die in respect of the other. Thus there was born true God in the entire and perfect nature of true humanity, complete in his own properties, complete in ours (*totus in suis, totus in nostris*).

Patristic writers such as Athanasius argued that the total thrust of the biblical witness to and Christian experience of Jesus of Nazareth required him to be conceptualized as both divine and human. For example, Athanasius makes the point that it is only God who can save. God, and God alone, can break the power of sin, and bring us to eternal life. An essential feature of being a creature is that one requires to be redeemed. No creature can save another creature. Only the creator can redeem the creation. Having emphasized that it is God alone who can save, Athanasius then makes the logical move which the Arians found difficult to counter. The New Testament and the Christian liturgical tradition alike regard Jesus Christ as Saviour. Yet, as Athanasius emphasized, only God can save. So how are we to make sense of this?

The only possible solution, Athanasius argues, is to accept that Jesus is God incarnate. The logic of his argument at times goes something like this:

1   No creature can redeem another creature.
2   According to Arius, Jesus Christ is a creature.
3   Therefore, according to Arius, Jesus Christ cannot redeem humanity.

At times, a slightly different style of argument can be discerned, resting upon the statements of Scripture and the Christian liturgical tradition.

1   Only God can save.
2   Jesus Christ saves.
3   Therefore Jesus Christ is God.

Salvation, for Athanasius, involves divine intervention. Athanasius thus draws out the meaning of John 1: 14 by arguing that the "word became flesh": in other words, God entered into our human situation, in order to change it.

A second point that Athanasius makes is that Christians worship and pray to Jesus Christ. This represents an excellent case study of the importance of Christian practices of worship and prayer for Christian theology. By the fourth century, prayer to and adoration of Christ were standard features of the way in which public worship took place. Athanasius argues that if Jesus Christ is a creature, then Christians are guilty of worshipping a creature instead of God – in other words, they had lapsed into idolatry. Christians, Athanasius stresses, are totally forbidden to worship anyone or anything except God himself. Athanasius thus argued that Arius seemed to be guilty of making nonsense of the way in which Christians prayed and worshipped. Athanasius, argued that Christians were right to worship and adore Jesus Christ, because by doing so, they were recognizing him for what he was – God incarnate.

It was this awareness that Jesus of Nazareth required to be understood in both divine and human terms which eventually led to what is known as the "Chalcedonian definition of faith" – the famous assertion that Jesus is truly divine and truly human. Maurice Wiles summarizes the reasons for this development as follows (Wiles 1967, 106):

> On the one hand was the conviction that a saviour must be fully divine; on the other was the conviction that what is not assumed is not healed. Or, to put the matter in other words, the source of salvation must be God; the locus of salvation must be humanity. It is quite clear that these two principles often pulled in opposite directions. The Council of Chalcedon was the church's attempt to resolve, or perhaps rather to agree to live with, that tension. Indeed, to accept both principles as strongly as did the early church is already to accept the Chalcedonian faith.

Pressure on space limits our confirmation of the convergence between the other factors noted by Loder and Neidhardt and those which can be discerned as shaping doctrinal development in the early church. It is, however, important to notice that many of the arguments set out during the early patristic period for the "dual nature" of Christ are primarily functional. In other words, the focus of the arguments can be seen to rest on what it is that Jesus of Nazareth achieved. There is no doubt that patristic writers drew ontological conclusions from their functional analysis. In other words, if Jesus truly behaved as God, then the case could be made that he was God. A number of modern writers have argued that it is not necessary to draw such ontological conclusions (which may reflect a particular interest in ontology in the patristic period); it is quite possible to rest content with the assertion that Jesus behaves in divine and human ways.

The pressure for clarification of the nature of quantum phenomena came from experimental observations which precipitated a theoretical crisis, demonstrating that existing conceptualities simply could not account for the phenomena. The pressure for clarification of the nature of Jesus of Nazareth arose through a growing awareness, fuelled by intense debate and controversy, that Jesus simply could not be described in terms of any one existing idea. In each case, the temptation to reduce the phenomena to existing notions was resisted, on account of the serious distortions introduced. To explain the phenomenon, either new use had to be made of existing categories, or radically new categories had to be introduced. Bohr's approach was to retain existing categories ("classic models"), while recognizing that such ordinary language can have specialized extensions which allow it to illuminate other domains. The implications of this approach are considerable, not least in that they illustrate the way in which complex domains can be illuminated by known domains.

Conclusion

"*A picture* held us captive and we could not get outside it" (Wittgenstein 1968, 48). This chapter has explored the way in which the natural sciences and religions aim to represent a complex world in ways which can be understood and visualized. As we have seen, it is a remarkably rich and complex area of human inquiry, where parallel after parallel can be discerned between the two disciplines, without in any way compromising their distinctive identities and concerns. Although it is not correct to assert that either or both the sciences and religions are committed to forms of realism, it is clear that a sufficiently significant section of both communities adopts some form of "critical realism" to make a genuine convergence of views possible in a number of key areas, particularly in relation to the use of models, analogies, and metaphors.

Discussion in this section has focused primarily on the manner in which Niels Bohr argued that classical models could be used to visualize non-classical phenomena. It is important to appreciate that Bohr was making no ontological claims whatsoever; his concern lay rather in the manner in which we were able to model phenomena which were otherwise impossible to visualize. In some ways, the force of Bohr's position has been eroded, not least on account of the realization that manners could be devised to represent quantum phenomena without recourse to two mutually exclusive models. Even if this point is conceded, however, Bohr has made a point of theological importance, which will be explored further in what follows – that a complex or inaccessible phenomenon may be described by using models which are derived from known and understood situations.

For Bohr, classical models which were, at first sight, inconsistent and mutually incompatible could be deployed to explain different aspects of a more complex system (note, again, that any given aspect of the phenomenon, according to Bohr, can only be represented by *one* of the mutually exclusive models). The need for such models, and the precise areas of their validity, required to be established by experimentation. In other words, the aspects of "particle" and "wave" models which were not appropriate as means of representing the phenomenon to be modeled could not be established *a priori*, but required to be demonstrated experimentally. (To the extent that they could be predicted, those predictions rested on prior experimental investigations, so that any such predictions would thus be *a posteriori* rather than *a priori* in nature.)

The theologian is unable to appeal to present experimentation, or the results of past experimentation, in this manner. Whereas the scientific community takes its ideas from such experimental approaches, the religious community takes them from revelation. As we have stressed, this is one of the most fundamental of differences between the natural sciences and religion, despite the possibilities for bridging the divide through an appeal to natural theology (see pp. 98–118). Nevertheless, both the scientific and religious communities have developed ways of dealing with models which appear to conflict as an integral and accepted of depicting and discussing the phenomena with which they are concerned, and the real entities which are held to lie behind them. This is potentially an area of continuing discussion for the future.

In Place of a Conclusion: Beyond Conflict

Commenting on the scientific search for the origins of the universe, the noted astronomer Robert Jastrow notes how modern science finds itself asking precisely the same questions as those posed in earlier generations by religious thinkers (Jastrow 1978, 115–16):

> It is not a matter of another year, another decade of work, another measurement, or another theory; at this moment, it seems as though science will never be able to raise the curtain on the mystery of creation. For the scientist who has lived by his faith in the power of reason, the story ends like a bad dream. He has scaled the mountains of ignorance; he is about to conquer the highest peaks; as he pulls himself over the final rock, he is greeted by a band of theologians who have been sitting there for centuries.

One must allow for at least a degree of poetic licence at this point; nevertheless, the point seems to have been well made. For some, science has made theology redundant, and is able to give the correct answers to questions rightly raised but wrongly answered by well-meaning religious thinkers in the past. Doubtless that viewpoint will continue to be represented and defended. On the basis of this model, the encounter which ensues after the scientist hauls himself over that final rock will be a nasty little scuffle over who sits where. This work, and the larger project of which it is part, offers a somewhat different answer, in the belief that it is both correct and of potential importance to the development of both disciplines and communities.

It is perhaps inevitable that the present volume will seem inadequate to many. Important issues may have been identified; they have not, however, been discussed in the detail they require. Equally, other important issues have not even been touched on – including the vast ethical issues which are raised by the growth of technology, and the contributions of religions other than Christianity. It is intended to remedy these deficiences at later stages in the project. The present volume is intended simply to indicate the general lines of approach of future work which the present writer intends to undertake – more of a *Forschungsdarstellung* than a *Forschungsgeschichte*. It might be helpful to think of this volume as an attempt to justify a sustained intellectual engagement between two highly important aspects of human life and thought. The cumbersome title of the volume is intended to convey the idea of laying the foundations for a dialogue, even if the volume perhaps makes less of a contribution to that dialogue than might be desired. The conclusion to this volume, therefore, is not this brief final section, but a series of works which will follow in due course.

But some will expect to find some concluding remarks, following the conventional pattern. Not wishing to disappoint those who respect this convention, let me end by posing a question: what is the most significant difference between the natural sciences and religion?

One answer is suggested by George Herbert's poem "The Elixir," which speaks of the possibility of seeing beyond the natural order to discern the divine (Herbert 1941, 185):

> A man that looks on glass
> On it may stay his eye;
> Or if he pleaseth, through it passe
> And then the heav'n espie

A related point is made by philosopher of science Michael Polanyi, in his important yet somewhat difficult book *Knowing and Being*. Polanyi here attempts to deal with the question of meaning in nature. To focus on something is potentially to develop tunnel vision, and to fail to see the "big picture" of which it is part. "So long as you look *at* X, you are *not* attending *from* X to something else, which would be its meaning. In order to attend *from* X to its meaning, you must cease to look *at* X and *the moment you look at X, you cease to see its meaning*" (Polanyi 1969, 146).

This is a major theme of Christian theology – that the natural world, while wonderful in itself, offers a way to begin to discern the glory of God. For Calvin, the natural order is a theatre in which the glory of God is displayed to humanity , and through which something of the majesty of God can be known. The noted English literary critic and author C. S. Lewis addressed this issue in a remarkable sermon entitled "The Weight of Glory," preached before the University of Oxford on June 8, 1941. In this sermon, Lewis stressed the need to see beyond the present world, and discover that to which it points. Those who seek to find joy and beauty in the natural world will be disappointed, in that the beauty of that world is merely a sign of and signal to something which lies beyond it – something which is to be desired and grasped (Lewis 1965, 97–8):

The books or the music in which we thought the beauty was located will betray us if we trust to them; it was not *in* them, it only came *through* them, and what came through them was longing. These things – the beauty, the memory of our own past – are good images of what we really desire; but if they are mistaken for the thing itself they turn into dumb idols, breaking the hearts of their worshippers. For they are not the thing itself; they are only the scent of a flower we have not found, the echo of a tune we have not heard, news from a country we have not visited.

One can study the natural order, and stop at that point – or one can go on, and discern what lies beyond and behind it, realizing that, from a religious perspective, the natural order beckons us onwards to discover its creator. Perhaps one of the most significant differences between science and religion thus lies not in how they begin, nor even in how they proceed, but in how they end.

Notes

Chapter 1 Starting All Over Again

1 One might recall at this point that Sigmund Freud admitted that the application of scientific *methods* do not necessarily lead to a scientific *worldview*: see the careful studies of (Ricoeur 1970; Küng 1979).

2 At one level, the realization of the importance of social factors has led to the emergence of the "strong program" in the sociology of knowledge (Manicas and Rosenberg 1985), which stresses the role of social and cultural pressures in the generation and acceptance of scientific theories. This program can be seen at its most persuasive in Shapin and Schaffer's classic study of the status of experimental evidence in the controversy between Robert Boyle and Thomas Hobbes . The notion of "scientific truth," it is argued, is a social construct which is largely determined by social and cultural factors. This approach has met with vigorous resistance (see Norris 1997, 218–47, 265–94), not least on account of its seeming indifference to the strong record of explanatory and predictive successes of the natural sciences.

3 The survey was of no small influence in indicating the rise of agnosticism within American academia, and stimulating reactions from conversative Christianity (Larson 1989; Numbers 1992; Marsden 1994).

4 It must be stressed that the concerns which have been expressed do not imply the rejection of *all* forms of foundationalism but the specific form linked with the Enlightenment (Alston 1989; Czapkay Sudsduth 1995). Nor does it in any way lend weight to a rejection of the theory of knowledge in general. "The theory of knowledge is currently flourishing, perhaps as never before. There are some, of course, who loudly proclaim the death of epistemology. This seems to me to be less premature than confused: what they observe is the breakdown of *classical foundationalism*, which is only one epistemological program among several, even if a historically important one" (Plantinga 1993, v).

5 Stauffer, however, argues that Calvin does engage with Copernicus (although not by name) in the course of his exposition of 1 Corinthians 10: 19–22, in which he declares that some "say that the sun does not change position, and that it is the

earth which moves and turns (*c'est la terre que se remue et qu'elle tourne*)." Calvin subjects this position to criticism, which might be taken to imply that he knew of the Copernican hypothesis, and was opposed to it. However, the text cannot bear this weight of interpretation. Calvin appears to have been engaging with views which he found in the writings of the eleventh-century writer Adelmann of Liège (Marcel 1980, 193–4; Kaiser 1986). The subject of the text is in any case not cosmology, but the issue of whether Christians should eat meat that had previously been offered to idols.

6 It is therefore important to note that the legendary embellishment of the Wilberforce–Huxley encounter dates from the 1890s, thirty years after the event took place: see pp. 15–16.

7 For an excellent example, see (Brooke 1991).

8 In any case, more nuanced understandings of the nature of evolution are emerging, with concepts such as "symbiosis" being set alongside those of "conflict." A significant challenge to a pure Darwinian model of evolution through competition and conflict has been offered by Lynn Margulis. In a study of the origin of eukaryotic cells (Margulis 1970), Margulis argued that there were reasons for believing that certain aspects of cell structure might be explained by assuming that mitochondria were originally bacterial cells that had been incorporated into larger cells, leading to a process of symbiosis between the smaller cell and its host. The theory originally met with a curious mixture of ridicule and hostility, which gradually dissipated as evidence accumulated in favor of the theory – for example, when it became clear, through advanced sequencing studies, that mitochondrial proteins resembled those of bacterial cells rather than of host cells. The role of symbiosis in relation to evolution now seems to have found wide acceptance. It will be clear that the intrusion of a cooperative element forces at least a degree of modification to an evolutionary model dominated by conflict imagery.

9 Interestingly, Dawkins seems to espouse an outdated nineteenth-century positivism in relation to the sciences when he asserts that science is "based upon verifiable evidence," whereas religion claims an "independence from evidence" (Dawkins 1997, 27). Both statements reveal a lack of serious understanding of or engagement with either the philosophy of science or basic Christian theology.

10 It is important to note that *The Fundamentals* include a number of essays directly addressing Darwinism. Some are decisively and aggressively anti-Darwinian; others are cautiously welcoming or approving of his ideas (Livingstone 1986, 73–8). Writing in 1888, Benjamin B. Warfield – perhaps the most influential of all conservative Protestant writers in North America at this time, and widely cited with approval by later fundamentalist writers – had no hesitation in asserting that "we raise no question as to the compatibility of the Darwinian form of the hypothesis of evolution with Christianity" (Warfield 1932, 548). It is significant that from about 1920 onwards, this plurality of assessments of Darwinism within fundamentalism disappeared, being replaced with what appears to be an essentially monolithic hostility.

11 Nevertheless, the fact that certain forms of religion within Buddhism, Taoism, and Jainism have no central concern with such beings remains an important point of contention in this matter.

12 It will also be clear that the decision to focus on Christianity as a "single case study" avoids any precommitment to one specific model of religion – such as the "experiential," "functionalist," "structuralist" or "family resemblance" models (Alston 1967; Clarke and Byrne 1993, 3–27).

13 Some attempts to relate science and religion take the form of an assimilationism which fails to respect the distinct autonomies and integrities of the disciplines. An example of a recent work which appears to be vulnerable at this point is the highly engaging and stimulating work by Fritjof Capra, entitled *The Tao of Physics* (Capra 1992). Fascinating through Capra's conclusions may be, they appear to be derived without a due consideration of the very different methodologies of the specific forms of scientific and religious activity which he chooses to compare, with essentially verbal similarities being transposed in such a way as to suggest the existence of significant conceptual and methodological convergence (Polkinghorne 1996, 88). This may be regarded as a rather sobering example of a religious borrowing of scientific language without due attention to the detail of the scientific context.

14 In an important study of 1962, Harold K. Schilling explored in detail a number of parallels between religious and scientific inquiry, noting in particular the implicit assumption of the dependability of nature as a basis for scientific investigation (Schilling 1962). For Schilling, there are parallels between religion and science which on the one hand allow for genuine differences between the disciplines, yet on the other point to a significant degree of convergence which is too easily overlooked.

15 Given that readers of this book may be drawn from a variety of disciplines and interested in developing their knowledge of the fields on which this work impacts, I have been considerably more generous with bibliographical references than might be thought strictly necessary.

Chapter 2   The Quest for Order

1 For two recent biographies of Hawking, see (Ferguson 1991; White and Gribbin 1992).

2 Hawking's most recent biographers have expressed uncertainty over whether Hawking's references to God should be taken at face value, or be seen as intellectual teases (White and Gribbin 1992, 3).

3 For an excellent review of the scholarly literature, see (Preuss 1995, vol. 1, 226–39).

4 Isaiah 45: 7 is an important exception to this general categorization, and merits careful study in its own right (Deroche 1992).

5 The religious significance of chaos has been the subject of much reflection in recent years. From a Christian perspective, Philip Hefner has explored the positive role of chaos in the thinking of the philosopher Nicholas Berdyaev (Hefner 1984); Stuart Chandler offers insights from a Buddhist perspective (Chandler 1992).

6 The term "process theology" is not especially well defined, and can cause difficulties at points. For example, Robert Cummings Neville would be regarded as a "process thinker" by some, partly on account of his clear affinities with Alfred

North Whitehead. Yet Neville defends the notion of creation *ex nihilo* by God (Neville 1968), and offers a sustained critique of process theology at points of importance (Neville 1980). For a general survey see Fiddes (1993).

7 For an example of an uncritical response to White, see Cobb (1972). Apparently lacking the ability or willingness to criticize White at the historical or theological levels, Cobb calls for "a new Christianity" on the basis of this critique.

8 This fourth point is of especial importance, as it indicates a tension with the rise of technology, which permits humanity to by-pass natural limits. For reflection on this critical point, see Barbour 1980; Cooper 1991; Ferre 1993; Postman 1993; Guardini 1994.

9 One of the more regrettable aspects of the philosophical discussions of the nature of induction is a lack of attention to experimental studies of the manner in which the regularities of the world are discerned and assimilated. The work of Jean Piaget is of especial importance in this respect (Flavell 1963; Ginsburg and Opper 1979; Hundert 1989, 93–156).

10 It should be recalled that Newton did not speak of the "conservation of energy."

11 It may be of interest here to note that Albert Einstein explained the remarkable number of clergy who were interested in relativity as follows: "clergymen are interested in the general laws of nature and physicists, very often, are not" (Frank 1949, 349).

12 It should be noted that Einstein assumed that space–time coordinates were bosonic, and hence made no allowance for what are now termed "fermions."

13 As is now thought to be the case with "gauge symmetry," in which the infinitesimal parameters in a Lie symmetry group are replaced by arbitrary space–time functions (Young and Mills 1954; Sakurai 1960).

14 In particular, Aquinas argues that perfection corresponds to actuality, rather than potentiality. To the degree that something is in a state of potentiality, it may be said to lack actuality, and hence perfection (Kretzmann 1997, 131–8).

Chapter 3   The Investigation of the World

1 An interesting discussion, which should be noted at this point, concerns the notion of a "thought-experiment" (McAllister 1996). Some writers have held that such "experiments" are to be regarded as primarily argumentative (Norton 1991); others adopt the view that they can be see as an extreme form of experimentalism (Brown 1991; Sorensen 1992).

2 Quine, of course, was based in the United States of America. The development of Pierre Duhem's ideas within the discipline of the philosophy of science in France is of some importance to this analysis, particularly as it is encountered in the writings of Gaston Bachelard (1884–1962) and Georges Canguilhem (1904–) (see, for example, Bachelard 1938; Canguilhem 1968). Bachelard in particular is widely interpreted as arguing that, since scientific truth claims are so incorrigibly theory-laden, there are no adequate empirical means available for distinguishing between them (Lecourt 1975; Tiles 1984).

3 It may be noted at this point that the two most philosophically sophisticated schools of thought within western Christianity are generally agreed to be the

approach which derives from Thomas Aquinas, which is especially significant within modern Roman Catholicism, and that which derives from John Calvin and his successors, which is particularly influential within Protestantism, and is often referred to as the "Reformed" school.

4 It is interesting to note how Torrance appeals to the history of modern scientific thought as a corrective to theologically and philosophically deficient modes of argument. Torrance argues that both Kantian idealism (which attributes the regularities observed in the world to the structuring activity of the human mind) and scientific positivism (which postulates a direct correspondence between observation and theoretical constructs) can be refuted by an appeal to the history of scientific thought.

5 More accurately, the critical assumptions are that life requires elements heavier than hydrogen and helium, water, galaxies, and special types of stars and planets. All of these are, in principle, contestable.

6 It should be noted that the "accommodation" approach was also used extensively by Christian theologians in relation to the Darwinian controversy of the nineteenth century.

7 A theory could be described as *ad hoc* if it is devised for the specific and limited purpose of explaining known phenomena (sometimes also referred to as "retrodiction'). This is to be contrasted with predictive theories, which generate novel predictions not themselves contained in the known observations.

8 The history of the reception of Darwin's theory is, in fact, considerably more complex than these brief comments might suggest. The discovery of the physical basis of heredity initially led to the view that Darwin's theory was an irrelevance. A number of definitive studies of the history of biology to be published in the 1920s dismissed Darwin as an irrelevance in the light of the new genetic theories. It was only during the 1930s (primarily on account of R. A. Fisher's work on the effects of allele substitution) that an "evolutionary synthesis" between Darwinianism and genetics was achieved . This delay in achieving the neo-Darwinian synthesis allowed a series of imaginative theories to flourish during the 1920s, such as vitalism, holism and orthogenesis (Berry 1982).

Chapter 4   The Reality of the World

1 This radical empiricism was, of course, propagated by the Vienna Circle. Mach, it should be noted, was the first holder of a chair of the History and Theory of the Inductive Sciences at the University of Vienna, a position later held by Moritz Schlick (Gillies 1993, 17–20).

2 It has been argued that, since Plato's "ideas" are regarded by him as real, his philosophy should be styled "realist." This would result in the term "idealism" acquiring a more specifically subjectivist association, such as that found in Cartesianism (Burnyeat 1982).

3 The most positive statements concerning electrons are at (Fraassen 1980, 63–6).

4 It is significant that some of those theologians who adopt radically anti-realist epistemological stances often do so in response to intellectual pressures from outside the Christian tradition. A particularly illuminating example can be found in

the writings of the English radical theologian Don Cupitt, whose theology can be argued to be a series of responses to the rapidly shifting cultural milieu (White 1994; Thiselton 1995, 87–110).

5 Given his massive contribution to the question of "science and religion," it may be of interest to note that one of the earliest published writings of Thomas F. Torrance was a 1941 review of Thomas Reid's *Essays on the Intellectual Powers of Man* (Torrance 1990, 225). For further exchanges between Murphy and Wolterstorff, see (Murphy 1996; Wolterstorff 1996).

6 Recall here that Werner Heisenberg famously proposed in 1927 that it was intrinsically impossible to assign precise values to both the position and the momentum of a particle at any given moment (Atkins and Friedman 1997, 25–7).

7 The issues involved go beyond the scope of this work. For an exploration of some of the central issues, see the classic study of Robert Schreiter on "constructing local theologies" (Schreiter 1986).

8 On the "strong program" and its discontents, see (Latour and Woolgar 1979); Pickering 1984; Barnes 1985; Collins 1985; Fuller 1989; Norris 1979.

9 Kuhn's paradigm thesis is itself controversial, and its relevance to theology disputed (Strug 1984). Our concern here is with the specific role of the scientific community in accepting paradigms.

Chapter 5   *The Representation of the World*

1 This point could be developed further. For example, it could be argued that debates between theologians on the themes of "realism" and "instrumentalism" are transpositions of debates that are taking place within the philosophy of science, and have been imported into philosophical theology by writers who believed that there was something to be learned from them – such as Ian Ramsey, during his period as Nolloth Professor of the Philosophy of the Christian Religion at Oxford University (see, for example, Ramsey 1957; Ramsey 1964; Gill 1976, 87–105).

2 "Les raisonnements par analogie peuvent servir à expliquer et à éclaircir certains choses, mais non pas à les démontrer . . . Une analogie tirée de la ressemblance extérieure des objets. Pour en conclure leur ressemblance intérieure, n'est pas une regle infaillible; elle n'est pas universellement vrai."

3 It might possibly be objected that such a system could arise naturally, with some mathematical algorithm evolving by which certain disks are "frozen." Once more, it is necessary to stress the importance of the Turing Machine, and supremely the question: how can one decide when a Turing machine will stop? As Turing himself demonstrated, there is no algorithm by which the "halting problem" can be solved automatically. It would therefore be important for any who wished to justify the use of the analogy mentioned above to set out the manner in which this criticism can be met.

4 On Morgan, see Allen (1969) and Allen (1978).

5 "Force" and "mass" are good examples of irreducible metaphors which physics has continued to employ in this manner (Jammer 1957; Jammer 1961).

6 It is, of course, possible to draw a distinction between "primary" or "root" metaphors, which are an integral aspect of the Christian revelation (such as "God as

shepherd") and secondary metaphors which are derived from these root meta-phors, and are useful for communicating theological insights in specific local contexts.

7 Indeed, the tension here directly parallels a related tension we noted earlier (pp. 81–7) – the relation between experimentation and revelation.

8 "Mutual exclusiveness is frequently thought to be the sole condition of Bohr's notion of complementarity . . . This is a mistaken view: the notion of mutual exclusiveness and of joint completion are equally necessary, indeed complementary, ingredients in the meaning of Bohr's conception. In the genesis of the conception the notion of joint completion came first (in the acceptance of the wave-particle duality); the notion of mutual exclusiveness came later (in the acceptance of the uncertainty principle)" (Murdoch 1987, 61).

9 It needs to be noted that this is hardly a fair description of Bohr's approach.

10 For an excellent account of the issue of "visualizability', see the discussion of "redefining visualizability" in Miller (1984).

11 These remain unpublished, and have received scant attention in the literature. See, for example, the very brief reference in Pais (1991, 450, n. 101). There is an allusion to them in Baillie (1962, 217).

12 In view of that fact that a number of distinct viewpoints can be discerned within the Copenhagen school, we shall limit ourselves to the writings of Niels Bohr dating from the late 1920s.

13 This traditional reading of Barth's theological development has been challenged recently by McCormack (1995). It is perhaps too early to judge whether McCormack's challenge will cause this traditional reading to be revised.

14 Torrance does not make as much use of this term as one might expect. For examples of its use, see Torrance (1969, 149); Torrance (1971, 17–18); Torrance (1985, 42, 106).

Bibliography

Achinstein, P. "The Circularity of a Self-Supporting Inductive Argument." *Analysis* 22 (1962): 138–41.

Achinstein, P. *Concepts of Science: A Philosophical Analysis.* Baltimore: Johns Hopkins, 1968.

Achinstein, P. *Law and Explanation.* Oxford: Clarendon Press, 1971.

Achtemeier, P. M. "The Truth of Tradition: Critical Realism in the Thought of Alasdair MacIntyre and T. F. Torrance." *Scottish Journal of Theology* 47 (1994): 355–74.

Ackermann, R. "Experiment as the Motor of Scientific Progress." *Social Epistemology* 2 (1988): 327–35.

Ackermann, R. "The New Experimentalism." *British Journal for the Philosophy of Science* 40 (1989): 185–90.

Alexander, H. G. *The Leibniz–Clark Correspondence.* Manchester: Manchester University Press, 1956.

Alexander, S. "The Basis of Realism." *Proceedings of the British Academy* 13 (1913): 279–314.

Allen, G. "T. H. Morgan and the Emergence of a New American Biology." *The Quarterly Review of Biology* 44 (1969): 166–88.

Allen, G. *Thomas Hunt Morgan.* Princeton: Princeton University Press, 1978.

Alston, W. P. "Religion." *Encyclopaedia of Philosophy.* Ed. Paul Edwards. Vol. 7. New York and London: Macmillan, 1967, pp. 140–5.

Alston, W. P. *Epistemic Justification: Essays in the Theology of Knowledge.* Ithaca, NY: Cornell University Press, 1989.

Alston, W. P. *Perceiving God: The Epistemology of Religious Experience.* Ithaca, NY: Cornell University Press, 1991a.

Alston, W. P. "The Inductive Argument from Evil and the Human Cognitive Condition." *Philosophical Perspectives* 5 (1991b): 30–67.

Alston, W. P. *A Realist Conception of Truth.* Ithaca: Cornell University Press, 1996.

Altmann, S. L. *Icons and Symmetries.* Oxford: Oxford University Press, 1992.

Ammermann, N. *Subjekt, Logik, Empirie: Grundlegung und Möglichkeiten empirischer Theologie als Erforschung subjektiver Theorien.* Frankfurt am Main: Peter Lang, 1997.

Anderson, B. W. "A Stylistic Study of the Priestly Creation Story." *Canon and Author-*

ity: Essays in Old Testament Religion and Theology. Ed. George W. Coats and Burke O. Long. Philadelphia: Fortress Press, 1977, pp. 148–62.

Anderson, B. W. *Creation versus Chaos: The Reinterpretation of Mythical Symbolism in the Bible.* Philadelphia: Fortress Press, 1987.

Anderson, M. J. *Carl Linnaeus: Father of Classification.* Springfield, NJ: Enslow Publishers, 1997.

Angstrom, A. *Recherches sur le spectre solaire.* Uppsala: Uppsala University Press, 1868.

Appiah, A. *For Truth in Semiotics.* Oxford: Blackwell, 1986.

Aquinas, T. *Summa contra Gentiles.* Trans. Anton C. Pegis. 5 vols. Notre Dame, IN: University of Notre Dame Press, 1975.

Arbib, M. A., and M. B. Hesse. *The Construction of Reality.* Cambridge: Cambridge University Press, 1986.

Ariew, R. "The Duhem Thesis." *British Journal for the Philosophy of Science* 35 (1984): 313–25.

Armstrong, D. M. *What is a Law of Nature?* Cambridge: Cambridge University Press, 1983.

Atkins, P. W. *Creation Revisited.* Harmondsworth: Penguin, 1994.

Atkins, P. W., and R. S. Friedman. *Molecular Quantum Mechanics.* 3rd edn. Oxford: Oxford University Press, 1997.

Augustine. *Saint Augustine: Confessions.* Trans. Henry Chadwick. Oxford: Clarendon Press, 1991.

Ault, D. D. *Visionary Physics: Blake's Response to Newton.* Chicago: University of Chicago Press, 1974.

Austin, W. H. *Waves, Particles, and Paradoxes.* Houston: Rice University Press, 1967.

Avis, P. D. L. "Apologist from the World of Science: John Polkinghorne, FRS." *Scottish Journal of Theology* 43 (1990): 485–502.

Ayer, A. J. "What is a Law of Nature?" *The Concept of a Person.* Ed. A. J. Ayer. London: Macmillan, 1956, pp. 209–34.

Bachelard, G. *La formation de l'ésprit scientifique.* Paris: Corti, 1938.

Bagchi, D. V. N. *Luther's Earliest Opponents: Catholic Controversialists, 1518–1525.* Minneapolis: Fortress Press, 1991.

Baillie, J. *The Sense of the Presence of God.* London: Oxford University Press, 1962.

Balashov, Y. "Duhem, Quine, and the Multiplicity of Scientific Tests." *Philosophy of Science* 61 (1994): 608–28.

Banner, M. C. *The Justification of Science and the Rationality of Religious Belief.* Oxford and New York: Oxford University Press, 1990.

Barbour, I. G. *Issues in Science and Religion.* Englewood Cliffs: Prentice-Hall, 1966.

Barbour, I. G. *Myths, Models and Paradigms: A Comparative Study in Science and Religion.* New York: Harper & Row, 1974.

Barbour, I. G. *Technology, Environment, and Human Values.* New York: Praeger, 1980.

Barbour, I. G. *Religion in an Age of Science.* San Francisco: HarperSanFrancisco, 1990.

Barnes, B. *About Science.* Oxford: Blackwell, 1985.

Barnett, S. A. *Biology and Freedom: An Essay on the Implications of Human Ethology.* Cambridge: Cambridge University Press, 1988.

Barr, J. "The Image of God in the Book of Genesis: A Study of Terminology." *Bulletin of the John Rylands Library* 51 (1968): 11–26.

Barr, J. *Biblical Faith and Natural Theology.* Oxford: Clarendon Press, 1993.

Barrett, P. "Beauty in Physics and Theology." *Journal of Theology for Southern Africa* 94 (1996): 65–78.

Barrow, J., and F. J. Tipler. *The Anthropic Cosmological Principle.* Oxford: Oxford University Press, 1986.

Barrow, J. D. *Theories of Everything: The Quest for Ultimate Explanation.* Oxford: Clarendon, 1991.

Barth, K., and E. Brunner. *Natural Theology.* London: SCM Press, 1947.

Bartholomew, D. J. *God of Chance.* London: SCM Press, 1984.

Basile, B. "Galileo e il teologo 'Copernicano' Paolo Antonio Foscarini." *Rivista di letteratura italiana* 1 (1–983): 63–96.

Bateman, H. "The Transformation of the Electrodynamical Equations." *Proceedings of the London Mathematical Society* 8 (1910): 223–64.

Bateson, W., E. R. Saunders, and R. C. Punnett. "Further Experiments on Inheritance in Sweet Peas and Stocks: Preliminary Account." *Scientific Papers of William Bateson.* Ed. R. C. Punnett. Vol. 2. Cambridge: Cambridge University Press, 1905, pp. 139–41.

Battles, F. L. "God was Accommodating Himself to Human Capacity." *Interpretation* 31 (1977): 19–38.

Bauckham, R. "Moltmann, Jürgen." *The Blackwell Encyclopaedia of Modern Christian Thought.* Ed. A. E. McGrath. Oxford: Blackwell, 1993, pp. 385–8.

Bauckham, R. *Moltmann: Messianic Theology in the Making.* Basingstoke: Marshall Pickering, 1987.

Bauman, Z. *Postmodern Ethics.* Oxford: Blackwell, 1993.

Baur, J. "Theologisches Reden über die Schöpfung: christlich oder vor-christlich?" *Neue Zeitschrift für Systematische Theologie* 28 (1986): 124–38.

Bazer, O. "Schöpfung als Rede an die Kreatur durch die Kreatur." *Evangelische Theologie* 40 (1980): 316–33.

Beardsley, M. *Practical Logic.* New York: Prentice-Hall, 1950.

Bebbington, D. *Evangelicalism in Modern Britain: A History from the 1730s to the 1980s.* London: Hyman, 1989.

Behe, M. J. *Darwin's Black Box: The Biochemical Challenge to Evolution.* New York: Free Press, 1996.

Beier, U. *The Origin of Life and Death: African Creation Myths.* London: Heinemann, 1966.

Benin, S. D. *The Footprints of God: Divine Accommodation in Jewish and Christian Thought.* Albany: State University of New York, 1993.

Bennett, J. *Kant's Dialectic.* Cambridge: Cambridge University Press, 1974.

Bennett, J. A. "The Mechanics' Philosophy and the Mechanical Philosophy." *History of Science* 24 (1986): 1–28.

Berndt, R. M. "Some Aspects of Jaralde Culture, South Australia." *Oceania* 9 (1940): 164–85.

Bernhardt, R. "Ein neuer Lessing? Paul Knitters Theologie der Religionen." *Evangelische Theologie* 49 (1989): 516–28.

Bernstein, J. *Elementary Particles and their Currents.* San Francisco: W. H. Freeman,

1968.

Bernstein, J. *Three Degrees above Zero: Bell Laboratories in the Information Age.* New York: Scribner's, 1984.

Bernstein, J. *The Tenth Dimension: An Informal History of High Energy Physics.* New York: McGraw Hill, 1989.

Bernstein, R. J. *The New Constellation. The Ethical-Political Horizons of Modernity/ Postmodernity.* Cambridge: Polity Press, 1991.

Berry, R. J. *Neo-Darwinism.* London: Edward Arnold, 1982.

Berry, R. J. *God and the Biologist: Faith at the Frontiers of Science.* Leicester: Apollos, 1996.

Beversluis, J. "Reforming the 'Reformed' Objection to Natural Theology." *Faith and Philosophy* 12 (1995): 189–206.

Biagioli, M. *Galileo, Courtier: The Practice of Science in the Culture of Absolutism.* Chicago: University of Chicago Press, 1993.

Bird, P. A. "'Male and Female He Created Them': Genesis 1.27b in the Context of the Priestly Account of Creation." *Harvard Theological Review* 74 (1981): 129–59.

Black, M. "Self-Supporting Inductive Arguments." *Journal of Philosophy* 55 (1958): 718–25.

Blackwell, R. J. *Galileo, Bellarmine and the Bible.* Notre Dame, IN: University of Notre Dame Press, 1991.

Blaisdell, M. "Natural Theology and Nature's Disguises." *Journal of the History of Biology* 15 (1982): 163–89.

Bohm, D. *On Dialogue.* London: Routledge, 1996.

Bohr, N. *Niels Bohr: Collected Works.* Ed. Leon Rosenfield and Erik Rudiger. 6 vols. Amsterdam: North Holland, 1972–85.

Bohr, N. *The Philosophical Writings of Niels Bohr.* 3 vols. Woodbridge, CT: Ox Bow Press, 1987.

Born, M. *Einstein's Theory of Relativity.* New York: Dover Publications, 1965.

Bouma-Prediger, S. "Creation as the Home of God: The Doctrine of Creation in the Theology of Jürgen Moltmann." *Calvin Theological Journal* 32 (1997): 72–90.

Boyd, R. "Realism, Underdetermination, and a Causal Theory of Evidence." *Nous* 7 (1973): 1–12.

Boyd, R. "The Current Status of Scientific Realism." *Scientific Realism.* Ed. Jarrett Leplin. Berkeley: University of California Press, 1984, pp. 41–82.

Boyle, R. *The Works of the Honourable Robert Boyle.* Ed. Thomas Birch. 2nd edn, 6 vols. London: Rivingtons, 1772.

Bradley, J. "Across the River and Beyond the Trees: Feuerbach's Relevance to Modern Theology." *New Studies in Theology.* Ed. S. W. Sykes and D. Holmes. London: Duckworth, 1980, pp. 139–52.

Branley, F. M. *The Electromagnetic Spectrum.* New York: Crowell, 1979.

Brereton, M. G. "Symmetry in Physics." *Physics Bulletin* 25 (1974): 95–9.

Broberg, G. *Homo Sapiens: L. Studier i Carl von Linnés naturuppfatining och människolära.* Uppsala: Almqvist & Wiksell, 1975.

Brockliss, L. W. B. "Aristotle, Descartes and the New Science: Natural Philosophy at the University of Paris, 1600–1740." *Annals of Science* 38 (1981): 33–69.

Brody, N., and P. Oppenheim. "The Application of Bohr's Principle of Complementarity to the Mind-Body Problem." *Journal of Philosophy* 66 (1969): 97–113.

Brooke, G. J. "Creation in the Biblical Tradition." *Zygon* 22 (1987): 227–48.

"Brooke, J. H. "Science and the Fortunes of Natural Theology: Some Historical Perspectives." *Zygon* 24 (1989): 3–22.

Brooke, J. H. *Science and Religion: Some Historical Perspectives.* Cambridge and New York: Cambridge University Press, 1991a.

Brooke, J. H. *Telling the Story of Science and Religion: A Nuanced Account.* Cambridge: Cambridge University Press, 1991b.

Brotóus, V. N. "The Reception of Copernicus in Sixteenth-Century Spain: The Case of Diego de Zúñiga." *Isis* 86 (1995): 52–78.

Brown, H. "Alvin Plantinga and Natural Theology." *International Journal for Philosophy of Religion* 30 (1991): 1–19.

Brown, J. R. *The Laboratory of the Mind: Thought Experiments in the Natural Sciences.* London: Routledge, 1991.

Bruce, S., ed. *Religion and Modernization: Sociologists and Historians Debate the Secularization Thesis.* Oxford: Clarendon Press, 1992.

Brun, R. B. "Integrating Evolution: A Contribution to the Christian Doctrine of Creation." *Zygon* 29 (1994): 275–96.

Buchdahl, G. "History of Science and Criteria of Choice." *Minnesota Studies in the Philosophy of Science.* Ed. Roger H. Steuwer. Vol. 5. Minneapolis: University of Minnesota Press, 1970, pp. 204–30.

Bunge, M. "Analogy in Quantum Theory: From Insight to Nonsense." *British Journal for the Philosophy of Science* 18 (1967): 265–86.

Bunge, M. *Method, Model, and Matter.* Dordrecht, Holland: D. Reidel, 1973.

Burgess, A. J. "Irreducible Religious Metaphors." *Religious Studies* 8 (1972): 355–66.

Burnyeat, M. F. "Idealism and Greek Philosophy: What Descartes saw and Berkeley missed." *Idealism Past and Present.* Ed. G. Vesey. Cambridge: Cambridge University Press, 1982, pp. 19–50.

Burrell, D. *Analogy and Philosophical Language.* New Haven, CT: Yale University Press, 1973.

Butler, D. "God's Visible Glory: The Beauty of Nature in the Thought of John Calvin and Jonathan Edwards." *Westminster Theological Journal* 52 (1990): 13–26.

Byrne, P. A. *Natural Religion and the Nature of Religion.* London: Routledge, 1989.

Cairns, D. "Thomas Chalmer's Astronomical Discourses: A Study in Natural Theology." *Scottish Journal of Theology,* 9 (1956): 410–21.

Calinescu, M. *Five Faces of Modernity.* Durham, NC: Duke University Press, 1987.

Cameron, E. *The European Reformation.* Oxford: Oxford University Press, 1991.

Canguilhem, G. *Etudes d'histoire et de philosophie des sciences.* Paris: Vrin, 1968.

Cannon, S. F. *Science in Culture: The Early Victorian Period.* New York: Science History Publications, 1978.

Cantor, G. "The Reception of the Wave Theory of Light in Britain: A Case Study Illustrating the Role of Methodology in Scientific Debate." *Historical Studies in the Physical Sciences* 6 (1975): 109–32.

Capra, F. *The Tao of Physics: An Exploration of the Parallels between Modern Physics and Eastern Mysticism.* 3rd edn. London: Flamingo, 1992.

Caroti, S. "Un sostenitore napoletano della mobilità della terra: Il padre Paolo Antonio Foscarini." *Galileo e Napoli.* Eds. Fabrizio Lomonaco and Maurizio Torrini. Naples: Guida, 1987. 81–121.

Carr, B. J., and M. J. Rees. "The Anthropic Principle and the Structure of the Physical World." *Nature* 278 (1979): 605–12.

Carritt, E. F. *The Theory of Beauty.* 6th edn. London: Methuen, 1962.

Carroll, J. "The Humean Tradition." *Philosophical Review* 99 (1990): 185–219.

Carroll, J. W. *Laws of Nature.* Cambridge: Cambridge University Press, 1994.

Carroll, W. E. "San Tommaso, Aristotele e la creazione." *Annales Theologici* 8 (1994): 363–76.

Cartwright, N. *How the Laws of Physics lie.* Oxford: Clarendon Press, 1983.

Cassirer, E. *The Philosophy of the Enlightenment.* Princeton, NJ: Princeton University Press, 1951.

Castle, W. E. "Mendel's Law of Heredity." *Science* 18 (1903): 396–406.

Chadwick, H. *Early Christian Thought and the Classical Tradition.* Oxford: Clarendon, 1966.

Chadwick, O. *From Bossuet to Newman: The Idea of Doctrinal Development.* Cambridge: Cambridge University Press, 1957.

Chadwick, O. *The Secularization of the European Mind in the Nineteenth Century.* Cambridge and New York: Cambridge University Press, 1975.

Chalmers, A. F. "Curie's Principle." *British Journal for the Philosophy of Science* 21 (1970): 133–48.

Chandler, S. "When the World Falls Apart: Methodology for Employing Chaos and Emptiness as Theological Constructs." *Harvard Theological Review* 85 (1992): 467–91.

Chiste, W. "Sola ratione: Zur Begrundung der Methodus der intellectus fide bei Anselm von Canterbury." *Theologie und Philosophie* 60 (1985): 341–75.

Chitnis, A. C. *The Scottish Enlightenment.* London: Croom Helm, 1976.

Churchland, P. M. *Scientific Realism and the Plasticity of Mind.* Cambridge: Cambridge University Press, 1979.

Clark, S. R. L. "The Possible Truth of Metaphor." *International Journal of Philosophical Studies* 2 (1994): 19–30.

Clarke, B. L. "Natural Theology and Methodology." *New Scholasticism* 57 (1983): 233–52.

Clarke, M. L. *Paley: Evidences for the Man.* London: SPCK, 1974.

Clarke, P. B., and P. Byrne. *Religion Defined and Explained.* London: St. Martin's Press, 1993.

Clayton, P. *Explanation from Physics to Theology: An Essay in Rationality and Religion.* New Haven, CT: Yale University Press, 1989.

Clifford, R. J. "Cosmogonies in the Ugaritic Texts and in the Bible." *Orientalia* 53 (1984): 183–201.

Cobb, J. *Is it too late? A Theology of Ecology.* Beverly Hills: Bruce Books, 1972.

Cobb, J. B. *Sustainability: Economics, Ecology, and Justice.* Maryknoll: Orbis, 1992.

Cock, A. G. "William Bateson's Rejection and Eventual Acceptance of Chromosome Theory." *Annals of Science* 40 (1983): 19–60.

Coleman, W. "Bateson and Chromosomes: Conservative Thought in Science." *Centaurus*

15 (1970): 228–314.

Collins, H. M. *Changing Order: Replication and Induction in Scientific Practice.* Beverly Hills: Sage, 1985.

Condon, E. U., and G. Shortley. *The Theory of Atomic Spectra.* Cambridge: Cambridge University Press, 1964.

Connor, S. *Postmodernist Culture: An Introduction to Theories of the Contemporary.* Oxford: Blackwell, 1989.

Cooper, B. *Action into Nature: an Essay on the Meaning of Technology.* Notre Dame: University of Notre Dame Press, 1991.

Corr, C. A. "The Existence of God, Natural Theology and Christian Wolff." *International Journal for Philosophy of Religion* 4 (1973): 105–18.

Correns, C. "G. Mendels Regel über das Verhalten der Nachkommenschaft der Rassenbastarde." *Berichte der deutschen botanischen Gesellschaft* 18 (1900): 158–68.

Cotton, F. A. *Chemical Applications of Group Theory.* New York: Wiley, 1990.

Coulson, C. A. *Science and Christian Belief.* Oxford: Oxford University Press, 1955.

Coulson, C. A. "Fact and Fiction in Physics." *Bucknell Review* 9 (1960): 1–14.

Cowan, R. D. *The Theory of Atomic Structure and Spectra.* Berkeley, CA: University of California Press, 1981.

Craig, W. L. *The Cosmological Argument from Plato to Leibniz.* London: Macmillan, 1980.

Craig, W. L. "Barrow and Tipler on the Anthropic Principle vs. Divine Design." *British Journal for Philosophy of Science* 38 (1988): 389–95.

Craig, W. L. "What Place, Then, for a Creator? Hawking on God and Creation." *British Journal for Philosophy of Science* 41 (1990): 473–91.

Craig, W. L. "Theism and Big Bang Cosmology." *Australasian Journal of Philosophy* 69 (1991): 492–503.

Craig, W. L. "The Origin and Creation of the Universe: A Reply to Adolf Grünbaum. *British Journal for the Philosophy of Science* 43 (1992): 233–40.

Craig, W. L. "The Caused Beginning of the Universe: A Response to Quentin Smith." *British Journal for the Philosophy of Science* 44 (1993): 623–39.

Craig, W. L. "Creation and Big Bang Cosmology." *Philosophia Naturalis* 31 (1994): 217–24.

Craig, W. L. "Timelessness and Creation." *Australasian Journal of Philosophy* 74 (1996): 646–56.

Creel, R. E. *Divine Impassibility: An Essay in Philosophical Theology.* Cambridge: Cambridge University Press, 1986.

Crombie, I. M. "Theology and Falsification." *New Essays in Philosophical Theology.* Ed. Anthony Flew and Alasdair MacIntyre. London: SCM Press, 1955, pp. 109–30.

Crook, S. *Modernist Radicalism and its Aftermath: Foundationalism and Anti-foundationalism in Radical Social Theory.* London: Routledge, 1991.

Crutchfield, J. P., et al. "Chaos." *Scientific American* 255 (1986): 46–57.

Cunningham, E. "The Principle of Relativity in Electrodynamics and an Extension Thereof." *Proceedings of the London Mathematical Society* 8 (1909): 77–98.

Cupitt, D. *Taking Leave of God.* London: SCM Press, 1980.

Cupitt, D. *Only Human.* London: SCM Press, 1985.

Cupitt, D. *Radicals and the Future of the Church.* London: SCM Press, 1989.

Curie, P. "Symétrie dans les phénomènes physiques." *Journal de physique* 3 (1894): 393–415.

Cushing, J. T. "Electromagnetic Mass, Relativity and the Kaufmann Experiments." *American Journal of Physics* 49 (1981): 1133–49.

Czapkay Sudduth, M. L. "Alstonian Foundationalism and Higher-Level Theistic Evidentialism." *International Journalfor Philosophy of Religion* 37 (1995a): 25–44.

Czapkay Sudduth, M. L. "The Prospects for 'Mediate' Natural Theology in John Calvin." *Religious Studies* 31 (1995b): 53–68.

Dalley, S. *Myths from Mesopotamia: Creation, the Flood, Gilgamesh and Others.* New York: Oxford University Press, 1989.

Darden, L. "William Bateson and the Promise of Mendelism." *Journal of the History of Biology* 10 (1977): 87–106.

Darden, L. *Theory Change in Science: Strategies from Mendelian Genetics.* Oxford: Oxford University Press, 1991.

Darwin, C. *The Origin of Species.* Harmondsworth: Penguin, 1968

Darwin, F. *The Life and Letters of Charles Darwin.* 3 vols. London: John Murray, 1887.

Darwin, F., and A. C. Seward. *More Letters of Charles Darwin.* 2 vols. London: John Murray, 1903.

Davies, B. *The Thought of Thomas Aquinas.* Oxford: Clarendon Press, 1992.

Davies, P. *God and the New Physics.* New York: Penguin, 1984.

Davies, P. *The Mind of God: Science and the Search for Ultimate Meaning.* London: Penguin, 1992.

Davis, E. B. "Fundamentalism and Folk Science Between the Wars." *Religion and American Culture* 5 (1995): 217–48.

Dawkins, R. *The Blind Watchmaker: why the Evidence of Evolution reveals a Universe without Design.* New York: W. W. Norton, 1986.

Dawkins, R. *The Selfish Gene.* Oxford and New York: Oxford University Press, 1989.

Dawkins, R. "Is Science a Religion?" *The Humanist* January/February (1997): 26–39.

Day, J. *God's Conflict with the Dragon: Echoes of a Canaanite Myth in the Old Testament.* Cambridge: Cambridge University Press, 1985.

de Kreef, B., et al. "Lipid Asymmetry, Clustering and Molecular Motion in Biological Membranes and Their Models." *Nobel Foundation Symposium: Biological Membranes and Their Models.* Ed. S. Abrahamsson and I. Pascher. New York: Plenum Press, 1977, pp. 389–407.

de Marsais, C. C., and C. l'Abbé Yvon. "Analogie." *Encyclopédie; ou Dictionnaire raisoné des sciences, des arts et des métiers.* Ed. Denis Diderot and Jean Le Rond d'Alembert. Vol. 1. Paris: Briasson, David Le Breton, Durand, 1751, pp. 399–400.

de Vleeschauwer, H. J. "Wie Ich jetzt die Kritik der reinen Vernunft entwicklungsgeschichtlich lese." *Kant-Studien* 54 (1962): 351–68.

Delattre, R. *Beauty and Sensibility in the Thought of Jonathan Edwards.* New Haven, CT: Yale University Press, 1968.

Dennett, D. C. *Darwin's Dangerous Idea: Evolution and the Meaning of Life.* New York: Simon & Schuster, 1995.

Deroche, M. "Isaiah 45:7 and the Creation of Chaos." *Vetus Testamentum* 42 (1992): 11–21.

Deutsch, D. "Quantum Theory, the Church-Turing Principle, and the Universal Quantum Computer." *Proceedings of the Royal Society of London A* 400 (1985): 97–117.

Devine, P. E. "On the Definition of 'Religion'." *Faith and Philosophy* 3 (1986): 270–284.

Devitt, M. *Realism and Truth.* Oxford: Blackwell, 1984.

DeWitt, C. B. "Ecology and Ethics: Relation of Religious Belief to Ecological Practice in the Biblical Tradition." *Biodiversity and Conservation* 4 (1995): 838–48.

Diacu, F., and P. Holmes. *Celestial Encounters.* Princeton, NJ: Princeton University Press, 1997.

Dirac, P. "The Evolution of the Physicist's Picture of Nature." *Scientific American* 208. (5) (1963): 45–53.

Dolby, R. G. A. "Science and Pseudo-Science: The Case of Creationism." *Zygon* 22 (1987): 195–212.

Doore, G. "The Argument from Design: Some Better Reasons for Agreeing with Hume." *Religious Studies* 16 (1980): 145–61.

Dörrie, H. "Emanation: Ein unphilosophisches Wort in spätantiken Denken." *Parusia: Studien zur Philosophie Platons und zur Problemgeschichte des Platonismus.* Ed. J. Hirschberger and K. Flasch. Frankfurt am Main: Minerva, 1965, pp. 119–41.

Dowey, E. A. *The Knowledge of God in Calvin's Theology.* New York: Columbia University Press, 1952.

Draper, J. W. *History of the Conflict between Religion and Science.* New York: Daniel Appleton, 1874.

Draper, P. "Pain and Pleasure: An Evidential Problem for Theists." *Nous* 23 (1989): 331–50.

Drees, W. B. *Beyond the Big Bang Quantum Cosmologies and God.* La Salle: Open Court, 1990.

Dretske, F. I. "Laws of Nature." *Philosophy of Science* 44 (1977): 248–68.

Duce, P. P. "Complementarity in Perspective." *Science and Christian Belief* 8 (1996): 145–55.

Duhem, P. *The Aim and Structure of Physical Theory.* Princeton, NJ: Princeton University Press, 1954.

Dulles, A. *Models of Revelation.* Dublin: Gill & Macmillan, 1983.

Dummett, M. *Truth and Other Enigmas.* London: Duckworth, 1978.

Dyson, F. "The Scientist as Rebel." *Nature's Imagination: The Frontiers of Scientific Vision.* Ed. John Cornwell. Oxford: Oxford University Press, 1995. 1–11.

Eagleton, T. *The Illusions of Postmodernism.* Oxford: Blackwell, 1996.

Eco, U. *The Aesthetics of Thomas Aquinas.* London: Radius, 1988.

Edwards, J. *The Images of Divine Things.* Ed. Perry Millar. New Haven, CT: Yale University Press, 1948.

Edwards, P. "Russell's Doubts about Induction." *Mind* 68 (1949): 141–63.

Ehrhardt, A. *The Beginning: A Study in the Greek Philosophical Approach to the Concept of Creation from Anaximander to St John.* Manchester: Manchester University Press, 1968.

Einstein, A. "Zur Elektrodynamik bewegter Körper." *Annalen der Physik* 17 (1905): 891–921.

Einstein, A., B. Podolsky, and N. Rosen. "Can Quantum-Mechanical Description of

Physical Reality be Considered Complete?" *Physical Review* 47 (1935): 777–80.

Eiseley, L. *The Firmament of Time.* New York: Athenaeum Press, 1985.

Elders, L. *The Philosophy of Nature of St Thomas Aquinas.* Frankfurt am Main: Peter Lang, 1997.

Ellegerd, A. *Darwin and the General Reader: The Reception of Darwin's Theory of Evolution on the British Periodical Press, 1859–1872.* Gothenburg: Acta Universitatis Gothenburgensis, 1958.

Erdoes, R., and A. Ortiz. *American Indian Myths and Legends.* New York: Pantheon, 1984.

Evans, G. R. *The Language and Logic of the Bible: The Earlier Middle Ages.* Cambridge: Cambridge University Press, 1984.

Evans, L. T. "Darwin's Use of the Analogy between Artificial and Natural Selection." *Journal of the History of Biology* 17 (1984): 113–40.

Evans-Pritchard, E. E. *Theories of Primitive Religion.* Oxford: Clarendon Press, 1965.

Fairlamb, H. L. *Critical Conditions: Postmodernity and the Question of Foundations.* Cambridge: Cambridge University Press, 1994.

Fales, E. "Plantinga's Case against Naturalistic Epistemology." *Philosophy of Science* 63 (1996): 432–51.

Fantino, J. *La théologie d'Irénée: lecture des écritures en response à l'exégèse gnostique.* Paris: Editions du Cerf, 1994.

Fantino, J. "La rencontre entre science et théologie." *Revue des sciences religieuses* 71 (1997): 60–78.

Faye, J. *Niels Bohr: His Heritage and Legacy. An Anti-Realist View of Quantum Mechanics.* Dordrecht: Kluwer, 1991.

Ferguson, K. *Stephen Hawking: Quest for a Theory of Everything.* New York: Bantam Books, 1991.

Fermi, E. "Tentativo di una theoria dell'emissione dei raggi 'beta'." *Ricerca Scientifica* 4 (1933): 491–5.

Ferre, F. *Hellfire and Lightning Rods: Liberating Science, Technology, and Religion.* Maryknoll: Orbis, 1993.

Fester, R., and L. Margulis, eds. *Symbiosis as a Source of Evolutionary Innovation: Speciation and Morphogenesis.* Cambridge, MA: MIT Press, 1991.

Feuerbach, L. *Gesammelte Werke.* Ed. W. Schuffenhauer. Berlin: Akademie Verlag, 1973.

Fiddes, P. *The Creative Suffering of God.* Oxford: Clarendon Press, 1988.

Fiddes, P. "Process Theology." *The Blackwell Encyclopaedia of Modern Christian Thought.* Ed. A. E. McGrath. Oxford: Blackwell, 1993. 47–76.

Fine, A. "The Natural Ontological Attitude." *Scientific Realism.* Ed. J. Leplin. Berkeley, CA: University of California Press, 1984, pp. 83–107.

Fine, A. *The Shaky Game: Einstein, Realism and the Quantum Theory.* Chicago: University of Chicago Press, 1986a.

Fine, A. "Unnatural Attitudes: Realist and Instrumentalist Attachments to Science." *Mind* 95 (1986b): 149–79.

Fisch, H. "The Scientist as Priest: A Note on Robert Boyle's Natural Theology." *Isis* 44 (1953): 252–65.

Fishbane, M. "Jeremiah 4.:23–26 and Job 3:3–13: A Recovered Use of the Creation Pattern." *Vetus Testamentum* 21 (1971): 151–67.

Fitzpatrick, F. J. "The Onus of Proof in Arguments about the Problem of Evil." *Religious Studies* 17 (1981): 19–38.

Flavell, J. H. *The Developmental Psychology of Jean Piaget.* New York: Van Nostrand, 1963.

Fock, V. "Zur Theorie des Wasserstoffatoms." *Zeitschrift für Physik* 98 (1935): 145–54.

Fodor, J. "Observation reconsidered." *Philosophy of Science* 51 (1984): 23–43.

Fodor, J. *Christian Hermeneutics: Paul Ricoeur and the Refiguring of Theology.* Oxford: Clarendon Press, 1995.

Folse, H. *The Philosophy of Niels Bohr: The Framework of Complementarity.* Amsterdam: North Holland, 1985.

Folsing, A. *Albert Einstein: A Biography.* New York: Viking Books, 1997.

Force, J. E. *William Whiston: Honest Newtonian.* Cambridge: Cambridge University Press, 1985.

Ford, L. S. "An Alternative to *Creatio ex Nihilo.*" *Religious Studies* 17 (1981): 205–13.

Ford, L. S. "Contrasting Conceptions of Creation." *Review of Metaphysics* 45 (1991): 89–109.

Foster, M. B. "The Christian doctrine of Creation and the Rise of Modern Science." *Mind* 43 (1934): 446–68.

Fraassen, B. C. v. "The Pragmatics of Explanation." *American Philosophical Quarterly* 14 (1977): 143–50.

Fraassen, B. C. v. *The Scientific Image.* Oxford: Oxford University Press, 1980.

Fraassen, B. C. v. "Glymour on Evidence and Explanation." *Minnesota Studies in the Philosophy of Science* 10 (1983): 165–76.

Fraassen, B. C. v. *Laws and Symmetry.* Oxford: Clarendon Press, 1989.

Fraassen, B. v. "Empiricism in the Philosophy of Science." *Images of Science: Essays on Realism and Empiricism.* Ed. P. Churchland and C. Hooker. Chicago: University of Chicago Press, 1985, pp. 245–308.

Frängsmyr, T. *Geologi och skapelsetro: Föreställningar om jordens historia från Hiärne till Bergman.* Stockholm: Almqvist & Wiksell, 1969.

Frank, P. *Modern Philosophy and Its Science.* Cambridge, MA: Harvard University Press, 1941.

Frank, P. "Einstein's Philosophy of Science." *Reviews of Modern Physics* 21 (1949): 349–55.

Frankenberry, N. "Functionalism, Fallibilism and Anti-Foundationalism in Wieman's Empirical Theism." *Zygon* 22 (1987): 37–47.

Franklin, A. *The Neglect of Experiment.* Cambridge: Cambridge University Press, 1986.

Franklin, A. "Experimental Questions." *Perspectives on Science* 1 (1993): 127–146.

Fraser, H. *Beauty and Belief: Aesthetics and Religion in Victorian Literature.* Cambridge: Cambridge University Press, 1986.

Friedman, A. "Über die Krummung des Raumes." *Zeitschrift für Physik* 10 (1922): 377–86.

Friedman, M. "Explanation and Scientific Understanding." *Journal of Philosophy* 71 (1974): 5–19.

Fuller, S. *Philosophy of Science and its Discontents.* Boulder: Westview Press, 1989.

228

Bibliography

Galison, P. *How Experiments End.* Chicago: University of Chicago Press, 1987.

Galison, P. "Philosophy in the Laboratory." *Journal of Philosophy* 85 (1988): 525–7.

Galison, P. L. "Context and Constraints." *Scientific Practice: Theories and Stories of Doing Physics.* Ed. Jed Z. Buchwald. Chicago: University of Chicago Press, 1995, pp. 13–41.

Gardner, M. "HWAP, SAP, FAP and PAP." *New York Review of Books 33* (1987): 22–5.

Gascoigne, J. "From Bentley to the Victorians: The Rise and Fall of British Newtonian Natural Theology." *Science in Context* 2 (1988): 219–56.

Gascoigne, J. *Cambridge in the Age of the Enlightenment: Science, Religion and Politics from the Restoration to the French Revolution.* Cambridge and New York: Cambridge University Press, 1989.

Gaskin, J. C. A. "The Design Argument: Hume's Critique of Poor Reason." *Religious Studies* 12 (1976): 331–45.

Gates, S. J., et al. *Superspace: One Thousand and One Lessons in Supersymmetry.* Reading, MA: Benjamin & Cummins, 1983.

Gatewood, W. B. "From Scopes to Creation Science: The Decline and Revival of the Evolution Controversy." *South Atlantic Quarterly* 83 (1984): 363–83.

Gay, P. *Deism.* Princeton, NJ: van Nostrand, 1968.

Geertz, C. "Common Sense as a Cultural System." *Local Knowledge: Further Essays in Interpretative Anthropology.* Ed. Clifford Geertz. New York: Basic Books, 1983, pp. 73–93.

Gehrke, H. "Kosmos und Schöpfung: Erich Heintels Aneignung des Schöpfungsgedankens." *Neue Zeitschrift für Systematische Theologie* 35 (1993): 71–84.

Gibbins, P. *Particles and Paradoxes.* Cambridge: Cambridge University Press, 1987.

Gieryn, T. F. "Distancing Science from Religion in Seventeenth-Century England." *Isis* 79 (1988): 582–93.

Gilbert, G. N., and M. Mulkay. "Warranting Scientific Belief." *Social Studies of Science* 12 (1982): 383–408.

Gilbert, J. "Burhoe and Shapley: A Complementarity of Science and Religion." *Zygon* 30 (1995): 531–9.

Gilkey, L. *Maker of Heaven and Earth: the Christian Doctrine of Creation in the Light of Modern Knowledge.* Garden City: Doubleday, 1959.

Gilkey, L. *Creationism on Trial.* San Francisco: HarperCollins, 1985.

Gilkey, L. "Nature, Reality and the Sacred: A Meditation in Science and Religion." *Zygon* 24 (1989): 283–98.

Gill, J. H. *Ian Ramsey: To Speak Responsibly of God.* London: Allen & Unwin, 1976.

Gill, J. H. "Kant, Analogy and Natural Theology." *International Journal for Philosophy of Religion* 16 (1984): 19–28.

Gillespie, N. C. "Divine Design and the Industrial Revolution: William Paley's Abortive Reform of Natural Theology." *Isis* 81 (1990): 214–29.

Gillies, D. *Philosophy of Science in the Twentieth Century: Four Central Themes.* Oxford/Cambridge, MA: Blackwell, 1993.

Gilson, E. *History of Christian Philosophy in the Middle Ages.* London: Sheed and Ward, 1978.

Gingerich, O. "Is there a Role for Natural Theology Today?" *Science and Theology:*

Questions at the Interface. Ed. M. Rae, H. Regan, and J. Stenhouse. Edinburgh: T. & T. Clark, 1994, pp. 29–48.

Ginsburg, H., and S. Opper. *Piaget's Theory of Intellectual Development.* Englewood Cliffs, NJ: Prentice-Hall, 1979.

Gleick, J. *Chaos: Making a New Science.* New York: Penguin Books, 1987.

Glymour, C. *Theory and Evidence.* Princeton, NJ: Princeton University Press, 1980b.

Glymour, C. "Explanations, Tests, Unity and Necessity." *Nous* 14 (1980a): 31–50.

Godlove, T. F. *Religion, Interpretation and Diversity of Belief: The Framework Model from Kant to Durkheim to Davidson.* Cambridge: Cambridge University Press, 1989.

Goldberg, S. "The Abraham Theory of the Electron: The Symbiosis of Experiment and Theory." *Archive for History of Exact Sciences* 7 (1970): 7–25.

Golinski, J. "The Theory of Practice and the Practice of Theory: Sociological Approaches in the History of Science." *Isis* 81 (1990): 492–505.

Gombrich, E. H. *"Icones Symbolicae:* The Visual Image in Neoplatonic Thought." *Journal of the Courtauld and Warburg Institutes* 11 (1948): 163–92.

Gooding, D., T. Pinch, and S. Schaffer. *The Uses of Experiment: Studies in the Natural Sciences.* Cambridge. Cambridge University Press, 1989.

Gower, B. *Scientific Method: An Historical and Philosophical Inquiry.* London/New York: Routledge, 1997.

Grant, E. *Planets, Stars and Orbs: The Medieval Cosmos, 1200-1687.* Cambridge: Cambridge University Press, 1996.

Greenacre, G. "Two Aspects of Reception." *Christian Authority.* Ed. Gillian R. Evans. Oxford: Clarendon Press, 1988, pp. 40–58.

Greenwood, J. D. "Two Dogmas of Neo-Empiricism: The 'Theory-Informity' of Observation and the Duhem-Quine Thesis." *Philosophy of Science* 57 (1990): 553–74.

Gregory, F. *Nature Lost? Natural Science and the German Theological Traditions of the Nineteenth Century.* Cambridge, MA: Harvard University Press, 1992.

Griffin, D. R. *The Reenchantment of Science: Postmodern Proposals.* Albany: State University of New York Press, 1989.

Grillmeier, A. *Christ in Christian Tradition.* 2nd edn. London: Mowbrays, 1975.

Grislis, E. "Calvin's Use of Cicero in the *Institutes* I:1–5: A Case Study in Theological Method." *Archiv für Reformationsgeschichte* 62 (1971): 5–37.

Grube, D.-M. "Religious Experience after the Demise of Foundationalism." *Religious Studies* 31 (1995): 37–52.

Grünbaum, A. "The Duhemian Argument." *Philosophy of Science* 27 (1960): 75–87.

Grünbaum, A. "Is Falsifiability the Touchstone of Scientific Rationality? Karl Popper versus Inductivism." *Essays in Memory of Imre Lakatos.* Ed. R. S. Cohen. Dordrecht: Reidel, 1976, pp. 213–52.

Grünbaum, A. "The Pseudo-Problem of Creation in Physical Cosmology." *Epistemologia* 12 (1989): 3–32.

Grünbaum, A. "Narlikar's 'Creation' of the Big Bang Universe was a Mere Origination." *Philosophy of Science* 60 (1993): 638–46.

Guardini, R. *Letters from Lake Como: Explorations in Technology and the Human Race.* Grand Rapids, MI: Eerdmans, 1994.

Guerlac, H. "Theological Voluntarism and Biological Analogies in Newton's Physical Thought." *Journal of the History of Ideas* 44 (1983): 219–30.

Gunton, C. E. *A Brief Theology of Revelation*. Edinburgh: T. & T. Clark, 1995.

Hacking, I. *The Emergence of Probability: a Philosophical Study of Early Ideas about Probability, Induction and Statistical Inference*. Cambridge: Cambridge University Press, 1975.

Hacking, I. *Representing and Intervening: Introductory Topics in the Philosophy of Natural Science*. Cambridge: Cambridge University Press, 1983.

Hahn, R. "LaPlace and the Vanishing Role of God in the Physical Universe." *The Analytic Spirit*. Ed. Harry Woolf. Ithaca, NY: Cornell University Press, 1981. 85–95.

Hall, A. R. *Isaac Newton: Adventurer in Thought*. Cambridge: Cambridge University Press, 1996.

Hall, D. J. *Imaging God: Dominion as Stewardship*. Grand Rapids: Eerdmans, 1986.

Hamilton, V. *In the Beginning: Creation Stories from around the World*. New York: Harcourt Brace Jovanovich, 1988.

Hanson, N. R. *Patterns of Discovery: An Inquiry into the Conceptual Foundations of Science*. Cambridge: Cambridge University Press, 1961.

Hanson, H. R. *The Concept of the Positron*. Cambridge: Cambridge University Press, 1963.

Hanson, N. R. "A Picture Theory of Theory-Meaning." *What I do not Believe*. Ed. Stephen Toulmin and Harry Woolf. Dordrecht: D. Reidel, 1971. 4–49.

Harman, G. "The Inference to the Best Explanation." *Philosophical Review* 74 (1965): 88–95.

Harré, R. *Varieties of Realism: A Rationale for the Natural Sciences*. Oxford: Basil Blackwell, 1986.

Harré, R. *Laws of Nature*. London: Duckworth, 1993.

Harris, E. *Cosmos as Anthropos: A Philosophical Interpretation of the Anthropic Cosmological Principle*. New Jersey: Humanities Press, 1990.

Harrison, P. *'Religion' and the Religions in the English Enlightenment*. Cambridge: Cambridge University Press, 1990.

Harvey, D. *The Condition of Postmodernity. An Enquiry into the Origins of Cultural Change*. Oxford: Blackwell, 1989.

Hassan, I. *The Dismemberment of Orpheus: Toward a Postmodern Literature*. New York: Oxford University Press, 1982.

Hawking, S. *A Brief History of Time: From the Big Bang to Black Holes*. New York: Bantam Books, 1988.

Hawking, S. "Letters to the Editor: Time and the Universe." *American Scientist* 73 (1985): 12.

Hefner, P. "God and Chaos: the Demiurge versus the *Urgrund*." *Zygon* 19 (1984): 469–85.

Heimann, P. M. "Nature is a Perpetual Worker: Newton's Aether and Eighteenth-Century Natural Philosophy." *Ambix* 20 (1973): 2–24.

Heisenberg, W. *Physics and Beyond: Encounters and Conversations*. New York: Harper & Row, 1971.

Hempel, C. G. *Aspects of Scientific Explanation*. New York: Free Press, 1965.

Hempel, C. G., and P. Oppenheim. "Studies in the Logic of Explanation." *Readings in the Philosophy of Science.* Ed. B. A. Brody. Englewoods Cliffs, NJ: Prentice-Hall, 1970, pp. 8–27.

Hensley, J. "Are Postliberals Necessarily Antirealists? Reexamining the Metaphysics of Lindbeck's Postliberal Theology." *The Nature of Confession: Evangelicals and Postliberals in Conversation.* Ed. T. R. Philips and D. L. Okholm. Downers Grove, IL: InterVarsity Press, 1996, pp. 69–80.

Herbert, G. *The Works of George Herbert.* Ed. F. E. Hutchinson. Oxford: Clarendon Press, 1941.

Herrman, S. "Die Naturlehre des Schöpfungsberichtes." *Theologische Literaturzeitung* 6 (1961): 414–24.

Herschel, J. F. W. *Preliminary Discourse on the Study of Natural Philosophy.* London: Longman, Rees, Orme, Brown and Green, 1830.

Hesse, M. *Revolutions and Reconstructions in the Philosophy of Science.* Bloomington, IN: Indiana University Press, 1980.

Hesse, M. B. "Models and Analogy in Science." *Encyclopaedia of Philosophy.* Ed. Paul Edwards. Vol. 5. New York & London: Macmillan, 1967, pp. 354–9.

Hesse, M. B. *The Structure of Scientific Inference.* New York, NY: Macmillan, 1974.

Heyck, T. W. *The Transformation of Intellectual Life in Victorian England.* London: Croom Helm, 1982.

Heyd, M. "Un rôle noveau pour la science: Jean Alphonse Turrettini et les débuts de la théologie naturelle à Genève." *Revue de théologie et philosophie* 112 (1982): 25–42.

Hick, J. *Faith and Knowledge.* Ithaca, NY: Cornell University Press, 1957.

Hick, J. "Theology and Verification." *The Existence of God.* Ed. John Hick. London: Macmillan, 1964, pp. 252–74.

Hick, J. *God and the Universe of Faiths.* London: Macmillan, 1973.

Hiebert, E. "The Genesis of Mach's Early Views on Atomism." *Ernst Mach: Physicist and Philosopher.* Ed. R. Cohen and R. Seeger. Dordrecht: D. Reidel, 1970, pp. 79–106.

Hintikka, J. and G. Sandu. "Metaphor and the Varieties of Lexical Meaning." *Dialectica* 44 (1990): 55–78.

Hirosige, T. "Theory of Relativity and the Ether." *Japanese Studies in the History of Science* 7 (1968): 37–53.

Hirosige, T. "The Ether Problem, the Mechanistic World View, and the Origins of the Theory of Relativity." *Historical Studies in the Physical Sciences* 7 (1976): 3–82.

Hodge, C. *What is Darwinism?* New York: Scribner, Armstrong & Co., 1874.

Hodges, A. *Alan Turing: The Enigma.* London: Vintage, 1992.

Hoesterey, I., ed. *Zeitgeist in Babylon: The Postmodernist Controversy.* Bloomington, IN: Indiana University Press, 1991.

Hoitenga, D. J. *Faith and Reason from Plato to Plantinga: An Introduction to Reformed Epistemology.* Albany, NY: State University of New York Press, 1991.

Holland, J., et al. *Induction: Process of Inference, Learning and Discovery.* Cambridge, MA: MIT Press, 1986.

Hommel, H. "Wahrheit und Gerechtigkeit: Zur Geschichte und Deutung eines Begriffspaars." *Antike und Abendland* 15 (1969): 159–86.

Hon, G. "On Kepler's Awareness of the Problem of Experimental Error." *Annals of Science* 44 (1987): 545–91.

Hon, G. "Towards a Typology of Experimental Error: an Epistemological View." *Studies in History and Philosophy of Science* 20 (1989): 469–504.

Hon, G. "Is the Identification of Experimental Error contexually dependent? The Case of Kaufmann's Experiment and its Varied Reception." *Scientific Practice: Theories and Stories of Doing Physics.* Ed. Jed Z. Buchwald. Chicago: University of Chicago Press, 1995, pp. 170–223.

Hones, M. J. "Reproducibility as a Methodological Imperative in Experimental Research." PSA 1990. Ed. A. Fine, M. Forbes and L. Wessels. Vol. 1. East Lansing: Philosophy of Science Association, 1990. 585–99.

Honner, J. *The Description of Nature: Niels Bohr and the Philosophy of Quantum Physics.* Oxford: Clarendon Press, 1987.

Hooykaas, R. "Science and Reformation." *Journal of World History* 3 (1956): 136–8.

Hooykaas, R. *G. J. Rheticus' Treatise on Holy Scripture and the Motion of the Earth.* Amsterdam: North Holland, 1984.

Hort, F. J. A. *The Way, The Truth, The Life: The Hulsean Lectures for 1871.* Cambridge: Cambridge University Press, 1893.

Howson, C. "The Last Word on Induction." *Erkenntnis* 34 (1991): 73–82.

Hoye, W. J. *Actualitas omnium actuum: Man's Beatific Vision of God as apprehended by Thomas Aquinas.* Meisenheim: Hain, 1975.

Hundert, E. M. *Philosophy, Psychiatry and Neuroscience: Three Approaches to the Mind. A Synthetic Analysis of the Varieties of Human Experience.* Oxford: Clarendon Press, 1989.

Hunt, B. J. "The Origins of the FitzGerald Contraction." *British Journal of the History of Science* 21 (1988): 67–76.

Hutten, E. H. *The Language of Modern Physics: An Introduction to the Philosophy of Science.* London: Allen & Unwin, 1956.

Huxley, T. H. "Biogenesis and Albiogenesis." *Collected Essays.* Ed. T. H. Huxley. Vol. 8. London: Macmillan, 1894, pp. 227–91.

Huyssteen, W. Van. "Experience and Explanation: The Justification of Cognitive Claims in Theology." *Zygon* 23 (1988): 247–61.

Huyssteen, W. Van. *Theology and the Justification of Faith: Constructing Theories in Systematic Theology.* Grand Rapids, MI: Eerdmans, 1989.

Inui, T., Y. Tanabe, and Y. Onodera. *Group Theory and Its Applications in Physics.* New York: Springer, 1990.

Inwagen, P. v. "Genesis and Evolution." *Reasoned Faith: Essays in Philosophical Theology.* Ed. Eleonore Stump. Ithaca, NY: Cornell University Press, 1993, pp. 93–127.

Irvine, W. *Apes, Angels and Victorians: A Joint Biography of Darwin and Huxley.* London: Weidenfield and Nicholson, 1956.

Jacob, J. R., and M. C. Jacob. "The Anglican Origins of Modern Science: The Metaphysical Foundations of the Whig Constitution." *Isis* 71 (1980): 251–67.

Jacob, M. C. *The Newtonians and the English Revolution 1689–1720.* London: Harvester, 1976.

Jaki, S. L. *Lord Gifford and his Lectures.* Edinburgh: Scottish Academic Press, 1986.

Jameson, F. *Postmodernism, or the Cultural Logic of Late Capitalism.* London: Verso,

1992.

Jammer, M. *Concepts of Force: A Study in the Foundations of Dynamics.* Cambridge, MA: Harvard University Press, 1957.

Jammer, M. *Concepts of Mass in Classical and Modern Physics.* Cambridge, MA: Harvard University Press, 1961.

Jammer, M. *The Conceptual Development of Quantum Mechanics.* New York: McGraw-Hill, 1966.

Jammer, M. *The Philosophy of Quantum Mechanics.* New York: John Wiley & Sons Inc., 1974.

Jastrow, R. *God and the Astronomers.* New York: Norton, 1978.

Jauch, J. M., and E. L. Hill. "On the Problem of Degeneracy in Quantum Mechanics." *Physical Review* 57 (1940): 641–5.

Jenson, R. W. *The Triune Identity.* Philadelphia: Fortress, 1982.

Jevons, W. S. *The Principles of Science.* New York: Dover, 1958.

Johnson, G. *Fire in the Mind: Science, Faith and the Search for Order.* New York: Alfred A. Knopf, 1995.

Jones, L. G. "Alasdair MacIntyre on Narrative, Community and the Moral Life." *Modern Theology* 4 (1987): 53–69.

Jones, R. "Realism about What?" *Philosophy of Science* 58 (1991): 185–202.

Jüngel, E. "Von der Dialektik zu Analogie: Die Schule Kierkegaards und der Einspruch Petersons." *Barth Studien.* Ed. Eberhard Jüngel. Zurich: Benziger Verlag, 1982, pp. 127–79.

Jüngel, E. *God as the Mystery of the World.* Edinburgh: T. & T. Clark, 1983.

Kaiser, C. B. "Christology and Complementarity." *Religious Studies* 12 (1976): 37–48.

Kaiser, C. B. "Calvin, Copernicus and Castellio." *Calvin Theological Journal 21* (1986): 5–31.

Kaiser, C. B. "Quantum Complementarity and Christological Dialectic." *Religion and Science: History, Method, Dialogue.* Ed. W. Mark Richardson and Wesley J. Wildman. New York: Routledge, 1996, pp. 291–8.

Kaiser, O. "Dike und Sedaqa. Zur Frage nach der sittlichen Weltordnung." *Neue Zeitschrift für Systematische Theologie und Religionsphilosophie* 7 (1965): 251–75.

Kantorovitch, A., and Y. Ne'eman. "Serendipity as a Source of Evolutionary Progress in Science." *Studies in History and Philosophy of Science* 20 (1989): 505–30.

Kaufmann, W. "Über die Konstitution des Elektrons." *Annalen der Physik 19* (1906): 487–553.

Kellenberg, B. J. "Unstuck from Yale: Theological Method after Lindbeck." *Scottish Journal of Theology* 50 (1997): 191–218.

Kempfi, A. "Tolosani versus Copernicus." *Organon* 16–17 (1980–1): 252.

Kepel, G. *La revanche de Dieu: chrétiens, juifs et musulmans à la reconquête du monde.* Paris: Seuil, 1991.

Kerr, F. "Aesthetic Theory." *The Blackwell Encyclopaedia of Modern Christian Thought.* Ed. A. E. McGrath. Oxford: Blackwell, 1993, pp. 1–2.

Kitcher, P. *Abusing Science: The Case against Creationism.* Cambridge, MA: MIT Press, 1982.

Klauber, M. "Jean-Alphonse Turrettini (1671-1737) on Natural Theology: The Triumph of Reason over Revelation at the Academy of Geneva." *Scottish Journal of Theology* 47 (1994): 301–25.

Kleiner, S. A. "Problem Solving and Discovery in the Growth of Darwin's Theories of Evolution." *Synthese* 62 (1981): 119–62.

Kleiner, S. A. "The Logic of Discovery and Darwin's Pre-Malthusian Researches." *Biology and Philosophy* 3 (1988): 293–315.

Knight, C. "An Authentic Theological Revolution? Scientific Perspectives on the Development of Doctrine." *Journal of Religion* 74 (1994): 524–41.

Knight, D. A. "Cosmogony and Order in the Hebrew Tradition." *Cosmology and Ethical Order: New Studies in Comparative Ethics.* Ed. R. W. Lovin and F. E. Reynolds. Chicago: University of Chicago Press, 1985, pp. 133–57.

Knitter, P. *No Other Name? A Critical Survey of Christian Attitudes Towards the World Religions.* Maryknoll, NY: Orbis, 1985.

Kosso, P. *Observability and Observation in Physical Science.* Dordrecht: Kluwer Academic Publishers, 1989.

Kragh, H. *An Introduction to the Historiography of Science.* New York: Cambridge University Press, 1987.

Kreitzer, L. J. "Eschatology." *Dictionary of Paul and His Letters.* Ed. Gerald F. Hawthorne, Ralph P. Martin, and Daniel G. Reid. Downers Grove, IL: InterVarsity Press, 1993, pp. 253–69.

Kretzmann, N. *The Metaphysics of Theism: Aquinas's Natural Theology in Summa contra Gentiles I.* Oxford: Clarendon Press, 1997.

Krips, H. *The Metaphysics of Quantum Theory.* Oxford: Clarendon Press, 1987.

Kristeller, P. O. *The Philosophy of Marsilio Ficino.* New York: Columbia University Press, 1943.

Kruger, C. B. "The Doctrine of the Knowledge of God in the Theology of Thomas F. Torrance." *Scottish Journal of Theology* 43 (1990): 366–89.

Kuhn, T. *The Structure of Scientific Revolutions.* Chicago: University of Chicago Press, 1962.

Kuhn, T. *Black-Body Radiation and the Quantum Discontinuity.* Oxford: Clarendon Press, 1978.

Kuhn, T. S. *The Structure of Scientific Revolutions.* 2nd edn. Chicago: University of Chicago Press, 1970.

Küng, H. *Freud and the Problem of God.* New Haven, CT: Yale University Press, 1979.

Küng, H. *Does God Exist?* London: Collins, 1980.

Lafferty, P., and J. Rowe. "Science." *The Hutchinson Dictionary of Science.* Ed. Peter Lafferty and Julian Rowe. Oxford: Helicon, 1993, pp. 523–4.

Lange, M. "Armstrong and Dretske on the Explanatory Power of Regularities." *Analysis* 52 (1992): 154–9.

Langford, J. R. "Science, Theology and Freedom: A New Look at the Galileo Case." *On Freedom.* Ed. Leroy S. Rouner. Notre Dame, IN: University of Notre Dame Press, 1989, pp. 108–25.

Larmor, J. *Aether and Matter.* Cambridge: Cambridge University Press, 1900.

Larson, E. J. *Trial and Error: The American Controversy over Creation and Evolution.* New York: Oxford University Press, 1989.

Larson, E. J., and L. Witham. "Scientists are still keeping the Faith." *Nature* 386 (1997): 435–6.

Larson, J. L. *Reason and Experience: The Representation of Natural Order in the Work of Carl von Linne.* Berkeley, CA: University of California Press, 1971.

Larson, J. L. *Interpreting Nature: The Science of Living from Linnaeus to Kant.* Baltimore: Johns Hopkins Press, 1994.

Latour, B., and S. Woolgar. *Laboratory Life: The Social Construction of Scientific Facts.* Beverly Hills, CA: Sage, 1979.

Laudan, L. "Grünbaum on the Duhemian Problem." *Philosophy of Science* 32 (1965): 295–9.

Laudan, L. *Progress and its Problems: towards a Theory of Scientific Growth.* Berkeley, CA: University of California Press, 1977.

Laudan, L., and J. Leplin. "Empirical Equivalence and Underdetermination." *Journal of Philosophy* 88 (1995): 449–72.

Laudisa, F. "Einstein, Bell and Nonseparable Realism." *British Journal for the Philosophy of Science* 46 (1995): 309–29.

Lecourt, D. *Marxism and Epistemology: Bachelard, Canguilhem and Foucault.* London: New Left Books, 1975.

Lee, T. D. "Symmetry Principles in Physics." *Elementary Processes at High Energies.* Ed. A. Zichichi. New York: Academic Press, 1971, pp. 306–19.

Leeming, D. A. *A Dictionary of Creation Myths.* New York: Oxford University Press, 1995.

Leftow, B. *Time and Eternity.* Ithaca, NY: Cornell University Press, 1991.

Lehmann, P. "Barth and Brunner: The Dilemma of the Protestant Mind." *Journal of Religion* 20 (1940): 124–40.

LeMahieu, D. L. *The Mind of William Paley: A Philosopher and His Age.* Lincoln: University of Nebraska Press, 1976.

Lenoir, T. "Practice, Reason, Context: The Dialogue between Theory and Experiment." *Science in Context* 2 (1988): 3–22.

Leplin, J., ed. *Scientific Realism.* Berkeley, CA: University of California Press, 1984.

Leplin, J. "Methodological Realism and Scientific Rationality." *Philosophy of Science* 53 (1986): 31–51.

Leuba, J. H. *The Belief in God and Immortality: A Psychological, Anthropological and Statistical Study.* Boston: Sherman, French & Co., 1916.

Levenson, J. D. *Creation and the Persistence of Evil: The Jewish Drama of Divine Omnipotence.* Princeton, NJ: Princeton University Press, 1994.

Levenson, M. *Genealogy of Modernism.* Cambridge: Cambridge University Press, 1984.

Levi, I. "Induction as Self-Correcting according to Peirce." *Applications of Inductive Logic.* Ed. L. Jonathan Cohen and Mary Hesse. Oxford: Clarendon Press, 1980. 127–39.

Levin, M. "Realisms." *Synthese* 85 (1990): 115–38.

Lewis, C. S. *Screwtape Proposes a Toast.* London: Collins, 1965.

Lewis, D. *Counterfactuals.* Oxford: Blackwell, 1973.

Lewis, L. M. *The Promethean Politics of Milton, Blake and Shelley.* London: University of Missouri Press, 1992.

Lighthill, J. "The Recently Recognized Failure of Predictability in Newtonian Dynamics." *Proceedings of the Royal Society of London Series A* 407 (1986): 35–50.

Lindbeck, G. *The Nature of Doctrine*. Philadelphia: Westminster, 1984.

Lindberg, D. C., and R. L. Numbers. "Beyond War and Peace: A Reappraisal of the Encounter between Christianity and Science." *Church History* 55 (1984): 338–54.

Liss, T. M., and P. L. Tipton. "The Discovery of the Top Quark." *Scientific American*, September 1997 (1997): 36–41.

Livingstone, D. N. "B. B. Warfield, the Theory of Evolution and Early Fundamentalism." *Evangelical Quarterly* 58 (1986): 69–83.

Livingstone, D. N. *Darwin's Forgotten Defenders: The Encounter between Evangelical Theology and Evolutionary Thought*. Grand Rapids, MI: Eerdmans, 1987.

Livingstone, D. N. "Darwinism and Calvinism: The Belfast-Princeton Connection." *Isis* 83 (1992): 408–28.

Loder, J. E., and W. J. Neidhardt. *The Knight's Move: The Relational Logic of the Spirit in Theology and Science*. Colorado Springs: Helmers & Howard, 1992.

Loder, J. E., and W. J. Neidhardt. "Barth, Bohr and Dialectic." *Religion and Science: History, Method, Dialogue*. Ed. W. Mark Richardson and Wesley J. Wildman. New York: Routledge, 1996, pp. 271–89.

Logan, A. H. B. *Gnostic Truth and Christian Heresy: A Study in the History of Gnosticism*. Edinburgh: T. & T. Clark, 1996.

Lohfink, N. "God the Creator and the Stability of Heaven and Earth: The Old Testament on the Connection between Creation and Salvation." *Theology of the Pentateuch*. Ed. Norbert Lohfink. Edinburgh: T. & T. Clark, 1994, pp. 116–35.

Long, E. T. "Experience and Natural Theology." *Philosophy of Religion* 31 (1992): 119–32.

Lorentz, H. A. "Electromagnetic Phenomena in a System moving with any Velocity smaller than that of Light." *Proceed ings of the Royal Academy of Amsterdam* 6 (1904): 809–31.

Lorentz, H. A. *The Einstein Theory of Relativity*. 3rd edn. New York: Brentano, 1920.

Lorenz, E. N. "Deterministic Nonperiodic Flow." *Journal of the Atmospheric Sciences* 20 (1963): 130–41.

Lough, J. *Essays on the Encyclopedie of Diderot and d'Alembert*. London: Oxford University Press, 1968.

Louth, A. *The Origins of the Christian Mystical Tradition: From Plato to Denys*. Oxford: Clarendon Press, 1981.

Lovell, B. *The Individual and the Universe*. New York: New American Library, 1961.

Lowinger, A. *The Methodology of Pierre Duhem*. New York: Columbia University Press, 1940.

Lucas, J. R. "Wilberforce and Huxbey: A Legendary Encounter." *Historical Journal* 22 (1979): 313–30.

Lucas, J. R. *Space, Time and Causality: An Essay in Natural Philosophy*. Oxford: Oxford University Press, 1984.

Lundin, R. *The Culture of Interpretation. Christian Faith and the Postmodern World*. Grand Rapids: Eerdmans, 1993.

Lyon, D. *Postmodernity*. Buckingham: Open University Press, 1994.

Lyotard, J.-F. *The Postmodern Condition: A Report on Knowledge*. Manchester: Manchester University Press, 1992.

Lyttkens, H. *The Analogy between God and the World.* Uppsala: Almquist & Wiksells, 1952.

MacCormac, E. R. "Scientific and Religious Metaphors." *Religious Studies* 11 (1975): 401–9.

MacDonald, S. "Aquinas's Parasitic Cosmological Argument." *Medieval Philosophy and Theology* 1 (1991): 119–55.

Mach, E. *Popular Scientific Lectures.* Chicago: Open Court Publishing, 1898.

Mach, E. *The Analysis of Sensations and the Relation of the Physical to the Psychical.* Chicago: Open Court Publishing Co., 1906.

Mach, E. *History and Root of the Principle of the Conservation of Energy.* Chicago: Open Court Publishing Co., 1911.

MacIntyre, A. *Whose Justice? Which Rationality?* London: Duckworth, 1988.

MacKay, D. M. "'Complementarity' in Scientific and Theological Thinking." *Zygon* 9 (1974): 225–44.

MacKenzie, D. "From Kwajelein to Armageddon? Testing and the Social Construction of Missile Accuracy." *The Uses of Experiment.* Ed. D. Gooding, T. Pinch, and S. Schaffer. Cambridge: Cambridge University Press, 1989. 409–35.

MacKinnon, E. "Complementarily." *Religion and Science: History, Method, Dialogue.* Ed. W. Mark Richardson and Wesley J. Wildman. New York: Routledge, 1996, pp. 255–70.

Macquarrie, J. *Jesus Christ in Modern Thought.* London: SCM, 1990.

Manicas, P. T., and A. Rosenberg. "Naturalism, Epistemological Individualism and 'The Strong Programme' in the Sociology of Knowledge." *Journal for the Theory of Social Behaviour* 15 (1985): 76–101.

Manuel, F. E. *The Religion of Isaac Newton.* Oxford: Clarendon Press, 1974.

Marcel, P. C. *Calvin et Copernic.* Saint Germain-en-Laye: Société Calviniste de France, 1980.

Margulis, L. *Origin of Eukaryotic Cells: Evidence and Research Implications for a Theory of the Origin and Evolution of Microbial, Plant and Animal Cells on the PreCambrian Earth.* New Haven, CT: Yale University Press, 1970.

Margulis, L. *Symbiosis in Cell Evolution: Microbial Communities in Archean and Proterozoic Eons.* 2nd edn. New York: W. H. Freeman, 1993.

Marsden, G. *Fundamentalism and American Culture: The Shaping of Twentieth Century Evangelicalism 1870–1925.* New York: Oxford University Press, 1980.

Marsden, G. M. *The Evangelical Mind and the New School Presbyterian Experience.* New Haven: Yale University Press, 1970.

Marsden, G. M. *Reforming Fundamentalism: Fuller Seminary and the New Evangelicalism.* Grand Rapids, MI: Eerdmans, 1987.

Marsden, G. M. *The Soul of the American University: From Protestant Establishment to Established Nonbelief.* New York: Oxford University Press, 1994.

Marshall, I. H. *The Origins of New Testament Christology.* 2nd edn. Downers Grove, IL: InterVarsity Press, 1992.

Martin, M. "Does the Evidence confirm Theism more than Naturalism?" *International Journal for Philosophy of Religion* 16 (1984): 257–62.

Marty, M. E. "What is Fundamentalism? Theological Perspectives." *Fundamentalism as an Ecumenical Challenge.* Ed. H. Küng and J. Moltmann. London: SCM, 1992, pp. 3–13.

Marx, K. *Marx–Engels Gesamtausgabe.* Ed. A. Adoratskii. Berlin: Marx–Engels Verlag, 1932.

Mascall, E. L. *Existence and Analogy.* London: Darton, Longman & Todd, 1966.

Massey, M. C. "The Literature of Young Germany and D. F. Strauss's *Life of Jesus.*" *Journal of Religion* 59 (1979): 298–323.

Masuzawa, T. *In Search of Dreamtime: The Quest for the Origin of Religion.* Chicago: University of Chicago Press, 1993.

Maudlin, T. *Quantum Nonlocality and Relativity.* Oxford: Blackwell, 1994.

Maurer, A. A. *About Beauty: A Thomistic Interpretation.* Houston, TX: Center for Thomistic Studies, 1983.

May, G. *Creatio Ex Nihilo: the Doctrine of Creation out of Nothing in Early Christian Thought.* Edinburgh: T&T Clark, 1995.

May, H. F. *The Enlightenment in America.* Oxford: Oxford University Press, 1976.

May, R. M. "Simple Mathematical Models with Very Complicated Dynamics." *Nature* 261 (1976): 459–67.

Mayr, E., and W. B. Provine. *The Evolutionary Synthesis: Perspectives on the Unification of Biology.* Cambridge, MA: Harvard University Press, 1980.

Mayr, O. *Authority, Liberty and Automatic Machinery in Early Modern Europe.* Baltimore: Johns Hopkins University Press, 1986.

McAllister, J. W. "Truth and Beauty in Scientific Reason." *Synthese* 78 (1989): 25–40.

McAllister, J. W. "The Evidential Significance of Thought Experiment in Science." *Studies in History and Philosophy of Science* 27 (1996): 233–50.

McCluskey, S. C. "Gregory of Tours, Monastic Timekeeping, and Early Christian Attitudes to Astronomy." *Isis* 81 (1990): 9–22.

McCormack, B. L. *Karl Barth's Critically Realistic Dialectical Theology: Its Genesis and Development 1909–1936.* Oxford: Clarendon Press, 1995.

McFague, S. *Metaphorical Theology: Models of God in Religious Language.* London: SCM, 1983; Philadelphia: Fortress, 1985.

McGrath, A. E., C. G. Morgan, and G. K. Radda. "Positron Lifetimes in Phospholipid Dispersions." *Biochimica at Biophysica Acta* 466 (1976a): 367–72.

McGrath, A. E., C. G. Morgan, and G. K. Radda. "Photobleaching: A Novel Fluorescence Methbod for Diffusion Studies in Lipid Systems." *Biochimica at Biophysica Acta* 426 (1976b): 173–85.

McGrath, A. E. "The Influence of Aristotelian Physics upon St Thomas Aquinas's Discussion of the Processus Iustificationis." *Recherches de théologie ancienne et médiévale* 51 (1984): 223–9.

McGrath, A. E. *Luther's Theology of the Cross: Martin Luther's Theological Breakthrough.* Oxford: Blackwell, 1985.

McGrath, A. E. *Iustitia Dei A History of the Christian Doctrine of Justification.* 2 vols. Cambridge: Cambridge University Press, 1986a.

McGrath, A. E. *The Making of Modern German Christology. From the Enlightenment to Pannenberg.* Oxford: Blackwell, 1986b.

McGrath, A. E. *The Intellectual Origins of the European Reformation.* Oxford: Blackwell, 1987.

McGrath, A. E. *The Genesis of Doctrine*. Oxford: Blackwell, 1990.

McGrath, A. E. (ed.). *Blackwell Encyclopaedia of Modern Christian Thought*. Oxford/ Cambridge, MA: Blackwell, 1993a.

McGrath, A. E. *Reformation Thought: An Introduction*. 2nd edn. Oxford: Blackwell, 1993b.

McGrath, A. E. "Theology and Experience: Reflections on Cognitive and Experiential Approaches to Theology." *European Journal of Theology* 2 (1993c): 65–74.

McGrath, A. E. *The Christian Theology Reader*. Oxford/Cambridge, MA: Blackwell, 1995a.

McGrath, A. E. *Evangelicalism and the Future of Christianity*. Downers Grove, IL: InterVarsity Press, 1995b.

McGrath, A. E. *Christian Theology: An Introduction*. 2nd edn. Oxford/Cambridge, MA: Blackwell, 1996a.

McGrath, A. E. "An Evangelical Evaluation of Postliberalism." *The Nature of Confession: Evangelicals and Postliberals in Conversation*. Ed. T. R. Philips and D. L. Okholm. Downers Grove, IL: InterVarsity Press, 1996b, pp. 23–44.

McGrath, A. E. *An Introduction to Christianity*. Oxford/Cambridge, MA: Blackwell, 1996c.

McGuire, J. E. "Force, Active Principles and Newton's Invisible Realm." *Ambix* 15 (1968): 154–208.

McGuire, J. E. "Atoms and the 'Analogy of Nature': Newton's Third Rule of Philosophizing." *Studies in History and Philosophy of Science* 1 (1970): 3–58.

McMullin, E. "Two Ideals of Explanation in Natural Science." *Midwest Studies in Philosophy* 9 (1984): 205–20.

McWilliams, W. *The Passion of God: Divine Suffering in Contemporary Protestant Theology*. Macon, GA: Mercer University Press, 1985.

Meland, B. E. "The Empirical Tradition in Theology at Chicago." *The Future of Empirical Theology*. Ed. B. E. Meland. Chicago: University of Chicago Press, 1969, pp. 1–62.

Mellor, D. H. "Probable Explanation." *Australasian Journal of Philosophy* 54 (1976): 231–41.

Mermin, D. "Quantum Mysteries for Anyone." *Journal of Philosophy* 78 (1981): 397–408.

Mermin, N. D. "Is the Moon there when Nobody looks? Reality and the Quantum Theory." *The Philosophy of Science*. Ed. Richard Boyd, Philip Gasper and J. D. Trout. Cambridge, MA: MIT Press, 1991, pp. 501–16.

Metzger, H. *Attraction universelle et religion naturelle chez quelques commentateurs anglais de Newton*. Paris: Hermann, 1938.

Michelson, A. A., and E. W. Morley. "On the Relative Motion of the Earth and Luminiferous Ether." *American Journal of Science* 34 (1887): 333–45.

Midgley, M. *Science as Salvation: A Modern Myth and its Meaning*. London: Routledge, 1992.

Milbank, J. *Theology and Social Theory. Beyond Secular Reason*. Oxford: Blackwell, 1993.

Mill, J. S. *A System of Logic*. Collected Works. Ed. J. M. Robson. 8 vols. Toronto: University of Toronto Press, 1974.

Millar, D. "Falsification versus Induction." *Science, Belief and Behaviour*. Ed. D. H. Mellor. Cambridge: Cambridge University Press, 1980, pp. 109-29.

Millar, P. D. "Cosmology and World Order in the Old Testament: The Divine Council as Cosmic-Political Symbol." *Horizons in Biblical Theology* 9 (1987): 53–78.

Miller, A. I. *Imagery in Scientific Thought: Creating 20th-Century Physics*. Boston–Basel–Stuttgart: Birkhauser, 1984.

Moltmann, J. *Theology of Hope*. London: SCM, 1967.

Moltmann, J. *The Crucified God. The Cross of Christ as the Foundation and Criticism of Christian Theology*. London: SCM, 1974.

Moon, F. C. *Chaotic and Fractal Dynamics*. New York: John Wiley & Sons, 1992.

Moonan, L. *Divine Power: The Medieval Power Distinction up to Its Adoption by Albert, Bonaventure and Aquinas*. Oxford: Clarendon Press, 1994.

Moore, J. R. *The Post-Darwinian Controversies: A Study of the Protestant Struggle to come to terms with Darwin in Great Britain and America, 1870–1900*. Cambridge: Cambridge University Press, 1979.

Moore, J. R. "Evangelicals and Evolution: Henry Drummond, Herbert Spencer and the Naturalisation of the Spiritual World." *Scottish Journal of Theology* 38 (1985): 383–417.

Morgan, T. H. *The Theory of the Gene*. New Haven: Yale University Press, 1926.

Morris, C. "Science." *Dictionary of Science and Technology*. Ed. Christopher Morris. San Diego, CA: Academic Press, 1992. 1926.

Morris, H. *History of Modern Creationism*. San Diego: Master Book Publishers, 1984.

Morris, H. M. *Scientific Creationism*. El Cajon: Master Books, 1985.

Morris, H. M. *The Long War against God: The History and Impact of the Creation/Evolution Debate*. Grand Rapids: Baker, 1989.

Morrison, J. D. "Heidegger, Correspondence Truth and the Realist Theology of Thomas Forsyth Torrance." *Evangelical Quarterly* 59 (1997): 139–55.

Mothersill, M. *Beauty Restored*. Oxford: Clarendon Press, 1984.

Müller, E. F. K. *Die Bekenntnisschriften der reformierten Kirche*. Leipzig: Georg Böhme, 1903.

Müller, H.-P. "Eine neue babylonische Menschenschöpfungserzählung im Licht heilschriftlicher und biblischer Parallelen: Zur Wirklichkeitsauffassung im Mythos." *Orientalia* 58 (1989): 61–85.

Murdoch, D. *Niels Bohr's Philosophy of Physics*. Cambridge: Cambridge University Press, 1987.

Murphy, N. "Postmodern Apologetics, or why Theologians *must* pay attention to Science." *Religion and Science: History, Method, Dialogue*. Ed. W. Mark Richardson and Wesley J. Wildman. New York: Routledge, 1996, pp. 104–20.

Murphy, N. "Relating Theology and Science in a Postmodern Age." *CTNS Bulletin* 7.4 (1987): 1–10

Murphy, N. "From Critical Realism to a Methodological Approach: Response to Robbins, van Huyssteen and Hefner." *Zygon* 23 (1988): 287–90.

Murphy, N. *Theology in the Age of Scientific Reasoning*. Ithaca: Cornell University Press, 1990.

Mutschler, H.-D. "Schöpfungstheologie und physikaler Feldbegriff bei Wolfhart Pannenberg." *Theologie und Philosophie* 70 (1995): 543–58.

Napier, B. D. "On Creation-Faith in the Old Testament." *Interpretation* 16 (1962): 21–42.

Nash, J. *Loving Nature: Ecological Integrity and Christian Responsibility.* Nashville: Abingdon, 1991.

Needham, P. "Aristotelian Chemistry: A Prelude to Duhemian Metaphysics." *Studies in History and Philosophy of Science* 27 (1996): 251–69.

Nelson, D. E. "Confirmation, Explanation and Logical Strength." *British Journal for the Philosophy of Science* 47 (1996): 399–413.

Nelson, K. V. "Evolution and the Argument from Design." *Religious Studies* 14 (1978): 423–43.

Nelson, M. T. "Naturalistic Ethics and the Argument from Evil." *Faith and Philosophy* 8 (1991): 368–79.

Neuhaus, R. J. *The Naked Public Square: Religion and Democracy in America.* 2nd edn. Grand Rapids: Eerdmans, 1986.

Neville, R. C. *God the Creator: On the Transcendence and Presence of God.* Chicago: University of Chicago Press, 1968.

Neville, R. C. *Creativity and God.* New York: Seabury Press, 1980.

Newton-Smith, W., and S. Lukes. "The Underdetermination of Theory by Data." *Proceedings of the Aristotelian Society* 52 (1978): 71–91.

Newton-Smith, W. "Modest Realism." *Proceedings of the Philosophy of Science Association.* Ed. A. Fine and J. Leplin. Vol. 2. East Lansing, MI: Philosophy of Science Association, 1988, pp. 179–89.

Newton-Smith, W. H. *The Rationality of Science.* London: Routledge & Kegan Paul, 1981.

Niditch, S. *Chaos to Cosmos: Studies in Biblical Patterns of Creation.* Chico, CA: Scholars Press, 1985.

Niebuhr, H. R. *The Meaning of Revelation.* New York: Macmillan, 1960.

Norris, C. *The Truth about Postmodernism.* Oxford: Blackwell, 1993.

Norris, C. *Against Relativism: Philosophy of Science, Deconstruction and Critical Theory.* Oxford: Blackwell, 1997.

Norton, J. "Thought Experiments in Einstein's Work." *Thought Experiments in Science and Philosophy.* Ed. T. Horowitz and G. J. Massey. Savage, MD: Rowan and Littlefield, 1991, pp. 129–48.

Numbers, R. L. "Creationism in 20th-Century America." *Science* 218 (1982): 538–44.

Numbers, R. L. "Science and Religion." *Osiris* 1 (1985): 59–80.

Numbers, R. L. *The Creationists: The Evolution of Scientific Creationism.* New York: Knopf, 1992.

Oakley, F. *Omnipotence, Covenant and Order: An Excursion in the History of Ideas from Abelard to Leibniz.* Ithaca, NY: Cornell University Press, 1984.

Ockham, W. *Opera Philosophica et Theologica.* New York: St Bonaventure Publications, 1966.

O'Connor, D. "On Failing to resolve Theism-versus-Atheism Empirically." *Religious Studies* 26 (1990): 91–103.

Odom, H. H. "The Estrangement of Celestial Mechanics and Religion." *Journal of the*

History of Ideas 27 (1966): 533–58.

O'Donaghue, N. "A Theology of Beauty." *The Analogy of Beauty: The Theology of Hans Urs von Balthasar.* Ed. John Riches. Edinburgh: T. & T. Clark, 1986, pp. 1–10.

O'Donnell, J. *Hans Urs von Balthasar.* London: Chapman, 1992.

O'Donnell, J. J. *Trinity and Temporality.* Oxford: Oxford University Press, 1983.

O'Donovan, J. "Man in the Image of God: The Disagreement between Barth and Brunner Reconsidered." *Scottish Journal of Theology* 39 (1986): 433–59.

O'Donovan, O. *Resurrection and Moral Order.* Grand Rapids: Eerdmans, 1986.

Oeschlaeger, M. *Caring for Creation: An Ecumenical Approach to the Environmental Crisis.* New Haven: Yale University Press, 1994.

O'Flaherty, W. D. *Hindu Myths.* Harmondsworth: Penguin, 1975.

O'Hear, A. *Experience, Explanation and Faith.* London: Routledge & Kegan Paul, 1984.

O'Higgins, J. "Hume and the Deists." *Journal of Theological Studies* 22 (1971): 479–501.

O'Neill, J. *The Poverty of Postmodernism.* London: Routledge, 1994.

Oser, F. K., and K. H. Reich. "The Challenge of Competing Explanations: The Development of Thinking in Terms of Complementarity of Theories." *Human Development* 30 (1987): 178–86.

Packer, J. I. *The Evangelical Anglican Identity Problem.* Oxford: Latimer House, 1978.

Packer, J. I. *God has spoken.* Grand Rapids: Baker Book House, 1988.

Pagano, S. M., ed. *I documenti del processo di Galileo Galilei.* Vatican City: Pontifical Academy of Sciences, 1984.

Pagels, H. R. *The Cosmic Code: Quantum Physics and the Language of Nature.* Harmondsworth: Penguin, 1984.

Pais, A. "The Early History of the Theory of the Electron: 1897–1947." *Aspects of Quantum Theory.* Ed. A. Salam and E. P. Wigner. Cambridge: Cambridge University Press, 1972, pp. 79–92.

Pais, A. *Niels Bohr's Times, in Physics, Philosophy and Polity.* Oxford: Clarendon Press, 1991.

Palmer, H. *Analogy.* London: Macmillan, 1973.

Pals, D. L. *Seven Theories of Religion.* New York: Oxford University Press, 1996.

Pannenberg, W. "The Appropriation of the Philosophical Concept of God as a Dogmatic Problem of Early Christian Theology." *Basic Questions in Theology II.* London: SCM Press, 1971, pp. 119–83.

Pannenberg, W. "The Doctrine of Creation and Modern Science." *Zygon* 23 (1988): 3–21.

Parker, T. H. L. *Calvin's Doctrine of the Knowledge of God.* Edinburgh: Oliver & Boyd, 1969.

Parusnikova, Z. "Is a Postmodern Philosophy of Science Possible?" *Studies in History and Philosophy of Science* 23 (1992): 21–37.

Peacocke, A. *Creation and the World of Science.* Oxford and New York: Oxford University Press, 1979.

Peacocke, A. *The Sciences and Theology in the Twentieth Century.* Notre Dame, IN: University of Notre Dame Press, 1981.

Peacocke, A. *Intimations of Reality.* Notre Dame, IN: University of Notre Dame Press, 1984.

Peacocke, A. *Theology for a Scientific Age: Being and becoming Divine and Human.* London: SCM Press, 1993.

Pedersen, O. *Galileo and the Council of Trent.* Vatican City: Specolo Vaticana, 1983.

Peitgen, H.-O., H. Jürgens, and D. Saupe. *Chaos and Fractals: New Frontiers of Science.* New York, Berlin and London: Springer-Verlag, 1992.

Pelikan, J. *The Mystery of Continuity: Time and History, Memory and Eternity in the Thought of St Augustine.* Charlottesville, VA: University of Virginia Press, 1986.

Penrose, R. "The Role of Aesthetics in Pure and Applied Mathematical Research." *Bulletin of the Institute of Mathematics and Its Applications* 10 (1974): 266–71.

Penrose, R. *The Emperor's New Mind.* London: Vintage, 1990.

Peters, T. "Theology and the Natural Sciences." *The Modern Theologians: An Introduction to Christian Theology in the Twentieth Century.* Ed. David F. Ford. 2nd edn. Oxford/Cambridge, MA: Blackwell, 1997, pp. 649–68.

Peterson, M. L. *Reason and Religious Belief: An Introduction to the Philosophy of Religion.* Oxford: Oxford University Press, 1991.

Phillips, D. Z. *Religion without Explanation.* Oxford: Blackwell, 1976.

Philips, D. Z. *Faith after Foundationalism.* London: Routledge, 1988.

Pickering, A. "The Hunting of the Quark." *Isis* 72 (1981a): 216–36.

Pickering, A. "The Role of Interests in High-Energy Physics: The Choice between Charm and Colour." *The Social Process of Scientific Investigations: Sociology of the Sciences.* Ed'. K. D. Knorr, R. Krohn, and R. D. Whitley. Dordrecht: Reidel, 1981b, pp. 107–38.

Pickering, A. *Constructing Quarks: A Sociological History of Particle Physics.* Chicago: University of Chicago Press, 1984, pp. 68–79.

Pickering, A. "Knowledge, Practice and Mere Construction." *Social Studies of Science* 20 (1990): 68–79.

Pickering, A. "From Science as Knowledge to Science as Practice." *Science as Practice and Culture.* Ed. Andrew Pickering. Chicago: University of Chicago Press, 1992, pp. 1–26.

Pickering, W. S. F. "Secularization." *The Blackwell Encyclopaedia of Modern Christian Thought.* Ed. A. E. McGrath. Oxford: Blackwell, 1993, pp. 593–8.

Pike, N. *God and Timelessness.* London: Routledge & Kegan Paul, 1970.

Pinch, T. J. "Towards an Analysis of Scientific Observation: The Externality and Evidential Significance of Observation Reports in Physics." *Social Studies of Science* 15 (1985): 1–20.

Pinnock, C. H. "Climbing out of a Swamp: The Evangelical Struggle to Understand the Creation Texts." *Interpretation* 43 (1989): 143–55.

Pisi, P. *Prometo nel culto attico.* Rome: Edizioni dell Ateno, 1994.

Placher, W. C. *Unapologetic Theology: A Christian Voice in a Pluralistic Conversation.* Louisville, KY: Westminster/John Knox, 1989.

Plantinga, A. "The Probabilistic Argument from Evil." *Philosophical Studies* 35 (1979): 1–53.

Plantinga, A. "Reason and Belief in God." *Faith and Philosophy: Reason and Belief in God.* Eds. Alvin Plantinga and Nicholas Wolterstorff. Notre Dame: University of

Notre Dame, 1983, pp. 16–93.

Plantinga, A. *Warrant and Proper Function.* New York: Oxford University Press, 1993a.

Plantinga, A. *Warrant: The Current Debate.* Oxford: Oxford University Press, 1993b.

Plotnik, K. *Hervaeus Natalis OP and the controversies over the real presence and transubstantiation.* Munich: Schoningh, 1970.

Plotnitsky, A. *Complementarity: Anti-Epistemology after Bohr and Derrida.* Durham, NC: Duke University Press, 1994.

Pöhlmann, H. G. *Analogia entis oder analogia fidei? Die Frage nach Analogie bei Karl Barth.* Göttingen: Vandenhoeck & Ruprecht, 1965.

Poincaré, H. *Les méthodes nouvelles de la méchanique celeste.* Paris: Gauthier-Villars, 1892.

Poincaré, H. "Sur la dynamique de l'electron." *Rendiconti del circolo matematico di Palermo* 21 (1906): 129–76.

Polanyi, M. *Knowing and Being Essays.* London: Routledge & Kegan Paul, 1969.

Polikarov, A. "On the Nature of Einstein's Realism." *Epistemologia* 12 (1989): 277–304.

Polkinghorne, J. *One World: The Interaction of Science and Theology.* Princeton: Princeton University Press, 1986.

Polkinghorne, J. *Science and Creation: The Search for Understanding.* London: SPCK, 1988.

Polkinghorne, J. *Reason and Reality.* London: SPCK, 1991.

Polkinghorne, J. *Scientists as Theologians: A Comparison of the Writings of Ian Barbour, Arthur Peacocke and John Polkinghorne.* London: SPCK, 1996.

Poole, M. "A Critique of Aspects of the Philosophy and Theology of Richard Dawkins." *Science and Christian Belief* 6 (1994): 41–59.

Pope, A. *The Poems of Alexander Pope.* Ed. J. Butt. London: Methuen, 1963.

Popper, K. R. *The Logic of Scientific Discovery.* New York: Science Editions, 1961.

Popper, K. R. *Realism and the Aim of Science.* London: Hutchinson, 1983.

Post, H. R. "Correspondence, Invariance and Heuristics." *Studies in History and Philosophy of Science* 2 (1971): 213–55.

Postman, N. *Technopoly: The Surrender of Culture to Technology.* New York: Vintage, 1993.

Pratt, V. *Religion and Secularization.* London: Macmillan, 1970.

Prestige, G. L. *Fathers and Heretics.* Oxford: Oxford University Press, 1940.

Preus, S. J. *Explaining Religion: Criticism and Theory from Bodin to Freud.* New Haven, CT: Yale University Press, 1987.

Preuss, H. D. *Old Testament Theology.* 2 vols. Louisville, KY: Westminster John Knox Press, 1995.

Prigogine, I., and I. Stengers. *Order out of Chaos: Man's New Dialogue with Nature.* New York: Bantam Books, 1984.

Prigogine, I. *The End of Certainty: Time, Chaos and the New Laws of Nature.* New York: Free Press, 1997.

Pugh, J. C. *The Anselmic Shift: Christology and Method in Karl Barth's Theology.* Berlin/New York: Peter Lang, 1990.

Quine, W. V. O. *From a Logical Point of View.* Cambridge, MA: Harvard University Press, 1953.

Quinn, P. L. "Creation, Conservation and the Big Bang." *Philosophical Problems of the Internal and External Worlds.* Ed. John Earman et al. Pittsburg, PA: University of Pittsburg Press, 1993, pp. 589–612.

Railton, P. "A Deductive-Nomological Model of Probabilistic Explanation." *Philosophy of Science* 45 (1978): 206–26.

Railton, P. "Probability, Explanation and Information." *Synthese* 48 (1981): 233–56.

Ramsey, I. T. *Religious Language. An Empirical Placing of Theological Phrases.* London: SCM, 1957.

Ramsey, I. T. *Models and Mystery.* London: Oxford University Press, 1964.

Raven, C. E. *Natural Religion and Christian Theology.* 2 vols. Cambridge: Cambridge University Press, 1953.

Rawlyk, G. A. *Champions of the Truth: Fundamentalism, Modernism and the Maritime Baptists.* Montreal/Kingston: McGill–Queens University Press, 1990.

Redhead, M. *Incompleteness, Nonlocality and Realism: A Prolegomenon to the Philosophy of Quantum Mechanics.* Oxford: Clarendon Press, 1987.

Redhead, M. L. G. "Symmetry in Intertheory Relations." *Synthese* 32 (1975): 77–112.

Reich, K. H. "The Relation between Science and Theology: The Case for Complementarity Revisited." *Zygon* 25 (1990): 369–90.

Reich, K. H. "The Relation between Science and Theology: A Response to Critics of Complementarity." *Studies in Science and Theology.* Ed. G. V. Coyne, S. J. Schmitz-Moorman, and K. Schmitz-Moorman; Yearbook of the European Society for the Study of Science and Religion. Geneva: Labor et Fides, 1994, pp. 284–91.

Reich, K. H. "A Logic-Based Typology of Science and Theology." *Journal of Interdisciplinary Studies* 7 (1996): 149–67.

Reid, T. *Essay on the Intellectual Powers of Man.* Ed. B. Brody. Cambridge, MA: MIT Press, 1969.

Reines, C. "Beauty in the Bible and the Talmud." *Judaism* 24 (1975): 100–7.

Rescher, N. *Scientific Realism: A Critical Appraisal.* Dordrecht: D. Reidel, 1987.

Richardson, W. M., and W. J. Wildman. "Religion and Science: History, Method, Dialogue." New York: Routledge, 1996.

Ricoeur, P. *Freud and Philosophy: An Essay on Interpretation.* New Haven, CT: Yale University Press, 1970.

Rinpoche, L. N., et al. *The Assisi Declarations: Messages on Man and Nature from Buddhism, Christianity, Hinduism, Islam and Judaism.* Geneva: World Wildlife Fund, 1986.

Robinson, N. H. G. "The Problem of Natural Theology." *Religious Studies* 8 (1972): 319–33.

Rolston, H. *Science and Religion: A Critical Survey.* Philadelphia: Temple University Press, 1987.

Rosen, E. "Calvin's Attitude towards Copernicus." *Journal of the History of Ideas* 21 (1960): 431–41.

Roth, P. A. "Will the Real Scientists Please Stand Up? Dead Ends and Live Issues in the Explanation of Scientific Knowledge." *Studies in History and Philosophy of Science* 27 (1996): 43–68.

Rothbart, D. "The Semantics of Metaphor and the Structure of Science." *Philosophy of*

Science 51 (1984): 595–615.

Rowe, W. L. *The Cosmological Argument.* Princeton, NJ: Princeton University Press, 1975.

Rowe, W. L. "The Problem of Evil and Some Varieties of Atheism." *American Philosophical Quarterly* 16 (1979): 335–41.

Rowe, W. L. "Evil and the Theistic Hypothesis: A Response to Wykstra." *International Journal for Philosophy of Religion* 16 (1984): 95–100.

Rowe, W. L. "The Empirical Argument from Evil." *Rationality, Religious Belief and Moral Commitment.* Ed. R. Audi and W. J. Wainwright. Ithaca: Cornell University Press, 1986, pp. 227–47.

Rudwick, M. J. S. "Senses of the Natural World and Senses of God: Another Look at the Historical Relation of Science and Religion." *The Sciences and Theology in the Twentieth Century.* Ed. Arthur R. Peacocke. London: Oriel Press, 1981, pp. 241–61.

Rudwick, M. J. S. *The Great Devonian Controversy: The Shaping of Scientific Knowledge among Gentlemanly Specialists.* Chicago: University of Chicago Press, 1985.

Ruelle, D. *Chance and Chaos.* Harmondsworth: Penguin, 1993.

Ruse, M. "Darwin's Debt to Philosophy: An Examination of the Influence of the Philosophical Ideas of John F. Herschel and William Whewell on the Development of Charles Darwin's Theory of Evolution." *Studies in the History and Philosophy of Science* 66 (1975): 159–81.

Russell, B. *The Problems of Philosophy.* London: Oxford University Press, 1912.

Russell, B. *Religion and Science.* London: Oxford University Press, 1935.

Russell, B. *History of Western Philosophy.* 2nd edn. London: George Allen & Unwin, 1961.

Russell, C. A. "The Conflict Metaphor and its Social Origins." *Science and Christian Faith* 1 (1989): 3–26.

Russell, R. J., N. Murphy, and A. Peacocke. *Chaos and Complexity: Scientific Perspectives on Divine Action.* Vatican City State: Vatican Observatory and Berkeley: Center for Theology and Natural Sciences, 1995.

Sakurai, J. J. "Theory of Strong Interaction." *Annals of Physics* 11 (1960): 1–48.

Salmon, W. "Epistemology of Natural Science." *A Companion to Epistemology.* Ed. Jonathan Dancy and Ernest Sosa. Oxford: Blackwell, 1992, pp. 280–99.

Salmon, W. C. *Scientific Explanation and the Causal Structure of the World.* Princeton: Princeton University Press, 1984a.

Salmon, W. C. "Scientific Explanation: Three Basic Conceptions." *Philosophy of Science Association* 2 (1984b): 293–305.

Santmire, H. P. "The Genesis Creation Narratives Revisited." *Interpretation* 45 (1991): 366–79.

Sassower, R. "Postmodernism and Philosophy of Science: A Critical Engagement." *Philosophy of the Social Sciences* 23 (1993): 426–45.

Sassower, R. "Prolegomena to Postmodern Philosophy of Science." *Continental and Postmodern Perspectives in the Philosophy of Science.* Ed. B. E. Babich, D. B. Bergoffen, and S. V. Glyn. Aldershot: Avebury, 1995. 13–30.

Schilling, H. K. *Science and Religion.* New York: Charles Scribner's Sons, 1962.

Schmid, H. H. *Gerechtigkeit als Weltordnung: Hintergrund und Geschichte des alitestamentlichen Gerechtigkeitsbegriffs.* Tübingen: Mohr, 1968.

Schmid, H. H. "Schöpfung, Gerechtigkeit und Heil: 'Schöpfungstheologie' als Gesamthorizont biblischer Theologie." *Zeitschrift für Theologie und Kirche* 70 (1973): 1–19.

Schmitt, C. B. "Towards a Reassessment of Renaissance Aristotelianism." *History of Science* 11 (1973): 159–93.

Schoen, E. L. *Religious Explanations: A Model from the Sciences.* Durham, NC: Duke University Press, 1985.

Schöpf, H.-G. "Newton zwischen Physik und Theologie." *Neue Zeitschrift für Systematische Theologie* 33 (1991): 262–81.

Schreiner, S. E. *The Theater of His Glory: Nature and the Natural Order in the Thought of John Calvin.* Durham, NC: Labyrinth Press, 1991.

Schreiter, R. J. *Constructing Local Theologies.* Maryknoll, NY: Orbis, 1986.

Searle, J. "Rationality and Realism: What is at stake?" *Daedalus* 122 (1993): 55–83.

Selby, R. C. *The Principle of Reserve in the Writings of John Henry Newman.* Oxford: Oxford University Press, 1975.

Seng, K. P. "The Epistemological Significance of Homoousion in the Theology of Thomas F. Torrance." *Scottish Journal of Theology* 45 (1992): 341–66.

Shapere, D. "The Concept of Observation in Science and Philosophy." *Philosophy of Science* 49 (1982): 485–525.

Shapin, S., and S. Schaffer. *Leviathan and the Air-Pump: Hobbes, Boyle and the Experimental Life.* Princeton, NJ: Princeton University Press, 1985.

Shapiro, R. *Origins: A Skeptic's Guide to the Creation of Life on Earth.* New York: Summit Books, 1986.

Sharpe, E. J. *Comparative Religion: A History.* New York: Charles Scribner's Sons, 1975.

Shaw, W. H., and L. R. Ashley. "Analogy and Inference." *Dialogue* 22 (1983): 415–32.

Sher, R. *Church and University in the Scottish Enlightenment.* Princeton, NJ: Princeton University Press, 1985.

Sherry, P. *Spirit and Beauty: An Introduction to Theological Aesthetics.* Oxford: Clarendon Press, 1992.

Sircello, G. *A New Theory of Beauty.* Princeton, NJ: Princeton University Press, 1975.

Sloan, P. R. "The Buffon-Linnaeus Controversy." *Isis* 67 (1976): 356–75.

Smith, J. E. "Prospects for Natural Theology." *The Monist* 75 (1992): 406–20.

Smith, Q. "Atheism, Theism and Big Bang Cosmology." *Australasian Journal of Philosophy* 69 (1991): 48–66.

Smith, Q. "A Big Bang Cosmological Argument for God's Nonexistence." Faith *and Philosophy* 9 (1992): 217–37.

Smith, Q. "Anthropic Explanations in Cosmology." *Australasian Journal of Philosophy* 72 (1994): 371–82.

Sober, E., *The Philosophy of Biology.* Boulder, CO: Westview Press, 1993.

Söhngen, G. "Rectitudo bei Anselm von Canterbury als Oberbegriff von Wahrheit und Gerechtigkeit." *Sola Ratione.* Ed. H. Kohlenberger. Stuttgart: Friedrich Frommann Verlag, 1970, pp. 71–7.

Sommerville, C. J. "Is Religion a Language Game? A Real World Critique of the Cultural Linguistic Theory." *Theology Today* 51 (1995): 594–9.

Soontiëns, F. "Evolution, Teleology and Theology." *Bijdragen, tijdschrift voor filosofie en theologie* 53 (1992): 394–406.

Sorabji, R. *Time, Creation and the Continuum: Theories in Antiquity and the Early Middle Ages.* London: Duckworth, 1983.

Sorensen, R. A. *Thought Experiments.* New York: Oxford University Press, 1992.

Sosa, E. "The Foundations of Foundationalism." *Nous* 14 (1980): 3–25.

Soskice, J. "Theological Realism." *The Rationality of Religious Belief.* Ed. W. J. Abraham and S. Holtzer. Oxford and New York: Clarendon Press, 1987, pp. 105–19.

Soskice, J. M. *Metaphor and Religious Language.* Oxford: Clarendon Press, 1985.

Spinoza, B. *Opera: Lateinisch und Deutsch.* Ed. Konrad Blumenstock. Darmstadt: Wissenschaftliche Buchgesellschaft, 1980.

Sproul, B. C. *Primal Myths: Creation Myths around the World.* San Francisco: HarperCollins, 1991.

Stackhouse, J. G. *Canadian Evangelicalism in the Twentieth Century: An Introduction to Its Character.* Toronto: University of Toronto Press, 1993.

Stannard, R. *Science and the Renewal of Belief.* London: SCM Press, 1982.

Stauffer, R. "Calvin et Copernic." *Revue de l'Histoire des Religions* 179 (1971): 31–40.

Steck, O. H. "Alttestamentliche Impulse für eine Theologie der Natur." *Theologische Zeitschrift* 34 (1978): 202–11.

Stephens, W. P. *The Theology of Huldrych Zwingli.* Oxford: Clarendon Press, 1986.

Stewart, I. *Does God Play Dice: The Mathematics of Chaos.* Oxford: Blackwell, 1989.

Stolnitz, J. "'Beauty': Some Stages in the History of an Idea." *Journal of the History of Ideas* 22 (1961): 183–204.

Stout, J. *The Flight from Authority: Religion, Morality and the Quest for Autonomy.* Notre Dame, IN: University of Notre Dame Press, 1981.

Striedl, H. "Der Humanist Johann Albrecht Widmanstetter (1506–1557) als klassischer Philologe." *Festgabe der bayerischen Staatsbibliothek.* Wiesbaden: Harrassowitz, 1953, pp. 96–120.

Strug, C. "Kuhn's Paradigm Thesis: A Two-Edged Sword for the Philosophy of Religion." *Religious Studies* 20 (1984): 269–79.

Sullivan, R. E. *John Toland and the Deist Controversy.* Cambridge, MA: Harvard University Press, 1982.

Sulloway, F. J. "Darwin and his Finches: The Evolution of a Legend." *Journal of the History of Biology* 15 (1982): 1–53.

Sutherland, S. R. *God, Jesus and Belief: The Legacy of Theism.* Oxford: Blackwell, 1984.

Swift, L. "Basil and Ambrose on the Six Days of Creation." *Augustiniana* 21 (1981): 317–28.

Swinburne, R. "Falsifiability of Scientific Theories." *Mind* 73 (1964): 434–6.

Swinburne, R. *The Coherence of Theism.* Oxford: Clarendon Press, 1977.

Swinburne, R. *The Existence of God.* Oxford: Clarendon Press, 1979.

Swinburne, R. "The Argument from the Fine-Tuning of the Universe." *Physical Cosmology and Philosophy.* Ed. John Leslie. New York: Macmillan, 1990, pp. 154–73.

Swinburne, R. *Revelation: From Metaphor to Analogy.* Oxford: Clarendon Press, 1992.

Sylla, E. D. "The a posteriori Foundations of Natural Science. Some Medieval Commentaries on Aristotle's *Physics.*" *Synthese* 40 (1979): 147–87.

Tanner, K. "Respect for Other Religions: A Christian Antidote to Colonialist Discourse." *Modern Theology* 9 (1993): 1–18.

Tatarkiewicz, W. "The Great Theory of Beauty and Its Decline." *Journal of Aesthetics and Art Criticism* 31 (1972): 165–80.

Tennant, F. R. *Philosophical Theology.* 2 vols. Cambridge: Cambridge University Press, 1930.

Thagard, P. "The Best Explanation: Criteria for Theory Choice." *Journal of Philosophy* 75 (1976): 76–92.

Thiel, J. E. *Nonfoundationalism.* Minneapolis, MN: Fortress, 1994.

Thiemann, R. F. *Revelation and Theology: The Gospel as Narrated Promise.* Notre Dame, IN: University of Notre Dame Press, 1985.

Thiselton, A. C. *New Horizons in Hermeneutics: The Theory and Practice of Biblical Interpretation.* London: HarperCollins, 1992.

Thiselton, A. C. *Interpreting God and the Postmodern Self: On Meaning, Manipulation and Power.* Edinburgh: T. & T. Clark, 1995.

Thompson, J. *Modern Trinitarian Perspectives.* Oxford: Oxford University Press, 1994.

Thompson, P. E. S. "The Yahwist Creation Story." *Vetus Testamentum* 21 (1971): 197–208.

Tiles, M. *Bachelard: Science and Objectivity.* Cambridge: Cambridge University Press, 1984.

Tirrell, L. "Reductive and Nonreductive Simile Theories of Metaphor." *Journal of Philosophy* 87 (1991): 337–58.

Todd, D. D. "Plantinga and the Naturalized Epistemology of Thomas Reid." *Dialogue* 35 (1996): 93–107.

Tooley, M. "The Nature of Laws." *Canadian Journal of Philosophy* 7 (1977): 667–98.

Torrance, I. R. "A Bibliography of the Writings of Thomas F. Torrance 1941–1989." *Scottish Journal of Theology* 43 (1990): 225–62.

Torrance, T. F. *Theological Science.* Oxford: Oxford University Press, 1969.

Torrance, T. F. "The Problem of Natural Theology in the Thought of Karl Barth." *Religious Studies* 6 (1970): 121–35.

Torrance, T. F. *God and Rationality.* London: Oxford University Press, 1971.

Torrance, T. F. *Space, Time and Resurrection.* Edinburgh: Handsel Press, 1976.

Torrance, T. F. "God and the Contingent World." *Zygon* 14 (1979): 329–48.

Torrance, T. F. *The Ground and Grammar of Theology.* Belfast: Christian Journals Ltd, 1980.

Torrance, T. F. *Reality and Scientific Theology: Theology and Science at the Frontiers of Knowledge.* Edinburgh: Scottish Academic Press, 1985.

Torrance, T. F. "Realism and Openness in Scientific Inquiry." *Zygon* 23 (1988): 159–69.

Torrance, T. F. *The Christian Doctrine of God: One Being, Three Persons.* Edinburgh: T. & T. Clark, 1996a.

Torrance, T. F. "Revelation, Creation and Law." *Heythrop Journal* 37 (1996b): 273–83.

Toulmin, S. *The Return to Cosmology: Postmodern Science and the Theology of Nature.* Berkeley: University of California Press, 1982.

Toulmin, S. *Cosmopolis: The Hidden Agenda of Modernity.* New York: Free Press, 1990.

Towler, R. *The Need for Certainty: A Sociological Study of Conventional Religion.* London: Routledge & Kegan Paul, 1984.

Trefil, J. S. *The Moment of Creation: Big Bang Physics from before the First Millisecond to the Present Universe.* New York: Scribner, 1983.

Trembath, K. R. *Divine Revelation: Our Moral Relation with God.* New York: Oxford University Press, 1991.

Trigg, R. *Rationality and Science: Can Science Explain Everything?* Oxford: Blackwell, 1993.

Trousson, R. *Le thème de Prométhée dans le litérature europeene.* Geneva: Droz, 1976.

Tuana, N. "Quine on Duhem: An Emendation." *Philosophy of Science* 45 (1978): 456–62.

Turner, F. M. "Rainfall, Plagues and the Prince of Wales: A Chapter in the Conflict of Science and Religion." *Journal of British Studies* 13 (1974): 46–65.

Turner, F. M. "The Victorian Conflict between Science and Religion: A Professional Dimension." *Isis* 69 (1978): 356–76.

Turner, H. E. W. *The Patristic Doctrine of Redemption: A Study of the Development of Doctrine during the first Five Centuries.* London: Mowbray, 1952.

Uebel, T. E. "Anti-Foundationalism and the Vienna Circle's Revolution in Philosophy." *British Journal for the Philosophy of Science* 47 *(1996):* 415–40.

Urbach, P. "What is a Law of Nature? A Humean Answer." *British Journal of Philosophy of Science* 39 (1988): 193–210.

Valentini, B. P. *Commentatorium et disputationum in Genesim tomi quatuor.* 4 vols. Rome: George Ferrarius, 1591–95.

van Bavel, T. "The Creator and the Integrity of Creation in the Fathers of the Church." *Augustinian Studies* 21 (1990): 1–33.

van den Brink, G. *Almighty God: A Study of the Doctrine of Divine Omnipotence.* Kampen: Kok Pharos, 1993.

van Till, H. J. "Basil, Augustine and the Doctrine of Creation's Functional Integrity." *Science and Christian Belief* 8 (1996): 21–38.

Vaught, C. G. "Metaphor, Analogy and the Nature of Truth." *New Essays in Metaphysics.* Ed. Robert C. Neville. Albany, NY: State University of New York Press, 1987, pp. 217–36.

Vico, G. *The New Science.* Trans. T. G. Bergin and M. H. Fisch. Ithaca, NY: Cornell University Press, 1968.

von Balthasar, H. U. *The Glory of the Lord: A Theological Aesthetics.* 7 vols. Edinburgh: T. & T. Clark, 1982–.

von Hoftsen, N. "Skapelsetro och uralstringshypoteser före Darwin." *Uppsala Universiteits Årsskrift* 2 (1928): 31–6.

von Rad, G. *Old Testament Theology.* 2 vols. London: SCM Press, 1975.

Vuillemin, J. "On Duhem's and Quine's Theses." *Grazer Philosophische Studien* 9 (1979): 69–96.

Wachtmann, C. *Der Religionsbegriff bei Mircea Eliade.* Frankfurt am Main/Berlin: Peter Lang, 1996.

Waismann, F. *The Principles of Linguistic Philosophy.* London: Macmillan, 1965.

Ward, K. *Divine Action.* London: HarperCollins, 1990.

Ward, K. *Religion and Revelation: A Theology of Revelation in the World's Religions.* Oxford: Clarendon, 1994.

Ward, K. *God, Chance and Necessity.* Oxford: One World, 1996.

Ward, K. *Religion and Creation.* Oxford: Oxford University Press, 1996b.

Warfield, B. B. *Studies in Theology.* New York: Oxford University Press, 1932.

Wartofsky, M. *Feuerbach.* Cambridge: Cambridge University Press, 1982.

Warwick, A. "The Sturdy Protestants of Science: Larmor, Trouton and the Earth's Motion through the Ether." *Scientific Practice: Theories and Stories of Doing Physics.* Ed. Jed Z. Buchwald. Chicago: University of Chicago Press, 1995, pp. 300–43.

Warwick, A. C. "On the Role of the FitzGerald-Lorentz Contraction Hypothesis in the Development of Jospeh Larmor's Electronic Theory of Matter." *Archives for History of the Experimental Sciences* 43 (1991): 29–91.

Watts, F. "Are Science and Religion in Conflict?." *Zygon* 32 (1997): 125–38.

Webster, J. B. "Creation." *The Blackwell Encyclopaedia of Modern Christian Thought.* Ed. A. E. McGrath. Oxford: Blackwell, 1993. 94–7.

Weinandy, T. G. *The Father's Spirit of Sonship: Reconceiving the Trinity.* Edinburgh: T. & T. Clark, 1995.

Weinberg, S. *Dreams of a Final Theory: The Search for the Fundamental Laws of Nature.* London: Hutchinson Radius, 1993.

Weitzenfield, J. S. "Valid Reasoning by Analogy." *Philosophy of Science* 51 (1984): 137–49.

Welch, C. "Dispelling Some Myths about the Split between Theology and Science in the Nineteenth Century." *Religion and Science: History, Method, Dialogue.* Ed. W. Mark Richardson and Wesley J. Wildman. New York: Routledge, 1996, pp. 29–40.

Wencelius, L. *L'ésthétique de Calvin.* Geneva: Slatkine, 1979.,

Wess, J., and J. Bagger. *Supersymmetry and Supergravity.* 2nd edn. Princeton: Princeton University Press, 1992.

Westman, R. S. "The Melanchthon Circle, Rheticus and the Wittenberg Interpretation of the Copernican Theory." *Isis* 66 (1975): 165–93.

Westman, R. S. "Proof, Poetics and Patronage: Copernicus' Preface to *De Revolutionibus.*" *Reappraisals of the Scientific Revolution.* Ed. David C. Lindberg and Robert S. Westman. Cambridge: Cambridge University Press, 1990, pp. 167–205.

White, A. D. A *History of the Warfare of Science with Theology in Christendom.* 2 vols. London: Macmillan, 1896.

White, L. "The Historical Roots of Our Ecological Crisis." *Science* 155 (1967): 1203–7.

White, S. R. *Don Cupitt and the Future of Doctrine.* London: SCM Press, 1994.

White, W., and J. Gribbin. *Stephen Hawking: A Life in Science.* New York: Bantam Books, 1992.

Whitney, E. "Lynn White, Ecotheology and History." *Environmental Ethics* 15 (1993): 151–69.

Wilde, A. *Horizons of Assent: Modernism, Postmodernism and the Ironic Imagination.* Baltimore, MD: Johns Hopkins University Press, 1981.

Wiles, M. F. *The Making of Christian Doctrine.* Cambridge: Cambridge University Press, 1967.

Wilkinson, D. A. "The Revival of Natural Theology in Contemporary Cosmology."

Science and Christian Belief 2 (1990): 95–115.

Williams, M. *Groundless Belief? An Essay on the Possibility of Epistemology.* New Haven: Yale University Press, 1977.

Williams, R. " 'Religious Realism': On Not Quite Agreeing with Don Cupitt." *Modern Theology* 1 (1984): 3–24.

Williams, R. *Arius: Heresy and Tradition.* London: DLT, 1987.

Wilson, C. A. "Rheticus, Ravetz and the 'Necessity' of Copernicus' Innovation." *The Copernican Achievement.* Ed. Robert S. Westman. London: University of California Press, 1975, pp. 17–39.

Wilson, E. B. *The Cell in Development and Inheritance.* New York: Macmillan, 1896.

Witten, E. "Duality, Spacetime and Quantum Mechanics." *Physics Today* 50(5) (1997): 28–33.

Wittgenstein, L. *Philosophical Investigations.* 3rd edn. Oxford: Blackwell, 1968.

Wolf, M. "Theology, Meaning and Power: A Conversation with George Lindbeck on Theology and the Nature of Christian Difference." *The Nature of Confession: Evangelicals and Postliberals in Conversation.* Ed. T. R. Philips and D. L. Okholm. Downers Grove, IL: InterVarsity Press, 1996, pp. 45–66.

Wolff, R. P. *Kant's Theory of Mental Activity.* Cambridge, MA: Harvard University Press, 1963.

Wolterstorff, N. *John Locke and the Ethics of Belief.* Cambridge: Cambridge University Press, 1996a.

Wolterstorff, N. "Entitled Christian Belief." *Religion and Science: History, Method, Dialogue.* Ed. W. Mark Richardson and Wesley J. Wildman. New York: Routledge, 1996b, pp. 145–50.

Worrall, J. "Fresnel, Poisson and the White Spot: The Role of Successful Predictions in the Acceptance of Scientific Theories." *The Uses of Experiment: Studies in the Natural Sciences.* Ed. David Gooding, Trevor Pinch and Simon Schaffre. Cambridge: Cambridge University Press, 1989, pp. 135–57.

Worrall, J. "Structural Realism: The Best of both Worlds?" *Dialectica* 43 (1989b): 99–124.

Worthing, M. W. *Foundations and Functions of Theology as Universal Science: Theological Method and Apologetic Praxis in Wolfhart Pannenberg and Karl Rahner.* Frankfurt am Main/Berlin: Peter Lang, 1996.

Wright, C. *Realism, Meaning and Truth.* 2nd edn. Oxford/Cambridge, MA: Blackwell, 1993.

Wright, D. F. "Accommodation and Barbarity in John Calvin's Old Testament Commentaries." *Understanding Poets and Prophets.* Ed. A. Graeme Auld. Sheffield: JSOT Press, 1993, pp. 413–27.

Wright, N. T. *The New Testament and the People of God.* Minneapolis, MN: Fortress, 1992.

Wykstra, S. J. "The Humean Objection to Evidential Arguments from Suffering: On Avoiding the Evils of 'Appearance'." *International Journal for Philosophy of Religion* 16 (1984): 73–93.

Yang, C. N., and R. L. Mills. "Conservation of Isotopic Spin and Isotopic Gauge Invariance." *Physical Review* 96 (1954): 191–5.

Yeo, R. R. "William Whewell's Philosophy of Knowledge and its Reception." *William Whewell: A Composite Portrait*. Ed. Menachem Fisch and Simon Schaffer. Oxford: Clarendon Press, 1991, pp. 175–99.

Young, F. M. "Adam and Anthropos: A Study of the Interaction of Science and the Bible in Two Anthropological Treatises of the Fourth Century." *Vigiliae Christianae* 37 (1983): 110–40.

Young, R. "Malthus and the Evolutionists: The Common Context of Biological and Social Theory." *Past and Present* 43 (1969): 109–45.

Young, R. M. "Darwin's Metaphor: Does Nature Select?" *Monist* 55 (1971): 442–503.

Young, R. M. *Darwin's Metaphor: Nature's Place in Victorian Culture*. Cambridge: Cambridge University Press, 1985.

Young, R. M. "Darwin's Metaphor and the Philosophy of Science." *Science as Culture* 16 (1993): 375–403.

Zahar, E. "Why did Einstein's Programme supersede Lorentz's?" *British Journal for the Philosophy of Science* 24 (1973): 95–123; 233–62.

Zahar, E. "'Crucial' Experiments: A Case Study." *Progress and Rationality in Science*. Ed. G. Radnitzky and G. Andersson. Dordrecht: Reidel, 1978, pp. 71–97.

Zee, A. *Fearful Symmetry: The Search for Beauty in Modern Physics*. New York: Macmillan, 1986.

Zekiean, L. *L'interioriso agostiniano: la struttura onto-psicologica dell 'interioriso agostiniano e la 'memoria sui'*. Genoa: Studio editoriale di culture, 1981.

Ziegenaus, A. *Die trinitarische Ausprägung der göttlichen Seinsfülle nach Marius Victorinus*. Munich: M. Hueber, 1972.

Zolbrod, P. G. *Dine Bahane: The Navajo Creation Story*. Albuquerque, NM: University of New Mexico Press, 1984.

Index